THE PUDDING
THAT TOOK
A THOUSAND
COOKS

MICHAEL SYMONS

THE PUDDING
THAT TOOK
A THOUSAND
COOKS

The story of cooking in civilisation and daily life

VIKING

Viking
Penguin Books Australia Ltd
487 Maroondah Highway, PO Box 257
Ringwood, Victoria 3134, Australia
Penguin Books Ltd
Harmondsworth, Middlesex, England
Penguin Putnam Inc.
375 Hudson Street, New York, New York 10014, USA
Penguin Books Canada Limited
10 Alcorn Avenue, Toronto, Ontario, Canada M4V 3B2
Penguin Books (N.Z.) Ltd
Cnr Rosedale and Airborne Roads, Albany, Auckland, New Zealand
Penguin Books (South Africa) (Pty) Ltd
4 Pallinghurst Road, Parktown 2193, South Africa

First published by Penguin Books Australia Ltd, 1998

Design by Sandy Cull, Penguin Design Studio
Typeset in 10.5/14pt Minion by Midland Typesetters, Maryborough, Victoria
Printed in Australia by Australian Print Group, Maryborough, Victoria

National Library of Australia
Cataloguing-in-Publication data:

Symons, Michael, 1945– .
  The pudding that took a thousand cooks: the story
  of cooking in civilisation and daily life.

  Bibliography.
  Includes index.
  ISBN 0 670 87740 9.

  1. Cookery – Social aspects. 2. Cookery – History.
  I. Title.

392.37

One of my fascinations writing this book has been how cooking has brought its own negations: the most indispensable people have been belittled, policy decisions have been based on money not food, cooperation has brought division.
In the hope that we might share more convivially, I dedicate this book
To the meal makers
To the true economists
To mothers of sons taken for war

CONTENTS

PREFACE

Between us, we have eaten an enormous number of meals. We have
nibbled, gorged and hungered our way through history. Cooks have
been in charge – finding, sharing and giving food meaning. We
could not have survived without them. They have been everywhere,
yet writers have hardly noticed. In fact, I suggest that this is the first
book devoted to the essential duties and historical place of cooks.

If this is, with few qualifications, the world's first book on the
world's most important people, it implies a surprising intellectual
oversight. Nearly two and a half millennia ago Plato warned against
an interest in cooks, and Western scholars have largely complied.
Almost without exception, they have failed to inquire into the chief
occupation of at least half the people who have ever lived. Even
thinkers must eat.

Cookery books are so consumable that French chef Raymond
Oliver compares them to wooden spoons: 'one is astonished at the
number which have disappeared' (1967: 209). Likewise, so much
dietary advice has been circulated that, almost a century and a half
ago, an English author counted 'upwards of seventeen hundred works
extant on the subject . . . Sufferers may study the question till they are
driven mad by doubt and dyspepsia, and difference of opinions'
(Doran 1859: 16).

We have devoured innumerable books on how and what to cook,
and even some about certain cooks and aspects of cooking, but this
abundance makes the central gap even more peculiar. There are so
many texts *for*, and so few *about*, cooks. No writer has got up from

a meal, so to speak, publicly in awe. Why have cooks expended so much energy? Why the neglect? Even in books where cooks could scarcely be kept out, I have been bemused that the index is more likely to refer to 'Cook, Captain' than to 'Cook' plain and simple. Not unusually, the excellent *Eating in America: A history* (1976) by Waverley Root and Richard de Rochemont includes three references to the navigator and none to cooks.

Cookery is at once 'sufficiently familiar to every housekeeper; and, its luxurious refinements too copiously detailed in manuals and directories' to require enlargement, 'were it even a topic that at all deserved consideration in a work of this nature'. This is the way 'Cookery' was dismissed in 1823 by the editors of the sixth edition of the *Encyclopaedia Britannica*.

Cooks have always been in the background – both ever present and unnoticed. Their contributions have seemed too common, pervasive, trivial, unproblematic. Cooks generally have been women, and their achievements overlooked as inglorious and private. They have been restricted to the chopping-board and spice rack. But while each of the cooks' actions might be infinitesimal, the results have multiplied into civilisation.

Only the vulgar would 'see no more to a kitchen than saucepans and no more to dinner than dishes', French food critic Grimod de La Reynière protested two centuries ago. Once made the 'object of serious study or profound thought', the gastronomic arts expand to 'embrace all three realms of nature, and the four corners of the globe, all moral considerations and all social relationships' (1987: 185–6). That's more like it; but he and other gastronomic thinkers, such as Jean-Anthelme Brillat-Savarin, have tended to pay more attention to enjoying than to preparing dinners.

Virtually every archaeological dig, every diary, every street-scape tells the cooks' tale. We do not lack evidence, and can appropriate much scholarship. But no one has tried to pull all this together. Since the nineteenth century, we have become so hyper-specialised that we scarcely know any longer how to place cooks within the great scheme of things. As evidence of consequent conceptual sloppiness, we slip unthinkingly from 'cooking' as heating food (the dictionary meaning) to something much, much more.

Unmindful of culinary history, let alone the basic physics, we blur the distinction between 'roasting' and 'baking'. English even lacks a collective noun for the heat source – cooking fire, brazier, stove, oven and so forth.

If 'we are what we eat', cooks have not just made our meals, but have also made us. They have shaped our social networks, our technologies, arts and religions. Cooks deserve to have their story told often and well. We need to invent ways to think about them, and to revise our views about ourselves in their light. Having to traverse the entire globe and its peoples since the first cook picked up her stone 'knife', a book truly commensurate with the place of cooks in human history would be massive. I offer an introductory essay, a faint sketch of awesome consequences.

In quest of cooks, we initially enter the kitchen of just one Sydney chef, Phillip Searle (Chapter One). The book then relates how certain novelists have portrayed women cooks (Chapter Two) and finds the gastronomic tradition often appreciative (Chapter Three). Having traced the development of the cooking fire (Chapter Four), existing assumptions about what cooks do are examined (Chapter Five). I then set out my own suggestions, which centre on cooks as sharers. This explains why cooks specialise in sauces (Chapter Six), why their key tool is the knife (Chapter Seven) and how they are behind festivals, beauty and love (Chapter Eight).

Much flows from the sharing of food, not the least the possibility of sharing tasks. Then, increasing culinary specialisation gives shape to history. In exploring this, the second part of the book summarises a case for cooks as builders of civilisation (Chapter Nine). It takes up some ideas about the emergence of human beings (Chapter Ten), the settling down with crops and livestock (Chapter Eleven) and the rise of temple civilisations (Chapter Twelve). Magnificent banquets are the centrepieces of empires (Chapter Thirteen); professional cooks have long fed cities (Chapter Fourteen); industrialisation brings both liberation and alienation (Chapter Fifteen); and the tour concludes at a banquet orchestrated by the chef we met at the opening (Chapter Sixteen).

This has been no instant project. I learned just how much our eating says about ourselves when writing a gastronomic history of modern Australia, *One Continuous Picnic* (1982). The puzzle of the historic prejudice against food intellectualism then led me to complete a PhD in the sociology of cuisine (1991), followed by a study of present-day eating, *The Shared Table* (1993). With cooking partner Jennifer Hillier, I ran the Uraidla Aristologist Restaurant in the Adelaide Hills for fifteen years. Mainly, since an early age I have been a keen diner.

In an obscure footnote in his journal for 15 August 1773, the literary biographer James Boswell defines the human as the 'Cooking Animal'. It is not tool-making that separates us from the rest of nature, he writes. It is not memory, judgement and all the faculties and passions of our minds that make us unique. But 'no beast is a cook' (1924: 179 n.1). This book honours Boswell's intuition. It sets out to explain ourselves and our world through cooks. It finds civilisation to be a culinary creation.

The italics in quotations are in the original sources, except where stated otherwise.

CHAPTER ONE

To Pick One Cook

Hovering over an industrial city spreading beside the Pacific, an angel tunes into the tangled whispers of human thought, watching over silliness and drama, and brushing comfort when and where it will. Suddenly drawn to comprehend, this angel descends past Sydney's opera house, art gallery, library, museum and botanical gardens. On wings of inquiry it glides across the cathedral, conservatorium of music and hospital. It floats over the hotels, department stores and shopping complexes. It circles the stock exchange, banks and corporate towers. It glances towards the sporting stadiums and beaches.

Subtropical foliage protects a sombre former manse at a busy intersection, where Oxford Street meets four other roads and the gates to Centennial Park. The angel drifts towards the corner, lands on the short garden path, steps onto the porch and pushes through the heavy door. White-covered tables stand in the rooms to the left and ahead past a desk. Off to the right a swing door hides a kitchen. It is not time yet for a meal.

I lead the angel through the 'wrong' door; we enter the kitchen. We are greeted by an old friend not in formal chef's hat, nor even pressed white jacket and apron, but casual pyjamas and sandals. The cook, lithe and short-haired, is thumbing a hand-written, well-greased book of recipes. That's between proving rolls, shelling mussels and slicing the ginger that he preserves each year. He is culinary artist Phillip Searle. This might appear to be an unusual place for an inquiring angel to seek the heart of humanity. Nonetheless, this visitation starts on a midsummer's afternoon in 1994, in the increasingly forgotten kitchen of a great and favourite chef at a restaurant called Oasis Seros.

Born in Dubbo in rural New South Wales, in 1950, Phillip Searle emerged in Sydney as a radical art student. He went wild with luxuries to stage extravagant feasts. He and his good friend, Ned, ate themselves 'to death' through Europe. When the Troisgros restaurant was closed at Roanne, France, they took a train to the Tour d'Argent in Paris. Diverted from a trip to Bangkok to live in Adelaide, and with a copy of Michel Guérard's *Cuisine Gourmande*, Phillip fell into cooking at Reilly's Café, an unpretentious place to which he brought minor fame. Then, during the 1982 Festival of Arts, he encountered Barry Ross, who was seeking a new chef for a small restaurant called Possum's. Phillip's artistry became even more renowned out of Adelaide than in, so he and Barry shifted to Sydney, opening Oasis Seros in February 1987.

Preparing for the evening meal, Phillip works alongside long-time assistant Tom Claessen. They move easily around the space, rotating from job to job. One flips tongs with practised wrist. The other stirs saucepans on blue rings. Repeatedly, one tastes and the other touches. What are they, as cooks, really doing?

CULTURAL ACCOUNTS

A restaurant such as Oasis Seros is a venue in which to overindulge sensual pleasures, to flaunt wealth, to escape. Amid the crystal, white linen and slippery plywood chairs, Phillip Searle sells distinction and distraction to stressed and sybaritic citizens. In the expensively casual Sydney way, his customers seize the rewards and show them off.

We often hear that we cook (or others cook for us) to make a point: to manifest religious impulses, to prove that we belong to a certain social class, to display how cultivated we are. Just as we first take up and later reject Coca-Cola as a signifier of sophistication, we head for places like Oasis Seros, as French sociologist Pierre Bourdieu says, to make 'distinctions'. We each belong to what he calls a *habitus*, a social and cultural position bound up with countless preferences. Under the heading 'form and substance', Bourdieu speaks of a historic shift from solid meals to food as a sign. He also finds more and more spending on appearance as he moves up the social scale. The 'middle classes are *committed* to the symbolic', he writes (1984: 253).

Reflecting Bourdieu's 'de-materialisation' thesis, Australian sociologist Joanne Finkelstein sees food becoming less a source of nutrition and more a 'commodity and an entertainment'. The growth of fastfoods and gimmick foods also suggests the 'successful recasting of foodstuffs into items of fashion', she writes in her book *Dining Out* (1989: 45–6). She categorises dining-out spots: 'A sense of family unity is sold with the McDonald's hamburger, romance with the dark-hued interior of the bistro mondain, sophistication and worldliness with a meal taken in a fête spéciale' (4). The taste for creative cooking (such as Phillip Searle's) demonstrates that 'food is not a banal and simple ingredient in the maintenance of life but rather a cultural event and form of aesthetic in which its arrangement and colouring should be appreciated as if they were works of art' (156).

For Finkelstein, who nurses the old academic contempt for dining, the restaurant's fantasising and mannered interaction blocks both analysis and direct communication. 'Dining out allows us to act in imitation of others, in accord with images, in response to fashions, without need for thought or self-scrutiny.' By preventing the examined life, she argues, dining out is a 'constraint on our moral development and, subsequently, a rich source of incivility' (5). By reducing meals to signs and images, she finds a confusion 'between what is enduringly valuable and what is temporarily valued' (103). We become preoccupied by 'trivial matters such as where to dine' (155).

Almost the inverse of gloss and refinement, the reality is abrupt: Phillip and Tom are flanked by a bank of three stainless-steel stoves and metal benches with refrigerators beneath. There is a salamander, a deep-fryer, a heavy-duty mixer; nearby an ice-cream machine. Arrayed about the stove are twenty ladles on the right, a dozen tongs above, a dozen spoons, three whisks, scissors, strainers on the left, and surrounding bowls, moulds, steamers, sieves, a dozen frying pans, a dozen sautéing pans.

Above the stoves is a rangehood and, above the central bench, various implements dangle on hooks from an iron frame harnessed with chains to the roof. It is a room of bodies and metal, and pum-melling, hacking, singeing, scorching. Come to think of it, at any one moment little food is in evidence – hidden in plastic containers, steel bowls and, mostly, in the refrigerated cupboards and a walk-in cool room still temporarily installed through a side door. Against the heavy stone walls, the two cooks are like gnomes in a festooned and partially tiled dungeon. In this backroom we seriously doubt that cooks are slaves to style. We begin to see the substance.

Obeying the world's rawest rules, Phillip guts, slashes, smooths and puts on the plate. He chops, slices, bubbles, frizzles, moulds, coats and displays. Peel back the finery and we find he feeds us. Well before food is a cultural indicator, it is physical nourishment.

Phillip's kitchen offers an epitome of what is to come. Further chapters will bring out three aspects of what cooks do, as they acquire, distribute and organise human sustenance.

ACQUISITION

This kitchen is well looked after, but cooking is messy, dirty work. We feel this acutely when dressed in our best, our shirt pressed, our feathers preened. We might get splattered or brush against a wet or oily surface. The work involves bare hands, sticky fingers, licks of this and that, whacks on fleshy lumps, hissing lids and miscellaneous smells. It is also dangerous, the basic tools being either very sharp or very hot.

It is messy because cooks bring the country to the city. They secure the colours of gardens, the smell of soils, the infinities of oceans, the invigoration of breezes. They import bits of harmonious, contented nature, where animals devour plants and each other. With razor-sharp knife, bludgeoning pestle, sizzling pan, cooks round up ingredients. This is a calculated engagement with the material world. Most items must be cleaned, stripped of feathers, scraped of scales, dislodged from pods, pulverised.

While notional centres of Sydney might today include one of the cathedrals, the glass towers of the financial district, or the opera house, harbour and bridge, in a previous era the city might have been thought to radiate from the docks, or the General Post Office, or the web of rails from Central Station. And before that, we might

4

have sought out the market. This was the central exchange point for the morning's produce. Historically, temples and churches were set up in the market square. But in Sydney this physical heart, where cooks once congregated, has been transplanted to an anonymous suburb.

At the time of the angel's visit, Phillip Searle feels increasingly distant from the rest of the food industry, working mornings alone: 'I'm a complete isolate these days'. He seeks the best supplies but finds it impossible to get out to the wholesale market at Flemington. Most days he visits Chinatown, where the market used to be. He buys spring onions, watercress, Chinese cabbage, ginger and garlic, and dry goods. Every night he leaves a message on the answering machine of Connie Simon, who trades under the name of East Side Providores. She is asleep, about to head for the market. He might have rung during the day to check what's about, such as the first strawberry guavas.

As well as getting pork from Chinatown, Phillip uses two or three butchers who deliver. A supplier flies up guinea fowl and squab pigeon from Victoria. He gets Peking–Aylesbury ducks from the man who grows all the ducks for Chinatown. Still with their head and feet on, they are 'pumped' with an air compressor to puff the skin apart from the body. As to fish: Barry Ross goes to the fish market every day. 'He picks everything out by hand.'

Phillip and Barry have bought a house two hours away in the Blue Mountains. Barry stays increasingly on the 'farm', growing produce. 'At present it's the wild mushroom season,' Phillip says. 'On Monday I spent four hours in the forest, mushrooming; I love the distinctive sounds, patterns of light.' He works with nature, then puts it on a pedestal. With Phillip's kitchen door closed, diners do not see the physical processes involved. But, far from being immaterial, people are condemned to be bodies, to be animals, absolutely embedded in nature. Cooks haul choice morsels in.

DISTRIBUTION

The restaurant is filling up, and Phillip and Tom go hard at it. Non-stop. They have adapted to the pressure, racing not to prove themselves but to get the job done. When a restaurant is working well, it churns along, whirling according to practised routines. It drags nature into its vortex. The pair attend the flames, and do much else. They tug, tear and crack. They wash, squash and trim. They roll, shave and pinch. They fold, crease and interleave. Eventually, they make neat, tamed parcels, strips, clumps and pools, almost as if they have not touched the food. They wipe drips clean.

After gathering ingredients, the second main task of cooks is sharing. Especially in the slicing, chopping, carving and arranging, it is possible to see that, essentially, cooks allocate food among diners. More fundamentally than the application of heat, and at the basis of the cultural transformation of garnered nature, cooking is dividing up. That is why we cook even in a heating sense – to make safe, to keep for a later date, to make appetising – all so as to distribute. Cooks have long stored food as dried fruit, cheese, beer, ham, pickles, jam, biscuits. Phillip candies ginger so he can apportion it over the months. He is also an ice-cream specialist, his most celebrated dish being what a restaurant guidebook sees as a 'chequer-board ice-cream of star anise, pineapple, vanilla and a fine pencil line of liquorice looking like a divine Paul Klee miniature' (Schofield 1989: 106). The frozen mosaic is a wonder of slicing, slicing to share.

Given the duty to share, the key culinary virtue becomes generosity. In Phillip's case the generosity is, perhaps, detached. In the kitchen he is totally immersed. He wallows in food and, once it is tamed, he despatches it. He throws his all into the dish, and that's it. Or so he says. 'I'm not like other cooks: I do it all for me. Occasionally, I might say to Barry, "Did they like that?". I don't know one of my customers just as a customer. I have to eat it to make sure it's perfectly harmonious food, or whatever. Once I've got that far I'm satisfied.' Out of the restaurant, among friends, he says, it is different. 'I really enjoy the idea of cooking for a group of people; when this has been the case there hasn't been one person who hasn't asked, "What can I do?".'

Some diners come to escape. Some diners come to flaunt their wealth, their fashionability, their good taste. Many also come to forge and affirm commercial alliances, to celebrate anniversaries, to discharge obligations, to court. They come to talk, to exchange, to win. But, at a deeper level even than sharing lives, all diners come to share food. In getting us together, cooks sustain social liaisons. Cooks hold us in bonds and networks – with the world and one another.

ORGANISATION

To recommend old favourites from the menu: 'Steamed prawn cakes with prawn sauce', an extraordinarily refined sponge roll on a bisque-like sauce; 'Roast glazed duckling with steamed ginger buns', duck steamed from the inside; and, for dessert, the already mentioned 'Chequerboard ice-cream'. Whatever we choose, Phillip's creations look strikingly simple, belying a complexity of flavour and construction, much effort and artistry.

Phillip Searle remains hidden in the kitchen, an invisible presence. Are we sure that he's even on tonight? And yet the experience has him written all over it.

Relatively few other chefs could claim to have invented as many dishes coherent enough to stay on the menu year after year and to be taken up elsewhere. Phillip is always improving his craft, plundering the whole world through books, travel and eating. 'I haven't a ravenous appetite. However, I'll go to great lengths to get what I feel like. One day I'd kill for a laksa. In Chinatown there's a north Chinese restaurant with handmade noodles and brisket soup. I'll keep going until I know what I've eaten.'

Phillip says that he is 'not entirely produce-inspired . . . it comes out of my head, I'm not sure from where'. He gives as an example his candied-fruit pudding, which came from having to make a Christmas pudding with duck eggs and olive oil, so that he worked from a duck-egg mayonnaise. Before our eyes, between sheets of greaseproof paper, he meticulously rolls out his most extraordinary invention, 'glass' biscuit pastry. Just sugar, butter and flour, but so thin and toffee-like you can see through it.

His physical artistry also pushes him to create spectacular banquets. For the Fourth Symposium of Australian Gastronomy in Sydney in 1988, he provided a long table spread with quails, each cooked in clay, and hammers to crack the shells open. Subsequently, for a restaurant-industry dinner, he came up with the 'Bombe Oasis'. 'It took ages, four months, thinking about it all the time' – a miniature ice-cream pyramid meticulously covered on two faces by thin layers of meringue, and on the other two faces by his 'glass' biscuit.

But why particular recipes? Why the cultural richness of *dishes*? Why the particular cuisines of localities and individuals? As a provisional answer, the mixing and matching of ingredients help in both physical and social sustenance. We need a 'balanced' meal, the ingredients balanced for the benefit of both our individual physical bodies and fair distribution within the group. Standard combinations are practised ways to achieve such harmony.

In formulating ways of summoning bits of nature and sharing the sustenance, Phillip anticipates, plans, orders, organises, controls, studies, reads, experiments, explains, and rationalises as he records his recipes in exercise books. Cooks provide a mixed diet for their charges and, for this, they arrange attractive, coherent statements (perhaps with an emphasis on the latter in restaurants).

The perfection, the geometry, the colouring, the 'look' are important for dissemination. Indeed, this is how art emerges: the culture of distribution gains its own existence. Dishes attract and distribute; this signalling and balancing accumulate their own rules and meanings that take the eye beyond the plate. In what is technically known as *service à la russe*, instead of diners helping themselves to one big pot or scatter of pots, the chef prepares each person a plate. In *à la carte* this goes further so that we order individually, according to whim. In this way, chefs lift the art of distribution to its highest level.

Cooks make routines out of this juggling act of gathering and distributing. Employing what is available in that season and that location, and expanding on practised culinary techniques and equipment, cooks shape the activities of those around them. This achievement requires them to develop recipes, not just narrow, stove-based rigmaroles, but culture as a whole, culture being the overall recipe for living. In other words, recipes are the core of culture.

AT THE HEART

'My role is like that of an alchemist – transubstantiation, that's basically what cooking is, and the question of science comes into it. I quite often become literally fascinated by, for example, making sourdough bread. All it is is sea salt, water and ground-up wheat – from these basics you end up with a loaf. The magic fascinates me.' As we have seen, this alchemist is also a butcher, host, recipe-keeper, artist, poet. He also farms out jobs to specialists. While Phillip makes superior sourdough bread, he and innumerable other cooks commission an ever-increasing division of labour.

Criss-crossing this broad city, the angel finds domestic kitchens, hotel kitchens, office kitchens, airline kitchens and fastfood factories. All these cooks employ farmers to send the foods. They call upon rail workers to cart coal, grain and people to kitchens. They rely on industrialists to produce equipment, such as the best steel knives. They subcontract theatrical companies to provide after-dinner entertainment. They invite government to protect and enhance the 'pursuit of happiness', as that great epicurean Thomas Jefferson declared.

Phillip Searle and the other cooks giving life to a thriving city such as Sydney are connected to everything. Very occasionally, a van turns in to deposit provisions. A few cars eventually bring customers. But every vehicle is at the beck and call, in one way or another, of cooks. The traffic lights stand sentinel to people heading for other eating places, to meals at home. Teenagers in their parents' cars grab takeaway from conspicuous hamburger outlets. Trucks roar to restock supermarkets. Buses take workers to 'earn a crust'.

In investigating what cooks do and how they have shaped us, I rethink this Pacific city as a sprawling culinary machine. It is a complex kitchen, intricate and messy, made from a multitude of little ones – Phillip's kitchen multiplied.

Cooks such as Phillip Searle can be relegated to the job of pandering to important people. Or, as I prefer, they can be placed at the focus of society. Cooks command the kitchen of culture. They work at the maelstrom at the centre of our world; they stir the mighty pudding of civilisation.

At the risk of getting carried away, I suggest that with cooks such as Phillip we get to the *guts* of cities such as Sydney, 'guts' being colloquially the 'belly as the source of appetite'. I can also say that with cooks we get to the *heart*, the heart distributing the body's goodness. The heart also connotes love, and love is about others' well-being, about cooking. And we reach the *soul*; it is the spiritual or immaterial part, our cities' culture.

WHY PHILLIP?

Chefs have become celebrities. As much an energetic publicist as an artist, the French chef Alexis Soyer became a household name in England last century, even if gourmets judged him 'more likely to earn his immortality by his soup-kitchen than by his soup' (Hayward 1853: 77). More recently, Paul Bocuse, Joël Robuchon and others have marketed their names worldwide. Within a smaller clientele, Phillip Searle has received acclaim as among the very best, the cooks' cook. Compared to the historic anonymity of cooks, he has been spoiled. I come in praise of all cooks, so why have I not accompanied the angel into the kitchen of the unknown cook? Out of the literally billions working as I write, and even more over history, why start back at Oasis Seros?

Perhaps partly because professionals like Phillip Searle are clearly labelled 'cook'. While domestic cooks could be viewed as both doing less (their duties being steadily taken over by the modern food industry, of which Phillip is a part) and doing more (child-minding, cleaning, washing), he represents the cook in the extreme (one of his favourite words). He has been completely, ridiculously dedicated, which ought to tip off even the most disdainful angel that cooking can (at least on occasion) be engrossing. Besides, at this moment in history, he commands the foods and the techniques of the world, making him a global cook, all cooks rolled in one. There is a simpler reason: he has cooked some of my most memorable meals. He is an exceptional cook, but, for all that, he is merely the opening cook, who introduces all the others.

The next few chapters circle widely, as the angel meets cooks through time and place – in reality, as we will confirm before we finish, Phillip Searle has long since moved on from Oasis Seros. The angel will find that a book about cooks is also about cooking. From a highly appreciative slant, the work of cooks will tend to blur with that of others. And I am certainly not just talking about professionals, or even just about domestic cooks, but about humanity.

I might have adopted the neologism '*her*-story' and spoken of 'the cook, she', but I have chosen the plural 'cooks', largely in an attempt to avoid the reification of The Cook against cooks in their diversity and totality. When I quote other works, the sex of the cook can shift disconcertingly: some authors assume that their cook is a man employed in a large household or restaurant; others assume that theirs is a woman employed in a less grand household or at the myriad hearths throughout history. Nevertheless, in broad terms, women have maintained and improved the culture surrounding essential caring. Men have left for the public domain, ascending the pyramids. They have become the professionals, including chefs. Phillip Searle is a singular, male cook, but because the vast majority have been women, the next chapter starts again entirely in the kitchens of women.

PART ONE

WHAT DO COOKS DO?

CHAPTER TWO

Distributing Goodness

What Katy Did is the story, its author announces, of a girl 'who planned to do a great many wonderful things, and in the end did none of them, but something quite different – something she didn't like at all at first, but which, on the whole, was a great deal better than any of the doings she had dreamed about'. In short, Katy gave up her silly ambitions and settled down to run a household. Susan Coolidge (Sarah Chauncey Woolsey, 1835–1905) published the 'Katy' stories in the late nineteenth century, when teenage girls already needed persuading to see life as cooking and regulating the home. In lauding the traditional role, the novel betrays the essentials of cooks and their world.

Katy Carr is the eldest of six children, growing up in a thriving North American town. Dr Carr has lost his wife, and fidgety Aunt Izzie endeavours to take over. For half of *What Katy Did*, Katy leads a turbulent child's life, misunderstood by Aunt Izzie. Then Cousin Helen, whom illness has confined to a sofa, visits. She is so good that, upon becoming crippled, she released her sweetheart, predicting that he would love somebody else well enough to marry. Dr Carr affirms: 'Cousin Helen is half an angel already, and loves other people better than herself ... She's an example to us all, Katy, and I couldn't ask anything better than to have my little girls take pattern after her' (Coolidge 1957: 99–100). The very next day, Katy falls from a swing.

Now herself confined to bed, Katy can no longer pursue her ambitions to 'Study, and help people, and become famous'. However,

Cousin Helen reveals the opportunity to go to God's school, 'The School of Pain', where Katy is to learn the 'beautiful' lessons of Patience, Cheerfulness, Making the Best of Things, Hopefulness and Neatness (123–6).

So that she might appeal to others, Katy should keep her room and herself pretty and, in dealing with people, pick them up by the smooth rather than the rough handle. As Cousin Helen encourages, a sick person is always available. 'If people love her, she gets naturally to be the heart of the house' (131). When Aunt Izzie dies of typhoid fever, someone else will have to manage the housekeeping, taking charge of the three or four servants. Katy announces to her father: 'I wish you would let *me* try . . . I shall be fourteen in two weeks' (161).

Every morning, after the breakfast dishes are put away, Debby ties on a clean apron, and comes upstairs for orders. At first Katy finds planning dinner great fun, but it grows tiresome. 'Let me see – there is roast beef – leg of mutton – boiled chicken . . . Debby, you might roast the chickens. Dear! – I wish somebody would invent a new animal!' So Katy sends for every recipe book in the house. 'Dr Carr had to eat a great many queer things in those days. But he didn't mind, and as for the children, they enjoyed it. Dinner-time became quite exciting, when nobody could tell exactly what any dish on the table was made of' (163–4).

Trapped indoors, Katy has stepped prematurely into her mother's place and, after four years as an invalid, she is finally recovered sufficiently to descend downstairs on her mother's birthday. The family have secreted Cousin Helen in the house to greet her.

'You have won the place, which, you recollect, I once told you an invalid should try to gain, of being to everybody "The Heart of the House".'

'Oh, Cousin Helen, don't! . . . I haven't been brave . . . It's too delightful to have you praise me – but you mustn't. I don't deserve it.'

But although she said she didn't deserve it, I think that Katy did! (192).

What Katy Did promotes domestic values. Not destined for the public arena and workforce, Katy ceases outdoor adventures. She learns to become a carer: neat, patient, cheerful, hopeful, making the best of things. 'But there was Love in the Pain. I see it now' (186). This concept of womanliness promotes resignation. And yet Katy finds genuine rewards in serving and routine. She delights in happy surprises, good menus, kind actions, family togetherness. Supporting its sentimental themes and moral lessons with vigorous writing, the book also affirms cooking. While awarding Katy servants to do the work, Susan Coolidge, unlike the majority of novelists, does not ignore and downgrade cooks and the diffused tasks of housekeeping.

Holding the 'threads of the house firmly in her hands' (165), Katy is a true economist, both etymologically and historically. The original meaning of *oikonomia* – from the Greek words *oikos* for 'house' and *nemo* for 'manage' – is 'household management'. When Xenophon, a disciple of Socrates, wrote his *Oikonomikos (Economics)*, it concerned precisely what Katy did – the wifely supervision of stores, meals and servants.

Until the nineteenth century, economics remained just this, the study and stewardship of the household. Thus in the *Oxford English Dictionary* we find such uses as: 'three great ministers, who could exactly compute ... the accompts [accounts] of a kingdom, but who were wholly ignorant of their own œconomy' (1727). Around two centuries ago 'political economy' borrowed the name. This was by way of metaphor. The overall political economy was like the household, greatly multiplied. (Similarly, the science of ecology was to generalise the *oikos* into the natural 'household'.) Eventually, the usurpers dropped the 'political', leaving just 'economics', and the real economists had to practise 'home economics'.

What Katy Did features what historian Fernand Braudel terms 'material life', which is an 'extremely elementary economy' covering the earth in a 'rich layer' and which can be compared to the eighteenth-century conception of the 'natural economy', as against the superior, sophisticated 'artificial economy' (1982: 21–2).

THE LONG WINTER

Another novel aimed at young women, and not embarrassed about its domestic interests, is *The Long Winter*, published in 1940 by Laura Ingalls Wilder (1867–1957), whose series of pioneering reminiscences of her North American childhood also includes *Little House on the Prairie*.

The Ingalls family live on the Dakota prairie with few features beyond the swampy grass of the Big Slough and the wide sky. The mother and four daughters maintain a 'tidy shanty', their sewing stitches being 'so exactly alike that you could not tell them apart' (Wilder 1968: 31). But winter comes early, and they leave the claim for their more airtight dwelling in the isolated town. During an unprecedented succession of blizzards, housework is conducted close to the stoves and starvation. Nothing makes cooks more noticeable than provisions running out.

From the jug of cold water Laura takes to Pa out on the mowing machine – 'the heat there smelled as good as an oven when bread is baking' (8) – cooking is described on every second page. When an early, bitter frost kills the kitchen garden, ever-resourceful Ma makes tomato pickles and a green pumpkin pie. Early in the winter, they enjoy hot cakes with crisped slices of fat pork and the brown-and-amber grease from the pan, and dried-apple sauce and sugar syrup, even if there is no butter, for Ellen (the cow) is nearly dry (99). When the flour finishes they convert the coffee-grinder to grinding wheat. They extinguish the heating stove, and cluster all day around the 'cookstove' (110). The school closes. The kerosene for the lamp runs out. The superintendent finally gives up his attempts to get trains through. Coal beats brushwood for steady heat, but that gone, they burn hay tied tediously into 'sticks'. Their menu becomes brown-bread toast and tea for breakfast and potatoes for the second meal of the day (171). Pa's hands become too cold to play his fiddle. Yet, even in the worst, Ma reminds him, 'I'll have a hot meal ready and waiting by the time you come in' (180–1).

Laura Ingalls Wilder evokes a simple physical, social and cultural environment. She draws the reader into Laura's subjective states: brave, happy, tired, frightened. Being safe at home, with her family and a steaming cup of ginger tea, 'must be a little bit like Heaven' (76). Mainly, though, the dramatic structure is provided by the long winter itself, the suspense of whether they, like the train, will finally get through. Snowed in for seven months – 'only the blizzard and the coffee mill's grinding, the cold and the dusk darkening to night

again, were real' (232) – certain basics stand out.

Pa is responsible for a specialised aspect of the food system, acquisition, which takes him outdoors growing, hunting, purchasing and being prepared to slaughter Ellen and her heifer calf (183). Even during the worst blizzards, he is forever coming and going, feeding the animals, trying to clear the railroad tracks, negotiating the last supplies and keeping up with the scant news.

And Ma sustains indoors. She does not like to see women working in the fields: 'Only foreigners did that. Ma and her girls were Americans, above doing men's work' (10). Crucially, she is in charge of sharing what Pa has fetched. This is how, for instance, she divides twelve potatoes: 'Little Grace needed only one, the others had two apiece, and Ma insisted that Pa take the extra one'. With the heaviest labour, Pa has to keep his strength up, she says (171). And this is how Ma bakes the last wheat into little breakfast biscuits: 'I thought I made them all the same', she protests, but Pa is still somehow able to get the biggest, she the next, then Mary, with Laura and Carrie having two suspiciously alike and Grace the smallest (238).

Ma is also the guardian of culture, responsible for culinary lore, knowing how to improvise. When the potatoes have been exhausted, she thaws some specially hidden salt codfish with which to make welcome gravy for the coarse bread (190). She is also in charge of mealtime stories, so that a little butter that had been kept aside is 'what the cobbler threw at his wife' – that is, his awl, or his last (104).

Eventually, a Christmas barrel, kept frozen by the blizzards safely aboard a train, brings a feast of turkey and cranberry in May. Up at dawn, Laura all day helped Ma 'bake and stew and boil the good things for next day's Christmas dinner' (245).

> When all the chairs were drawn up to the well-filled table, Ma looked at Pa and every head bowed.
>
> 'Lord, we thank Thee for all Thy bounty.' That was all Pa said, but it seemed to say everything (248).

THE CULT OF DOMESTICITY

These books are examples of *Bildungsroman* (German for 'training novel'), in which a young person learns to become, for instance, a good wife and mother. Readers can put themselves in the main character's place. While we might smile at their old-fashioned charm, the 'Katy', 'Laura' and similar series have held numerous young people enthralled, and the way of life has definite pluses, such as cooking usually being done in the company of mothers, daughters, sisters, cousins and friends.

As these training novels make plain, men have left the hearth, heading off on various errands; as a doctor, Katy's father becomes almost invisible. It had so long been the custom that men worked outside and women inside that it had seemed inevitable. However, the message needed spelling out, especially with changes in the nineteenth century, as in another largely autobiographical example, *Little Women; Good Wives*. In this double volume of Louisa May Alcott, published in 1868–69, the character of Jo March must repress her literary ambitions to do a course in plain cooking and get down to married life. Similarly, after pursuing a university education, the protagonist of *Anne of Green Gables*, published by Canadian L.M. Montgomery in 1908, chooses rural domesticity over urban intellectualism.

Since time immemorial, the public sphere has claimed and has been accorded authority. Nonetheless, when domestic duties are spelled out, they can gain a nobility. While 'private' comes from the Latin for 'deprived', these novels find richness around the stove. They uphold the resourceful (in these cases, North American) values of the relatively self-sufficient family (Fellman 1990).

Such novels reflect what historians have termed a 'cult of domesticity', promoted notably in Britain between 1780 and 1820 by the branch of Protestants known as the Evangelicals, who also led the struggle against slavery and for feminism (Hall 1979). In the United States and from a famous family of progressive Christians (her sister wrote *Uncle Tom's Cabin*), Catharine Beecher defends domesticity in her *Treatise on Domestic Economy* of 1841. Women's duties are not 'petty, trivial, or unworthy', she declares. Instead, they are the 'most important, the most difficult, and the most sacred and interesting duties that can possibly employ the highest intellect' (144). For one thing, unlike the man's job, which is necessarily 'limited to a particular department', the housewife is preoccupied by 'ten thousand little disconnected items' (136).

Laura Ingalls Wilder's heartfelt warmth is replaced in Beecher's case, however, by moralism from on high. Beecher argues for women's freedom, but the limited freedom that lets a woman choose to which man she will submit domestically (3). Even more para-doxically, Beecher blames the general view 'that women's business and cares are contracted and trivial' not on the mystifications of patriarchy, but on private overemphasis on clothing, housing and the 'gratification of the appetite' (142–3). Instead, according to her, women are important (and equal and free) because their prime responsibility is to maintain and improve moral standards. Every woman ought to start with the assumption that 'religion is of more consequence than any worldly concern', and the 'mere gratification of appetite is to be placed *last*' (145–6).

So far, these have been girls' books (which might well be read by adults beneath the covers), but the next depictions of cooks bring us closer to 'serious' art. Simultaneously, we find a lessening in acceptance of domesticity.

'BABETTE'S FEAST'

'Babette's Feast' is a short story written under a male-sounding name, Isak Dinesen. But this is again written by a woman, a Dane, Karen Blixen (1885–1962), also known for her autobiographical novel *Out of Africa*. Part of her collection *Anecdotes of Destiny*, first published in 1958, 'Babette's Feast' became the basis of Gabriel Axel's 1987 film, much loved for its careful reconstruction of a dinner of a lifetime.

Two elderly ladies, living on the stark Berlevaag Fjord in Norway, have inherited the pious, widely admired but declining sect founded by their father. Like Catharine Beecher's model housewife, these Lutherans renounce the pleasures of this world, for the earth is 'but a kind of illusion', and the true reality is the 'New Jerusalem toward which they were longing' (Dinesen 1986: 23). As young women, both daughters had been kissed fleetingly on the hand by an admirer, but their liaisons had been abbreviated by their father, the dean, who kept them beside him in favour of the heavenly ideal (25).

The disappointments of both thwarted suitors eventually revisit the sect. One of the men, a touring French opera singer, recalls his Norwegian romance by sending on a political refugee, Babette, who remains as cook for the sisters. Karen Blixen tells us that 'within a week Babette cooked a split cod and an ale-and-bread-soup as well as anybody born and bred in Berlevaag' (36).

The centenary of the founder's birth is to be celebrated on 15 December 1883. A very plain supper with a cup of coffee is the most sumptuous meal to which the daughters have ever asked any guest to sit down. However, Babette, who has worked for them twelve years without seeking any favour, has asked if she can give a 'real French dinner' (42–3). She spends the entire proceeds of a lottery win on imports from home, and throws herself into elaborate preparations. Despite granting Babette's wish, the sect members have made a pact that 'they would, on the great day, be silent upon all matters of food and drink. Nothing that might be set before them, be it even frogs or snails, should wring a word from their lips' (46–7).

This is when the other disappointed suitor returns, the now worldly General Loewenhielm. As an accidental guest, he is taken aback by the wines and dishes. 'Incredible! . . . It is Blinis Demidoff!'

He recognises the Veuve Cliquot 1860, which the sect members presume is some kind of lemonade that 'agreed with their exalted state of mind and seemed to lift them off the ground, into a higher and purer sphere'. It is, they realise, when man has 'firmly renounced all ideas of food and drink that he eats and drinks in the right spirit'. When Babette sends in 'Cailles en Sarcophage', the general suspects a miracle, since that dish was the creation of 'the greatest culinary genius of the age', unusually a woman, who had been 'turning a din-ner at the Café Anglais into a kind of love affair – into a love affair of the noble and romantic category in which one no longer distinguishes between bodily and spiritual appetite or satiety!' (56–8).

Afterwards, Babette sits on the chopping block, surrounded by more black and greasy pots and pans than her mistresses have ever seen. She is 'as white and as deadly exhausted as on the night when she first appeared and had fainted on their doorstep' (64). Babette explains that in Paris she had cooked for the very people she had fought against as a communard. And yet she grieved for them.

> 'You see, Mesdames . . . those people belonged to me, they were mine.
> They had been brought up and trained, with greater expense than you,
> my little ladies, could ever imagine or believe, to understand what a
> great artist I am. I could make them happy. When I did my very best I
> could make them perfectly happy'(68).

In some ways our lives are long and passed in devotion – either to grinding labour or to some timeless, higher world. In other ways our lives are brief, with only one chance at deliverance. 'Babette's Feast' intertwines the eternal and transitory. Just as one religious leader's moment of truth can sustain the hopes of an entire congregation, and a brush with love can sustain old age, preparing one fine, Parisian meal can redeem years of cooking split cod and ale-and-bread soup. Exemplifying the cook's dedication, in Paris Babette has loved her class enemies. After twelve years on the Berlevaag Fjord, she asks to vary the menu just once.

Providing a heroine condemned to drudgery, two domineering sisters, windfall transformation, spectacular banquet and excel-lence recognised by a distinguished aristocrat, Blixen has written a

DISTRIBUTING GOODNESS

modern, inspired 'Cinderella'. The authorities rate the story of the 'woman of the cinders' as the 'best known folktale in the world'. The earliest recorded version is Chinese, from the ninth century AD, and more than 500 versions come from Europe alone, including those of Charles Perrault and the Grimm brothers (Leach 1972: 233–4).

With 'Cinderella' proverbial for a 'person or thing of unrecognised or disregarded merit or beauty', the story's appeal testifies to both the lack of recognition and the timelessness of cooking – the scene being repeated infinitely through history and across places. Cinderella is liberated from the 'banal' in its older senses of 'compulsory' and hence 'common to all'.

Early in the nineteenth century, gourmand Dr William Kitchiner spoke of the pleasures of the table being enjoyed 'above *a Thousand times in a Year, every Year of our Lives!!!*' (1821: 7), and these meals have to be cooked. Like Sisyphus condemned to roll his stone, cooks are trapped in motion: complete one meal and prepare the next. The repetition is staggering. But we should not be overwhelmed because, as Albert Camus reminds us in the *Myth of Sisyphus* (1942), Sisyphus could delight at seeing his labour roll down the other side.

HIGH VERSUS LOW CULTURE

Good cooking, like its associated crafts, relies on this very predictability. It depends on routines. It demands a practised hand, keen eye and grounded intuition, rather than any frenzied leap of creation. Katy is trapped upstairs with plenty of quiet thinking time. When things run smoothly down below, it is because 'Aunt Izzie's regular, punctual ways were so well understood by the servants, that the house seemed almost to keep itself' (Coolidge 1957: 163). 'Babette's Feast' asks us to stand in awe at the enormousness of shared accomplishments and the vanity of our own ambitions.

Anthropologist Clifford Geertz urges that culture needs to be seen not as complexes of concrete behaviour patterns but as a 'set of control mechanisms – plans, recipes, rules, instructions (what computer engineers call "programs") – for the governing of behaviour' (1973: 44). Note the word 'recipe' in there – culture can be viewed as our recipes for life. Or, the other way around, the shape of the

25

activities of cooks and their helpers is culture. Culture gains its force through repetition, routine, reiteration, recapitulation, rigmarole, ritual, rhythm, regulation, reproduction – recipes.

The very repetitiveness of cooking is part of the reason why many Western intellectuals have snubbed it. On the contrary, the less the procedure varies between hearths and from one culture to the next, the more fundamental it must be. Of course, there are innumerable variations between cultures, but it has been, for example, traditionally the women who do the cooking and men the talking.

High culture is altogether different. High culture (usually male) claims importance, greatness, transcendence, originality. It disguises its material dependence and disowns its humble beginnings. Just as the word 'economy' has come to stand against itself (the public economy denying its household origins), the word 'culture' has been used to mean high culture, which distances itself from the everyday.

The contrast between the uniqueness of art and the banality of the cooks' offerings shows up in attitudes to plagiarism. Where the former is a personal statement, which cannot be stolen, the essence of the latter lies in its sharing. In the prefaces to cookery books, certainly in former days, writers customarily lamented the lack of originality of predecessors, and protested their own. However, as the Victorian English writer A.V. Kirwan explains: 'Cookery is, above all others, a traditional and practical art, and unless receipts [recipes] have stood the test of time and experience, and general approval, they are little worth' (1864: 64). The word 'plagiarism' comes from the Greek for kidnapping, and cooks 'kidnap' hour after hour.

A London-based defender of Chinese cuisine, F.T. Cheng, muses: 'A nation, though uncultured, may, all of a sudden or at times, produce a genius, whether in art or in literature, but only a people of culture can have a good cuisine; because the former is particular and transient, whereas the latter is general and permanent' (1954: 18). So it is a significant achievement when the novelist, like the still-life painter, brings out the beauty, the drama, the tragedy of the familiar, the bowl of fruit that might look the same but is continually replenished.

There are no rules, but while most novelists keep cooks in the background, they do tend to deal more than other creative artists with personal feelings, intimate relationships and everyday experiences. In their one-to-one form, novels are adapted to the private. And to the extent that they actually do represent women's lives, they do not entirely ignore domestic cooks. In the narratives already discussed, the mundanity of cooking is thrown into relief and even sometimes given meaning by its antithesis, which might be a teenage accident, an exceptionally hard winter, a French extravaganza or, as in the examples to follow, a passionate love affair and a husband fleeing the nest.

LIKE WATER FOR HOT CHOCOLATE

Like Water for Hot Chocolate reveals the passion behind the drudgery of cookery. It brings wild impulses and banality into conflict: a cook is kept by her duties from her lover. Laura Esquivel's exuberant book appeared in 1989, was made into a film in 1991 and translated into English in 1992. Parodying a popular form of 'calendars for young ladies' (de Valdes 1995), it looks back to Mexico earlier in the twentieth century.

The protagonist is condemned to cook. Tita was born prematurely 'right there on the kitchen table amid the smells of simmering noodle soup, thyme, bay leaves and coriander, steamed milk, garlic and, of course, onion' (Esquivel 1993: 9). And she maintains a deep love for the kitchen and kitchen gardens – 'for Tita the joy of living was wrapped up in the delights of food' – but at a cost. She is prevented from marrying Pedro by having to look after her embittered mother, whose secret is that she, too, has been frustrated in love. The book does not weep long, though, over the powerlessness of the individual against tradition, since the empowerment of tradition is also represented – especially by the overwhelmingly good servant cook, Nacha, from whom Tita learns and takes over.

Tita is trapped in an everyday universe, both spirited and earthy. Sometimes the physical world rises up in metaphors: 'The anger she felt within her acted like yeast on bread dough' (137). When her eyes meet Pedro's, she understands 'how dough feels when it is plunged into boiling oil' (18). True knowledge comes from physical intimacy: 'Only the pan knows how the boiling soup feels' (35). Esquivel explains that the expression 'like water for *hot* chocolate' (shortened for the film title) means that a person is 'on the verge of boiling over' (138), presumably like simmering or seething.

In the magic of everyday life, the emotional and physical worlds interpenetrate, as when Tita cries while chopping onions, and when people are drawn together by the warmth of the stove. The story is interlarded with instructional passages. Tita twists a quail's neck too nervously, so that the poor bird runs pitifully around the kitchen. 'She realised that you can't be weak when it comes to killing: you have to be strong or it just causes more sorrow' (47). Recipes are also part of the narrative, as when Tita prepares 'Quail in rose petal sauce', which so inflames guests.

Tita's chores: 'She had to get up, get dressed, get the fire going in the stove, fix breakfast, feed the animals, wash the dishes, make the beds, fix lunch, wash the dishes, iron the clothes, fix dinner, wash the dishes, day after day, year after year' (98–9). The difficulty in portraying such monotony is solved by compressing a virtual lifetime into a few pages: the lovers are not united for twenty-two years, during which much food flows across the table. Mind you, at thirty-nine, Tita is 'still as sharp and fresh as a cucumber that had just been cut' (213). Simultaneously, the book comes in '12 monthly parts', which relay the seasonal recurrence.

The book favours cooks and their command of their world: having sister Gertrudis and her fifty hungry troops staying at the house had 'not made Tita feel oppressed by extra work, instead it had provided her with a real peace' (170). Personifying the dilemmas of tradition, Esquivel constructs the characters around Tita in pairs, starting with her mother and the family cook. Of her two suitors, Pedro is the strong, silent traditionalist and John Brown the man of science. John, with 'his peace, serenity, reason', has 'shown her the way to freedom' (157), but she decides in favour of her original love. Of her two sisters, Gertrudis succeeds with decided *élan* in the man's military world, while the slothful Rosaura remains at home, psychically incapacitated.

In the end, Tita passes on to her niece Esperanza a valuable education in 'the secrets of love and life as revealed by the kitchen'. However, Esperanza belongs to the new world and, in her, we finally find the cook as a complete person, 'so self-confident, so intelligent, so perfectly prepared, so happy, so capable, and at the same time, so feminine and womanly, in the fullest sense of the word' (216). This cyclical novel concludes in a mighty conflagration. Upon the couple finally getting together, Pedro dies. Grief consumes Tita; she consumes matches; and the cook's fire consumes all. The ashes of the hero and heroine and their household fertilise fabulous fruits and vegetables, which are tasted by our story-teller in her youth. Tita's grandniece cries as she returns to the first recipe in the book (222).

The first two novels discussed above were already caught in this changing world, advocating the traditional Cinderella role for modern, literate girls. Babette, too, cooked for an older social order undergoing revolutionary change. *Like Water for Hot Chocolate* makes visible similar gains and losses of modernity, targeted not only by novels but by the collection of explanations from historical sociology. For example, Karl Marx focuses on the emergence of the working class, Max Weber on increasingly soulless organisations, and Emile Durkheim on the more fluid manufacture of value systems.

Our ways, our recipes, were once handed down by our mothers. They were the very embodiment of repetition, the tried and true. Needless to say, complex, global sharing requires a very different, flexible, many-stranded culture. Where once people grew, preserved and cooked their own food, and maintained personal control, the emerging generations belong to an era of global distribution of food and information. Instead of relying on our ancestors' customs, we rely on the latest knowledge and the goodwill of unknown contemporaries. Rather than being embedded in ritual, we plunge from the cutting edge. Where traditional cooking practices held their own authority and actions were undertaken because they always were, now practices are 'rationalised'. Once hands-on, cooking is now mostly by remote control.

Laura Esquivel understands this well. Her book looks back, nostalgically, only a generation or two to the traditional kitchen of Tita and virtually all women. 'Tita was the last link in a chain of cooks who had been passing culinary secrets from generation to generation since ancient times', she writes. Tita had learned so well from the family cook that 'it seemed Nacha herself was in Tita's body doing all those things' (45–7). In the novel the traditional characters learn their culture from lived experience; we read it.

HEARTBURN

I loved to cook, so I cooked. And then the cooking became a way of saying I love you. And then the cooking became the easy way of saying I love you. And then the cooking became the only way of saying I love you . . . Would anyone love me if I couldn't cook?

Ephron 1986: 119

Nora Ephron's quite autobiographical novel *Heartburn* is about a very modern couple (New York Jews in Washington and then in therapy) whose marriage seems fine until she learns, when seven months pregnant, that he's having an affair. Ephron, a journalist who moved to Hollywood as a screenwriter and director, had been married to Carl Bernstein, the *Washington Post* columnist involved in the Watergate exposé. My copy is the revised edition that was published in 1986 (which presumably makes it the less bitter version), the year *Heartburn* also became a film, subject to the constraints of a marital separation agreement (Ephron 1985).

The first of the book's twin themes is the regularity and even dullness of the private domain. The narrator, Rachel Samstat, explains:

I love the everydayness of marriage, I love figuring out what's for dinner and where to hang the pictures and do we owe the Richardsons, but life does tend to slow to a crawl. The whole summer Mark was secretly seeing Thelma Rice while pretending to be at the dentist, I was cooking.

Perfecting a vinaigrette is 'not exactly the stuff of drama', but she could not believe Mark would 'risk losing that vinaigrette' (Ephron 1986: 17). The thickening of a white sauce is a 'sure thing in a world where nothing is sure' (117).

Rachel writes cookbooks, 'very personal and chatty . . . Then, of course, the television show came along, which made the books sell even better' (19). This thinly disguised recounting of Ephron's real-life drama is pegged with actual recipes. There's nothing like mashed potatoes when you're feeling blue, Ephron writes. So a recipe says to add just as much melted butter and salt and pepper as you feel like. 'Eat immediately. Serves one' (112). The first person narrator decides: 'I haven't managed to work in any recipes for a while. It's hard to work in recipes when you're moving the plot forward' (89). Counterpointing culinary routine is sexual boredom: 'it's hard to compete with *anyone* new in the sack if you're the spouse who's been around for years' (39). She is incredulous that someone could be so sexually driven that he might actually skip lunch (59).

The novel's complementary theme is that men come from an alien world. They are the Other. Rachel knows so little about them. The housekeeper, Lucy Mae Hopkins, had 'given up men for Jesus forty years earlier, and she couldn't understand why anyone else wouldn't'. Men are so inadequate. 'It's true that men who cry are sensitive to and in touch with feelings, but the only feelings they tend to be sensitive to and in touch with are their own' (78–9). Men are so self-centred. The 'Jewish prince doesn't mean, "Where's the butter?" He means, "Get me the butter". He's too clever to say "Get me" so he says "Where's"' (22).

With the 'major concrete achievement' of the women's movement in the 1970s being the Dutch treat, Ephron writes that household duties were also to be divided: 'thousands of husbands agreed to clear the table. They cleared the table. They cleared the table and then looked around as if they deserved a medal' (74). Rachel's husband, Mark Feldman, a Washington newspaper columnist, is always saying: 'Maybe I can get a column out of it'. Rachel could feel nothing happened to her because 'every time something *did* happen, Mark got a column out of it' and 'made it all seem as if it had happened to him' (80–1). Arthur Siegel would declare: 'Pesto is the quiche of the seventies', whereupon Mark would turn it into a column (90). This is the universal phenomenon of the public world being lifted up from and being sustained by the private – of the man relying on the home for vitality.

Why does Ephron make Rachel a cook, albeit a cookery writer? It is not simply that she is a New York chatterer who needs to pass on recipes. It is to reassert the original economy. It is a cry, in the face of heartbreak, for the comfort of banality. The target of the book is inadequate men (or one inadequate man) who cannot cope with domestic life. At the book's climax the passions of domesticity triumph over public personas. Rachel briefly accepts her husband back, and, at the final dinner party, throws her contribution, Key lime pie, in his face (recipe included).

Routine can be presented as drab, but it is raw culture, the real thing, subtly changing, engaged and vibrant. Its very mundanity draws us on. Its reiteration gives us momentum. The repeated round of cooks – in all its variation – is staggering. Yet this endows human life with rhythm, which gets taken up in ritual, which grows into meaning. When we think of culture, we are encouraged to think of the exceptional, and the more extraordinary the better. *Heartburn* shows the 'shock of catapulting from the peanut-butter-and-jellyness of my life into High Drama' (42). But the 'high' is but a whirl in the icing: eye-catching, indicative, but more shape than texture, more style than substance. It is the unshared recipe.

In this chapter, women novelists have provided sympathetic insights into the accomplishments and enthusiasms of women cooks, mainly domestic and loosely fictionalised. They have juxtaposed the exceptional with the utterly ordinary, which gives an inkling of the taken-for-granted *economy* and *culture* based in cooking. We now turn to another category of written sources, when prosperous gentlemen have become appreciative diners.

CHAPTER THREE

'A Good Bank Account, a Good Cook, and a Good Digestion'

A group of well-to-do gourmands surrender to a well-cooked dinner, chewing, chatting and comparing notes. It could be at a mansion, club or eating-house at any time over the past few thousand years. Eventually, as it surely must, the conversation comes around to the meal – the source of the ingredients, the execution of recipes and, even if shielded by steward and waiters, the cook(s). The plan in this chapter is to check out such dinner-table appreciation of cooks as has been committed to paper – here we borrow the privileged diners' stance on specialist cooks, who, like the diners, were typically male. Swiss–French political philosopher Jean-Jacques Rousseau sums up the situation: 'Happiness: a good bank account, a good cook, and a good digestion' (Cohen and Cohen 1960: 301).

The eighteenth-century English literary critic Dr Samuel Johnson, who launched such *mots* as 'When a man is tired of London he is tired of life' and 'Patriotism is the last refuge of a scoundrel', performed at table for the likes of portraitist Joshua Reynolds, writer Oliver Goldsmith, politician Edmund Burke and actor David Garrick. When the conversation got around to meals on Friday, 5 August 1763, Johnson proclaimed:

> Some people ... have a foolish way of not minding, or pretending not to mind, what they eat. For my part, I mind my belly very studiously, and very carefully; for I look upon it, that he who does not mind his belly will hardly mind anything else.

As to cookery, at dinner on Wednesday, 15 April 1778, Johnson boasted:

> I could write a better book of cookery than has ever yet been written; it should be a book upon philosophical principles. Pharmacy is now made much more simple. Cookery may be made so too. A prescription which is now compounded of five ingredients, had formerly fifty in it. So in cookery, if the nature of the ingredients be well known, much fewer will do.

He then jumped on a Miss Seward: 'Women can spin very well; but they cannot make a good book of Cookery', a humiliation that illustrates a frequent characteristic of such gatherings – men take pride of place.

The great biographer James Boswell (1740–95) provides these epigrams in his *The Life of Samuel Johnson, LL.D.* (1970: 331, 942–3). In the area of culinary insight, the loyal reporter far outdid his clubbish hero. In conversation with Edmund Burke, James Boswell proposed a ground-breaking definition of human nature. He recalled that an ancient philosopher had defined 'Man' as a 'two-legged animal without feathers', whereupon his sparring partner had had a cock plucked and set down as 'Philosophick Man'. Boswell also accepted Benjamin Franklin's proposition that 'Man' is a 'tool-making animal' – but not every person makes tools. Attempting to do better, Boswell announced:

> My definition of *Man* is, 'a Cooking Animal'. The beasts have memory, judgement, and all the faculties and passions of our mind, in a certain degree; but no beast is a cook.

While a trick monkey might roast chestnuts, Boswell continued, that surely just keeps people humble. 'Man alone can dress a good dish; and every man whatever is more or less a cook, in seasoning what he himself eats.' Incidentally, Boswell recalls this conversation in his *Journal of a Tour to the Hebrides* for 15 August 1773 to demonstrate that, contrary to Johnson's view, Burke had wit. Burke's riposte had been that he now saw the 'full force of the common proverb, "There is *reason* in roasting of eggs" ' (Boswell 1924: 179–80 n.1). This saying usually suggests that even the most ridiculous-seeming action might have a good explanation.

Homo sapiens, the 'cooking animal', became a familiar dictum in the eighteenth and nineteenth centuries. Crusty dictionaries of quotations ascribe versions to other authors, which suggests that the term did the dinner-table rounds. 'Man is an animal that cooks his victuals' is attributed in the *Nuttall* dictionary to Edmund Burke (borrowed, we have to infer, from Boswell). The *Benham* dictionary finds that 'The greatest animal in creation, the animal who cooks' was coined a century later by humorist Douglas Jerrold.

But 'great men' have not always been so discerning. Before continuing with diners' appreciation, I must confront an opposing view. The ancient Greek philosopher Plato decried cooks.

PLATO'S WARNING

Western learning's most influential exponent set it against culinary affairs. Through the voice of Socrates, Plato (427?–347 BC) declares in *Gorgias* that cookery 'isn't an art at all'. It is a 'kind of knack gained by experience' that is aimed at 'gratification and pleasure' (462d; 1960: 43). Cookery does not employ rational calculation, but follows routine (501a; 107). In the same work, Plato throws scorn on Sarambus the retailer in wine, Thearion the baker and Mithaecus the author of the Sicilian cookery book. These people might win praise by cramming and fattening bodies, but they have merely given the Athenians their fill of what they desired, rather than what would have served their best interests (518bd; 134–5). Little wonder that philosophers at Plato's Academy, the ancient Greek forerunner of our universities, gained notoriety for smashing a casserole to bits because it was too fancy, the cook being expected to 'abstain from such far-fetched importations' (Athenaeus 137f; 2: 129).

Diogenes the Cynic is said to have teased Plato about sailing to Syracuse in Sicily for the sake of the luxurious dishes, for which, with fertile agriculture, good fishing and trading cities, the island's cooks were famous. No, replied Plato, he had lived on olives and suchlike. 'Why then', inquired Diogenes, 'did you need to go to Syracuse?' (Diogenes Laertius 1925, 2: 27). In his *Seventh Letter*, Plato says he found 'nothing whatever to please me in the tastes of a society devoted to Italian and Syracusan cookery, where happiness was held to consist in filling oneself full twice a day, never sleeping alone at night, and indulging in the other pursuits that go with such a way of living' (326bc; 1973: 116). In *The Republic*, Socrates, Plato's teacher and literary mouthpiece, explains what is wrong with Sicilian cooking. Just as elaborate music produces indiscipline, 'elaborate food produces disease'. It is disgraceful that an idle life has filled our bodies with gases and fluids, like a stagnant pool, and driven the medical professional to invent names like flatulence and catarrh (404d–5d; 1974: 167–8).

Plato mocks those deceived by bodily appetites.

> They bend over their tables, like sheep with heads bent over their pasture and eyes on the ground, they stuff themselves and copulate, and in their greed for more they kick and butt each other with hooves and horns of steel, and kill each other because they are not satisfied, as they cannot be while they fill with unrealities a part of themselves which is itself unreal and insatiable (586ab; 412).

Instead, according to Plato, the members of his ideal state would feast, along with wine, on wheaten loaves and barley-cakes. Prompted that this sounds 'pretty plain fare for a feast', Socrates accepts some *opsa*. One translator calls these a 'few luxuries', but they are merely things to have with the bread and cake. Socrates lists the basic *opsa* of salt, olive oil, cheese and 'different kinds of vegetables from which to make various country dishes'. Additionally, for dessert, the citizens might get 'figs and peas and beans, and myrtle-berries and acorns to roast'. On this diet, Plato's citizens 'will lead a peaceful and healthy life, and probably die at a ripe old age, bequeathing a similar way of life to their children' (372bd; 121–2). While vegetarian writers pick out the lack of meat, the more pointed absence is fish, since Athenians saw fish-eating as synonymous with gourmandise (the habits of a gourmand).

Plato remains the greatest philosophical hero of all time, with many practitioners agreeing with A.N. Whitehead that the 'safest general characterisation of the European philosophical tradition is that it consists in a series of footnotes to Plato' (for example, Lovejoy

1964: 24). Anti-gastronomic arguments, both explicit and otherwise, usually follow the same shape. Not long ago French intellectual Roland Barthes accepted 'we do not see our own food or, worse, we assume that it is insignificant. Even – or perhaps especially – to the scholar, the subject of food connotes triviality or guilt' (1979: 167). What should we make of such antagonism?

Plato's warning against cooks – as mere seducers of the palate, with this-worldly preoccupations and apathetic to theoretical principles – accompanies his philosophical dualism. Entranced by an eternal world of 'forms', of which our world is an inferior copy, he decides that the mind is linked to the higher things, such as logic, eternal values and spiritual truth, whereas food, its cooking and enjoyment are naturally part of the lower, physical and transient world. The difficulty for dualists is to explain how unlikes might interact, especially how mind might synchronise with body. Plato's immediate solution is that the higher instincts ought totally to dominate the lower, reason rule the senses, and so on.

In a more sophisticated model, Plato splits systems into three, such that the higher aspect controls the lower through an intermediary (for a sociological explanation, see Durkheim 1960). Accordingly, in the *Republic*, the ideal state comprises three social classes: the philosopher kings; the middle class, with military powers; and the third class, which undertakes the basic life-support tasks of agriculture, handicrafts and so on (500bc; 296–7). The three social classes are matched by a threefold psychology, in which the soul is differentiated into reason, spirit and appetite. Plato accords primacy to self-control, in which thought or reason, mediated by the emotions, controls appetite (431a; 201).

Likewise, in his cosmological exposition, the *Timaeus*, Plato speaks of the three-tiered arrangement of the human anatomy – the head at the top, the heart in the middle and the stomach below. The part of the soul associated with reason lies in the head; indeed, the divine part attaches us as if by roots to the heavens and so keeps the whole upright (90ab; 1971: 121). The seat of courage, passion and ambition (the heart) is located near the head to be 'well-placed to listen to the commands of reason and combine with it in forcibly restraining the appetites when they refused to obey' (70a; 97–8). Meanwhile, the appetite for food and drink and other natural needs is found in the 'kind of manger for the body's food' (the stomach) to be 'as far as possible from the seat of deliberation, and cause the least possible noise and disturbance, so leaving the highest part of us to deliberate quietly about the welfare of each and all' (70d–71a; 98).

According to Plato, the designers of the human anatomy foresaw that people would be seduced by cooks. Accordingly, they 'wound the bowels round in coils, thus preventing the quick passage of food, which would otherwise compel the body to want more and make its appetite insatiable, so rendering our species incapable through gluttony of philosophy and culture, and unwilling to listen to the divinest element in us' (73a; 100).

Plato's nature is also divisible in three. Endowed with the power of reason, human beings stand above all other species. While animals lack rationality, they share the human power of locomotion, and so come midway in the hierarchy. Having neither thought nor loco-motion, plants are purely 'nutritive' or 'vegetative'.

Many aspects of Plato's hierarchical world still seem tantalisingly accurate. We still think of God on 'high'. We speak of 'top dogs', 'upper class', 'high' art, 'higher' mathematics, 'superstructure' and so on. Freud subdivides the psyche into superego, ego and id. Belonging to the higher species, vegetarians refuse to eat the intermediate category.

However, in a series of religious, scientific, political and other upheavals in recent centuries, the hierarchical view of the world has been demystified. Our philosophical ideas are no longer quite so authoritarian, and we are more likely to speak of interdependent systems. We are more secular, democratic and empirical. In total, we no longer let Plato bluff us about cooks.

Significantly, Plato spoke against cooks when he was at the table, or, more precisely, at symposia, which were conversational, after-dinner drinking parties. In much of his writing, his conceit is that he has jotted down table talk, with Socrates as the principal speaker. The trouble is that Plato did not just make a science of dinner-party conversation; he fought for its privileged status. He sought to en-shrine debate as the most 'important' part of the meal. He exalted its exponents, the philosophers. Plato became so entranced with one aspect of the meal, the rationality, that he put it on a pedestal, and vilified the rest. Cooks would fail if they only sat around adoring and adorning the beauty of their own minds. However important formal argument, our world includes a lot more.

To some degree, this book is an extended response to Plato; but I have another interest in his thought. Despite himself, Plato helps analyse what cooks do (Symons 1996). Cooks perform three duties, I propose in this book, which correspond to Plato's three functions: the organisation, distribution and getting of food. Plato just makes the mistake of overstating the philosophers' interest in logical argument.

As an illustration, consider a 'dish'. Is a 'dish' a recipe, and thus cultural and seemingly eternal? This is the prescription that Dr Johnson would provide in a cookery book based 'upon philosophical principles'. Or is a 'dish' a plate of food, and thus material and ephemeral? This is what Plato's school would smash as 'too fancy'. The answer is that it is both. However, this leaves the problem of how they interact: how does the recipe (culture) relate to the physical sustenance (nature)? My answer, adapted from Plato, is that they are connected by cooks. The cooks follow the recipe to produce the plate of food. In the other direction, the succession of cooks devises and hands on the recipe. In stressing the 'eternal' recipe, Plato has just elevated one part of the dialectic.

Rather than promote 'rational' philosophers by maligning 'practical' cooks, let us move back nearer the table and edge closer to the kitchen. There we immerse ourselves in a whirl of smells, sights, emotions, bodies, achievements and jests, as well as fine thoughts. In enjoying meals, we appreciate cooks, or should.

GREEK GASTRONOMERS

In marked contrast to Plato, well-to-do Athenian men at the time were usually food mad; they were educated gourmands. Today we are jolted by reports of ancient excess and by the near-invisibility of slaves and women; life was both expensive and cheap. And yet such assumptions are jumbled up with refined sensibility, humour and thoughtfulness.

Plato's contemporaries told stories about gourmands such as Philoxenus, famous for plunging his hands into hot water and gargling with it so that he might not shrink from hot food. Another of the same name would tramp a city followed by slaves carrying oil, wine, fish paste, vinegar and other relishes so that he might season any cooking he found. Aristoxenus, the hedonist philosopher, 'used to water the lettuce in his garden at evening with wine and honey', calling them 'blanched cakes produced by the earth for him'. Rather than a long life, Melanthius prayed for a long gullet, 'that he might linger long over his pleasures' (Athenaeus 5e–7c; 1: 23–31).

When one invited Philocrates to dinner, one was said to invite two, or even three, his appetite was so huge. It was also said that when Philocrates was invited for dinner at 8, he arrived promptly at 8 a.m., apologising for any tardiness (8bc; 1: 33–5). Gourmands complained: 'Were it not for the doctors, there wouldn't be anything stupider than the professors' (666a; 7: 67).

We have begun to dip into the jam-packed compilation made by Athenaeus, a Greek living in Rome nearly six centuries after the time of Plato but looking back at the greatness of Greek culture. He provides the world's richest single collection of table talk. Perhaps best left as in the Greek, *The Deipnosophists* (*deipnon* means 'meal'), the title of the treasure trove has been variously translated, from *The Sophists at Dinner* to something less literal such as *The Learned Banquet* or *The Gastronomers*. The work masquerades as a discussion between two-dozen dinner guests, who quote chunks of literature on the various aspects of the meal as it progresses. The anonymous author of a separate Epitome (summary) announces that Athenaeus:

> contrived to bring into his book an account of fishes, their uses and names with their derivations; also vegetables of all sorts and animals of every description; historians, poets, philosophers, musical instruments, innumerable kinds of jests; he has also described drinking-cups in all their variety, the wealth of kings, the size of ships, and other matters so numerous that I could not easily mention them all (1ab; 1: 3).

This gastronomic work is not on many shelves partly because it is so cumbersome. The available English translation took Harvard professor Charles Burton Gulick twenty-five years, which is a mighty task even if 'often interrupted' (7: ix). Admittedly, the translation only takes up the right-hand pages (with the Greek on the left), but it comes to seven volumes, totalling about 3500 pages. And this is thought to be just half the original.

Athenaeus cites 1250 authors, gives titles of more than 1000 plays and quotes in excess of 10 000 lines of verse. One of the guests complains of the others' 'word-diarrhoea' (159e; 2: 227). It is so long that the author has to dismiss the guests to take up again on a second and then third day, even for a while dropping the pretence of a meal altogether.

Athenaeus lists no fewer than eighteen authors of works with the title *The Art of Cookery* (516c; 5: 323). One especially sad loss, given its reputation, is the epic poem of the Sicilian Archestratus, seemingly republished under various titles, translated as *Gastronomia*, *The Art of High Living*, *The Art of Dining*, *The Art of Fine Cookery* (4e; 1: 19) and, according to the authors of a partial reconstruction, most probably *The Life of Luxury* (Archestratus 1994: 35). Archestratus travelled the entire world known to the Greeks documenting the 'delights of the belly' (Athenaeus 278d; 3: 251).

Ancient theatre-goers enjoyed comedies of manners preoccupied with cooking. The cook was a stock character; notably, in so-called Middle Comedy, the cook was the 'dominant' figure (Norwood 1931: 42). Aristophanes wrote such titles as *Masters of the Frying Pan* and *Men of Dinnerville*, and ended his career with *Aiolosicon*, about the renowned and wily chef Sicon. Indeed, the stage cook flourished for a century or so from around the time that Plato became Socrates's student (407 BC), so that while Plato dismissed cooks, his contemporaries were agog.

For a special meal Athenians would go to the marketplace (*agora*) to hire a cook, who would troop along with assistants and equipment. This gave narrative structure to the plays, as they followed the full sequence of purchasing, hiring the cook, preparing, slaughtering the animal and holding the party. Joining the 'scholars at dinner', we find a lively picture of ancient cooks.

THE COOKS

A cook boasts in Hegesippus's comedy *Brothers* that, when catering at a funeral feast, 'I take the lid from the pot and make the mourners laugh'. He can be like the Sirens of old, the fragrance of his cooking so attractive that anyone passing down the alley will become glued to the door, until rescued by a friend with stopped nostrils. The cook reveals: 'Why, I know of many persons seated here in the audience who have eaten up their estates for my sake' (Athenaeus 290ce; 3: 303–5).

Boasting great learning and skill, cooks pored over cookery books early in the morning (404b; 4: 331) and burned lamps late into the night. As fast as someone can list another fish, the cook in Antiphanes's *Philotis* responds with the correct method of cooking (662bc; 7: 49). Straton devises a mad conversation in his play *Phoenicides* in which the employer misunderstands the cook's arcane terminology. When the cook uses a fancy word for guests as conversationalists, the employer assumes this is the name of a particular guest, and so denies that any 'Articulates' has been invited. 'And so there is going to be no Epulator [feaster] present at all?' the cook asks again. 'Epulator? No, at least I think not.' The cook, who now fears no one is coming, drives the employer to further distraction with pretentious terms for the proposed foods (382bd; 4: 229).

The cook created by Philemon the Younger decrees: 'A man isn't a cook merely because he comes to a customer with a soup-ladle and carving-knife, nor even if he tosses some fish into a casserole; no, Wisdom is required in his business' (291e; 3: 309). The word for 'wisdom' is a favourite of the philosophers. In the play *Linus* by Alexis, Heracles is invited to improve himself by choosing from a library of tragedies, histories and similar classics. When he selects a book entitled *Cookery*, Linus recognises: 'You are a philosopher, that's very plain' (164c; 2: 247).

In the *Foster Brothers* by Damoxenus, a cook says that, as a follower of philosopher Epicurus, he follows the laws of nature. As a learned cook he must know what ingredients go together, 'for what possible good can come when one individual quality is mixed with another and twisted together in a hostile grip? Distinguishing these things clearly is a soulful art, not washing dishes or reeking with smoke'. The philosophical cook does not even enter the kitchen: 'I sit near by and watch, while others do the work; to them I explain the principles and the result' (102af; 1: 439–41).

The cook in *The False Accuser* by Sosipater declares himself a true heir of Sicon. 'He was the founder of the art. He taught us, first, to practise astrology; to follow that up immediately by architecture. He had by heart all the treatises on nature. Capping it all, he used to say, came the science of strategy.' That is, the cook has to understand the stars to follow the seasons, architecture to lay out the kitchen correctly (with plenty of light, no unwanted draughts and yet sufficient ventilation for the smoke), and military methods to ensure proper order and timing (378b–379a; 4: 211–15).

Having to coordinate smoke, flame and bustle so that foods reach the table on time, cooks have often been compared to generals, as in *The Law-giver* by Dionysius. Anyone can dress dishes, carve, cook sauces, blow the fire, 'but the cook is something else'. A cook has to take account of who is dining, the manner of serving, at what moment or in what way to dress the food, any number of questions (405a; 4: 333–5). A cook named Seuthes, described by comic poet Poseidippus, stands up to the 'whole drinking rabble', clamouring for their dinner: 'the general of profound genius stands his ground and receives the attack' (377c; 4: 209).

Mind you, the crowning glory of the cook's art is a certain amount of puffery. In *Dancing-girls* Poseidippus depicts a cook as arguing that effrontery or cheek is the best seasoning. The art's finishing touch is a boastful pretence (376e–377a; 4: 207). In Demetrius's play *The Areopagite* the cook metaphorically leaps off the stage, proclaiming his superiority to the person playing him: 'what I have accomplished in this art of mine, no play-actor has ever accomplished' (405e; 4: 337). When King Nicomedes was twelve days' journey from the sea in midwinter he desired an anchovy. His cook Soterides took a fresh turnip and cut it in long, thin slices, shaping each just like an anchovy. He parboiled each strip, poured oil on it, sprinkled on salt, spread on the top exactly forty poppy seeds, and delighted the king. In reporting this, the comic poet Euphron comments: 'The cook and the poet are just alike: the art of each lies in his brain' (7df; 1: 31–3). While the great majority of cooks had inquiring minds in matters of history and the use of words, the exasperated suggestion in *The Cauldron* by Alexis is that: 'You're a much better speech-writer, as it now turns out, than cook' (383be; 4: 233–5).

In *The Law-giver* a professional expounds the difference between a cook and a mere kitchen mechanic, with lofty strictures on the inadequacy of the textbook of Archestratus, and a panegyric on simplicity. Bring me, he says, the person 'with knowledge of many sumptuous banquets, I'll make him forget them all, Simias, if I can only show him an omelette, and set before him a dinner redolent of the Attic breeze' (405bd; 4: 335). In the fourth century BC two such cooks were credited with a revolution akin to the introduction of a *nouvelle cuisine*. They were Sophon of Acarnania and Damoxenus of Rhodes, who had been fellow pupils of Labdacus of Sicily. According to Anaxippus in *Behind the Veil*, they did away with spices and preferred quick cooking.

> These men, to be sure, wiped out the old trite seasonings from the cookery-books, and utterly abolished from our midst the mortar; I mean, for example, caraway-seed, vinegar, silphium, cheese, coriander, seasonings which Cronus [mythological king of the (former) golden age] used; all of these they have removed . . . they themselves, governor, desired only oil and a new stewpan, and a fire that was quick and not blown too often (403e–4a; 4: 329).

In Philemon's play *The Soldier* the cook boasts: 'What a tender fish I had, how perfectly did I serve it! Not drugged with cheese, not decked on top with herbs, but even when baked it looked exactly like what it was when alive. So mild and gentle was the fire I gave it . . . ' It was no wonder that the diners behaved like hens, with the first man to discover the dish running about, holding it fast, with the others close at his heels (288df; 3: 295–7).

GASTRONOMY

We may live without poetry, music, and art;
We may live without conscience, and live without heart;
We may live without friends; we may live without books;
But civilized man cannot live without cooks.

He may live without books – what is knowledge but grieving?
He may live without hope – what is hope but deceiving?
He may live without love – what is passion but pining?
But where is the man that can live without dining?

'Owen Meredith', Lucile (1860)

Dinner-party writing has rarely attained the level of important scholarship or literature, but has remained largely anecdotal, derivative, pretentious and fun. The authors have not been philosophers, but essayists, playwrights, epigrammatists and cookery-book dabblers who keep the conversation circulating. They have paid undue attention to the fanciness of the dish, the vintage of the wine and the joviality of the company. Their topic has been the after-hours spending of fortunes rather than the making of them. Yet gastronomic authors, in their predominantly masculine and upper-class way, have often recognised cooks.

To cooks, employers 'commit their dearest interests', as the ebullient Launcelot Sturgeon affirms (1823: 202). Jean-Anthelme Brillat-Savarin concludes a grave lecture on frying by reminding his cook that, 'from the instant when my guests have set foot in my house, it is *we* who are responsible for their well-being' (Meditation 7; 1971: 131). William Kitchiner counsels that any 'Master, who wishes, to enjoy the rare luxury, of a table regularly well served in the best style, must treat his Cook as his friend' (1821: 18–19).

Showing that the great men have been in frequent communication with their culinary staff, Alexandre Dumas writes that the Duc de Nivernais – whose palate was meant to be so well developed that he could tell if the white of a poultry wing came from the same side as the gall – was sufficiently conscientious to have a new dish served 'for eight days in a row, and to taste them each day, in order to give his directions in such a way that the new dish would finish up virtually perfect'. Similarly, despite the devastation of the Hanoverian war leaving his chefs little more than a stray ox with which to entertain the defeated princes and princesses, Marshal Richelieu devised an elaborate menu employing the beast's tail, tongue, kidneys, brains and so forth, both as flesh and consommés and aspics. In this way he demonstrated that he understood the practical aspects 'better

45

than the best maître d'hôtel' (Dumas 1979: 58–61).

Many hosts have been a type of supervisory cook, and when the gastronomers have transcribed light-hearted table banter, it was partly because, with Plato in the ascendant, it seemed audacious to talk about food as one might talk about, say, art or religion. Ultimately, however, a happy eater has difficulty denying cooks, and adulating cooks can mean inquiring into what they do and even situating them in the wider world. Meeting and sometimes exceeding those specifications, a string of authors pops up throughout this book, including Athenaeus, Grimod de La Reynière, Brillat-Savarin, Baron von Rumohr, Launcelot Sturgeon, Thomas Walker and Robert Farrar Capon, and not all in the Western tradition.

Yüan Mei

Yüan Mei (1715–97) has been described as a Chinese 'official who got into trouble with his superiors and went into retirement at the early age of 40. Chiefly known as a poet' (Giles 1965: 260). In his literary collection *Hsiao-ts'ang-shan fang wen chi*, this great eighteenth-century gourmand includes an affectionate and informative biography of his cook, Wang Hsiao-yü (Spence 1977: 292).

'When he first came', writes Yüan Mei, 'and asked what was to be the menu for the day, I feared that he had grand ideas, and I explained to him that I came of a family that was far from rich'. Very well, he replied merrily, and produced a plain vegetable soup that was 'so good that one went on and on taking it till one really felt one needed nothing more . . . ' Wang explained that: 'If one has the art, then a piece of celery or salted cabbage can be made into a marvellous delicacy; whereas if one has not the art, not all the greatest delicacies and rarities of land, sea or sky are of any avail . . . '

Wang insisted on doing all the marketing himself, saying, 'I must see things in their natural state before I can decide whether I can apply my art to them'. He never made more than six or seven dishes, and if asked for more, would refuse. At the stove, 'he capered like a sparrow, but never took his eyes off it for a moment, and if when anything was coming to a boil someone called out to him, he took not the slightest notice, and did not even seem to hear'.

Yüan Mei once asked his cook why, when he could easily have

got a job in some affluent household, he had preferred to stay all these years with him. 'To find an employer who appreciates one is not easy', Wang replied.

> But to find one who understands anything about cookery is harder still. So much imagination and hard thinking go into the making of every dish that one may well say I serve up along with it my whole mind and heart. The ordinary hard-drinking revellers at a fashionable dinner-party would be equally happy to gulp down any stinking mess. They may say what a wonderful cook I am, but in the service of such people my art can only decline. True appreciation consists as much in detecting faults as in discovering merits. You, on the contrary, continually criticise me, abuse me, fly into a rage with me, but on every such occasion make me aware of some real defect; so that I would a thousand times rather listen to your bitter admonitions than to the sweetest praise. In your service, my art progresses day by day. Say no more! I mean to stay on.

But when Wang had been in the household not quite ten years, he died, and 'now I never sit down to a meal without thinking of him and shedding a tear', records Yüan Mei (Waley 1956: 52–3).

In 1797, the last year of his own long life, the poet published his cookery book, *Sui-yüan Shih-tan* (*Recipes from Sui Garden*). It seems, however, that at least a draft had been circulating for some years. Whenever he had particularly enjoyed a dish at a friend's house, Yüan Mei had been in the habit of sending around his cook to take a lesson in it (Waley 1956: 195). Prefacing the recipes with a dozen pages of general tips and observations, Yüan Mei extols simplicity, preferring the homely tastes of chicken, pork, fish and duck. He writes:

> Cookery is like matrimony. Two things served together should match. Clear should go with clear, thick with thick, hard with hard, and soft with soft. I have known people mix grated lobster with birds'-nest, and mint with chicken or pork! The cooks of today think nothing of mixing in one soup the meat of chicken, duck, pig, and goose. But these chickens, ducks, pigs, and geese, have doubtless souls; and these

souls will most certainly file plaints in the next world as to the way they have been treated in this . . .

Don't eat with your ears! By this I mean do not aim at having extraordinary out-of-the-way foods, just to astonish your guests. For that is to eat with the ears, not with the mouth. Beancurd, if good, is actually nicer than birds'-nest . . .

Don't eat with your eyes! By this I mean do not cover the table with innumerable dishes and multiply courses indefinitely. For this is to eat with the eyes, not with the mouth (Giles 1965: 260–1).

In one of his wonderful poems on old age Yüan Mei complains that, when young, he could dream only of great things to eat and drink. Now that he is old and ugly, and the fancy clothes he always wanted do not suit him at all, the choicest foods are at his table, 'But I only manage to eat a few scraps'. He is inclined to petition his Creator:

Let me live my days on earth again,
But this time be rich when I am young;
To be poor when one is old does not matter at all (Waley 1956: 191).

GRIMOD DE LA REYNIÈRE

As a wealthy young man before the French Revolution, Alexandre-Balthazar-Laurent Grimod de La Reynière (1758–1837) was an eccentric host, who held what purported to be his own funeral supper. After the revolution, and in more reduced circumstances, he invented modern food journalism. He founded the *Jury des dégustateurs*, which met to pronounce upon Parisian food and thereby promote shops and restaurants. His series of reports on how to eat well in Paris, the *Almanach des Gourmands*, appeared annually from 1803 until 1808 and then biennially until 1812. Among other publications, his *Manuel des Amphitryons* (1808) provides advice on dinner parties for the host or amphitryon (from the character in Molière's comedy also of that name). His exuberant style inspired a rash of imitators, particularly in London, but virtually nothing has yet been translated into English.

Grimod was a hearty eater, whose robust sense of humour

breaches our own sense of good taste. He declares, for example, that
when the little *ragoût* (stew) of thrush in a juniper dressing is well
made, one could 'eat one's own father in this sauce' (1987: 213).
Another story concerns the 'subtle Capuchin'. Some youthful rascals
provide spit-roasted sucking pig, warning that whatever the monk
does to the pig they will do to him. If he should lop off a limb, they
will promptly remove his, and so on. The unruffled monk sticks his
finger in the pig's anus and sucks it. 'Gentlemen', he says, 'I heartily
beg of you to carry out your menaces' (210).

Declaring vigorously in favour of cooks, Grimod warns that
'having no cook means having no friends', no matter were the host
'as witty as Voltaire or as warm-hearted as Beaumarchais' (173). He
recognises that the cook is surrounded by the 'deleterious vapours
and pestilential exhalations of the charcoal . . . the glare of a scorching
fire, and the smoke so baneful to the eyes and the complexion'. This
was like the smoke and fire of the soldier, except that for the cook

> every day is a fighting day, that her warfare is almost always without
> glory, and most praiseworthy achievements pass not only without
> reward, but frequently without even Thanks; – for the most consummate
> Cook is, alas! seldom noticed by the master, or heard of by the guests;
> who, while they are eagerly devouring his Turtle, and drinking his
> Wine, – care very little who dressed the one, or sent the other (Kitchiner
> 1821: 18).

The delicacy of one's table, Grimod contends, depends on the
care taken in regularly purging the cook with medicine. The cook's
palate must be 'extremely delicate, almost virginal'. However, the
necessity of frequent tasting, along with the constant smell of the
ovens, the smoke fumes and the need to drink often-poor wine at
frequent intervals 'all contrive to vitiate a cook's taste buds'. The
palate 'ends up as callous and insensitive as the conscience of an
old judge'. The only way to help the cook recover is purging. As
soon as the stews are too spicy and overseasoned, it is time to call
on an apothecary. Grimod sets out a regimen of dieting, cleansing
and resting, together with a purgative based on 'Calabriar manna',
senna, cassia and Seidlitz powders. This is no jest, he protests, and

any cook who refuses is not destined to greatness. 'You who would maintain a delicate, refined and distinguished table, have your cooks purged regularly. There is no other way' (Davidson 1988: 38–9).

BRILLAT-SAVARIN

I soon saw, as I considered every aspect of the pleasures of the table, that something better than a cook book should be written about them; and there is a great deal to say about those functions which are so ever-present and so necessary, and which have such a direct influence on our health, our happiness, and even on our occupations.

Brillat-Savarin 1971: 20

While Grimod de La Reynière led the upswelling of gastronomic literature in Europe in the early nineteenth century, Jean-Anthelme Brillat-Savarin (1755–1826) was the more philosophical and eventually more celebrated (MacDonogh 1992). Not the self-promoting food celebrity, this legal figure surprised even friends when, in the last weeks of his life, he released his long-digested classic, *La Physiologie du goût* (*The Physiology of Taste*). Historian Theodore Zeldin judges the work 'important because it provided a justification of concern about food, but written with wit and style, so that it acquired the *cachet* of a literary masterpiece' (1977: 745).

Brillat-Savarin's book has a 'double purpose', he announces: firstly, to set forth the basic theories of gastronomy, that it might assume the 'rank among the sciences which is incontestably its own', and, secondly, to defend gourmandism from the 'gluttony and intemperance with which it has for so long and so unfortunately been linked' (Transition; 1971: 343). The twenty opening aphorisms, intended to serve as a 'lasting foundation for the science of gastronomy', tend to follow his advice for the progression of the courses in a dinner, 'from the most substantial to the lightest' (Aphorism XI). The first reads: 'The Universe is nothing without the things that live in it, and everything that lives, eats'. He again stresses consumption rather than production in his second aphorism: 'Animals feed themselves; men eat; but only wise men know the art of eating'.

Towards the end of the book Brillat-Savarin credits Aphorism IX to his legal colleague Monsieur Henrion de Pansey: 'I consider the discovery of a new dish, which excites our appetite and prolongs our pleasure, much more important than the discovery of a star. We can always see plenty of the latter'. And there was more: 'I shall never feel that the sciences have been adequately represented', the magistrate continued, 'nor sufficiently honoured, so long as I do not see a cook installed in the first ranks of the Institute [of learned Academies, founded in 1795]' (Varieties XXV; 411). While Brillat-Savarin writes as a diner and rarely ventures into the kitchen, his axioms provide a context for the serious consideration of cooks, and we shall have cause to return to his 'philosophical history of cooking'.

The Physiology of Taste even includes an appendix of songs. In his ditty 'The choice of sciences', Brillat-Savarin eschews history ('a tale devoid of cheer'), preferring 'wine that's old!'; astronomy ('Stray without me in the skies'); Greek philosophy (which, even when studied endlessly, 'Never taught me anything'); and the physic ('All the drugs that ever were/Only help a man to die'). Instead, Brillat-Savarin calls on gastronomy (the theoretical branch) and gourman- (the practical), and declares: 'Now by Cookery I swear,/Which doth make us whole again:/Cooks surpass all other men!' (Varieties XXIV; 409).

In his concluding 'Historical Elegy' (Varieties XXVII; 414), Brillat-Savarin remembers a time before cooks, when Adam and Eve found their humanity.

> First parents of the human race, whose feastings are historical, what did you not lose for a ruddy apple, and what would you not have given for a truffled turkey hen? But in your Earthly Paradise you had no cooks, no fine confectioners!
>
> I weep for you!

SPECIALISTS OF THE TABLE

Brillat-Savarin concedes that cooking could be no more than a craft, skill or Plato's knack while it 'was practised solely by paid servants, while its secrets stayed below ground in the kitchens, while the cooks kept their knowledge to themselves and wrote only books of directions'. However, a serious interest in eating and drinking takes curiosity well beyond the table into the tiers of sciences – and Brillat-Savarin specifies natural history, physics, chemistry, cookery, business and political economy. He writes that the proper concerns of gastronomy extend to the '[cultivation] which produces, the commerce which exchanges, the industry which prepares, and the experience which invents means to dispose of everything to the best advantage'. An intelligently planned feast is like an epitome of the world, each of its parts duly represented (Meditation 3; 1971: 50–3).

Another, even more earnest culinary authority of the early nineteenth century, Baron Karl Friedrich Freiherr von Rumohr (1785–1843), protests that writing about food is not just writing about the 'whims of the rich' and that 'whenever cooking is mentioned, we are only too ready to think of delicacies' (1993: 45). Paying serious attention to the table draws diners beyond and then helps explain the wider economy and society. If that is the case, diners have to concern themselves with issues such as the class division between cooks and diners (the one giving and the other receiving), public intrusions upon the private, relations with nature and so on.

The gastronomic tradition is often more profound than it makes out, and so it should be – the goal is the good life, after all. All the same, for help on cooks we must often excuse ourselves from the genial tables of gourmets to join the sober desks of scholars, starting with those in the food area, such as Jack Drummond and Anne

Wilbraham, Reay Tannahill, and K.C. Chang's team, and then moving on to physics, archaeology, literary analysis, women's studies and many other domains.

French anthropologist Claude Lévi-Strauss reports that 'adequate data about culinary practices in various parts of the world is lacking, anthropologists having paid little attention to the subject' (1978: 490). Yet, along with Lévi-Strauss himself, anthropological authorities such as Audrey Richards, Mary Douglas, Marvin Harris and Jack Goody assist in my account. Among the most useful adjuncts to gastronomy, a somewhat broadened historical sociology draws on such scholars as Georg Simmel, Emile Durkheim, Max Weber and, more recently, Fernand Braudel, Norbert Elias, Ernest Gellner, Claude Fischler, Anne Murcott, Stephen Mennell and others (Symons 1991). Perhaps most unexpectedly, I have gleaned much from Karl Marx. This is the 'philosophical' Marx, rather than the 'political' and 'economic'.

KARL MARX

Karl Marx (1818–83) only depicts his communist utopia in one sentence. No longer dependent on a narrowly specialist livelihood, he writes, he will be able to 'do one thing today and another tomorrow, to hunt in the morning, fish in the afternoon, rear cattle in the evening, criticise after dinner, just as I have a mind' (Marx and Engels 1976: 53). Like Plato, Marx proposes philosophising 'after dinner', but he also intends to become more wholly and more practically involved – hunting, fishing and, I would hope, doing traditional women's chores as well.

In working out how to achieve this, Marx starts with eating and drinking. He emphasises 'real, corporeal *man*, man with his feet firmly on the solid ground, man exhaling and inhaling all the forces of nature' (1977: 135–6). In other words Marx is very concerned with the 'metabolic' interchange between human beings and nature. In this he was influenced by food science through Ludwig Feuerbach, Baron Liebig and Jakob Moleschott. Unfortunately, when Marx uses the word *Stoffwechsel*, it has been translated neutrally as 'material reaction' or 'exchange of matter' rather than its more usual 'metabolism' (Schmidt 1971: 87, 218 n.129).

To understand history we need to recognise that: 'Men can be distinguished from animals by consciousness, by religion or anything else you like. They themselves begin to distinguish themselves from animals as soon as they begin to *produce* their means of subsistence, a step which is conditioned by their [physiology]' (Marx and Engels 1976: 37). This is reminiscent of Boswell's talk of the 'cooking animal', except that 'cooking' has become 'producing'. For Marx, in producing our food, we also produce our social relationships, technology, consciousness, history and alienation.

The production of the physical means of subsistence is primary production. The 'second premise' of history is that this production requires the subsidiary production of, for example, digging-sticks and pots. If clothing and shelter are seen as essentially means of adaptation to wider habitats, then the production of clothing and shelter even fits under secondary production. Human beings must also 'produce' the social relations of production, such as the division of labour. The 'third premise' is that production must be reproduced – people propagate not just their kind, but also re-create social relations and culture.

As part of production, we make ourselves. As Marx explains: 'Hunger is hunger, the hunger gratified by cooked meat eaten with a knife and fork is a different hunger from that which bolts down raw meat with the aid of hand, nail and tooth. Production thus produces not only the object but also the manner of consumption ... Production thus creates the consumer' (1973: 92). This lets him say: 'The *forming* of the five senses is a labour of the entire history of the world down to the present' (1977: 96). Just as we to some extent produce ourselves, we 'produce' nature, as when commerce transplants the cherry tree (Marx and Engels 1976: 45). And we also produce cultural artefacts, including ideas. Theorists, ideologists and philosophers are the 'producers of "the concept"' (70). Despite the self-delusions of philosophers, consciousness is 'from the very beginning a social product' (49–50).

In his theories of history Marx finds special significance in the division of labour, the far-reaching consequences of which include alienation. Rather than the idealistic portrayal of humanity estranged from some great truth, Marx proposes that alienation is the fracturing of the productive interchange between nature, culture, society and the individual. Tragically, through production itself, people lose sight of the centrality of production. Their *life activity* appears 'merely as a means' to existence: 'Life itself appears only as a *means to life*' (1977: 68). This is a direct rebuttal of Plato's hero Socrates, for whom eating appears only as a *means to* living (Athenaeus 158f; 2: 223), when it *is* living. Philosophising is a means to cooking, not the other way around.

Appreciation

As the great French chef Antonin Carême (1783–1833) advises: 'Cookery is a difficult art; a generous host knows how to appreciate its grandeur and dignity' (Kirwan 1964: 407). A twentieth-century successor, Raymond Oliver, appeals: 'After all, the cook, however good or bad, is an artist whose single vocation is to make others' lives happier. He works only for the pleasure of his fellows, twice a day, for ever' (1967: 194).

Presenting Chinese ways for Westerners, Chinese–American author Lin Yutang affirms: 'Only in a society wherein people of culture and refinement inquire after their cooks' health, instead of talking about the weather, can the art of *cuisine* be developed. No food is really enjoyed unless it is keenly anticipated, discussed, eaten and then commented upon' (1939: 319).

Culinary appreciation has extended much further than China and the gentlemanly circles already mentioned. In Part Two of this book, we discover that gastronomic government has been practised by kings, emperors and caliphs and, in a relatively democratic form, by Greek symposia. Like them, we can only eat better, the better we appreciate what cooks do – which now takes us to the nostalgic heart of the kitchen, the hearth.

CHAPTER FOUR

'An Empire of Smoke'

Perhaps the oldest surviving written close-up of someone cooking is the Latin poem *Moretum*. Long ascribed to Virgil, but written by an unknown successor probably between 8 and 25 AD, the 123 lines describe the preparation of a basic meal in order to convey the hand-to-mouth grind of peasant life (Kenney 1984; Davidson 1988: 20–2).

On a dark winter's morning, Simulus gropes for the hearth and eventually coaxes the embers into fire. He fetches grain from a 'miserable heap' in a cupboard. His right hand turns the grinding stone rapidly, with the left feeding it, until he changes arms from weariness. Singing an uncouth country song, he sieves the meal, the flour falling away from the black husks. He piles the flour on a smooth board, pours on warm water, and works the mixture until it becomes cohesive, occasionally sprinkling it with salt. He smooths the kneaded dough into regular rounds, marking each loaf into eight segments. He puts the bread on a swept part of the hearth, covers it with crocks and then heaps coals on top.

So that bread alone should not displease his palate, Simulus finds an accompaniment. He has no meat-rack by the hearth with, say, a salted chine of pork, only a round cheese pierced through the middle with a string. So our 'far-seeing hero' contrives another resource, the poet tells us. A kitchen garden lies next to his hovel, the tiny estate costing nothing but his labour – if there is ever a respite from ploughing. He is expert in entrusting the seeds to the earth and in leading the nearby streams around the crops. Here flourish cabbage, beet, sorrel, mallows and elecampane, leeks, lettuce, radishes and gourds. However, this is the public's produce, which every eight days he sells in town. His own hunger is subdued by red onions, chives, watercress, endive, rocket and, as he chooses today, garlic, parsley, bushy rue and coriander.

Simulus sits again beside the bright fire and, with mortar and pestle, mashes the herbs with salt, cheese, a little olive oil and vinegar. Round and round goes his right hand, the ingredients gradually losing their own properties and becoming one (or, in the poet's Latin, 'e pluribus unus'). Often the sharp smell goes right up his nostrils, so that he passes judgement on his dinner as he wipes his streaming eyes with the back of his hand. Finally, he forms the mass into a ball to produce a perfect *moretum* (which commentators have called 'country salad' and 'herbed cheese', and which reminds me of pesto). With bread and *moretum*, he can leave to do the ploughing, 'with the fear of hunger banished, and free from care for that day'.

Simulus is an unusual domestic cook in being a man (perhaps the poet wanted a man to do women's work to emphasise the lowliness of this mock-heroic scene). He appears to cook merely for himself (although he might live with an African woman glimpsed in the poem). He uses no obvious cooking pot. Otherwise, much else is universal. So much cooking throughout the world for perhaps 10 000 years has been done with a small fire, a storage bin, a water jug, stones for arduous milling, and a mortar and pestle for preparing herbs and spices.

Cooks have scrounged for fuel, whether wood, brush, peat, charcoal or cattle-dung. Then they have needed a light, obtained by scratching together sticks or flints, striking matches, or borrowing embers. They have puffed at the fire, perhaps using blowpipes, bellows or fans, and they have adjusted the temperature, according to descriptions such as 'fine little fire', 'coals without flame', and 'graceful fire' (Scully 1995: 92), and *wu-huo* ('military' heat for fast frying) and *wen-huo* ('civil' or 'literary' heat for slower cooking) (Spence 1977: 273–4). Squatting on the hard dirt floor, cooks have baked various kinds of breads, roasted birds or bits of meat, and concentrated on a pot of porridge, soup, bean stew or vegetables. The fire has demanded equipment, often sparse, even if a dictionary could be compiled of the totality of hooks, cranes, firedogs, cauldrons, pans, ladles, and so on. Rather than have to start all over again the next day, cooks have covered the embers with broken pottery. Archaeologists have found these 'potsherds' left in fireplaces since the beginning. The word 'curfew' for a regulation to extinguish fires at a fixed hour derives from the French *couvrir* (cover) and *feu* (fire).

In the ancient Greek play *The Areopagite* by Demetrius, a showy cook declares: 'This art of mine is an empire of smoke' (Athenaeus 405e; 4: 337). In the Roman play *Pot of Gold*, Plautus calls a cook a 'fire-worshipper' (1965: 26). According to English poet John Lydgate's mid-fifteenth-century epigram: 'Hoot ffir and smoke makith many an angry cook' (Kurath and Kuhn 1959: 373). Little wonder that members of the Cooks' Guild played Hell's Mouth in medieval morality plays. In early editions, *Mrs Beeton's Book of Household Management* advocates that cooks and kitchen-maids go against fashion and wear short dresses, especially in the kitchen ('short' still being around the ankles). The modern trailing skirt is 'absurd, dangerous, out of place, and extravagant' – dangerous because it might catch fire (1880: 35). Hearth death has been common, and fire has devastated huts, hamlets and the City of London.

The fire gives my spiralling observations focus, and I choose the word advisedly, for *focus* is the Latin for 'hearth'. This is the cooks' spot on the map, the crucible of the magic. For half a million years, or maybe even three times that, human beings have clustered around a fire – it is the source of light and warmth and is where cooks distribute good things.

Prometheus stole fire from the gods and became the Titan benefactor of human beings. In retaliation, Zeus not only chained Prometheus to a mountain, where an eagle preyed on his liver, but burdened people with Pandora and her box of evils. Corresponding myths within other traditions grant the utmost debt to fire. And not just any fire, writes prehistorian Catherine Perlès – not the fire that permits defence or attack, not the fire that warms or illuminates, not that which has served, since the beginnings, to shape tools, but the culinary fire (1979: 9). This chapter stares at the hearth, from which the 'cooking animal' radiates, never leaving.

BASIC COOKING METHODS

The added aromas are one of the most common reasons given for cooking. At the time of Jean-Anthelme Brillat-Savarin, the justification for cooked meats was a chemical called osmazome. French chemists found in *bouillon* (meat stock) a 'mucous extractive substance' that was soluble in water and alcohol, did not taste like jelly and, when cooked, developed an aromatic flavour (McGee 1990: 287). It was named 'osmazome' from two Greek words *osme* for 'scent' and *zomos*, 'soup' or 'sauce'. Chemically, the single substance was almost immediately replaced by the idea of numerous flavour compounds – at least 600 in cooked beef (298). Nevertheless, as the scientific cook Harold McGee advocates: 'Whatever it is about a roast that inspires such devotion deserves a name, and in the absence of a better one, osmazome serves admirably' (296).

Among the complicated chemical changes that take place when foods are heated, browning is when intense roasting, broiling, baking or frying produces a flavourful crust. As Brillat-Savarin lectures his own cook, frying adds a kind of gift-wrapping, or what he calls 'la *surprise*' (Meditation 7; 1971: 127–31). One browning process, the caramelisation of sugar, creates various sour, sweet, bitter, fragrant and brown-coloured chemicals. Another, the Maillard reaction, named after its French discoverer, provides bread crusts, chocolate, coffee beans, dark beers, roasted meats and nuts. Of the utmost culinary importance, the high temperatures required to produce caramelisation and Maillard browning are not possible in boiling and steaming, whose results are plainer and blander (McGee 1986: 608–9).

For their part, in an attempt to understand cooking, physicists speak of three forms of energy transfer. Just heating a pan of water involves (1) radiation from a heat source, (2) conduction through the pan, and (3) convection in the water. In everyday life, we seldom find pure examples of these forms. Still, the basic physics contributes to our appreciation of the principal methods used by cooks (McGee 1986: 614–19).

When we cook with the infra-red radiation before glowing coals, we speak of *roasting*. But the intense heat can brown the surface too quickly and penetrate too slowly through conduction, leaving a

charred roast cold and uncooked inside. Brillat-Savarin's Aphorism XV acknowledges this trickiness: 'We can learn to be cooks, but we must be born knowing how to roast'. While roasting is done before the fire, *baking* is done in the oven, a distinction that stove manufacturers have successfully blurred, but which is much too important to lose. In stressing that baking meat is 'in many respects objectionable, and should never be done if any other method is available', an old *Encyclopaedia Britannica* explains that baked meat 'has never the delicate flavour of roast meat' (1910, 7: 75). The temperature of glowing coals and elements is about 1100°C (2000°F) and gas flames closer to 1650°C (3000°F), but oven walls only reach a fraction of this, about 260°C (500°F), although admittedly doing so from all directions.

When we still use the radiation of coals but place the food on a gridiron or grill, I use the trusty, old term *broiling*. Some prefer 'grilling', but the convention borrowed here is that *grilling*, while closely related, is done under a heated iron or salamander.

Beyond basic physics, cooking methods differ in the medium – air, water and oil. Just as baking relies to some extent on the convection of hot air, *steaming* relies on currents of steam and *boiling* on currents of hot water. The boiling point of water is insufficient to brown food, but, given that the entire surface of the food is in contact with the cooking medium, the method is efficient. A further advantage is that, in McGee's words, boiling 'takes no finesse at all' (1986: 616). Or, as John Cordy Jeaffreson puts it in his *A Book about the Table*, 'The pot needs no watching. Indeed, there is an old adage which forbids the cook to watch his boiler' (1875, 1: 243). In *stewing*, cooks do not discard the liquid – 'It is the cheapest method', explains a vast edition of *Mrs Beeton's Book of Household Management*, 'little fuel [is] used. Nothing is wasted ... The cheapest and coarsest meat can be used; and very little attention is needed' (1909: 116). The other main cooking medium, oil, gives *frying*. In *pan-frying*, a layer of oil brings the food into better contact with the pan (improving conduction), lubricates and prevents stick-ing, and supplies a little flavour. Because oils can be made relatively hot, frying also browns. In *deep-frying*, food is immersed in hot oil, and so, relying on convection, it physically resembles boiling but at browning temperatures.

'Numerous as the receipts are, the processes of cookery are but few', claims an 1824 supplement to the *Encyclopaedia Britannica* (4: 343). But is this right? I have now described nine methods, and authorities enumerate both fewer and many more. Cookery writer Elisabeth Rozin manages to get it down to three – dry-heat cooking, wet cooking and fat or oil cooking (1983: xiii). As Geoffrey Chaucer puts it in his General Prologue, the Cook on the Canterbury pil-grimage 'koude rooste, and sethe [boil], and broille, and frye,/ Maken mortreux [stews], and wel bake a pye'. These are the same six methods 'commonly spoken of' more than 500 years later, according to *Mrs Beeton's* (1909: 112). However, both lists omit steaming, and fail to distinguish between pan- and deep-frying.

At the points of his 'culinary triangle', anthropologist Claude Lévi-Strauss places boiled, roasted and smoked – then adds another three: broiled, fried and braised (1966). This ignores stewing and baking, but adds *smoking* and *braising*. Braising is an important hybrid process, in which something is fried lightly and then stewed–steamed, with the lid carrying, in the old days, extra coals. This explains the name – the French *braise* for 'coals' also leads to the English word 'brazier'. French scholar Jean-François Revel speaks of the 'seven major types of cooking': boiling, deep-frying, baking, grilling, braising, cooking in a sauce (stewing), and cooking in a frying pan (sautéing) (1982: 226). From those already listed, he omits roasting, steaming, smoking and, if we are to believe the *Larousse Gastronomique* (Montagné 1961), he should also have distinguished at least between braising (*braisage*) and pot-roasting (*poêlage* and, without moisture, *à l'étuvée*), and between boiling (*ébullition*) and poaching (*pochage*). We have begun to appreciate that real cooks cannot be reduced to a finite battery of techniques.

Dried abalone requires hour upon hour of slow simmering, while sliced kidney requires only three or four seconds in a hot wok – such a range of contrasts leaving Chinese cooks with numerous cooking verbs (Lai 1984: 15–17). Taking us back well over 1000 years, scholar Edward H. Schafer finds the most common words in T'ang literature are: *chien* ('parch', 'dry-fry', 'reduce liquid content by heating'), *ch'ao* ('stir-roast' in a pan), *chu* ('decoct'), *ao* ('dry-fry'), *chih* ('spit-roast', 'barbecue', 'broil'), *p'eng* ('cook', especially boiling), and *p'ao* ('roast', 'bake', especially in a wrapping) (1977: 116).

Introducing Western home cooks to just eight of the major Chinese techniques, Emily Hahn describes steaming, stir-frying, deep-frying, shallow-frying (slower than stir-frying in a heavy pan), red-cooking (braising, the name coming from the colouring soy sauce provides), clear-simmering (slow cooking in light broth), smoking and roasting (1969: 37–43). Another modern American introduction lists twenty Chinese methods (some obscure to me), adding boiling, pot-stewing, meeting, splashing, plunging, rinsing, cold-mixing, sizzling, salting, pickling, steeping and drying (Chang 1977: 31).

The list now includes steeping or infusing (as in preparing tea). But what about steam extraction (as in espresso coffee)? Is it true that rice is actually cooked by absorption? What about toffee-making? Where do we put pressure-cooking? Reluctantly, I append microwaving. With an arcane kind of radiation, microwaves shake only polar molecules such as water, quickly heating food, while the air and container, composed of non-polar molecules, remain unaffected. Microwaves do not give crusts, nor much else, I gather.

Briefed on the chemistry of browning, the physics of heat transfer and its messy gastronomic realities, we return to the hearth itself – to the camp-fire, bread oven, range, microwave ... But wait! We lack a generic term for these. Talking of 'fire' distracts from its containment. 'Fireplace' and 'stove' seem mutually exclusive. Modern textbooks might resort to 'heat source', 'cooking station' or possibly 'cooker'. The Latin *focus* might display a classical education. The lack of a general name exposes a strange poverty of culinary theory for a fire-centred species. Fires, cookers and pots have innumerable local names. But we stop speechless at the plurality. I make do with 'hearth', and now hold up for inspection the principal forms historically, which are the roasting fire, the pot, the oven, the brazier and the range.

'PHILOSOPHICAL' HISTORIES OF COOKING

Under 'Cuisine', the 1987 edition of the *Encyclopaedia Britannica* declares that: 'World cuisine is traditionally divided into regions according to the common use of major foodstuffs, especially grains and cooking fats'. We visit Central and South America for corn (maize); northern Europe for wheat, rye and animal fats; and the Middle East and Mediterranean for lamb, olive oil, lemons, sweet peppers and rice; and travel from India to Indonesia for lavish spices, coconuts and seafood. Even within one nation, Italy's northern cuisine of butter and rice contrasts with the south's wheat pasta and olive oil. China, likewise, can be divided into rice regions and noodle regions. The *Britannica*'s definition is an exercise in what an earlier edition called 'comparative cookery' (1910, 7: 74), and I now attempt something similar with the historical and geographical distribution of the basic hearths and their equipment.

Nineteenth-century authorities were likely to claim that cooks began with steak tartare (raw mince patty), which, as myth has it, was 'cooked' under the saddle of a galloping Tartar warrior. Then, as Isabella Beeton continues, 'fire was discovered'. People used fire first for drying, but then found meat placed on burning fuel was better than raw. Spits followed, removing the meat to a suitable height from the burning fuel. As for the introduction of stewing, the authorities knew from the Bible that, as Beeton explains, the 'Jews, coming out of their captivity in Egypt ... undoubtedly possessed kettles; and in one of these, Esau's mess of pottage, for which he sold his birthright, must have been prepared' (1861: 258–9). She uses 'kettle' in the general sense of a vessel for boiling over a fire. A 'mess of pottage' is used proverbially in reference to Genesis 25:29–34, in which Jacob (who stands for Israel) is cooking a lentil stew, when Esau (the older nation of Edom) comes in from the field so hungry that he is persuaded to sell his inheritance for a serve.

Publishing his *Geist der Kochkunst* (*The Spirit of Cookery*) in 1822, Baron von Rumohr joined the speculation about people eating raw meat and then attemping to heat it up under their saddles. Eventually, they discover heat, water and salt, the 'three elements' of cookery, 'external digestion aids, so to speak' (1993: 65). Because the roast is probably the original cooked food, Rumohr gives pride of place to the 'English, or rather the Homeric method' (73). (Roasting has often been called the Homeric method, because Homer speaks of roasted rather than boiled meat.)

Rumohr recognises the significance of boiling and stewing, since people could now 'combine animal products with the nutritious and aromatic products of the plant kingdom, creating a new end-product. For the first time it was possible for the art of cookery to be developed in all directions' (85). While not necessarily discovering them, the French are 'responsible for the spread of all chopped and mixed dishes'. He also credits the French with the invention of meat stocks, which distinguish modern European cookery.

> Only the French, who produce good [olive] oil only along their southernmost coast, and a little butter only in the extreme North of the country, found themselves obliged to find a substitute for the fats they needed. As so often happens, this pressure drove them to utilise meat stocks, with delicious results, opening a new era in world history (49–50).

The steak tartare, the roasted joint, the *pot au feu*, fine French sauces: there is an appealing logic to this culinary procession, but we should not embrace it willy-nilly. First, the authors underestimate the antiquity of most culinary methods. Prehistorian Catherine Perlès is not convinced that palaeolithic cooking would have been limited to roasting. Organic materials, such as bark containers used for boiling, would have left fewer archaeological traces. In fact, since the remotest use of fire, all known hunter–gatherer techniques would have been technically feasible. Food might have been smoked, dried, broiled directly on hot stones or on spits and skewers, baked in buried ovens or clay moulds, or boiled in skins or stomachs (1979: 7–8).

Even more importantly, a fuller history lifts Eurocentric eyes towards the East, where we find two very handy and ancient types of fire-pot, perhaps no longer familiar to Westerners but still in popular use. Inspecting these basic hearths, we shall sweep from the fire of forests, with plentiful meat and flames, to the fire of finesse, with charcoal or manure and meticulous preparation.

THE ROASTING FIRE

In the long-standing culinary antagonism between England and France, Grimod de La Reynière is struck that:

> these arrogant and greedy islanders, who persecute, destroy and despise all the other nations of Europe, have nothing to say for themselves when it comes to cookery. They know only how to half roast a joint: this scorching process owing rather more to the intense heat of their burning coals than to talent . . . When it comes to fowl, game, or little trotters, French roasters may still be assured of their superiority (1987: 179–81).

Yet a good roaster is even rarer than a great cook, declares Grimod. If the joint is 'mean, burnt or tough, all the excellent dishes that preceded it are forgotten and a dismal silence reigns' (207). The simple roast is rarely accomplished properly, echoes A.V. Kirwan. Getting it just right depends on 'a congeries of circumstances and contingencies which are eternally varying' (1864: 164). This adulation of roasters is almost lost on us, but, when the English roast was still at its peak, Dr William Kitchiner devoted several pages of his *Cook's Oracle* to instructions (1821: 95–102).

Let the fire, Kitchiner advises, 'be proportioned to the dinner to be dressed, and about three or four inches longer, at each end, than the thing to be roasted – or the ends of the meat cannot be done nice and brown'. From an hour to half an hour before beginning to roast, put a few coals on the fire, choosing their size according to the size of the joint and the time required. After that, throw wetted cinders on the back. 'If the thing to be roasted be thin and tender, the fire should be little and brisk – when you have a large joint to roast, make up a sound, strong fire, equally good, in every part of the grate . . . Give the Fire a good stirring before you lay the joint down', he continues. When the joint is thicker at one end, slant the spit so that the thickest part is nearest the fire. Since the ends of a

pig must have more fire, a protective metal plate or 'Pig iron' is hung in front of its middle part. And, as Kitchiner cautions, 'A sucking Pig, like a young Child, must not be left for an instant' (174).

Machines for turning spits are called 'jacks' (a word often used for a specialist, as in 'steeple-jack', and then a labour-saving contrivance). For the jack to work well, Kitchiner writes, keep it oiled and wiped. Never leave the winders on or they will fly off and hit a meddlesome servant (97). When half-done, remove the spit and drip-ping pan, and 'stir up your fire thoroughly, that it may burn clear and bright for the Browning'. With half an hour to go, make the gravy – he explains how to 'froth' it by dredging the dripping pan with a little flour. He approves the old '*Quarter of an hour to the Pound*' rule (99). This means that the 'Noble Sir-Loin of Beef of about fifteen pounds' will require 3½ to 4 hours. The 'Warmer the weather, and the staler killed the Meat is – the less time it will require' (161). When cooking something smaller, 'If your fire is clear and sharp, thirty minutes will roast a young, and forty a full grown Rabbit' (187).

Filling a chapter with English lore on 'Spits and Jacks', Jeaffreson speaks of the boys who acted as broach-turners or turnspits in medieval English kitchens as among the 'lowest drudges'. Wandering beggars also sought employment operating the handles. People were notoriously replaced by dogs caged in treadmills, lifting their feet 'in futile attempts to run forwards' (1875, 1: 246–7). In the sixteenth century, Europeans had weight- and spring-driven jacks, and in 1660 diarist Samuel Pepys examined a smoke-jack that was turned by a fan in the chimney. Jeaffreson reports a musical contraption that played melodies to inform the cook of the progress of up to 130 joints gyrating at the same time.

Chickens were done to a turn when the organ had played its twelfth tune; the completion of the eighteenth air was the signal for withdrawing hares and pheasants; but the largest pieces of beef and venison were not ready for the board until the twenty-fourth melody had been played out (255–6).

In simpler kitchens, the meat was often suspended on a wind-up device called, from its shape, a bottle-jack. With a bottle-jack pulled by the dead weight of the suspended meat, Jeaffreson comments: 'Human ingenuity achieved one of its proudest triumphs when it thus compelled a mass of unconscious flesh to prepare itself for the table' (259).

An open fire throwing out plenty of heat has been no problem where fuel has been abundant and climates dark and cold. Also, it could be used for much more than roasting. As Rumohr explains, a good fireplace, one where it is 'possible to cook without crying', has space for a number of spits. All kinds of kettles and pots can be hung from adjustable hooks and cranes, stood on nearby trivets and ledges, or perched warm atop the firedogs. And the main fire can be surrounded by secondary hearths, to which well-burned coals can be shifted for casseroles (1993: 66).

Grimod compares the roast to the *salon* or principal room of a house. Like the room upon which the host spends all spare cash, the roast is the 'dish that has cost him most money, and on which he hopes to content and feast his guests' (Kirwan 1864: 163). Given the costs of both fuel and meat, the roast has enjoyed high status, linked to men, ceremony, wealth and Englishness. Meanwhile, the French have been more famous for the products of the humble pot.

THE STEWING POT

The widespread reliance on stewing goes back earlier than Esau's 'mess of pottage', virtually to the beginnings of agriculture. Since pots became increasingly common about 8000 years ago, cooks have nestled them in the coals, dangled them from a hook, stood them on three stones and lent them a trivet (Latin, 'three-legged'). Of earthenware and then metal, pots evolved into cauldrons, stock pots, saucepans, casseroles, poaching kettles, tea-kettles and more. As preliminary human stomachs, pots have 'digested' as no other.

Jeaffreson explains: 'Whilst the rich, with slaves to turn their spits, accepted the boiler as a contrivance for multiplying the luxuries of the table, the poor adapted it as an instrument for cooking with the least possible trouble and cost' (1875, 1: 243).

The romantic idea is that the stew improves with age, with the pot retaining souvenirs of meals past. A prized domestic possession among the settlers of Dutch Guiana in the nineteenth century was a stew that had lasted for thirty years without the pot ever being cleaned. Lévi-Strauss mentions this homeliness when contrasting boiling as an 'inner' method to roasting as an 'outer' one. Cooked in or out of a receptacle, the boiled and roasted evoke the 'concave' and 'convex' respectively, he says. Boiling is used in domestic or 'endo-cuisine' (the humble *la poule au pot*), while roasting belongs to outward-looking 'exo-cuisine' offered to guests. Given that boiling conserves all the meat and its juices, it suggests 'plebeian' economy, where roasting involves 'aristocratic' destruction and waste (1978: 481–4).

Lévi-Strauss's analytical 'oppositions' between boiling and roasting can be explained more mundanely. Although I have referred to the costliness of roasting, for hunters and herders, meat can be relatively plentiful and require less equipment if roasted. By contrast, the stewpot belongs to settled agriculture with its denser populations and heavier environmental loads. Here, livestock is more useful for milk, fibre and locomotion than for extravagant roasts. Besides, farming communities rely on the storage of cereals, which are, importantly, boiled, to provide porridges, dumplings and the like. The pot also produces sauces to accompany breads, noodles and so on. Additionally, stored grains facilitate urban living and greater job specialisation. So, women look after domestic cooking, while men conduct public ceremonies, perhaps based on the sacrifice of a beast too big for domestic consumption.

Such is agricultural society's dependence that just about every national group could find its heritage in the pot. This includes even Hitler's Germany. With dreams of an austere but hearty past, Hitler exhorted Germans to 'return' to the so-called *Eintopf* or one-pot meal. Within a few years of the word *Eintopf* entering dictionaries, the law decreed that Germans had a duty to set aside one Sunday per month, from October to March, for nothing but one-pot meals,

and to donate savings to winter relief for the poor. The
first *Eintopfsonntag* (One-pot
Sunday) was celebrated on
5 October 1933, and cookery
books quickly gained *Eintopf*
sections. Typical of the underground humour it provoked,
one joke went: 'Which *Eintopf*

dish is most widespread in Germany?' Answer: '*Gedämpfte Zungen*' –
'steamed' or 'silenced' tongues (Gordon and Jacobs-McCusker 1989:
60–2).

Meanwhile, in Zambia, known as Northern Rhodesia when studied
by Audrey Richards in the 1930s (1939: 90–5), Bemba women relied,
with very occasional roasting, on pots for boiling, stewing and
brewing, which took four or five days. Indeed, the Bemba word for
'stew', *ukuipika*, is also the general term for cooking. The women
cooked in earthenware pots of various shapes and sizes that sat on
fixed clay tripods over wood fires on the floor of their huts. Daily,
they threshed the main crop, millet, which was stored outdoors in
circular granaries of lathes and plaster about 3 metres high. The
women pounded the grain in a high wooden mortar with stout
poles, then sifted it in a big, open basket. After further pounding
and winnowing, they ground the grain under a small stone. Adding
the millet to water boiling in an *inongo* (pot), about 70 centimetres
in diameter, they stirred it with a flat spoon that required both
hands. Within two or three minutes, the *ubwali* (porridge) was done.
They scraped it into serving baskets, and patted it into smooth balls.
Lumps of *ubwali* were torn off and dipped in *umunani* (sauce),
preferably a rich meat gravy, but probably vegetables cooked in a
smaller pot or little serving bowl.

The most common dish for the ancient Chinese was *keng* (meat
and/or vegetable stew). It was cooked in a *ting* (cauldron). Ceramic
versions of the *ting* nearly 8000 years old have been found at Cishan,
Hebei Province. These three-legged vessels were made of bronze in
the Shang Dynasty (Bahn 1992: 104, 135). They became so important
that two texts from the Chou Dynasty, which started in the twelfth

century BC, refer to the *ting* as the prime symbol of the state (Chang 1977: 11). Today, Chinese sand-pots (sand-tempered earthenware) are still indispensable for stews and casseroles. The finest restaurants make a speciality of sand-pot stews – 'only a seasoned cook (with a set of seasoned sand-pots) will attempt such a subtle, gentle, slow art', E.N. Anderson writes (1988: 186). Boiling is also important, not only as the usual method of preparing grain, from rice to noodles, but also because soup (from thin clear soup to thin stew) is a key part of virtually every meal and even snacks (138). While Western cooks serve soup first, in China they finish with the broth.

By the time the potato arrived in Ireland from South America in the early eighteenth century, the English had been regularly destroying shocking numbers of the Irish, along with their culture and agri-culture (it is claimed that by 1653 Oliver Cromwell's troops had killed five-sixths of the population) (Salaman 1949: 226). During this long-term distress, the Irish took to and relied upon the potato, which was cheaply produced, exceptionally nutritious and kept safely in the ground. Apart from when they occasionally added mashed potato to bread dough, the Irish peasantry wisely refrained from peeling the potatoes and simply boiled them in a cauldron. Once cooked, the potatoes were tumbled out to drain in a shallow wicker basket called a *skeehogue*. With no table in the hut, the family sat with the *skeehogue* on their knees and ate without knife or fork. Any mashing was done with a wooden or perhaps iron beetle, a heavy-headed tool with a handle. The Irish cauldron was usually 30 to 40 centimetres in diameter, and perhaps ribbed. It had two handles down the straight part of the side to where it bulged, and three legs. It was either hung above an open fire or set directly over the ashes. Pottery versions were in use as early as 1500 BC; bronze forms cropped up 1000 years later, replaced by iron from the sixteenth century (593–4).

Long the centre of Irish life, virtually that same household item has been trusted from one side of the world to the other. In North America, the cauldron (known as the 'kettle') was still the single most important and expensive item in the settlers' baggage during the westward expansion in the nineteenth century (Tannahill 1988: 97).

The fame of its roasts merely distracts from the entrenched reality in England, too, of porridges, gruels, olios, skillies and other kinds of stews. In the medieval kitchen, as Jeaffreson realises, the 'Populace fed habitually from the pot, and, save on highly festal occasions, never sniffed the smell of "crackling" '. Even in the late-fourteenth-century royal recipe book *Forme of Cury* (*Cury* means 'cooking'), for one dish cooked with the spit, twenty messes came from the pot (Jeaffreson 1875, 1: 243). Pottage, eaten daily by everyone, high and low, was a general soup or stew, the word coming from 'pot'. The commonest pottages were vegetable, made with red or green cabbage, lettuces, leeks, onions and garlic (Brears et al. 1993: 104–5). 'Frumenty' was an aristocratic pottage of hulled wheat boiled in milk and seasoned with cinnamon and sugar, and similar to 'mortress' (or 'mortrews').

Perhaps surprisingly, given the accusations against the complication of elegant French cuisine, it arose with the humble *ragoût* (stew).

* * *

Looking back in 1791, the Reverend Richard Warner notes that, already at the time of Richard II, French cooks were fashionable in England, equalling their descendants 'in the variety of their condiments, and in their faculty of disguising nature, and metamorphosing simple food into complex and non-descript gallimaufries' (xxxii). In the English climate, cattle can be fattened through the year and meat kept till tender, Warner explains. By contrast, in the south of France art is required for 'making *bad meat, eatable*' (125).

In Jane Austen's *Pride and Prejudice* (1813), Mr Hurst was an 'indolent man, who lived only to eat, drink, and play at cards' and had nothing to say to Elizabeth as soon as 'he found her prefer a plain dish to a ragout' (1972: 81). Providing recipes for 'honest JOHN BULL', Kitchiner 'rejected some *Outlandish Farragoes*' that had been received into some books 'for the sake of swelling the volume', but which would never be received by an Englishman's stomach (1821: 134). The ever-sensible Thomas Walker, writing in London in 1835, recommends: 'I should adopt the simple English style for my regular diet, diversifying it occasionally with the more complicated French style' (1928: 32).

According to Grimod de La Reynière:

> *Ragoûts* are practically non-existent when it comes to English cooking, which is limited to boiled chicken, a most insipid dish, and that thing which they call 'plump' [plum] pudding ... Only with the aid of French cooks do a number of lords maintain a good table in London (1987: 179–80).

As already noted, Rumohr judges in 1822 that while the French were 'sorely in need' of incorporating English roasting into their cookery, they were responsible for spreading the meat stocks that distinguish a new, more 'refined and sensitive' European taste (1993: 51). Stocks became the foundations of many delicate sauces (to which I return later). Brillat-Savarin accepts that soup – when *bouillon* (stock) has been augmented with vegetables and bread or flour pastes – is found at its best in France. 'This is not too surprising: soup [*le potage*] is the basis of our national diet, and centuries of experience have brought it to its present perfection' (Meditation 6; 1971: 76). In agreement, *Mrs Beeton's* records:

> The French *bourgeoise* cookery is an essentially slow process, by which the natural flavours of the substances are extracted by gentle means, and at the same time other flavours are blended so artfully with them that no particular one predominates. Stews, ragouts, and braises largely replace the joint which appears almost daily on our tables (1909: 1526).

The competition between the English and French was by the eighteenth century between the hefty roast and the 'made dish'. While any mixing of ingredients has been termed a 'made dish', this often meant a French stew, as Kitchiner's important *Cook's Oracle* shows.

MADE DISHES

Under this general head we range our Receipts for HASHES, – STEWS, – and RAGOUTS, &c.; of these there are a great multitude, affording the ingenious Cook an inexhaustible store of variety: – in the French kitchen they count upwards of 600, and are daily inventing new ones.

In fact, he continues, 'MADE DISHES are nothing more than Meat, – Poultry, or Fish, stewed very gently till they are tender with a thickened Sauce poured over them' (1821: 140). His book includes an 'Ingenious and Economical System of FRENCH COOKERY' which will 'teach you how to supply your Table with elegant little Made Dishes, &c. at as little expense as Plain Cookery' (141). Kitchiner acclaims a stew for happily combining frugality, nourishment and palatableness – 'and you get half a Gallon of excellent BROTH into the bargain'. However, he advises the Mistress to call it 'RAGOUT BEEF' – 'this will ensure it being eaten with unanimous applause; – the homely appellation of *Shin of Beef stewed* is enough to give your Genteel eater, a locked jaw' (392).

Kitchiner's recipes for 'made dishes' include sandwiches, eggs fried with bacon, bubble and squeak, curries, and alamode beef. This last was the speciality of 'alamode' beef shops that boiled down scraps of beef to a thick soup or stew. (Interestingly, the French phrase *à la mode* for 'in fashion' had been Anglicised by Kitchiner's time, only to become French again more recently.) Kitchiner complains that in scouring 180 volumes of cookery, he:

> could not find one Receipt that approximated to any thing like an accurate description of the way in which this excellent dish is actually dressed ... the whole of the secret seems to be the thickening [of] the gravy of Beef that has been *very slowly* stewed, and flavouring it with Bay leaves and Allspice (1821: 398).

While the celebrated French cuisine has been credited to the stew-pot, we ought to acknowledge that good cooking requires more than good sauces, and that cooks had made technical advances elsewhere than France and earlier by thousands of years. Arab cooking had invigorated Western Europe during the important cultural influx in the late medieval period. Before that, cooks had prospered in a long list of civilisations in and around Mesopotamia (modern Iraq) and the eastern Mediterranean. Meanwhile, highly controlled techniques became commonplace through India and China. These all relied on three further basic cooking devices or hearths: the oven, the brazier and the range.

THE OVEN

I am not sure which spelling to choose here, since the subject of this section comes in so many variants across North Africa, through the Middle East and northern India, and back through time. The most familiar word in English is 'tandoor' from the Hindustani (as in 'tandoori chicken'). Other spellings in the *Oxford English Dictionary* include *tenur*, *tenner*, *tendour*, *tendoor*, *tandur* and the Turkish *tandir*. All relate to the Persian, Arabic and Hebrew *tannūr*. The *tannūr* is often mentioned in the Jewish Bible. Even further back, nearly 4000 years ago, the Assyrians had the *tinūru*.

Clay ovens – and I settle for 'tannur' – have been excavated in Jarmo in Iraq (5000 BC), Tepe Sialk in Iran (3300 BC), Mohenjo-daro in the Indus Valley (2500 BC) and Egypt (2000 BC, and probably much earlier) (Lerche 1981). In the Mohenjo-daro example, Mortimer Wheeler reports finding in the courtyard of a large house a 'circular bread-oven, 3ft 8ins in diameter and 3½ feet high, resembling bread-ovens still widely used in Asia' (1968: 50). Eveline J. van der Steen, an archaeologist who has closely studied fifty bread ovens uncovered at Tell Deir 'Alla in the Jordan Valley, and dating back as many as 1000 years BC, measured internal diameters between 30 and 75 centimetres (1992). The smallest tend to be inside and were apparently also used in winter for heating. The largest tend to be outside, in what was probably the village square, and have double walls for insulation.

In shape, the classic tannur is like a barrel or beehive entered from the top and perhaps with an 'eye' or air vent at the base. It is usually made of clay and, in fact, may have started as a clay-lined hole in the ground. It is like a dumpy chimney, with a fire at the bottom variously fuelled with wood, charcoal, or dung-and-straw cakes. Since the fire is contained, the tannur uses fuel efficiently. Distinctively, the baker reaches in with sticks to press a thin round of dough against the hot interior wall. The two sides of the flatbread are cooked simultaneously – by contact with the wall and by radiation from the fire. The bread sticks to the inside wall so long as it retains moisture; the baker peels it off just before it drops, perhaps holding it a few more seconds above the radiant heat. Baking might only take one minute, so three or four people might work on a production line, from rolling the dough to the actual baking (Lerche 1981: 189–90). In order to save fuel, large tannurs tend to become communal facilities, operated by specialised bakers.

This is the oven for flatbreads. Variations on the tannur are used to this day in baking what is often known in English as 'pitta' bread (modern Greek for 'cake'); in Arabic as *khubz*; in Persian, Punjabi and Urdu as *nan*, and in Hindustani as *chapati* (179). In the ancient world, flatbread meant barley. Since barley can be grown in poor and alkaline soil, it came to be preferred to wheat in Mesopotamia, explains cultural anthropologist A. Leo Oppenheim. Egypt became the wheat land (with barley for beer), and the regions in between used the cereal that best responded to local conditions (1977: 14). In the ancient world, 'Mesopotamia proper is the land of barley, beer and sesame oil, while towards the west one reaches the *Kultur-kreis* [regime] of wheat, wine and olive oil' (44).

Thicker breads needed longer cooking on the floor of the oven, which required a chamber oven entered from the side. So, wheat-growers developed the typical leavened bread oven of clay, stone or brick. About 10 000 years ago, in the eastern Mediterranean, ovens were constructed to parch cereal grains before threshing and to bake bread. These ovens were a single chamber in which the fuel was burned and then raked out and the grain or un-baked bread inserted (Renfrew and Bahn 1996: 319).

While large ovens have been mainly restricted to specialist

bakers, home cooks in the heavily forested regions of northern Europe had plentiful fuel and a great need for heating. Their wooden houses have contained brick ovens, cube-shaped and perhaps as high as a person. A traveller in Russia in the 1630s noted that 'in winter they sleep on flat-topped stoves, like bake-ovens' (Smith and Christian 1984: 18). With ovens in constant use, these cooks became proficient at breads and pastries. Additionally, coals could be raked to the front for various purposes, and pottages, gruels and stews could be left inside to cook with the residual heat.

Even in the early twentieth century, in the peat districts on the east and west coasts of England, cooks employed the old arrangement – a fire burning on a stone hearth, with a wide chimney above. Vegetables or puddings were cooked in saucepans or pots suspended over the fire. They also had a large oval iron vessel, termed a 'hang-over oven' (or Dutch oven), used for baking pies, puddings and cakes. It had a depressed lid, like a braising pan, which was filled with hot peat, so that a gentle heat was applied from above and below. A separate room, the back kitchen or scullery, included a brick oven, in which bread and joints of meat were baked, but this oven was fired up once or at most twice weekly (Beeton 1909: 48–9).

While Kitchiner acclaims the superiority of roasting, he admits some baked meats have been eaten with as much satisfaction. 'BAKING is one of the cheapest, and most convenient ways of dressing a Dinner in small families; and I may say that THE OVEN is often *the only Kitchen a poor man has*, if he wishes to enjoy a joint of Meat at home with his family.' We are not to imagine that poor people used 'Dutch' or 'camp ovens', let alone managed the luxury of their own brick ovens, which were expensive to build and even more to run. The point is, of course, that small householders took their joints to the baker. This becomes clear when Kitchiner adds, 'if the meat be poor, no Baker can give satisfaction' (1821: 92).

So, ovens perform a range of duties, not just baking bread, and including, in horizontal ovens, stewing in pots. In the vertical tannur, chickens and other meats are inserted on skewers. The tannur also offers an open invitation for pots and pans to be placed on top. In that simple action, the tannur converts from an oven to a brazier.

THE VERSATILE BRAZIER

The heroes in Homer's epics roasted their beasts, but they belonged to the relatively backwoods era before the extraordinary flourishing of classical Athens. The denser population and over-exploitation of forests made both meat and firewood too expensive. In the meantime, however, as victors in the long wars with the Persians, Athenians returned with new culinary techniques, equipment and even the practitioners themselves. Of relevance, Athens became the Mediterranean centre of pottery. All in all, it is no surprise that Athenians enclosed their cooking fires in pots, fed by charcoal, which were both convenient to use and light to transport.

Braziers are portable stoves designed to carry stewpots, casseroles, gridirons and pans, with lids for baking. They come in many shapes. Some Greek ones were like little barrel-shaped tannurs. Others were squat, open, enclosed or flat, the *eschara* shallow enough just to contain a few coals, over which could be placed meats on skewers. Braziers were flexible enough to boil staples, fry flatbread or delicately broil fish. They epitomised what H.D.F. Kitto calls the 'startling difference between the Homeric and the classical Greek diet; in Homer, the heroes eat an ox every two or three hundred verses, and to eat fish is a token of extreme destitution; in classical times fish was a luxury, and meat almost unknown' (1957: 34).

Bread, the basis of Athenian eating, was commonly baked in commercial ovens. But flour could be ground domestically, using timber mortars or stones, the dough kneaded on a kneading table, and the result baked either 'under the ashes' – that is, under an earthenware cover heaped with charcoal – or in a portable oven (Sparkes and Talcott 1964). Athenaeus provides an evaluation of the results.

> Bread baked in the ashes is heavy and hard to digest because the baking is uneven. That which comes from a small oven or stove causes dyspepsia and is hard to digest. But bread made over a brazier or in a pan, owing to the admixture of the oil, is easier to excrete, but steam from the drying makes it rather unwholesome (115e; 2: 41–3).

Overall, the more sophisticated Greek cooking implied a society of many specialists, including men who worked in the woods burning charcoal, and street hawkers who sold the charcoal by the basket in Athens (Glover 1942: 83). Potters had their own quarters, and sold braziers and a wide range of pots and pans. Students of ancient Greek architecture find no chimneys, but that does not mean smoky rooms; as it is almost pure carbon, charcoal burns without appreciable flame or smoke, and the balmy nights required little heating of houses.

Of course, Greeks in no way invented the brazier, whose pedigree is much more ancient. In Bronze Age Crete, where an earlier civilisation was centred on Knossos, hearths faded out about 4000 years ago, leaving portable braziers 'common enough in Minoan houses and palaces' (Hutchinson 1962: 244–5). Braziers had by then occupied Asia, too, and stayed. A most descriptive name is *hibachi* from the Japanese words *hi* (fire) and *hachi* (bowl or pot), even if this name is used within Japan just for the hand-warmer rather than the little cooker.

'Chinese cooking is cooking of scarcity. Whatever the emperors and warlords may have had, the vast majority of Chinese spent their lives short of fuel, cooking oil, utensils, and even water', comments anthropologist E.N. Anderson. This points to the use of braziers. Originally made of pottery, these are now often old galvanised buckets (1988: 182). While foods are frequently boiled and steamed, the brazier also offers the most famous Chinese method, stir-frying or *ch'ao*.

The division in Chinese cooking between *fan* and *ts'ai* – the rice (or other cereal) and its accompaniment – is reflected in the modern kitchen with the rice cooker and the *wok* (Cantonese) or *kuo* (Mandarin). The wok is the standard curved pan ideal for stir-frying, as well as for deep-frying, boiling and, with racks in it, steaming. Its main function in south Asia (where it is known as a *kuali* in several languages) is quick stewing and evaporation (184–5). Stir-frying is likely to have been a Han invention, which makes it about 2000 years old. Although it is not directly mentioned in the texts, Anderson infers this from the great stress on slicing foods thinly and evenly and the presence of pottery model woks in the archaeological record. He also mentions models of large kitchen ranges with apertures for the curved bottoms of woks (52).

THE RANGE

'The big stove is an impressive creation', Anderson writes. 'It seems to have reached its final form just before the Han Dynasty.' Standing 60 centimetres to a metre high and up to 2 metres square, the Chinese stove is of brick or adobe construction. A stokehole opens into a fuel-burning chamber. Above, holes serve as burners. Pans fit tightly on them, so little heat is lost. With good insulation, even a tiny amount of poor fuel will cook a lot of food (1988: 182). Such a heat source – which we can call a range – is, effectively, a set of braziers permanently in place and perhaps stoked as one fire. It has long been a feature of substantial kitchens in lands where the brazier has been the mainstay. The range was common in ancient Meso-potamia and ancient Rome. In the city of Ur, Leonard Woolley excavated a 'restaurant', dated about 1900 BC, and he describes the kitchen as largely 'taken up by a solid brick range in the top of which were the troughs for the little charcoal braziers on which the cooking was done, and alongside this the circular bread-oven' (1954: 186).

In *The Cooking of India*, Santha Rama Rau recalls her grandmother's pre-Partition Kashmiri Brahman kitchen in Allahabad, in northern India. It had to be 'spotlessly, almost neurotically clean'. Children were banned, so were shoes, and Rau's grandmother herself 'had to bathe and put on clean clothes before she could go in'. Nonetheless, the floor had a foundation of dried mud, over which a thin layer of fresh cow-dung was spread by hand. It set hard and odourless within half an hour. Her grandmother was so convinced of the polish's efficacy that the kitchen had to be resurfaced with cow-dung after every meal (1969: 11).

As for cooking arrangements, along the back wall was the *chula* or range, which was fed firewood, charcoal or dung cakes. Its framework could be built by a bricklayer or one of the menservants, 'but the tricky part was the plastering and surfacing of the *chula* inside and out'. The mud had to be moulded to provide the right draught for the fire, the right draw for the burners and the right distribution of heat. Then, the woman of the house smoothed all surfaces with cow-dung. 'One of my aunts, I remember, had quite a local reputation for expert and elegant *chula* building', records

Rau. The pots and pans included *degchis* (saucepans of different sizes and depths), *karhais* (woks), *tavas* (very heavy iron pans for making wheat cakes), and large earthenware pots for slow cooking. This range was quite versatile, permitting the main categories of cooking. Even without an actual oven, baking could still be accomplished with the Dutch oven – that is, with a pot placed in hot ashes and with further glowing charcoal piled on its cover (11–12).

THE COOK'S ROOM

Dividing cooks' hearths into roasting fires, stewpots, ovens, braziers and ranges, I have given the broadest geo-historical picture, panning from west to east, towards the tropics and forward in time. But such generalities seem so much nonsense in comparison to the complicated reality. In our rough and ready world, cooks never quite manage to copy the eternal forms. Besides, at almost any hearth, we might take, for example, a roast from the skewer, a bean soup from the pot, a pie from the oven, a delicate fish from the pan, and a cheese from its straw hiding-place.

In *Food in England*, historian Dorothy Hartley demonstrates the ingenuity of traditional cooks, so that a medieval cauldron would not just cook a single stew, but various items contained in earthenware jars, covered in flour paste and wrapped in linen. 'An entire dinner could be cooked in one iron pot, which would simultaneously supply the bath before dinner and the washing-up water after', she writes (1954: 36–7). Good recipe books have also set real cooks in their cultural and geographical context, and certainly at their hearths, surely nowhere more extensively than in the twenty-seven volume *Foods of the World* series issued by Time-Life (1968–71), which assigned top photographers and knowledgeable authors, including Santha Rama Rau, just quoted. Another work produced by a team, *The Cook's Room: A celebration of the heart of the home* (Davidson 1991a), might be glossy but still cannot help demonstrating the richness of global culinary heritage.

The traditional kitchens of the town of Sille in Turkey, for example, contain various kinds of fixed and portable cookers, reports Nevin Halici (1991: 178). The fixed cookers include the *tandir* oven for baking bread, and the stone hearth in the wall for roasting and frying. Both are fuelled with wood. The portable cookers are two kinds of brazier, the *mangal* and the *maltiz*. The *mangal* brazier is used for cooking everyday vegetables, meat and rice, and is fuelled with oak, while the *maltiz* brazier burns coke to give the more intense heat needed for cooking sheep's heads, trotters and tripe.

To return to France, the open fireplace was the principal means of cooking in medieval times, with a spit turned in front for meat and hooks above for pots to boil vegetables. With ovens less known, baking was less available, Jean-François Revel claims, as were stews or meat sauces, 'for fireplaces provided no source of moderate heat' (1982: 93). In the seventeenth century, under 'Sun King' Louis XIV, the vast fireplace was supplemented with little braziers for more delicate cooking (189–90). Then, the eighteenth-century gastronomic revolution in French grand cooking – replacing 'admixtures' with subtler 'permeations' (171) – was achieved with the large *potager* or 'soup stove'. This was a range of twelve to twenty burners so that fires of different intensities were available, thanks to which slow cooking, rapid cooking, simmering, grilling and warming could continue simultaneously. The superior stove 'gave rise to registers as varied as those of an organ'. From then, three distinct branches of the art were recognised, practised by the *cuisinier* (chef), who ruled over the stoves, the *pâtissier* (pastry chef), who ruled over the ovens, and the *rôtisseur* (meat chef), who ruled over the spits. Grimod de La Reynière knew no cook can be 'at once great at the oven, great at the stove, and great at the spit' (Revel 1982: 190–1).

THE STEEL AGE

During the Industrial Revolution, well under way in England in the late eighteenth century, coal and iron came together, and nowhere more pervasively than in the new 'economy' stoves. Among numerous 'philosophers and artists' who set out to improve domestic heating and cooking, fame came to Count Rumford (1753–1814), the supplement to a contemporary *Encyclopaedia Britannica* records (1824, 4: 343). An American adventurer and prolific inventor who worked in Bavaria and London, Rumford (formerly known as Benjamin Thompson) made key contributions to physics, establishing that heat was not a substance and alerting science to convection. In addition, he recognised that scientific investigators might assist cookery, 'however low and vulgar it has hitherto generally been thought to be' (1969: 74).

When scoffers said Rumford would cook his dinner by the smoke from his neighbour's chimney, the point was that he used fuel otherwise escaping (Beeton 1909: 106). His long essay on the construction of more efficient kitchen fireplaces and appliances had associated him with so-called 'closed' or 'economy' stoves. With fireplaces not closed, the 'loss of heat and waste of fuel in these kitchens is altogether incredible', he writes. So he invented an oven that baked food in a separate chamber to avoid tainting food with flue gases. To confirm the advantages of 'roasting' in an oven, Rumford arranged a blind tasting of two legs of mutton from the same carcass, one being roasted before a fire, the other in the Rumford Roaster. The latter was unanimously preferred, the great publicist reports (1969: 160), although he had his sceptics.

In Germany, Baron von Rumohr greeted economy stoves as 'valuable discoveries', since they were ideal for boiling, stewing, baking and keeping food warm. 'They have, however, also given rise to that dried-up roast ... which intelligent housewives should banish from their cooking repertoire' (1993: 66–7). He warns that the 'effects of a good, blazing fire cannot be replaced by the so-called roasting machine, nor by any kind of oven, and least of all by a cooking pot or saucepan' (73). Rumford might have been an 'exact economist of Fuel', but he failed to appreciate the roast beef of Old England, Kitchiner protests: 'the Machines the Economical Grate-makers call ROASTERS, are in plain English, *Ovens*' (1821: 95).

Rumford despaired of ever converting the English. But by the end of the nineteenth century, although Edward Spencer devoutly prays such prejudice still exists, manufacturers had persuaded cooks that iron ranges were cheaper to run, cleaner, safer and more adjustable. He laments that the 'Roast Beef of Old England has become almost as extinct as a Dodo'. To save the cost of fuel, most English cooking was now performed by gas or steam. Spencer reports that:

> at many large establishments the food, whether fish, flesh, fowl, veg-
> etables or pastry, all goes, in a raw state, into a species of chest of drawers
> made of block-tin, in which receptacle the daily luncheons, dinners, and
> suppers are steamed and robbed of all flavour, save that of hot tin.

Meat was even steamed, he said, and alleged 'roasts' subsequently browned in the oven (1900: 75–6).

Around 1800 in the United States, too, women still stooped and lifted over a fireplace, using heavy iron pots and kettles (cauldrons) that sat directly on the coals or hung on a hinged crane. Affluent households had large fireplace ovens, along with extra iron im-plements, while in the poorer houses bread was baked in the ashes, with a dish-kettle the only piece of equipment (Larkin 1988: 29–30). The cast-iron 'cookstove' made its appearance in prosperous urban homes around 1820. The stove-top heating surfaces were at waist height and helped save lifting. The even heat was more comfortable than the blazing fire. The cookstove saved on firewood; however, where wood was abundant and cash scarce, farm women were tied longer to the fireplace (51–2). By the middle of the nineteenth century, dozens of American cookstove manufacturers busily exported, too. And, by century's end, Robert Wilhelm Bunsen's work had made gas a safe domestic fuel. The first all-electric kitchen

was on show at the Chicago World Fair in 1893 (Feild 1984: 135), and keen manufacturers cluttered kitchens with a thousand and one auxiliary gadgets.

THE FIRES GO OUT

In *The Cook's Oracle*, Dr Kitchiner reprints a 'Receipt to Roast Mutton', which is actually a nostalgic poem by Jonathan Swift. 'Gently stir and blow the fire', it goes, 'Lay the mutton down to roast ... Let the jack go swiftly round,/Let me have it nicely brown'd'. It is not a difficult poem. Quite the reverse, it is pointedly simple: 'On the table spread the cloth'; the roast is to be divided by knives 'sharp and clean'. The problem is that as we read through it we come across several perhaps unfamiliar words, not only 'stir and blow' and 'jack', but 'dripping', 'dress', 'dresser', 'small beer'. It is both simple and nostalgic, except that we have almost lost the words and the homely pleasures Swift summons up and Kitchiner still recognises (1821: 163–4 footnote).

'A bright, lively fire I reckon a most excellent dinner companion', writes Thomas Walker in 1835. He wants it 'one of the party. For instance, two or three at each side of the table, one at the top, and the fire at the bottom, with the lights on the mantelpiece' (1928: 47–8). On the other side of the world, F.T. Cheng recalls wintry days at table in China, cooking over a brazier with red-hot charcoal: 'The sight of the smokeless fire, the heat emitting from it, and the steam engendered by the bubbling soup contrast vividly with the snow-flakes falling down or flying about outside the window' (1954: 133). 'Gas and electricity have killed the magic of fire', remembers French author Simone de Beauvoir, mourning 'kindling live flames from inert wood' (1988: 472). Electric stoves are like a tin fiddle rather than a wooden violin, Robert Farrar Capon denounces, in fact, 'perhaps the biggest tin fiddle in the American household – the perfect example of a product which no professional ever uses, but which has been neatly fobbed off on the public'. At least, for him, gas gives greater control – 'You can *see* what you're doing . . . Fire is too old a friend to be forsaken for glowing rods' (1969: 138).

Writing in memory of the open fire of his boyhood, French philosopher Gaston Bachelard (1884–1962) recalls the black cauldron hanging from the notched teeth of the chimney hook, and his grandmother puffing through a tube to rekindle the flames. 'Everything would be cooking at the same time: the potatoes for the pigs, the choice potatoes for the family. For me there would be a fresh egg cooking under the ashes.' The egg was done when a drop of saliva would evaporate on the shell. Before getting the egg, he had to eat a soup of bread and butter boiled to a pulp. Once, he threw spoonfuls into the teeth of the crane, crying, 'Eat, chimney hook, eat!'. But when he was good, the waffle iron came out. 'As far back in time as we can go, the gastronomic value has always been more highly prized than the nutritive . . . ' People are 'a creation of desire, not a creation of need' (1987: 15–16).

Furthermore, Bachelard hazards, 'fire is more a *social reality* than a *natural reality*'. He puts this neatly: if children put their hands too close, their parents rap them over the knuckles with a ruler. 'Fire, then, can strike without having to burn' (1987: 10–11). For such reasons, he entitles his study, originally published in 1938, *The Psycho-analysis of Fire*. Sifting through passages from numerous authors, in order to place the fire (and its watcher) on the couch, he studies the pensive person, acclaiming the 'reverie in front of the fire, the gentle reverie that is conscious of its well-being' (14). For him, fire virtually defines good and evil.

> It shines in Paradise. It burns in Hell. It is gentleness and torture. It is cookery and it is apocalypse. It is pleasure for the *good* child sitting prudently by the hearth; yet it punishes any disobedience when the child wishes to play too close to its flames. It is well-being and it is respect. It is a tutelary and a terrible divinity, both good and bad. It can contradict itself; thus it is one of the principles of universal explanation (7).

According to Herodotus, ancient Egyptians believed fire to be a living creature that devours whatever it gets and, when it has eaten enough, dies with the food on which it feeds (*Histories* 3.16; 1972: 210). So, too, his successor, the Greek philosopher Heraclitus, who lived around 2500 years ago, proposed that the whole world was composed of fire and motivated by opposites, notably war and peace (Diogenes Laertius ix.1; 1925, 2: 409–25). Empedocles must have been staring at a steaming pot for he then advocated a view that prevailed in Europe for 2000 years, that everything is composed of four underived and indestructible substances – fire, water, earth and air.

By contrast, as Bachelard says, twentieth-century science has 'almost completely neglected the truly primordial problem' of fire. Chapters on fire in chemistry textbooks have become shorter, until it is '*no longer a reality for science*'. A prime area of concern has been 'suddenly broken down into smaller problems or set aside without ever having been solved' (1987: 2). The loss of the living elements of air, fire, earth and water – replaced by the periodic table – is the story, too, of osmazome, the secret of cooked meats, now broken down into innumerable flavour compounds. It is the story of cookery, fractured without ever being seen.

Human beings have gathered around fires for hundreds of thousands of years, making homes of stone, sticks and flickering shadows. Fires have been the many-eyed focus of civilisation. To the participants, the flames have scarcely seemed to change. But they have lately been lowered, until, almost in an instant, the eternal scene vanishes. Unwatched, the milk boils and burns. Invisibly, microwaves leave the pastry flaccid. The ardent flames are covered in a permanent curfew. The ancient Greek hearth god, Hestia, and her equivalents around the world have been exiled. Our households are no longer focussed. The home is no longer where the hearth is. This suggests the loss of centre, replaced by the darting gaze of the moderns. Seduced by glossy food photographs, we think we can replace roasting with baking.

City restaurants reclaim an antique inheritance by broiling over charcoal. Expensive country inns engage the nostalgic charm of logs. But, in the main, the flame represents a glimmer of its past glory. Individual hearths are extinguished in favour of the temples of the generating companies. We cook over gas and electricity, its energy derived through advanced physics from the atom. With baking done in factories, we lose sight of cooks.

But nor should we become too mesmerised by the human intimacy with fire. For all that staring into the coals seems to promise, it provides only the vaguest historical guidance. Worse, stoves tend to distract from what cooks actually do. Fire gives colour and taste, camouflaging what we are eating. If we concentrate on cooking in the heating sense, we miss the cooks for the smoke.

CHAPTER FIVE

What Do Cooks Do?

In his gently ridiculous 'A Dissertation on Roast Pig', composed two centuries ago, essayist Charles Lamb claims to retell the mythical discovery of cooking in China (1909: 215–24). A swineherd's son, left alone, accidentally set fire to the family shanty. Worse than his home being reduced to ashes, nine piglets perished. But an enticing odour assailed the boy; burning his fingers on the scorched skin, he put them in his mouth, 'and for the first time in his life (in the world's life indeed, for before him no man had known it) he tasted – *crackling!*'.

Upon his return, his father was persuaded to try another of the pigs, and the pair devoured the entire litter, swearing not to divulge their secret. After neighbours observed that the swineherd's cottage was burning down regularly, father and son were summoned to trial in Beijing. The obnoxious evidence was produced, and the verdict about to be pronounced, when the jury sought a taste. The verdict: not guilty. The shrewd judge winked at the decision, dismissed the court, and bought up all the pigs to be had. In a few days, his Lordship's townhouse was observed on fire. Then fires were seen in every direction. Fuel and pigs grew enormously dear. The insurance offices shut up shop, and slighter and slighter dwellings were built, until it was feared that the very science of architecture would be lost. Finally, a sage discovered that the flesh of swine, or any other animal, might be cooked without consuming a whole house. 'Then first began the rude form of a gridiron. Roasting by the string, or spit, came in a century or two later, I forget which dynasty', Charles

88

Lamb writes. The main moral he draws is that the dangerous experiment of setting houses on fire could have been justified by no other culinary object than roast pork. He knows no flavour comparable to that of the 'crisp, tawny, well-watched, not over-roasted, *crackling*'.

That is one theory of what cooks do – provide pork crackling. However incomplete Lamb's answer, at least he recognises the question. Why do so many cooks pound, chop, stir and eventually appear laden at the table? Why, in civilised parts of the world, are streets misted by hawkers' smoke? Why do Italians love pasta and Mexicans chilli? Why balance the salt? Why do the rich and powerful often sit down to layers of impressiveness? Why spend so much time and energy cooking (and so little asking the question)?

This chapter begins to face up to the culinary mystery: 'What do cooks do?'. The question can be tightly focussed: do cooks just stand at the stove, as we watched them doing in Chapter Four, or do they also shop and wash up, for instance? Beyond this, the search can en-compass the activities of cooks in relation to so-called bigger things such as families, religions, wars. That is, as well as 'what?', calling for a technical description, this chapter opens a deeper question, 'why?'. The food photographer shows a glistening close-up, or attaches a fish-eye lens to bring in the rest of the world.

MORE THAN HEATING

Take a bunch of English dictionaries, ladle out portions and chew them over – and prepare to be confused. To 'cook', according to the *Concise Oxford Dictionary*, is to 'prepare (food) by heating'. An office edition of *Funk & Wagnall's* speaks of preparing food for eating by the action of heat. The 1981 unabridged edition of *Random House Dictionary of the English Language* spells it out: 'to prepare (food) by the action of heat, as by boiling, baking, roasting, etc'. In an early edition in the nineteenth century, *Webster's* defines the verb more generally: 'To dress victuals for the table; to prepare for any purpose'. It is later modernised: 'To prepare food for eating'. A more recent edition again is actually a copy of the Random House work, specifying heating. The dictionary editors have converged on a demand that cooks employ heat. For speakers of good English, cooking is to boil the pot of potatoes, to steam the rice, to pop the corn, but not to chop, soak or arrange on plates, and certainly not to wash up afterwards.

According to Californian culinary investigator Harold McGee in his book *On Food and Cooking: The science and lore of the kitchen*, 'Cooking can be defined in a general way as the transfer of energy from a heat source to food' (1986: 610). Again, this definition hardly seems especially 'general' (his word) and even his book incorporates other processes, such as making mayonnaise and beer. True, in English, we do not like saying that we 'cook' a salad. However, a nicely washed and dressed bowl of lettuce is a credit to the cook.

Speaking of a Filipino tribe, an anthropologist notes that the 'Hanunoo regard as a "real" food only that which is prepared for human consumption by cooking ... A *meal* must include cooked food. In fact, meals are usually enumerated by the term: pag'apuy, "fire making" ' (Lévi-Strauss 1970: 336). On the other hand, the Philippines also offers *kinilaw* food, which has not been cooked by heat but by such means as marinating. The erudite Alan Davidson explains: 'Many kinilaw dishes are akin to the ceviche fish dishes of Latin America; but kinilaw covers a much more extensive dominion, including meat and vegetables and fruits as well as seafood' (1991b).

So, applying heat is close to the core of cooking, and in this book I sometimes use the verb 'cook' to mean 'prepare food by heating'. But the definition illustrates the stunted conceptualisation of cooking. More often, to 'cook' denotes food preparation generally, which I intend to show extends far into social, economic, cultural and moral life.

THE ARCHITECTURE OF COOKING

To design kitchens, architects ought to know what cooks do. Inspired by time-and-motion studies, the textbook answer is a triangle linking the three basic pieces of equipment – refrigerator, stove and sink. The idea is that cooks take food from the refrigerator, place it on the heat and then wash up. British architect John Prizeman, for example, complains about the tendency, especially in magazines, to recreate old-style farmhouse kitchens. Instead, the 'basic necessity is to make the kitchen as efficient as possible'. Prizeman's ergonomic 'cooking machine kitchen' relies on the triangular 'work flow diagram', which he summarises in the three activities 'Store, Cook, Wash' (1970: 6, 10).

Whizzing around a three-pointed 'cooking machine', cooks might look efficient, but this is a gross simplification. The authors of a UK government design bulletin in 1972 break down the 'Meal Preparation Process' into the sequence 'Prepare, Mix, Cook, Serve, Eat and Wash-up'. Under these headings, the authors list specialised operations: 'Unwrapping, Washing, Peeling, Chopping, Mincing, Adding water, Weighing, Measuring, Mixing, Baking, Boiling, Frying, Grilling, Keeping food and dishes hot, Putting food onto dishes or plates, Table laying, Eating, Clearing away, Disposing of waste, Stacking, Washing, Drying, Putting away'. Adding to the complications, even architects cannot help placing this labour in a wider social context, so that kitchens may also be used for 'eating, clothes-washing, children's play, studying, entertaining, watching TV, hobbies, general

household mending and cleaning jobs' (Department of the Environment 1972: 2, 11). House plans reveal further assumptions about the value of cooking – and the position of women – by locating the kitchen in the heart of the house or at the back, or by trying to reduce it entirely.

Other experts can be even more blinkered about culinary activity, as when economists see it as merely a set of expenditure decisions. Perhaps we get more help by returning to the great English authority, *Mrs Beeton's*.

MRS BEETON'S

Isabella Beeton (1836–65) and her husband, Sam, published *The Book of Household Management* in 1861. Subsequently revised and expanded by others, it was retitled *Mrs Beeton's* . . . after the death of Isabella. She left us with such vividly detailed instructions for cooks in prosperous households that the picture almost seems like a parody. As her first duty, on rising at 6 in summer and 7 in winter, the employed cook might set her dough for the breakfast rolls, Beeton suggests. In those 'numerous households' where only a cook and housemaid are kept, the cook might have to take personal charge of breakfast, while the housemaid is upstairs looking after the bedrooms. Before dinner, the cook can 'dish-up' food that might, without injury, stand on the hot plate or in the hot closet. The bell 'to serve' brings haste, but no hurry. The cook takes charge of the fish, soups and poultry, assisted by the scullery-maid, while the kitchen-maid handles the vegetables, sauces and gravies (1861: 41–3).

During the Victorian and Edwardian eras, domestic manuals such as *Mrs Beeton's* adopted a scientific tone, typically opening with an analytical paragraph or more setting out the cooks' goals. The great New Edition of 1909 offers six reasons why food is prepared and cooked.

1. To render mastication easy;
2. to facilitate and hasten digestion;
3. to convert certain naturally hurtful substances into nutritious foods;
4. to eliminate harmful foreign elements evolved in food (e.g. the tinea or tapeworm in beef and mutton; trichinae in pork; the ptomaines resulting from tissue waste);
5. to combine the right foods in proper proportions for the needs of the body;
6. to make it agreeable to the palate and pleasing to the eye.

The central theme is that cooks assist the bodily machine. 'Hurrying over our meals, as we do, we should fare badly if all the grinding and subdividing of human food had to be accomplished by human teeth', the authors state (1909: 108). Cooks also facilitate digestion, and a 'Digestive Time Table' shows, for example, that cabbage when pickled takes 4 hours and 30 minutes to digest, which is the maximum desirable, and when boiled takes a better 3 hours and 30 minutes. Among the foods taking only an hour are boiled rice and boiled tripe. Among those taking as long as 6 hours are old salted beef, roasted eel and raw stone fruit (124–5).

Reason 5 canvasses the cooks' responsibility for providing a balanced diet. 'Some foods are deficient in one respect, some super-abundant in another: a little addition here and there helps digestion and supplies the body with what it needs. All cooks do this in obedience to the natural promptings of the appetite.' To rice, rich in starch, cooks thus add butter and cream; with peas, they serve fat bacon; salt-fish has less nourishment than its egg sauce; beef steak is balanced by boiled potatoes (109).

Mrs Beeton's reasons read as if the mission of cooks is biochemical. Although 'no one will wish that any pleasure or beauty should be gratuitously foregone', the authority admits that the aesthetic explanation at the end of the list contradicts the second, presumably because deliciousness makes a person overeat (108). Grasping the laws that govern the application of heat by no means comprises the whole art of cookery. Accordingly, the book acknowledges that such nineteenth-century culinary artists as Louis-Eustache Ude, Antonin Carême and Charles Francatelli owe their fame to their ingenuity in originating new dishes, their skill in combining flavours in such perfect proportions that no particular ingredient predominates. Their influence in the 'direction of refinement and elegance eliminated much that was gross in the English mode of living' (1677).

Cooking is a momentous invention for improving the flavour of piglets. In the English language, it is the heating of food. For textbook architects, it revolves around storing, heating and washing up. And it is done to improve both the nutritive qualities of foods and the elegance of living. Between them, these sources peg out much ground, and add to aims raised in earlier chapters, such as Catharine Beecher's moral training. These divergent ideas by no means exhaust the possibilities. I have plucked suggestions from the writings of food historians, popular scientists, anthropological theorists, theologians and others. Even when grouped under headings (cooks as nutrition and pleasure providers and as social and cultural communicators), the proliferation indicates that cooks are involved in a bewildering array of tasks and/or that the question is far from settled.

Cooks as Nutrition Providers

The ancient nutritional idea that cooks soften food is supported by science populariser Lyall Watson, who sees cooking as 'in effect a sort of external, partial pre-digestion' (1971: 23). Food historian Reay Tannahill takes a similar nutritional direction: 'since heat helps to release protein and carbohydrate as well as break down fibre, cooking increases the nutritive value of many foods and makes edible some that would otherwise be inedible. Improved health must certainly have been one result of the discovery of cooking' (1988: 12–13). And not just heating food: traditionally, cooks have spent large stretches of the day helping ingestion by milling corn and grinding spices.

Numerous authors assert that cooks make food safe, and otherwise increase our success as a species. Suggestive of Charles Lamb, a Chinese legend credits the invention of fire for cooking to a certain Sui Ren. 'Realising that his companions were suffering stomach and intestinal ailments from eating raw food, Sui Ren bored the branch of a tree to produce fire, and cooked on it. The people enjoyed cooked food, grew healthier and gave Sui Ren his name, which means Firewood Man' (Lai 1984: 1). Harold McGee finds scientific support for such a rationale: 'Many toxins can be destroyed by heat or leached out of the plant by boiling water, and this was surely one fact in the development of cooking in prehistoric times' (1986: 137).

A related theory is that we cook to kill germs such as cholera and typhoid. So we need not only boil water, but heat food. Telling me this, horticultural scientist John Possingham wondered whether the success of engineers in providing clean water led to the United States becoming the country of salads.

Historian Madeleine Pelner Cosman addresses the multiple cookings of single dishes in medieval recipes. Why would a veal stew require four changes of pot and five separate cookings? Sometimes this was to plump dried food or eliminate the salt or other preservatives. However, there is another reason. 'Many medieval health manuals warn against the dangers of undercooked flesh. Given the uncertainties of food preservation, such was [a] reasonable precaution' (1976: 59). Perhaps the storage aspect just mentioned is central. Cooks make food microbiologically safe: they keep or preserve a lot of food, not just through heating but brewing, cheese-making, salting, pickling, candying, bottling, and the like.

Another key idea, especially when cooking is regarded as more than just heating, is that cooks encourage a mixed diet (*Mrs Beeton's* number 5). In this context, I cannot resist mentioning William Stark (1740–70), who is living (or dying) proof of culinary diversity. As a bright medical student in London, he was drawn to the study of foods by a chance conversation with Benjamin Franklin. It would afford him a 'singular pleasure', Stark declares (and we can read something into his quest for 'pleasure'), if he could confirm the healthiness of a 'pleasant and varied diet' after imposing a 'strict and simple' diet upon himself. Stark's meticulous journal (published posthumously in 1788) shows that, on 12 June 1769, he started by living on bread and water with occasional sugar. After ten weeks, he complained of swollen and bleeding gums and sore nostrils, which we now interpret as symptoms of scurvy. He then 'lived freely on animal food, milk, and wine; . . . when I felt myself quite recovered'. Stark next tried bread and cooked meats, which were not so hazardous. So he shifted to nothing but puddings. In a month scorbutic symptoms returned, relieved on Boxing Day by a quantity of blackcurrants. His next experiment was on the relative value of fat and lean meat. He then planned to study the effects of fresh fruit and vegetables, which would have cured his by then chronic scurvy, but for some reason he changed to a diet of honey puddings and Cheshire cheese. He died on 23 February 1770, a 'true martyr to science', to quote Jack Drummond and Anne Wilbraham (1939: 286–8). Stark had celebrated meals that are, to some minds, 'varied', and, to others, 'pleasurable'.

Cooks as Pleasure Providers

The last of *Mrs Beeton's* six reasons proposes an aesthetic or sensual dimension. An early *Webster's* dictionary declares that to 'cook' is to 'dress victuals' – using 'dress' in the sense of 'decorate or adorn'. Dr William Kitchiner acknowledges the nutritional objects, but then discloses that the ' "*chef-d'oeuvre*" of COOKERY, – is to entertain the Mouth without offending the Stomach' (1821: 138). His book might be consulted, then, to either 'diminish the expense, or increase the pleasures of Hospitality' (132–3). Dr J.L.W. Thudichum's tome of 1895 (*The Spirit of Cookery*) widens a dryly nutritional definition to the 'preparation of food in such a manner that *man shall derive the greatest nutritive and aesthetical advantage from its consumption*' (3).

This deliberate catering to pleasure goes a long way back. From recipes that are nearly 4000 years old, it seems that the ancient Babylonians took great care in balancing flavours in complete dishes. They did not just throw birds on the fire, but followed complicated recipes calling for as many as ten seasonings. Historian Jean Bottéro acknowledges the Mesopotamians' 'superior goal': the combination of flavours. We are entitled, he writes, to call this serious interest in food 'gastronomy' (1985: 44). Perhaps thinking of the Ngarrindjeri people of the Murray River estuary, an anthropologist reported in the *Official Year Book of the Commonwealth of Australia* in 1910 that: '[The Aborigine] is more of an epicure than a gourmand [meaning hearty eater] ... Cooking is certainly a fine art' (Smith 1910: 10–11). The challenge, then, is to understand this further level of the cooks' task. Why make food not just chemically healthy but also appealing to the senses and artistic imagination? Indeed, it has been suggested that sensory gratification is the whole point.

Along the lines of Charles Lamb's bucolic arsonists chancing upon the glories of pork crackling, Lewis Robert Wolberg imagines in his *The Psychology of Eating* a caveperson, his Adam, accidentally dropping meat beside the flames. 'To his surprise it tasted good. He smacked his lips ... The next day he deliberately placed his kill near the fire and to his great joy he experienced the same delicious taste. Because he craved his new pleasurable sensation he continued to broil his meat. And thus was born in these savage surroundings a new art – gastronomy' (1937: 4). Quoting this in *The Origin of Food*

Habits, H.D. Renner suggests that liking the cooked flavour is a learned reinforcement of changes made for other reasons. He supposes that the cooked taste would have been as off-putting to the cave dweller as steak tartare to those not accustomed to it. Instead, Renner argues that a mammal's first food, mother's milk, has always been warm, and so people use fire primarily to imitate that comforting experience. 'In our civilised mode of living we continually take advantage of this reflex action of warmth; every cup of tea is proof of it' (1944: 186–9).

Fascinated by the hundreds of extra flavour compounds of cooked foods, especially crusty bread and roasted pork, Harold McGee finds a parallel in ripe fruits, to whose explosions of flavours human beings are primordially attuned. 'Perhaps cooking with fire was valued in part because it transformed blandness into fruitlike richness', he proposes (1990: 304). Other flavours might appeal because various species already use these to attract us to distribute their seeds, and so on. 'In a sip of coffee or a piece of crackling there are echoes of flowers and leaves, fruit and earth, a recapitulation of moments from the long dialogue between animals and plants' (313).

But to the hedonist, the pleasure to be had from food, and developed into an art over history, is more than some fortunate by-product. It gives reason to the universe; it is God-given. When outlining a 'philosophical history of cooking', Jean-Anthelme Brillat-Savarin explains that the drive to produce banquets 'springs equally from the basic nature of man, who awaits with impatience the end of his life work, and from a kind of inquietude which tortures him, so long as the sum total of the life that is remaining to him is not filled to the brimming point with conscious enjoyment' (Meditation 27; 1971: 290). Elsewhere, he explains that the human being is 'incontestably, among the sentient creatures who inhabit the globe, the one who endures most pain'. This suffering makes people throw themselves towards the opposite extreme, giving themselves 'completely to the small number of pleasures which Nature has permitted'. People enlarge pleasures, perfect them, complicate them and finally worship them (Meditation 14; 180–1).

The aphorisms with which Brillat-Savarin opens *The Physiology of Taste* set out an even fuller theory that, in a metabolic universe, the basic drive of appetite is rewarded by pleasure, and cooks refine this. More particularly, in the first aphorism, he points to the significance of life in the world, 'and everything that lives, eats'. In an expanded version of the fifth aphorism, he says that, morally, gourmandism is an 'implicit obedience of the rules of the Creator, who, having ordered us to eat in order to live, invites us to do so with appetite, encourages us with flavour, and rewards us with pleasure' (Meditation 11; 148). Learning, he writes in his 'Parting Salute', is based on the 'two unshifting cornerstones of pleasure and of need' (Envoy; 439). In the seventh aphorism, the pleasures of the table are universal and at the centre of all others. And, justifying his gastronomy, the sixth states that the 'good life' is an 'act of intelligence, by which we choose things which have an agreeable taste rather than those which do not'.

*   *   *

In following their appetites, gourmands obey the biblical command 'O taste and see that the Lord is good' (Psalm 34:8). However, the more usual response has been the reverse: the dominant Western view has long cast cooks as the agents of the devil. This is the meaning of the old proverb 'God sends meat; the devil sends cooks'. As Plato argues, cooks divert our minds from higher things, leaving us bloated, diseased, apathetic and morally decadent. The ancient Roman educator Seneca considers that things went wrong once people 'began to seek dishes not for the sake of removing, but of rousing, the appetite'. 'Are you astounded at the innumerable diseases?' he exclaims; 'count the cooks!' (Epistle 95: 15, 23; 1925: 67, 73).

As such thinkers would have it, in a former golden age, people ate only raw fruit and nuts. With the culinary discovery of fire, they could eat meat and, with that, were cast from paradise. True believers in the golden age lament the lost innocence BC, Before Cooking. This has even been dated: 'The magiric [culinary] science, therefore, began in the year of the world 1656', writes Alexis Soyer (1853: 123). These days, the calculation might require a little explanation. According to God's covenant with Noah, outlined in Genesis 9:3,

'Every moving thing that lives shall be food for you'. That is, after the Flood, God added meat to the range of human foods and, by implication, the use of fire. From the calculations of Bishop Ussher, responsible for establishing biblical chronology in the early seventeenth century, the date could be fixed at 1656 years after the creation of the world in 4004 BC.

The main vegetarian argument for two or three millennia has been just this, that meat-eating is unnatural and that cooking made it possible. In classical times, vegetarians believed that Prometheus was rightly punished for stealing fire from the gods. Greek writer Plutarch in his youth thought that our repugnance at slaughter and eating raw meat proved just how 'unnatural' these are, since our distaste could only be overcome through cooking and spices (*Moralia* 995b; 1957: 553). While Plato does not make his own position clear, his ideas were readily developed into the most complete ancient vegetarian text extant, the *De Abstinentia* (*On Abstinence from Animal Food*) of Porphyry, who agrees, for instance, that 'sense is a nail by which the soul is fastened to bodies, through the agglutination of the passions, and the enjoyment of corporeal delight' (1965: 47). Only vegetable foods seem safely distant from carnal appetites.

In the *Canterbury Tales* of Geoffrey Chaucer, the Pardoner holds forth hypocritically against gluttony, complaining that cooks revive the appetite with sauces from spices of leaf, bark and root. Knocking the marrow out of bones, they cast aside nothing soft and sweet that might go through the gullet. And worse – they pander to the mere appetite.

> Thise cookes, how they stampe, and streyne, and grynde,
> And turnen substaunce into accident,
> To fulfille al thy likerous talent!

Borrowing this argument from Pope Innocent III's *De Contemptu Mundi* (*On Contempt for this World*), the Pardoner condemns cooks to transforming 'substance' into 'accidents'. According to eucharistic doctrine, consecrated bread and wine gain the 'substance' or essential qualities of the flesh and blood of Christ, while retaining the 'accidents' – that is, superficial properties (colour, weight, texture) perceived by the senses and appealing to those with a gluttonous ('likerous' or 'lecherous', related to 'lick') predisposition. This is yet another development of Plato's complaint.

The idea of seven deadly sins preoccupied some of the mightiest medieval minds, and the first among the seven was *gula*, gluttony. The dire and deadly sin to which a host of theologians ascribed Adam's loss of Eden was not pride but gluttony, writes Madeleine Pelner Cosman. Serious medieval literature inveighed against this 'apparelling' of food – creating a pretence of something else. Excessive adornment was called 'pride of the table'. These authorities condemned pastry and aspic designs, marzipan coats of arms, meat dishes such as 'cockentrice' (the front half of a chicken sewn to the back half of a suckling pig, and vice versa), and 'musician pies', which presented live instrumentalists in pastry. Such wonders, exciting the eye and ear as well as the palate, expressed too much wealth, too great a magnificence, and too worldly a pride. By pandering to their patrons' insatiable desires for novelty, cooks led them to other vices (1976: 116–23).

Writing on 'Cuisine' and related topics in the great French Enlightenment *Encyclopédie*, the Chevalier Louis de Jaucourt (1704–80) takes the line that 'cooking, which had been a simple art in the first ages of the world, subsequently became more elaborate and more refined century by century . . . it is impossible to reduce to a fixed order all the tricks for disguising natural foodstuffs that have been pursued, invented, and imagined by man's self-indulgence and unrestrained taste' (Bonnet 1979: 148). So people 'came to make an art out of the most natural activity'. He associates the important episodes in the treacherous art of cookery with corrupt and decadent princes. These are set against the simple, natural methods of the 'sober or poor' people (141). With a sigh, Jaucourt concedes that 'only savages can be satisfied with the pure products of nature, eaten without seasoning and as nature provides them. But there is a middle way between such coarseness and the over-refinement practised by our chefs' (143).

Similarly, Richard Warner argues in his *Antiquitates Culinariae*, published in 1791, that culinary artistry ends up subverting the nutritional goal. 'The *ars coquinaria*, or *art of cookery*, originated not in *Luxury*; but in *Necessity*. When the divine permission gave man the use of *animal food*, the inhibition of eating the blood with the flesh, made some mode of *dressing* the latter *necessary*', he writes. Animals can be lean and stringy, and, besides, require some condiment so that the flesh might keep.

> From this necessity then, arose the Art of Cookery, or practice of combining different kinds of food together, and seasoning, tempering, and correcting them with various herbs, spices, oily ingredients, etc. – an art, which so long as it confines itself to the purpose of rendering any food more digestible than it would be, in its natural, or simple state, is an useful art; but this purpose answered, use ends, and Luxury begins (125).

The author of the cumbersome *Pantropheon* of 1853 replies: 'Let us speak plainly: mankind has thrown on cooks all the faults of which they ought to accuse their own intemperance'. Referring to the need for Roman sumptuary laws, he continues: 'Why render the cook responsible for the extravagant tastes and follies of his age? Is it for him to reform mankind?' (Soyer 1853: 251–2).

Cooks are now scarcely accorded such power, and we can laugh at the ascription of villainy. Or can we? Moral language is now largely reserved to foods, which are 'pure', 'good', 'sinful', 'tempting' and so forth (Maddox, forthcoming). French philosopher Michel Foucault has written widely on the cultural 'disciplining' of the body, through physical training, plastic surgery and dieting (Coveney 1996). More subtly, serious scholarship still tends to demonise cooks. Cooks are complicit in the sin of conspicuous consumption, through which the rich demonstrate their wealth and assert their power by way of flamboyant, or even engagingly refined, feasts. Treating food as communication tends to reduce cooks to panderers, the unworthy role in which Plato cast them. This category of put-down, under the banner of sophisticated social and cultural studies, rewards further examination.

COOKS AS SOCIAL COMMUNICATORS

Q: Why do cooks prepare hors d'oeuvres of Beluga caviar?
A: That their rich employers might indicate their social status.

Social scientists use many such examples of food as a social indicator. Aware that 'food carries messages about social status and the relations between people', British sociologists Nickie Charles and Marion Kerr provide a neat example: 'a multi-coloured cake in the shape of a train with four candles means that a treasured child has reached her fourth birthday and is celebrating'. Charles and Kerr say that eating habits are 'fundamentally influenced, if not determined, by social factors such as gender, age and class'. They believe that this can occur because food is used to uphold and teach ideologies that reinforce the existing social order. They expressly follow two French writers, Louis Althusser and Pierre Bourdieu, in seeing that taken-for-granted practices within the family are 'constantly reproducing social divisions and ideologies'. More specifically, food is related to 'family and patriarchal familial ideology', which endows foods with particular connotations, such as the masculine strength provided by red meat (1988: 1–4). The 'provision of a proper meal seems . . . to symbolise the family' and a 'proper' meal is defined in terms of both the physical 'meat and two veg' and social requirements such as the woman doing the cooking and the family sitting down together (226).

Bourdieu bases his work *Distinction* on extensive surveys of French 'taste', correlating taste not with beauty and other aesthetic abstractions but with social position. He claims that: 'Taste classifies, and it classifies the classifier. Social subjects, classified by the classifications, distinguish themselves by the distinctions they make' (1984: 6). As raised in Chapter One, he argues that working-class people demand substantial meals, which other classes abandon in favour of food as a sign. 'The disappearance of economic constraints is accompanied by a strengthening of the social censorships which forbid coarseness and fatness, in favour of slimness and distinction.' School teachers, who are richer in cultural than in economic capital, pursue originality and cheapness, and so Italian and Chinese cooking (185).

However, social interpreters can get carried away with the 'social construction of reality', as if human relationships were the ultimate power in the world. While mighty culinary artists might show off refined sensibilities, peasant cooking can hardly be explained in equivalent terms – the aim of preparing honest gruel is not to signal lack of status. Besides, social relationships themselves need explaining, and culinary practices, in fact, structure social relations. Cooks are not mere victims of social forces, but intimately involved in creating them.

COOKS AS CULTURAL COMMUNICATORS

Six people are at a table eating spaghetti. They must be Italians. This guess relies on a simple connection between culture and cooking. In this case, we assume that being Italian decrees spaghetti, just as exposure to American corporate culture leads a teenager to demand cola and hamburgers. Another common example of this kind of logic is the religious taboo: being Muslim requires that pork is eschewed. An attempt to put this approach on a scientific footing was made by structuralists, a brand of scholars active especially within anthropology in the 1960s and 1970s. For them, cooks respond to the collective mind. Cooks, as mouthpieces, speak a non-vocal language that reflects deeper, mental 'structures'. As an example, anthropologist Mary Douglas describes her own cooking following a 'grammar' of one major stress and two minor (1972). She composes a plate of meat and two subsidiary vegetables. Within her cooking, a meal is properly one main course accompanied by two minor. And during the day, there is a main meal and two lesser ones. This kind of pattern is certainly intriguing, but fails to speak to me as the deep-seated cultural logic that is claimed.

The main figure in food structuralism is Claude Lévi-Strauss. Immersing himself in tribal myths from around the world, he endeavours to uncover their shared logic in four volumes of *Mythologiques*. The myths explain the origin of the stars, fire, cultivated plants and, especially, cooking. Cooking, 'it has never been sufficiently emphasised, is with language a truly universal form of human activity', he declares. The most famous result is his culinary triangle. In his words, people place foods on a 'triangular semantic field whose three points correspond respectively to the categories of the raw, the cooked and the rotted' (1966: 937). This is, to many readers, mystifying. Nevertheless, as a possible example of the triangle's universality, the architects' work-flow triangle mentioned earlier has at its three points the refrigerator (raw), stove (cooked) and sink (rotted).

Of 'polarities' arrayed in the triangle, the most important is *The Raw and the Cooked*, which became the title of the first volume, and through which Lévi-Strauss claims to establish 'the truly essential place occupied by cooking in native thought: not only does cooking mark the transition from nature to culture, but through it and by means of it, the human state can be defined with all its attributes' (1970: 164). As interpreted by anthropologist Edmund Leach, Lévi-Strauss decides: 'Men [presumably, in this case, people] do not *have* to cook their food, they do so for symbolic reasons to show that they are men and not beasts. So fire and cooking are basic symbols by which Culture is distinguished from Nature' (Leach 1970: 92).

The core idea is that cooking anoints raw materials as 'food'. Once Nature is cooked, according to well-established recipes, it belongs to Culture. A 'pig' becomes 'pork'. It can then be eaten. Again, it is worth giving space to Leach's interpretation:

> *Animals* just eat food; and food is anything which is available which their instincts place in the category 'edible'. But *human beings*, once they have been weaned from their mother's breast, have no such instincts. It is the conventions of society which decree what is food and what is not food, and what kinds of food shall be eaten on what occasions. And since the occasions are social occasions there must be some kind of patterned homology between relationships between kinds of food on the one hand and relationships between social occasions on the other (32).

This extends to tribal people who symbolically 'cook' other things to bring them more firmly into the cultural realm, such as when various Californian tribes placed pubescent girls or new mothers in ovens, hollowed out in the ground, before covering them with mats and hot stones (Lévi-Strauss 1970: 335–6).

Structuralists may be lofty and hard to fathom. They might try to deny the reality of the physical in favour of the cultural world – one of the most-quoted statements of Lévi-Strauss is that natural species are chosen not as 'good to eat' (*bonne à manger*) but as 'good to think [with]' (*bonne à penser*) (1963: 89). He means that we choose pheasant not as filling but because it is a thought, a status symbol. They might mystify cooking as a way of expressing ourselves, as language. But we should not be prevented from rejoicing that Lévi-Strauss conceives human beings as, essentially, cooking creatures.

Cooks provide physical sustenance, and they are involved, too, in culture. But how? Cooks certainly follow culture, so that Italian cooks serve spaghetti as a matter of course. But this top-down view has its limits. Importantly, the idea that culture determines cooking does not explain where this culture comes from. Italianness might dictate spaghetti-cooking, but why is spaghetti a part of Italian culture? Part of the answer must be that it gains its place through the labour of cooks. So, cooks maintain culture as much as it maintains them. In their everyday labour, cooks sustain not just physically, but also culturally.

Equally, do cooks set out to *symbolise* the difference between people and other animals, or do cooks *make* the difference, as I would prefer to suggest? Lévi-Strauss puts familiar ideas into fancy language, but at least he takes cooking seriously. Furthermore, he injects into intellectual discourse the slogan of the 'raw and the cooked', with 'cooking' referring to the cultural processing of much more than food.

COOKS AS CIVILISERS

After Lévi-Strauss, it is not easy to find even a brief account of what cooks do by an internationally respected socially or culturally orien-ted scholar. One exception is Dutch sociologist Johan Goudsblom. While Goudsblom accepts that it would take more than a few pages to cover all the implications of cooking and while, indeed, he writes well on an associated and also relatively neglected topic, *Fire and Civilization*, he still claims to sum up the 'main categories'. These are, first, the physiological consequences of cooking – extending the number of possible foods by predigestion, detoxification and pres-ervation. And, second, he writes that:

> cooking led human groups to cultivate eating habits of their own, by
> which they could distinguish themselves both from all other animals

and also from each other. Distinctions first developed in interspecies relationships were carried over into intraspecies relationships (1992: 36–7).

In this, Goudsblom covers two categories already canvassed: that cooks improve our nutrition and extend the menu, thereby increasing the range of human habitats, and that cooks speak languages to demonstrate that we are humans, refined bourgeoisie, patriarchal breadwinners and so on. But he omits several major possibilities we already know about – for example, that cooks facilitate a mixed diet. A more surprising omission is a further category: the ethical, where cooks either bring, or subvert, the good life.

Essayist Roland Barthes declares that one aspect of the 'ornamentation' of *Elle* magazine cookery – a smart, modern cookery 'based on coatings and alibis' – is that it is 'for ever trying to extenuate and even to disguise the primary nature of foodstuffs, the brutality of meat or the abruptness of sea-food' (1973: 78). This accords with cooks as tempters, on one hand, and a relatively sophisticated theory of alienation, on the other. More in line with the latter, sociologist Norbert Elias agrees that cooking helps hide brutality. In this, cooks are involved in an overall 'civilising process' (and we find more about this in Chapter Seven). By this term, he does not mean that 'civilising' is necessarily good or bad, just a trend. Putting it simply, having to coexist in increasingly complex societies, people have to be more self-restrained. Cooks are employed to 'disguise' the 'brutality' of feeding. This is reasonable enough, but are cooks now to be slaves of politeness, as they are of status? Nonetheless, it is especially surprising that Goudsblom overlooks this direction of thought since he is a great disciple of Elias.

A THOUSAND THINGS DONE WELL

This collection of fragments on the cooks' role has, I hope, been bewildering. Specialists see cooking in specialist terms: biologists view cooking biologically, cultural theorists culturally, dentists in terms of teeth, economists as a cost, and so forth. Such disciplinary commitments tend to limit cooks to technicians subservient to some 'greater' function. Existing attempts to define cooking are reductionist; that is, they tend to restrict cooks to one level.

Complementing the unacceptable limitations imposed by the various external and incidental viewpoints is their very multiplicity. Cooks appear to serve an incredible variety of ends. They are everywhere, allegedly distracting us from the spiritual and the true, shouting the human separation from other animals, conspiring with the rich and pretentious, expressing religious mysteries, giving plants and animals the stamp of human approval, making food safer and easier to chew and digest, contributing to the nutritional flexibility of the species, making hard lives more bearable, and so forth.

Two centuries ago, the pioneering food journalist Grimod de La Reynière decided that:

> In all truth one cannot be a decent cook without being at the same time a chemist, a botanist, a physician, a draughtsman and a geometer. One must also have a good nose, a keen ear and immense tact; someone not having these qualities would be continually perplexed by the hanging of meats, the seasoning of *ragoûts*, the roasting of meats, the marriage of materials or the condition of pastry. It is therefore of capital importance that a cook be provided with an extreme delicacy in all his senses and all his organs.
>
> But the physical qualities required pale into insignificance beside the moral ones or the talent necessary for this profession. Zeal, probity, impartiality, vitality, cleanliness, the ability to judge at a glance, *sang-froid*, deep understanding and intelligence, sobriety, vigilance, rigour, patience, moderation, a passion for work, a fondness for employers, etc. This is what is required of a cook worthy of the name; taking for granted an excellent nature, a good upbringing and an unflappable wisdom.

Given such a job description, it is little wonder that Grimod immediately congratulates any employer: 'Happy the Amphitryon having such a cook! He should treat him more as a friend than a servant, keep him entirely in his confidence, support him in all the setbacks of his profession, quote him at all times and spare no expense to achieve his glory and his fame' (1987: 173).

No less is expected of domestic cooks. In lectures to a girls' school, the English art and social critic John Ruskin speaks of three feminine virtues. They are 'to be intensely happy' (to 'dance'), to dress beautifully (yourselves, 'your houses, and your gardens'), and to cook.

> What does 'cooking' mean? . . . It means the knowledge of Medea, and of Circe, and of Calypso, and of Helen, and of Rebekah, and of the Queen of Sheba. It means the knowledge of all herbs, and fruits, and balms, and spices; and of all that is healing and sweet in fields and groves, and savoury in meats; it means carefulness, and inventiveness, and watchfulness, and willingness, and readiness of appliance; it means the economy of your great-grandmothers, and the science of modern chemists; it means much tasting, and no wasting; it means English thoroughness, and French art, and Arabian hospitality; and it means, in fine, that you are to be perfectly, and always, 'ladies' – 'loaf-givers' (1877: 137–8).

Successful cookery requires a thousand things done well. Indeed, cooks must possess the attributes of all the classical figures listed by Ruskin – Medea was noted for sorcery, Helen of Troy for beauty, Rebekah for cunning, the Queen of Sheba for wisdom, and so on. The amazing variety of cooks' duties should run counter to any thought of their insignificance. As he sees it, they have to be proper ladies ('lady' deriving, so the dictionary says, from 'loaf-kneader', along with 'lord' from 'loaf-keeper').

Cooks seem to do almost everything; in fact, I suggest that they *do* do almost everything. I want to take the lead from gastronomic writers such as Brillat-Savarin who place cooks at the heart of human affairs. Lifting our attention from the chopping-board, spice rack and saucepan, we see that the cooks' sleights-of-hand draw in the natural world as nourishment, gather around the human race as diners, and tie together customs and cultures. If we stand back, like Brueghel, we see cooks surrounded by a busy scene of musicians, priests, children, dogs and villagers ready to pounce on the good things. Cooks have so many connections, seem to serve so many masters, because they are at the centre of all activity. Cooks have fingers in all the pies.

At base, cooks are in charge of our feeding, and nothing demands closer attention. In the next chapter, I set out a comprehensive theory of my own.

CHAPTER SIX

'On the Physical and Political
Consequences of Sauces'

 Sauces have been acclaimed as the acme of cookery, certainly cookery in the sophisticated French style. They demonstrate a high degree of technical skill and often call for inordinate hours of careful preparation. They are nature transcended. They speak of the most legendary chefs, among them Taillevent, Vincent La Chapelle, Antonin Carême and Auguste Escoffier (Revel 1982). For such reasons, the editors of the *Encyclopaedia Britannica* early in the twentieth century went so far as to refer to cookery as the 'art of sauces'. With this, they deliberately lifted their sights above the 'mere necessities' of nutrition and dietetics to a concern with pampering and style. Historically, they pictured a steady increase in culture and wealth being matched by ever-more elaborate and 'decadent' ways to tickle the palate. 'Mere hunger, though the best sauce, will not produce cookery, which is the art of sauces. For centuries its elaboration consisted mainly of a progressive variety of foods, the richest and rarest being sought out' (1910; 7: 74). The old *Britannica* concentrates our minds usefully.

In narrowly nutritional terms, the explanations for sauces are familiar from the last chapter: predigestion, making food safe, and camouflaging meat. From a cultural viewpoint, sauces might also demonstrate our 'civilised' state. In the eighteenth-century *Encyclopédie*, Chevalier de Jaucourt writes about the *ragoût* as a 'sauce or seasoning used to titillate or stimulate the appetite when it has lost its edge'. This alludes to the derivation of *ragoût* from 'to revive the taste of' and suggests artificiality in food. De Jaucourt inclines to a negative evaluation in that 'combining and seasoning . . . is usually most pernicious to health, since *ragoûts* not only encourage excessive eating, but also cause the corruption of the humours. The simplest foodstuffs are the best for every kind of temperament' (Bonnet 1979: 142–3).

In discoursing on the 'Philosophy of Sauces' more than a century ago, J.L.W. Thudichum welcomes their invention because, he says, many solid foods are 'dry in substance, or unattractive in taste, or insufficiently or too strongly flavoured' (1895: 223–4). By stimulating the appetite and the digestive juices, sauces enhance both pleasure and nutritional value. Thudichum appends a further explanation: their importance as status symbols – 'their proper application reveals the man of taste, and their practical production is a constant opportunity for the exhibition of the minor qualities, such as dexterity, of a good cook' (226). In sum, Thudichum returns us to common suggestions for cooking overall – the bio-mechanical (improving palatability), the hedonist, and the expressive (a means for conspicuous consumption). So far, then, sauces have attracted similar interpretations to cooking generally, but there's more.

Salt

The world's oldest city, Jericho, which may be traced back as many as 12 000 years, probably grew up as a salt-trading centre alongside the Dead Sea. Beidha in modern Jordan might have been another early salt-trading town (Hamblin 1973: 19). Rome's 'salt road', Via Salaria, crosses to the Adriatic, and the first part of its course coincides with the route by which the Sabines came to fetch salt from marshes near the mouth of the Tiber. In 506 BC, according to Livy, the saltworks at Ostia, on both sides of the mouth of the Tiber, became a state monopoly. The word 'salary' comes from the Roman soldiers' salt-money, just as the ancient Greeks used 'some salt' for a charity hand-out. Venice started out on salt, which was shipped up the Po River, while in translation Salzburg is 'salt castle'.

E.M. Gale has written a book tracing the political and economic importance of salt in China back to its earliest history (there, as in so many places, salt was long a state monopoly). The salt tax has been called the most hated of all taxes and a major cause of the French Revolution. In *Das Salz*, published in Leipzig in 1875, M.J. Schleiden finds a connection between the salt tax and despotic government. He points out that ancient Egypt and Israel had a salt tax (as did the contemporary 'despotic governments' of Mexico and China), whereas neither Athens nor early republican Rome had one (Multhauf 1978: 8–12). Salt has been more pervasive on our tables (and so in our economics and politics) than we might usually notice.

When Simulus, the ancient Roman peasant described in Chapter Four, takes up mortar and pestle to prepare his enlivening *moretum*, he adds salt. In traditional Chinese cooking, free-running salt was almost never used, but it still came in fermented products such as soy sauce (Anderson 1988: 151). Such is its importance to cooks that Baron von Rumohr speaks of salt as one of the 'three elements' of cookery, along with heat and water. The English word 'sauce' originates in the Latin for 'salt'. Indeed, salt is so universally employed that sauces might well be explained as a means to add it.

The exceptionally informative American food writer Waverley Root speaks of the invention of cooking (in the sense of fire) as the first great gastronomic revolution. The second is the invention of seasoning, which was forced by the shift from hunting to herding and agriculture, often termed the Neolithic Revolution. People ate less game and more vegetables, 'which demanded salt for reasons of gastronomy (they were comparatively tasteless) and for reasons of health (they did not contain enough salt to meet human require- ments)'. To make matters worse, the new cereals contained virtually no salt. And, further, the momentous invention of cooking pots resistant enough to be placed over a fire enabled boiling, a 'more convenient method, requiring minimum attention from the cook: but while roasting conserves the salt content of meat, boiling leaches it out. It became necessary to find salt' (1980: 438–9).

It is generally agreed, confirms salt historian Robert Multhauf, that 'herbivorous animals and civilised men need additional salt' (1978: 4). This makes the involvement of cooks circular. Cooking removes salt. Our bodies need it. And so cooks put it back, often in sauces. The salt-replacement theory appears to have another flaw. Salt is only needed in minuscule proportions. If we heeded nutritionists' advice, we would never add any. If that is the case, we must merely be submitting to the crude demands of our taste buds, seeking salt and sweet and rejecting bitter. But this is not the only reason for adding salt, let alone making sauces.

As elsewhere, salt has long been a big industry in Russia. Rock salt has been mined, crystallised sea and lake salt collected, and, most importantly, brine pumped from underground and evaporated (this required large quantities of firewood). Besides being used for tanning hides and dyeing textiles, salt has preserved fish and cabbage to supplement grain-based diets over long winters. According to scholars R.E.F. Smith and David Christian, writing about Russian cuisine under the title *Bread and Salt*, the Russian word for hospitality is literally 'bread-salt' (1984: 5, 27–34). Accustomed to the taste of excessive salt through its near-universal use as a preservative, people have felt the need to add it.

FLAVOUR PRINCIPLES

In her *Ethnic Cuisine: The flavor-principle cookbook*, Elisabeth Rozin finds food systems, or cuisines, involve the selection of both foods and the basic techniques of preparing them. These are making physical changes (cutting up, separation and incorporation), altering the water content (soaking, drying and salting, freezing), and modifying the foods chemically (heating – dry, wet or fat cooking – and fermentation). And then there is the use of flavourings, the most 'crucial element in ethnic cuisine', according to Rozin. The distinctiveness of any cuisine relies on what she calls 'flavour principles', which are culture-specific, repetitive flavour combinations.

'Flavouring a dish with soy sauce, for example, almost automatically identifies it as Oriental', she says. This can be further broken down so that if you add garlic, brown sugar, sesame seeds and chilli to the basic soy, the seasoning is definitely Korean. She gives the Vietnamese flavour principle as fish sauce, lemon and chilli, and the Hungarian as paprika, lard and onions. In all, Rozin lists thirty-six flavour principles, with a few sub-categories such as when the soy sauce, rice wine and fresh ginger of China are supplemented by soy bean paste, garlic and sesame (Beijing), sweet–sour and hot (Szechuan), and black bean and garlic (Canton) (1983: xi–xviii).

Working with her social psychologist husband Paul, Elisabeth Rozin has gone on to treat flavour principles as a cuisine's stamp of approval for foods (Rozin and Rozin 1981). That is to say, cuisines replace instincts as guides to what to eat. As omnivores, and with only the faintest instincts, we are in danger of making mistakes. So, cooking according to entrenched rules, we eat only what is tested and approved. Because sauces add seasonings, salt and spices, and so operate like 'flavour principles', this is yet another possible hypothesis. Sauces are like little national flags.

This approach resembles that of Claude Lévi-Strauss in stressing cooking as a medium of communication. Sauces become 'good to think with', signalling proper eating. Yet such a 'bio-cultural' analysis can only be taken so far. It fails to explain the original suppression of animal instincts. More concretely, sauces themselves often provide goodness. Indeed, they are often nutritionally more valuable than, and are 'stretched' by, the staple.

*   *   *

As sauce artists, cooks are thus given the comprehensive nutritional, communicative and hedonistic responsibilities raised in the previous chapter. Every one of these suggestions is valid, yet none seems sufficient in itself. We must suspect, then, that cooks are not confronted squarely on their own merits. We need to break free from conventional assumptions to find a central role for cooks. I put them in charge of nothing less than our very lives. In feeding us, they connect with the rest of the natural world, while setting us off as social and cultural creatures. To show how, I pursue the purpose of sauces.

LAUNCELOT STURGEON

Launcelot Sturgeon, the exuberantly gastronomic author of *Essays, Moral, Philosophical, and Stomachical, on the Important Science of Good Living*, first published in London in 1822, provides clues in a pair of essays entitled 'On the physical and political consequences of sauces' and 'On the importance of forming good connexions; and on the moral qualities of the stomach'. Medical practitioners, he says, counsel against sauces 'because they induce us to eat to repletion'. But rather than an objection to sauces, this is the 'finest eulogium that could be passed'. If adopted, that sort of medical reasoning would not merely undermine the bodily constitution, but destroy the whole system of modern cookery, reducing 'us to a diet of plain roast and boiled' (1823: 81–2). Turning the medical advice on its head, Sturgeon upbraids cooks when sauces *lack* taste and satisfaction: cooks are lamentably deficient when 'they cheat us with false appearances, and give their sauces the semblance of richness, by the aid of mere colouring matter' (89–90).

An ambassador, Sturgeon confesses, once remarked that 'the English had twenty religions and only one sauce', presumably the 'eternal melted-butter' (82–3; and see Cohen and Cohen 1960: 97). This poverty was in obvious contrast to the French, who took pride in their cooks (1823: 193). However, now that 'our prejudices against foreign innovations are daily yielding to the dictates of an enlightened philosophy', such progress had been made that a contemporary catalogue of sauces extended to 'more than one hundred and eighty varieties' (84–5).

In mock scientific tones, Sturgeon asserts that: 'The duty of a good sauce is, to titillate the capillaceous extremities of the maxillary glands, and thus to flatter and excite the appetite'. Sauces not only vary the taste and form of dishes, and 'impart that relish which enables a man to eat three times as much as he could without them', they also add 'an attractive embellishment which may justly be compared to the finishing touch of the painter, or the toilette of a pretty woman' (80). These are hearty defences in the jokey tone of Sturgeon's inspiration, French gourmand Grimod de La Reynière. And sauces play an even greater role.

To uncover the 'political consequences of sauces', Sturgeon cata-logues various social 'connexions', claiming, for example, that family connections are 'commonly frigid', illicit connections are 'always frail', commercial connections 'often ruinous', and so forth. In other words, the bases of many social relationships are hazardous. However, he upholds an altogether different connection worth forming – '*the Connexion of Sauces*'. One of the 'greatest mysteries in the whole arcana of the sciences', their elements are simple – maybe just gravy or cream; 'it is their employment which is difficult'. Just as in a happy marriage each partner must yield to the other, 'so, in a good ragout, the substance, the seasoning, and the sauce, should all be blended in that exquisite concord which constitutes the foundation of good cookery and of all rational enjoyment' (87–9). So, the coming together of certain culinary materials is a marriage made in heaven.

Of course, Sturgeon intends a double meaning for the 'connexion of sauces'. Certainly, he extols the 'exquisite concord' of ingredients themselves. But he also reintroduces the earlier meaning of 'connexions', those social connections occasioned by the culinary connections of a good sauce. 'The importance of an art which thus binds the whole fabric of society must be at once apparent', he writes (89). I note that both connotations are reunited in the word 'liaison', which is both a 'relationship' and 'the binding or thickening agent of a sauce'.

The link between the harmony of sauces and the harmony of society is more than metaphoric. Sturgeon makes the strong claim that good sauces are the very basis of society and the balanced dish the root of 'all rational enjoyment'. The topic of '*Social Connexions*' springs naturally from that of sauce. 'The table is a magnet which not only attracts around it all those who come within its influence, but connects them together by ties which no one ever wishes to dissolve.' Sauces are not just a fancy bait, but the very glue of society. In fact, it is impossible to abstain from sauces and so society. He warns that 'if the stomach be unsound, the heart which is lodged in it must be corrupted; it therefore follows, that all abstemious people are people of bad heart'. Conviviality is stronger among epicures than others; they are 'more sociably disposed, more frank and cordial'. He has found that a 'good stomach is the parent of every social virtue' (90–2).

In 1815, after the fall of Napoleon, the emperors and princes of Europe (except, notably, that of Great Britain) formed a 'Holy Alliance' based 'upon the sublime truths which the Holy religion of Our Saviour teaches' (Evans 1990: 553). In this atmosphere, Sturgeon writes that:

the connexion between a good sauce, whereby the powers of the food are cemented, and a good stomach, wherewith the constitution is supported and the social system maintained, possesses the only legitimate title to respect, and is, in fact, the real secret of the HOLY ALLIANCE (1823: 92–3).

For him, meals are not just roasts and *ragoûts*, but gatherings of good people, brought by healthy stomachs and rewarded with good humour.

That the table brings not just good but all society is also suggested by Brillat-Savarin.

... every modification which complete sociability has introduced among us can be found assembled around the same table: love, friendship, business, speculation, power, importunity, patronage, ambition, intrigue; and this is why conviviality is a part of every thing alive, and why it bears fruits of every flavour (Meditation 14; 1971: 183).

Harmonious blends in sauces lead to harmonious blends in people. Drawn around the table by good sauces, people join successful social unions. Sauces are the liaisons of all liaisons. But why is this? What is so attractive about sauces? Sturgeon takes us much of the way. If we are finally to understand the reason we cook, the physical and political consequences of sauces need further spelling out. My proposal might seem obvious, and therein lies its power: the basic reason that stomachs gather around Sturgeon's sauces is sharing. The essential purpose of sauces is to dispense goodness.

SAUCES AS SHARING

While rarely raised as the reason to cook, the concept of sharing is at least familiar in discussions of certain kinds of sauces. I am thinking of how pasta or rice sauces are explained as eking out valuable ingredients, especially precious meat. We have heard how the Bemba horticulturists of Zambia dip pieces of millet *ubwali* in a stew-like *umunani* of vegetables or perhaps meat, fish, caterpillars, locusts, ants, and so on (Richards 1939: 46–9). And there are numerous other examples of companage (to use the medieval word deriving from the late Latin *companaticum* for a relish or accompaniment to bread). That is, the immediate reason for sauces is to add protein, salt and variety to staples, especially cereals. Through sauces, cooks distribute hard-won ingredients among the diners.

Historically, the need for sauces emerged with agricultural societies. The secret of cereals, root crops and pulses lies in their ability to be stored. Barley-cakes, bread, porridge, steamed rice, baked yams and so on tend to be bland and nutritionally incomplete. The carbohydrate cries out, especially to creatures attuned to saltiness and rich flavours, for a topping, perhaps a curry. Sauces become a way of adding piquancy, while rationing more expensive components.

In ancient Athens, meals were based on the staple, the *sitos*, of barley-cake and wheaten bread or perhaps lentil soup. This was taken with the *opson*, which might have been bitter herbs, cheese, eggs, fish (fresh, salted or dried) or, less frequently, meat (Dalby 1996: 22). Originally anything prepared by the use of fire, the *opson* came to mean any relish taken with bread and then, further, in Athens, to imply fish. Following on, the word for gourmand was *opsophagos* – those 'who gad about among the fishmongers' (Athenaeus 276ef; 3: 243–5). In his vegetarian phase, Plutarch recoils from taking life for 'a mere *opson*' (*Moralia* 994b; 1957: 547). The Greek *opson* was taken up in Latin and, from there, even found its way to the obsolete English words 'obsonation' for feasting and 'obsonator' for caterer.

This brings us back to Chinese cooking and the basic distinction between *fan* and *ts'ai*. In a narrow sense, *fan* means 'rice' or 'cooked rice', and *ts'ai* means 'greens' or 'vegetables'. In a broader sense, however, *fan* embraces all cereal and starchy dishes, among them porridge, steamed bread, dumplings, pancakes and noodles. And *ts'ai* refers to the accompaniments, whether vegetables, meat or fish. *Fan* are 'grain foods' and *ts'ai* 'dishes to go on rice'. The two types have to be in balance, although *fan* might win at home and *ts'ai* dishes be more numerous and prominent at feasts (Chang 1977: 7–8; Anderson 1988: 82, 154).

For a thousand years, Chinese have spoken of the Seven Necessities of even the poorest person. These come from the writings of Wu Tzu-mu in the late Southern Sung Dynasty, who said that 'the things that people cannot do without every day are firewood, rice, oil, salt, soybean sauce, vinegar, and tea. Those who are just slightly better off cannot do without *hsia-fan* and soup'. The *hsia-fan* is the 'food to help get the rice down' and this and the soup are both presumably made of vegetables, historian Michael Freeman explains (1977: 151). So, the Seven Necessities turn out to be rice and its least dispensable adjuncts.

An important family of French sauces derives from stocks known since the early eighteenth century as the *fonds* (foundations) of cuisine. The *Larousse Gastronomique* recommends that cooking in the grand manner requires a ready supply of '*broth, clear soup, veal stock, white* and *brown (thin* and *thick), juice* from *braised meat, poultry* and *game stock, fish stock* and *various jellies'*. When *roux* (a cooked paste of flour and fat, most likely butter) or another binding element is added, those stocks become the basic sauces (Montagné 1961: 934). Carême reduced the kitchen to three such sauces – *espagnole, velouté* and *béchamel* – which he prepared in large quantities and used with other flavourings to make compound sauces. The main rivals are egg-based sauces derived from mayonnaise and hollandaise (Mennell 1985: 147).

While a French sauce may well become so refined that it appears as a fashion and not a food item, it was once nutritionally dense. The refinement of the humble stewpot saw, for example, the notorious demand for fifteen pheasants from which to prepare a sauce for one. However, the result is not 'just' a rich sauce; the fifteen pheasants are still there, but the chef has so improved flavours that style seems to have taken over from sharing.

Sauces entice people to table, offering goodness. In giving eaters pleasure, sensory and aesthetic, they form those social connections that so entranced Launcelot Sturgeon. Togetherness on the plate goes with social mingling, which entails a complex of factors, as we shall explore.

Of course, sharing is not just the feature of sauces but cooking generally. Cooks are confronted, on one side, by photosynthesising plants and respiring animals, and, on the other, by feeding, digesting and excreting bodies with likes and dislikes. In the middle of this metabolic universe, as ringleaders in a many-ringed circus, cooks apportion, divide up, mete out. Distribution is at the heart, from rationing limited resources to showering *richesse*. In addition, I keep stressing that, to share food, cooks must first gather it in. And, as a third great 'moment' of cooking, the acquisition and distribution of food implies organisation. To share food, cooks must know and communicate the way this is done.

Set out more abstractly, my basic proposition is that any living system involves, first, a food-getting or energising aspect. Second, this sustenance has in some way to be stored and distributed, requiring a further sub-system. And, finally, these processes have to be organised, which involves a set of control mechanisms. These recall Plato's divisions (Chapter Three) of energising, distributive and organisational functions.

As a further fundamental principle, in sharing meals, cooks share tasks. Humans enjoy society's consolations for the benefits of physically sharing sustenance in return for the labour it demands. Historically, people cooperate in increasingly specialised ways, and this multiplies into civilisation. This differentiation, by which sharing evolves, becomes the underlying motif of the second half of the book.

It adds up to a busy schedule. Yet cooks are scarcely noticed amid the whirling brilliance of civilisation. Why? Because cooking quickly becomes so complex that its study, too, is broken down into self-important bits – nutritionists know the chemical properties of foods, architects the layout of kitchens, electrical engineers the laws of conduction, market researchers the weaknesses of shoppers, and so on, seemingly indefinitely. But these snap together again once all kinds of human activities are viewed as radiating out from cooking. Cooking is the point where production is directed, where social relationships are formed and maintained, and where the arts and sciences emanate. It is the starting-place of trades, the target of the marketplace, the object of philosophy. This is a quick summary of the broad principles behind cooks and their work. Let me take that again, more slowly.

DISTRIBUTION

So many of the most basic culinary actions, such as slicing, stirring and spooning out, are plainly distributive. The ancient Greek noun *dais*, which refers to a meal, feast, banquet and so to meat or food itself, derives from the verb *daitreuo*, to cut up or carve, to portion out, to distribute. That is to say, ancient Greeks understood a meal as a 'distribution'. Others have pursued the sharing idea of meals, but typically ignoring the cooks.

Wrestling with a philosophy of daily life, theologian Edmond Barbotin asks in *The Humanity of Man*: 'Why the art of cooking?'. He initially responds in the familiar terms that cooking 'acts as a kind of predigestion'. Along with Lévi-Strauss, he also views cooking as a way of humanising food, of cultural appropriation, which 'manifests itself in the distaste I have for food prepared in ways that differ from what I am used to'. Every book of recipes is a 'partial reflection' of people's image of themselves and the world, he writes (1975: 324).

As well as these familiar explanations, Barbotin speaks of meals as sharing. Coming from the Christian tradition, he offers bread as the paradigm.

> Bread is intended to be shared. The golden-crusted loaf on the table awakens my appetite and draws my hands to itself. My hands reach out, take the bread, cut or break it; then separate again to distribute the pieces. In giving the other his share, I withdraw the food from my own body towards which I was instinctively conveying it . . . My food is no longer centred on me alone: I assign it the body and life of another as its terminus and goal (328).

Furthermore, for him, the sharing of bread is the foundation for sharing ourselves. '*With the distributed food a fraternal meaning also circulates*' (329).

These are fine thoughts, except that, like too many male diners, Barbotin overlooks cooks. While crediting the table with intimate communion or a '*density of presence*' (321), he neglects its orchestrators. Emphasising the hand as a tool of giving, he forgets who might own it. When he is drawn to the bread, it is by the bread unaided. When shared, it is mysteriously already baked. Sadly, at the very point of celebrating sharing, he mystifies it.

Meals are also described as sharing in a seminal essay on the 'Sociology of the meal' published in 1910 by German sociologist Georg Simmel. He points to what he calls the 'material individualism' of meals. As he puts it: 'what I think, I can let others know; what I see, I can let them see; what I say, hundreds can hear – but what the individual eats, no one else can eat under any circumstances'. In a classic case of Simmel's fascination with paradoxes, he then points out that this selfishness brings people together with unparalleled force. Indeed, he says, the table brings us together more decisively than any elevated motive, and so this sharing is at the centre of our social universe. The meal orders our social lives, since it makes us come together at definite times, introduces social divisions between those admitted and not admitted, and then stimulates the intricacies of etiquette. Out of the brutality of eating unfolds the utmost cultural refinement and aesthetic expression (1994: 346–8). As Simmel expresses it, the socialisation enforced by our hunger 'promotes the overcoming of the sheer naturalism of eating' (350). But, again, he overlooks cooks. He effectively mythologises the world of male diners. This awe at the power of shared food needs redirecting to the people responsible, historically, the women of the household.

Similarly, other branches of learning – including those served by such journals as *Animal Behaviour*, *American Ethnologist* and *Current Anthropology* – deal with the issues surrounding food-sharing, exchange, cooperation and eventually commodification, but without making the link with cooking.

We keep *company* – that is, we share *panis*, bread. We share salt. We share sauces. In arranging this, cooks bring people together as a household. Cooks make families. Cooks also share in widening circles – contributing to communal feasts, providing hospitality to travellers, exchanging through markets. This makes the market a public table – in the sense of a place of food distribution. Cooks reach out, until today we share as far as the other side of the world. Note that food storage falls under the general heading of sharing; it is a form of distribution over time. Cooks take in provisions – and also dry, salt, pickle and ferment them – for allocation over the weeks and months. Not that this sharing is always fair.

The huts of a typical family of the Kwandu, a Herero people of south-west Angola, cluster around the sacred fire, which unites them with the spirits of their ancestors. The women do the cooking to one side of the front hut, belonging to the main man in that hearth group, and then serve in what anthropologist Carlos Medeiros describes as a 'rigid' manner. The married women approach the leading man, who sits facing the sacred fire, and offer him the food each has prepared. The man helps himself, taking first from his first wife and ending with his daughter-in-law. Then, it is the turn of his son to select in the same order. After the married men are served, the women seat themselves in a fixed formation on the cooking side; the married women help themselves in order until, lastly, the unmarried girls take food (1981: 59–63). In traditional Chinese villages, men and women ate at separate tables. The only exceptions were boys below five or six (who ate with their mother) and the wife of the most senior male (who sometimes joined the men). Meanwhile, cooking was undertaken by younger women, usually daughters-in-law (Hsu and Hsu 1977: 304). Such examples make clear that as much as we might prefer sharing to be free and fair, it rarely has been, and has (at least globally) worsened. World trade in just a handful of such commodities as wheat, sugar and soya beans favours global corporations and big estates to the detriment of village farmers. Nonetheless, even when distorted by powerful interests, cooks are still food distributors, so that rather than detract from the analysis of sharing, the realities of injustice make it all the more urgent.

I proffer sharing as a sound starting-point for understanding cooks and, through them, the world. Food-sharing presupposes and necessitates a mass of functions and realms, especially the division of labour. Rather than chase down our own meal like solitary beasts, we go about it collectively. We share the work and divide the spoils. The division of jobs lies behind the inequalities forced, as I see it, upon cooks. But I have again leaped ahead of myself and the second great moment of cooking.

ACQUISITION

An early eighteenth-century host, a Count Zinzendorff, jealously guarded his reputation for keeping the most elegant table in all Vienna. His kitchen was 'an epitome of the universe; for there were cooks in it of all nations, and rarities from every quarter of the globe'. The count appointed agents in any centre noted for its delicacies, and 'the carriages on which they were laden, came quicker and more regularly than the posts' (Sturgeon 1823: 26).

The cooks' responsibilities for acquisition are demonstrated, less extravagantly, in the bundles of private correspondence of the Paston family, who lived in East Anglia in England in the fifteenth century. Margaret Paston would use letters to her husband and son when in London to pass on family news and to urge the purchase of such luxuries as sugar, cinnamon, dates and almonds. 'Also I pray yow that ye woll send me datys and synamun as hastyly as ye may' (Davis 1971: 255).

In his cookery book, Dr William Kitchiner advises that a cook should examine the butcher's, baker's, butterman's, greengrocer's, fishmonger's, milkman's and washing bills every Monday before she presents them to her employer on Tuesday (1821: 20). Cooks are sharers and, as the necessary preliminary step, gatherers. Cooks extract, obtain, unpack. Cooks are the 'caterers', the root (related to the French *acheter*) originally meaning to 'buy'.

Acquisition is not just opening cupboards, packets and cans or even just shopping and running kitchen gardens, but scavenging, hunting, herding and farming. Cooks go out into the world to collect, catch and grow. They exploit forests, fields and markets. Before they can spoon out their offerings, they perform much podding, cleaning, grinding.

In the sharing of jobs, historically, the first such split is acquisition.

That is, in the sexual division of labour, men are sent off to hunt. Henceforth, as a generalisation, men take the public role, and women the domestic. Food acquisition grows beyond some home-craft into a largely male (until recently) public *industry*. Food *production* becomes conceptually distinguished from cooking and, in many ways, the dominant rival. Farmers appear as something much more important, at least economically, and yet are still cooks, part-cooks or cooks' helpers.

Speaking of exchange (sharing) and now production (acquisition) might sound like economics, the 'science of the production and distribution of wealth'. However, as Russian philosopher Nicolas Berdyaev affirms, the great task is to 'overthrow the rule of money and to establish in its place the rule of bread ... The kingdom of money is fictitious, the kingdom of bread is a return to realities' (1939: 178). Money is a distortingly one-dimensional abstraction. At meals, we share real, living food, friends, conversation, manners, religion and culture. Where specialists reduce cooking to such concerns as price, biochemistry, social position and cultural statement, the concept of sharing holds all these together in dynamic totality.

ORGANISATION

The preparation of meals precipitates numerous responsibilities. In the interests of usefully bold statements, I peg out a third main duty of cooks: organisation. The whole business of food acquisition and distribution calls for routines. Cooks *sustain sustenance* with recipes, tips and life's little instructions. Cooks are the guardians of traditions, etiquettes and rigmaroles.

I am thinking of cooks here not as minute-to-minute decision-makers, which they certainly are, so much as guardians of procedures. Along these lines, Victorian cookery books seem especially impressed by 'order'. Cooks, so the guides tell us, must be systematic. The essentials, as emphasised by Mrs Beeton's *Book of Household Management*, are 'cleanliness, punctuality, order, and method' (1861: 21). At close quarters, culinary routines might appear petty and uncreative, but, with domestic arts and crafts being the bases of public trades, the ramifications multiply. This third great moment of cooking overlaps with the anthropological notion of culture. The customs, rituals and performances of the table diffuse into civilisations.

Recording how cooks actually organise the world, recipes are a powerful set of instructions. The third, most stylish layer of the cooks' garb, then, is that of recipe-keepers and so culture-makers. Into this third heading, I also squeeze material culture – that is, the physical tools required for food-sharing. They are the physical versions of mental culture.

Following Marx, some intellectuals divide human activity into 'production' and 'reproduction'. The implication is that 'production' is the actual labour of extracting and processing, the 'real' work done by 'real' workers (who have at least implicitly been male). 'Reproduction' is supportive work (traditionally done by women), by no means limited to biological reproduction, and includes feeding and generally caring for workers. Within my scheme, reproduction is a genetic code of food production across an entire society.

That might seem like a wild wave of my arms, and so, a little less abstractly, let me stick to the recipe. Whether written or unwritten, the recipe is the essential, organising part that reveals the whole.

In merely listing ingredients, recipes show the first task is acquisition. Proverbially, they begin 'First catch your hare' and, commonly, 'Take ...' In some of the oldest recipe collections in English, such as a cookery manuscript dated 1381 (Warner 1791: 37–49), numerous sentences begin 'Tak wyte wyn' (Take white wine) and 'Tak partrichys rostyd' (Take roasted partridges). Others instruct 'Nym water' and 'Nym swete mylk' – the archaic 'nym' (or 'nim') again means 'take' (and relates to the German verb *nehmen*, to take, and the English adjective 'nimble', which is about taking quickly).

Yet another old direction starts 'Recipe brede gratyd, & eggis'. The *Oxford English Dictionary* cites this to show the origin of the word 'recipe', which is the Latin imperative for 'take'. Until the nineteenth century, this version would seem to have predominantly been used for medical prescriptions, leading to the abbreviation R or ℞. The more usual culinary name was 'receipt', which traces back to the feminine past participle of the same Latin verb, *recipere*. Presumably, 'recipe' eventually won out over 'receipt' as appearing more learnedly Latin.

Once cooks have 'taken', the same medieval recipes call on them to 'grind', 'dyce', 'shred', 'mynce', 'bray' (crush with mortar and pestle), 'quarter', 'quare' (cut into squares), 'swyng' (swinge or beat), 'alye' (mix) and 'medle' (mix). Many of these are blatantly dividing and distributing verbs – what has been acquired has then to be shared. Even using heat to 'frye', 'parboile', 'boyle' and 'seeth in gode broth' (seethe or boil) widens the access to the otherwise poisonous, inedible and indigestible.

In *The Forme of Cury*, an English collection dated around 1390, the recipes beginning 'Take . . .' almost as invariably conclude 'serve it forth' or 'messe it forth' (1791: 1–33). The word 'mess' has another interesting history, which again confirms the sharing. It has referred to a portion of food, a liquid food, a made dish, and a course of foods, all of which have been 'messed' forth – from the Latin *mittere*, to send. The word 'mess' has then been attached to animal fodder and thus the most frequent present-day use. Of relevance here, those sitting together at a banquet (usually in fours) and sharing from the same dish are also called a 'mess', leading to such surviving expressions as 'officers' mess'.

In summary, cooks 'take' and, having 'meddled' (mixed), they 'send'.

For to make a formenty [frumenty] on a fichssday [fish or fast day]. Tak the mylk of the hasel notis [hazel nuts], boyl the wete [wheat] wyth the aftermelk, til it be dryyd; and take and colour yt wyth safron; and the ferst mylk cast ther'to, and boyle wel, and serve yt forth (Warner 1791: 49).

Comprehending such an even faintly familiar old English memorandum would seem to require an immersion in the medieval world. Precisely! This is the point of any recipe – it opens out into the whole culture. It is a condensed survival guide, applicable to a set of physical and social circumstances.

THREE DIVISIONS OF COOKERY

'She is far more precious than jewels'; the good wife feeds and clothes her household with unflagging industry. 'She rises while it is still night', yet, at the end of a long day, 'Her lamp does not go out at night'. The ancient compilation of Proverbs concludes with an acrostic, each verse starting with a successive letter of the Hebrew alphabet and describing the ideal housewife of well over two millennia ago. This lifestyle 'recipe' remains sufficiently popular to be quoted, for example, at the opening of Isabella Beeton's *Book of Household Management* (1861: 1). Three of the verses exemplify the three basic ways to spend the long hours – as cooks take charge of food-gathering, food-sharing and its continuation. The woman is diligent in the acquisition of food – 'like the ships of the merchant, she brings her food from far away'. Her sharing extends generously: 'She opens her hand to the poor, and reaches out her hands to the needy'. And she is highly cultured: 'She opens her mouth with wisdom, and the teaching of kindness is on her tongue' (Proverbs 31:10–31).

In this chapter, I have sought the secret of sauces. This has been to understand what cooks do, and has led to my claim that their central task is sharing. In making some opening points about sharing, I have suggested that it implies two other important responsibilities, gathering food and maintaining procedures. What is shared has to be obtained, and both are done in definite ways. The familiar culinary recipes show this, and so, concluding this chapter, do more general 'recipes' of living.

Like Hebrew writers, ancient Greeks open vistas onto worlds that can seem at once distant (2000 years and more) and close (philosophically, artistically and gastronomically). As living voices, they are to us like their gods were to them. And while many of these venerated writers speak of exceptional doings, some concentrate on the small everyday things.

A pupil of philosopher Socrates, Xenophon (*c.* 430–*c.* 355 BC) gives a lesson in running a household in his *Oikonomikos*, using the then conventional guise of a dialogue with Socrates. We can read this as an essay on the cooks' three main activities. For Xenophon, the housewife is a queen bee. She takes charge of everything brought into the house, storing and distributing it when wanted. A man bringing supplies without someone to take care of them would be like drawing water in a bucket with holes. She is also responsible for passing on skills of housekeeping and management (1971: 49–51).

Fleshing that out, Xenophon says that, together, man and woman carefully allocate rooms, choosing the most secure for valuable bedding and vessels, the driest for corn, the coolest for wine, and so forth. They set apart such things as are consumed in a month from those reckoned to last a year. They divide the appliances (for spinning, grinding corn, cooking bread, washing, kneading and the table) into those for everyday use and state occasions. In household affairs, nothing is more important than Order, the proper arrangement and use of things (60–3). An army in confusion is easily beaten. 'But let Order hold sway, and that army is a sight of joy to friend; to foe, of wonder and dismay.' The most beautiful piece of arrangement that Xenophon's mouthpiece has ever seen is a great Phoenician merchant ship with 'the largest number of things arranged in the smallest possible space'. Likewise, if everything in the household has its place, it will not only always be at hand but also a single glance will reveal which gaps need attention. At the risk of ridicule, he admits being impressed by the beauty of 'even pots and pans when arranged in order'. The city is the same – everything in its proper place, so that a servant goes to market knowing where to fetch whatever is needed (54–9).

In Xenophon's work, we pick out the essentials of cooking. First, food must be obtained by the husband and the slaves whom the wife despatches outside. This is the basic division of labour, sending the man to fetch. Second, food has to be stored and distributed. While the husband may collaborate in general policy, such as selecting appropriate rooms, the woman remains in charge. She ensures that meals are properly prepared and allocated. She is also responsible for maintaining the cultural vigour of the enterprise, being entrusted with morale and instruction. She ensures that correct procedures are maintained, and not just the orderly storing Xenophon mentions. She has to be the 'guardian of the laws of our household', and to bestow praise and honour as well as disgrace and punishment (65). But she is also seen through the ideology of patriarchy – she must be timid, tamed, beautiful. Even for Xenophon, whom social critic John Ruskin republished in 1876 for the 'perpetual service of the peasantry' (Xenophon 1971: xvii), admiration for cooks goes hand-in-hand with belittling.

A Spoon in Every Sauce

Cooking might be unwanted drudgery to be cast off. It might be mindless frippery. It might be a physical solution to some purely material problem, such as widening the diet. It might maximise physical pleasures. Beyond this, it might be a cultural cypher, a religious trapping, a means of social expression, an art form. Serving the many suggested ends gives cooks an impressive stock of duties. But in each they tend to serve other gods. My proposal is that cooks are not mere servants of numerous other processes, but prime movers. Cooks – responsible for food acquisition and distribution, and the tools for these – sustain us on three major levels: the bodily, the social and the cultural. There is immense power in the mundane, that which is too familiar almost to be noticed. In terms again of Georg Simmel's paradox about the most elevated aspects of our lives arising from the lowest necessity, these higher, more refined matters are now all the more firmly rooted.

All in all, cooks have big responsibilities. Cooks are in touch with the seasons, the locations, the raw materials, the suppliers, the artisans, the institutions, the customs, the religious dictates, the costs, the clock, and so many other elements, not the least being the diners. Then, they must command every aspect of the actual preparation. The dough must be kneaded enough but not too much. The rice requires precise timing. If all goes well, the protein sources come together in an aesthetically pleasing sauce. When the ingredients are well disbursed, they taste 'balanced'. By a magic to be investigated further, the successful meal is harmonious on many levels, not the least the palate. Cooks taste the quality of the 'connexions'. In balanced sauces, they prove the sharing.

In Shakespeare's *Romeo and Juliet*, one of Capulet's servants says he will test the twenty cooks to be hired by whether they can lick their fingers, declaring ''tis an ill cook that cannot lick his own fingers' (IV.ii.6). An even earlier prescription for a good cook has caught many writers' imaginations. In his *Etat de la maison de Bourgogne*, Olivier de la Marche describes the role of the master cook at a fifteenth-century court.

He must command, order and be obeyed and should have a chair set between the buffet and the fireplace on which to sit and rest if need be, and this chair should be set in such a place that he can see and follow all that is being done in the kitchen. And he should have in his hand a large wooden stirring spoon for two purposes: first to taste stews and broths, and second to chase children out of the kitchen (Scully 1987: 199).

Cooks stir every sauce and the next two chapters magnify this involvement. I hold up a light to knives, and dip into truth, love and beauty. Later, I inquire after the world's first cook – what set her on this course?

CHAPTER SEVEN

Slices of Life

In an essay entitled 'The Measure of My Powers', American food writer M.F.K. Fisher tells the story of Ora, the family cook. 'She loved to cook, the way some people love to pray, or dance, or fight', Fisher writes. Ora spent almost the entire time in 'a kind of ecstasy in the kitchen', which helped set Fisher off on her own ecstasy. We are speaking of the United States in 1919, when the food writer was about ten and when servants were more typical. As a girl, Fisher paid particular attention to Ora's knife.

> She did almost everything with it, cut, and carved, and minced, and chopped, and even used it to turn things in the oven, as if it were part of her hand. It was a long one, with a bright curved point. She brought it with her to our house, and called it her French knife.

Ora usually took Sundays off, Fisher tells us, and one week did not return. It transpired that, after taking her mother to church, Ora had 'cut her into several neat pieces with the French knife'. She then ripped a tent to ribbons – Fisher did not know how the tent came in – and, finally, she cut her wrists and throat, expertly. 'The police told Father there wasn't a scratch or a nick in the knife.'

Cooks' knives have a violent, gruesome edge. They eviscerate geese and shred onions. If fingers are not burned in the kitchen, they are cut. Knives, too, are the direct progenitors of the spear, axe, dagger, cutlass and sword, the weapons of the hunter, warrior, pirate, ruffian and mad person. Yet knives are the cooks' oldest tool, the most essential and the most trusted. Their whole purpose is sharing. For the bulk of her life, Ora gutted and cored and slipped good things onto plates – her meals 'among the best I have ever eaten', swears Fisher (1990: 360–3).

In his dusty old *Spirit of Cookery*, J.L.W. Thudichum presumes, like so many others, that: 'The agent most essential for any kind of cooking is a *fire*' (1895: 51). Certainly, the fire archetypically transforms the 'raw' into the 'cooked'. But now that we see cooks as sharers, there is a more pervasive and more characteristic tool, transforming the 'raw' into the 'divided'. At perhaps three million years, the knife is more than double fire's age. Ora treasured her 'French knife' above all else, even seemingly, in a fit of insanity, above human life.

WHAT DO KNIVES DO?

Open a recipe book on any page and pick up a knife. The ingredients might well be: 1 large sliced onion, 1 teaspoon chopped celery, ¼ cup finely diced carrot, a slice of smoked ham 2 inches thick, chopped parsley. Then, instructions on other pages might include: 'Cut it into small strips', 'Slash the fat edge in several places', 'Spread it with the lobster mixture', 'Clean, skin and cut in 1½ inch pieces', 'Skin the lower ends of the stalks with downward strokes', 'Make two crosscut gashes on the flat side of each chestnut', 'Chill, then cut into basket shape as shown above', or 'Trim off the hard edges of the cake'. I sample these from a well-stained copy of Irma S. Rombauer and Marion Rombauer Becker's American classic *The Joy of Cooking* (1953), which runs to 1000 pages, each with three or more recipes, and each bluntly exhorting: dice, chop, cut, slice, peel, mince, scrape, spread, slash, shuck, trim ... Together, this is a lot of knife work.

'Visually, what most distinguishes Chinese food is the way in which ingredients are cut or fragmented ... the more uniformly the better', writes Hong Kong scholar T.C. Lai (1984: 10). Marvelling at the Chinese cook's 'knife-dance', F.T. Cheng says: 'The poet with his pen, the artist with his brush, the cook with his chopping-knife – they all are alike in having one aim: to do a fine job' (1954: 36–7).

The *tou* is probably Chinese cooks' most indispensable tool, advises

anthropologist E.N. Anderson. The word *tou* suggests cutters generally, which come in many shapes and sizes, from huge, thick, square, bone-hewing butchers' cleavers to tiny knives for slicing finely. A *tou* that comes to a point is used for boning and some kinds of slicing and slitting. But narrow-bladed knives like those of the West are little used – 'they are not versatile enough and do not pack enough mass to cut large chunks effectively' (1988: 183). Instead, the rectangular and versatile cleaver is:

> useful for splitting firewood, gutting and scaling fish, slicing vegetables, mincing meat, crushing garlic (with the dull side of the blade), cutting one's nails, sharpening pencils, whittling new chopsticks, killing pigs, shaving (it is kept sharp enough, or supposedly is), and settling old and new scores (Anderson and Anderson 1977: 364).

The conventional wisdom is that the highly cut-up Chinese cuisine (especially Cantonese) is the result of having to scrounge for food and fuel. Small pieces cook quickly. However, a finely chopped cuisine also shares most politely. We should recall that, against the background of *fan* (grains and other starchy foods), Chinese cooks offer *ts'ai* (vegetable and meat dishes), for which the cleaver and anvil work hard. Pork, for example, can be diced, sliced, shredded or ground, and combined with other meats, vegetables and spices, to produce utterly divergent dishes that spread the winnings around (Chang 1977: 8).

Let me take the heat off the fire, so to say, and, in quest of cooks, lay the hardworking knife on the table. The question of 'why do cooks cook?' might be rephrased as 'why do cooks use knives?'. And the answer has to be that knives share. The butcher's knife pokes a slice of sausage at the child. The pocket knife peels and quarters a pear. The spinning food-processor blade shreds vegetables. Since the earliest cooks first clasped a stone scraper, cutting implements have divvied up the bounty.

The cutting is handled in different ways, depending on culture. In fact, the use of knives does not depend on culture, it *is* culture. The knife itself is material culture, and the recipes are culture in the formal sense. Repeated chopping and slicing, out of the very mundanity of those actions, shape us. The cuts themselves become too familiar almost to be noticed, but culture is precisely the familiar, only brought into relief by the uncommonly skilled, the exceptional and aberrant.

Intrinsically social, the knife is the prime aid in distributing goodness. The knife is right there, its glint beckoning all to the table. It starts out a loving weapon. With cooks traditionally women, it is a female tool, but usurped by men, and sometimes terrifyingly, as we also investigate.

AN ABBREVIATED (WHITTLED) HISTORY

As explained in his guidebook in 1836, Christian Jurgensen Thomsen had rearranged the prehistory collections of the National Museum in Copenhagen into Stone Age, Bronze Age and Iron Age (Renfrew and Bahn 1996: 25). This influential 'Three Age System' refers essentially to cutting implements. Once of rock, then bronze, these venerable instruments are now of steel.

Archaeological textbooks contain photographs of rocks that, to the tutored eye, show deliberate fractures. With stone knives, the earliest cooks could cut through tough hides, scrape off meat, remove limbs, extract marrow, break open skulls to get at the brains, crack nuts, pound vegetables, hack out roots, and whittle and slice bark and reeds for making other simple implements such as containers and digging-sticks.

For at least 2.5 million years, stone cutters have helped extract, process and divide up food. Bronze is an alloy of copper, phosphorus, tin and zinc and its casting was well established in the Middle East by 3500 BC. Hammered iron was known in Egypt before 1350 BC, and, after the fall of the Hittite empire (1200 BC), migrants carried iron technology through southern Europe and the Middle East. Born into escalating industrialisation, Friedrich Engels (1820–95) regarded iron as the 'last and most important of all raw materials that played a revolutionary role in history, the last – if we except the potato' (1948: 159).

During the ancient Chinese dynasty of Chou, when bronze tools and weapons were first supplemented by iron, texts often refer to the culinary art as *ko p'eng*, namely, 'to cut and cook', a term still used in Japan. Meat might be cut in one of three ways: into pieces and chunks with bones (*hsiao*), slices (*tzu*) or mince (*hui*) (Chang 1977: 31, 33). Perhaps partly 2400 years old, a Taoist text, the *Chuang-tzu*, tells of the cook Ting. Unlike lesser cooks, who must constantly change knives, Ting claimed to have used the same cleaver to carve several thousand oxen, and 'after nineteen years the blade of the cleaver is as though it were fresh off the grindstone'. However, he revealed his secret as finding the 'gaps in the joints', through which he could insert the blade, which in his hands 'has no thickness'. He explained that in his 'love of the Way' he had 'advanced beyond skill'. He was guided no longer by his eyes, but by his spirit. The moral is that the person who cherishes life does not fight the environment, but adapts to it, passing through the gaps (Knechtges 1986: 52).

Several Han writers speak of mincing and slicing fish and meat to the thinnest degree nearly two millennia ago. Lu Hsü, a prisoner under Emperor Ming, was given a bowl of meat *keng* (soup or stew). He knew immediately his mother had come to see him: he recognised her cooking. 'When my mother cuts the meat, the chunks always come in perfect squares, and when she chops the scallions, the pieces always come in sections exactly one inch long' (Ying-shih Yü 1977: 68, 74).

During the T'ang Dynasty (still a good 1000 years ago), the term *kuai* for 'finely sliced' or 'minced' implied a refined technique of the most skilled chefs. The ancient poems of Tu Fu refer repeatedly to delicious 'snowflakes' of fish flying under an expert hand. He matches the images of 'silver threads of golden carp' with the 'frosty' glitter of a chopping knife. We read of a specialist who could chop so thinly that the slivers would be lifted by a current of air. On one occasion, it is said, a pile of such slivers formed during a storm turned into butterflies and flew away (Schafer 1977: 104).

The European diner has eaten with a knife that was at first pointed for spiking food, but with the adoption of forks in about the seventeenth century, its end could be round. According to C.T.P. Bailey, a historian of cutlery:

> In 1669 a royal edict of Louis XIV, probably issued with a view to discourage assassination at meal-times, made it illegal for anyone to carry pointed knives, for cutlers to make them, or for inn-keepers to put them on their tables; it also commanded that any existing knives with pointed blades should have their points rounded off (1927: 8–9).

In Britain, steel tools 'improved out of all recognition' after 1701, when the wearing of swords except by gentlemen was declared illegal and swordsmiths began to make domestic and garden tools and implements, writes a student of kitchen gadgetry, Rachael Feild, (1984: 259). Catharine Beecher, writing in the United States in 1841, recommends that 'Strong knives and forks, a sharp carving-knife, an iron cleaver and board, a fine saw ... chopping-tray and knife, an apple-parer, steel for sharpening knives, sugar-nippers ... ' be included in the 'Kitchen Furniture' (370).

The meat chopper had a wood handle, and was thereby distinguishable from the steel cleaver, which had blade and handle all of a piece, *Mrs Beeton's Book of Household Management* tells her British readers. The knives generally used by chefs were very pointed at the end, and slightly convex blades were preferable. They came in inch lengths from 6 to 12 inches (15 to 30 centimetres). The

French chopping knife was similar to the cook's knife but much stronger. With a wooden handle above a cutter, the mincing knife was used for chopping suet or meat. A semi-circular version was used for chopping in a wooden bowl (1909: 66–7).

Knife sharpeners and cleaners became vital pieces among the paraphernalia in grand Victorian households, for knives were forged from steel, which rusted and blunted quickly. Pedlars went from house to house sharpening scissors, knives and tools with knife-grinders on the backs of carts and then bicycles. In the 1920s, stainless steel put an end to cleaning blades (Feild 1984: 224–5).

MALE DUTIES

Over time, the cooks' basic tool has been modified and improved to serve a myriad tasks. In helping cooks gather, store and prepare, the rocks they first grasped have mutated into multifarious shapes, purposes and stories. They have become razors, scissors, scalpels, saws, chisels, hooks, swords, axes, planes, adzes, drills, trowels, secateurs, scythes, ploughshares, picks, spades . . . But should the likes of arrows, spears and daggers really be lumped under the heading of 'knives'? Let me speak more generally of the cutter producing and sharing food.

Far enough back in its ancestry, the cutter was less differentiated. It was a sharp and versatile stone. Surveying the impressive civilisation that thrived in the Indian subcontinent around four millennia ago, British archaeologist Mortimer Wheeler tends to dismiss 'simple chert [a flint-like quartz] blades which occur abundantly on all Harappan sites' and be more attracted to metal and much more impressive implements. And yet, even then, he cannot clearly distinguish between various copper and bronze spears, knives, short swords, arrowheads, barbed hooks, and axes, since the majority 'may have been used equally by the soldier, the huntsman, the craftsman or even by the ordinary householder' (1968: 73).

The history of sharing food has also been the history of sharing cutting tools, as knives – characteristically generous and in the hands of women – have been taken up and adapted by specialists, typically men who have aggrandised their instruments. Through ritual displays and propaganda, knife specialists have generated a mystique of bravery, authority, industry and skill. Men have seized the cooks' knife and called it the 'chefs' knife,' and made other tools seem utterly separate. Hunters extended it into spears. Farmers harnessed beasts to ploughs, the cutters of furrows. Military men claimed that swords provide security. As priests, men cut the earliest written messages into clay tablets. And, as we now observe, men became the butchers and carvers of meat.

Because the biochemistry of animals is like our own, meat tends to be of the highest benefit nutritionally. Being high on the food chain, meat is relatively expensive to obtain, and has tended to be hunted by men. For all such reasons, meat has usually been made the centrepiece of meals, allocated with pomp and machismo, most characteristically at the butcher's.

There were specialist butchers at least 9000 years ago. In one of the world's oldest towns, Beidha in Jordan, one house concentrated on making beads, while others concentrated on flint-making, and still others on butchering animals (Harris 1989: 394). In ancient Rome and Italy, the *lanius* (*laniare*, to cut up meat) probably kept the cattle he slaughtered for sale, while another type of butcher, the *macellarius* (*macellum*, market), was a retailer. These butchers would also have been involved with sacrificial animals for religious festivals and private offerings (Frayn 1995: 107–14). A temple menial called a *popa* assisted the priests, and took the leftovers for sale at a disreputable cookshop called a *popina* (Tanzer 1939: 41). A citizen might never have known whether meat sold in the market or served at a meal had come from a sacrifice (1 Corinthians 10:25–30).

Butchers eventually took the division of carcasses entirely into the marketplace. They became secular priests, presiding at commercial altars, popular distributors of meat, laughter and gossip. They formed

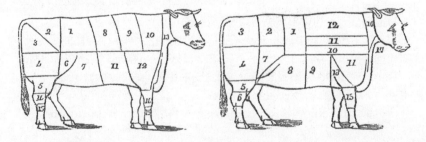

trade associations, setting prices, restricting entrance through apprenticeships, calling the law upon outside competitors and staging
fellowship dinners. Compiling a history of the tradition-encrusted
'worshipful company' of butchers of London, Philip E. Jones finds
the guild already recorded in 1179–80, with stalls congregated at
Eastcheap and St Nicholas Shambles. A surviving register for the
three years from November 1309 lists twelve young men bound as
apprentices, ten completing their terms and fourteen existing butchers
being admitted upon payment. In 1374, four butchers were placed
in the pillory and had their meat burned under them after a jury of
cooks found their meat to be bad (1976: 5, 132).

Rather than allocating according to strict hierarchical expectations,
dressed in religious meanings, butchers learned to divide beasts
into 'cuts', priced accordingly. The author of *Cookery and Domestic
Economy, for Young Housewives*, a slim 'work of plain practical utility'
published in Edinburgh in 1838, warns that pieces of meat differ
regionally in number, size and name. The book shows two outlines
of a bullock, Figure 1 marked for cutting on the English plan and
Figure 2 on the Scottish plan. The English carcass is cut 'more advan-
tageously for roasting and broiling', while the Scottish plan gives more
pieces for boiling ('The Mistress of a Family' 1845: 9–11).

We need to look harder at the handling of meat, for which men have
borrowed women's kitchen knives, reshaping and glorifying them.

THE DIVISION OF THE BEAST

Across the varying habitats of the Australian continent, Aboriginal
people developed a vast range of tools, mainly of wood and stone.
Nevertheless, as predominantly nomads, they transported very few.
In central Australia, women principally carried a digging-stick and,
in cool weather, a firestick. Meanwhile, the hunters carried spears
and a spear-thrower. Both women and men used a general-purpose
knife of stone that had a resin hand-grip. The men's knife was a
long, pointed stone flake. In one museum collection, such blades
range in length from 9 to 22 centimetres and in width from 3.3 to
8.6 centimetres. Where the men's blades were simple slivers of stone,
the women's knives were extensively trimmed, with rounded ends
(Mulvaney 1975: 74–5). They travelled light, but well prepared.

Ethnographic enthusiast Charles P. Mountford summarises the cooking methods of the Pitjantjatjara and Yankunytjatjara peoples he visited near the Mann and Musgrave ranges:

> The larger creatures are disembowelled and buried in a shallow trench already heated with a fire of dead branches; the smaller creatures, snakes, lizards, and birds, are usually grilled over the fire; and grass-seeds, reduced to a coarse flour between the grinding stones, mixed with water and buried in the ashes of the camp-fire.

Mountford observes in *Nomads of the Australian Desert* that the men often returned to camp empty-handed, but the women always brought in some food, at times not much nor particularly tasty, but usually sufficient for the family for yet another day. There was a great social difference in the distribution of the food. 'Although the women travel together in their search for food, each collects for her own family, her husband, her children, and for any male visitors who may be travelling with them.' By contrast, should a man spear one of the larger creatures, it is cut up and shared according to strict laws. Even though the hunter may have followed his prey for hours, and carried it back over a considerable distance, he neither cooks the creature, nor has any say in its division. In fact, among the desert people, the hunter receives by far the lesser share (1976: 49–50). While varying in detail throughout the continent, and modified by actual circumstances, fixed procedures controlled the division. For example, the explorer and pioneering anthropologist A.W. Howitt noted with respect to the Ngarigo people of south-eastern Australia:

> Of a kangaroo the hunter would take a piece along the backbone near the loin. The father would have the backbone, ribs, shoulders, and head. The mother the right leg, the younger brother the left foreleg. The elder sister would have a piece alongside the backbone, the younger sister the right foreleg. The father shares his portion thus: to his parents, tail and piece of backbone; and the mother shares her portions with her parents, giving them part of the thigh and the shin (1904: 759).

In other words, while Aboriginal women maintained basic subsistence, men were caught up in a web of kin and ritual obligations, which involved giving and receiving both food and other goods and services. This is the schism between hearth group and collective, between private and public domain. One style of cooking is female and the other male, and each has generated different social assumptions, tools and practices. Mountford declares that: 'Food-sharing is universal. There is no part in the culture where one feasts and another starves' (1976: 576).

SACRIFICE

Ritual sacrifice is an anthropological chestnut, and the usual impression is that an animal is killed merely in the expectation that the gods will smile. The needless killing represents a cleansing, a thanksgiving or even a bribe. This makes sacrifice pagan, bloodthirsty, incomprehensible. Such a slant might have suited colonial adventurers, devotees of colourful myth and perhaps even the original priests. However, it is possible to identify with sacrifice much more closely than that. Of course, I do not deny esoteric adornment, but the underlying action is incurably sensible.

Following influential sociological theories of Emile Durkheim at the dawn of the twentieth century, sacrifice might be viewed in terms of human togetherness. Worshippers have been, in fact, demonstrating, and learning, obedience to the community. In sending flesh up in smoke, they worship society as a god. Of course, cohesion is advanced by ceremony, but why is cohesion important in the first place? It turns out that the animal has typically not been lost but distributed among the worshippers. So, first and foremost, sacrifice is an elaborate version of the male slaughter and distribution of a carcass.

Peter Farb and George Armelagos, anthropologists of eating, write that: 'Because food is the human's most fundamental resource, offering food or abstaining from it are symbolic ways in all societies of showing devotion to supernatural powers'. They consider that meat is favoured in sacrifice because the sacrificers 'appear to be saying that they know they cannot afford it, but that their loss will be overcome by the even greater benefits to be obtained from the supernatural'. This symbolic significance cannot be denied, but Farb and Armelagos still go on to accept that, while, for example, Bantu ancestor-worship sacrifices might sound extremely wasteful, once the 'ancestral spirits have had their fill, the meat then of course becomes a great feast for humans' (1980: 125–6). According to Audrey Richards, the animal is 'divided with the utmost care according to the fixed kinship rules'. The beast is cut into separate portions, taken away and cooked and eaten by each household on its own hearth (1932: 187).

To take another example, when King Solomon sacrificed 22 000 oxen and 120 000 sheep at the dedication of his temple, it was enough to satisfy the mightiest of gods, let alone attract the Queen of Sheba's curiosity. Nonetheless, the protein went in a vast round of public meals, participated in by 'all Israel ... a great assembly' from distant places and whom Solomon only sent away on the eighth day (1 Kings 8:62–6).

A student of private life in ancient times, Paul Veyne, warns that in a Greek or Latin text the word 'sacrifice' always implies 'feast': 'Every sacrifice was followed by a dinner in which the immolated victim was cooked on the altar and eaten'. Great temples had kitchens and offered the services of their cooks. 'The flesh of the victim went to the participants in the ritual, the smoke to the gods.' The word for a man who made frequent sacrifices (*philothytes*) came to mean not a devout person but a host who gave good dinners, an amphitryon (1987: 195–6). The Greek *mageiros*, wielding his cleaver or *machaira*, was a priest, butcher and professional cook (Berthiaume 1982).

Classicist John Wilkins finds that the Greeks defined their culture 'above all by the ritual of animal sacrifice'. Typically, a domesticated beast was led to the altar, where its throat was cut; it was flayed, then the vital organs were removed and a portion burned for the gods. The rest was roasted and tasted by the leaders, while the other meat was jointed, boiled and shared among participants. The entrails and off-cuts were made into black and other puddings. 'In this system the gods were honoured, the community expressed its solidarity, and a rare chance to eat meat was enjoyed' (1991: 306). According to this view, people slaughtered to appease the gods and to hold together the common enterprise, but it was basically food-sharing.

A surviving inscription concerning the festival of *Panathenaia* shows that cattle sacrificed on the Acropolis in Athens were apportioned: 'to the senate committee 5 shares, to the 9 chief magistrates 3 shares, to the stewards of Athena 1, to the temple overseers 1, to the general and brigadiers 3, to the Athenians in the procession and to the girl basket bearers the customary amount'. The inscription goes on to provide for the distribution of further meat to the citizens at the *Kerameikos*, the potters' quarter at the edge of the city (307).

An Athenian sacrifice could also look like a family picnic, such as that in Menander's play, translated as *Bad-Tempered Man*. Here, a slave goes to the market to hire Sicon, a *mageiros* (sacrificer–cook), and purchase a sheep. The slave then sets off with four donkeys, loaded with the equivalent of picnic baskets packed by the women of the household. After the slave and the cook have set up at a country shrine to the god Pan, the women and other slaves arrive and, finally, well after the sheep has been slaughtered, the men. The luncheon jollity is enough for the bad-tempered man of the title to complain: 'The way these vandals sacrifice! They bring couches, wine-jars – not for the gods, for themselves . . . They offer the gods the tail-end and the gall-bladder, the bits you can't eat, and gobble the rest themselves'. Andrew Dalby notes in *Siren Feasts* that, while the women are clearly important in organising the proceedings, Menander keeps them almost invisible – like other Athenian literary works, the plays were 'dialogues among men: male depictions of a male world' (1996: 2–10).

Ritual sacrifice, then, is a way of publicly dispersing scarce flesh. All kinds of relationships and meanings and awarenesses develop around this key sharing event. The priests themselves construct a religious world view, in which they retain an important place. Certainly, the allocation can be so formalised it no longer even looks like cooking. My complaint is with mythologists who look at the world 'upside-down as in a *camera obscura*' (Marx and Engels 1976: 42), concentrating on just the symbolic trappings, and so consigning the body to the fire.

CARVING

A great platter of plump fowls, sows' udders, a hare and fish is decorated to make classical allusions. Delighted, the host Trimalchio keeps crying 'Carv'er! Carv'er!' (a weak pun), while a man runs up with a knife and, with his hands moving in time to the orchestra, slices up the victuals 'like a charioteer battling to the sound of organ music'. This glimpse of the carver's skill comes from the brilliant satire of *nouveaux riches* written by Petronius at the height of Nero's Rome, almost two millennia ago (1977: 51).

At the same ridiculous feast, a whole boiled calf is demolished by a character playing the warrior Ajax in a scene from Homer, 'slashing at the calf with a drawn sword like a madman. Up and down went his arm – then he collected the pieces on the point of his sword and shared them among the surprised guests' (71). Among further affectations, Trimalchio has named a favoured cook 'Daedalus', suggestive of inventiveness, and has bought him 'some carvers of Styrian steel as a present from Rome'. These are shown to the guests, who are encouraged to test the points on their cheeks (80).

The cutting-up of meat was already seen well before Petronius's time as a fine art. Distributing the main dishes was the axis around which palaces and mansions, and therefore aristocratic society, revolved. And just as we should not reduce animal sacrifice to 'superstition', we should not dismiss the redistributive significance of magnificent banquets. As the Roman Empire evaporated, it left ponds of civilisation centred on the great medieval halls. These public spaces were combined refectories, theatres, churches, meeting-rooms, parliaments, all centred on the fuss of carving.

The knife was the most common utensil at the medieval table (followed by the spoon), and guests would bring their own. A student of early English literature, Bridget Ann Henisch, has found a description of girls, who, running late for a wedding, take a shortcut across

a meadow and become plastered with mud. They clean their stockings and gowns with their knives as best they can, and press on to the roast beef. Increasingly, however, and starting in Italy, hosts provided knives to privileged diners. The proper use for a knife, Henisch writes, was to cut meat into manageable pieces that could then be picked up by hand. The knife was used to stab morsels from shared dishes, too. The knife and not the fingers reached for salt. In addition, large, heavy carving knives were provided and one or two can usually be seen scattered between the diners in contemporary illustrations. It was polite to carve for others (1976: 176–9).

Among the officers of the grand medieval household, the ewerer carried washing water and towel, the cupbearer fetched wine, the butler supervised butts of wine and ale, the surveyor controlled the surveying board to which the cook directed the platters, and so on. Among them, the panter, guardian of the lord's bread, used three knives at his breadboard: a chaffer, a parer, and a trencher knife for evening up the edges of the bread sliced specially for use as platters. The panter's fourth knife, the mensal knife, cut the choice 'upper crust' from rolls and breads for presentation to the master (Cosman 1976: 28–9).

The carver's was one of the most exalted of the domestic stations, and a prodigious number of rules and technical terms pertained to preparing and presenting fowl, flesh and fish. Wynken de Worde's *Booke of Kervinge* of 1508 opens with a complete list of terms used by professional carvers. He wants the expert to 'break' that deer, 'display' that crane, 'alay' (lay down) that pheasant, 'tranche' (slice) that sturgeon, and so forth (Warner 1791: xxxviii). Each animal required special knives, levers and hand positions, and most knives were held with two fingers and the thumb (Cosman 1976: 28–9). In his *Il Trinciante* (*The Carver*) of 1581, Vicenzo Cervio expected the carver to hold up the object on a fork in the left hand, while slicing off pieces with a knife held in the right (Wheaton 1983: 55).

The titles, responsibilities and implements of food service could be carried by noblemen and the sons of gentlemen. Serving could prove a means for political and professional advancement; Cardinal Morton predicted that the young Sir Thomas More, who was waiting on him, would prove a marvellous man (Cosman 1976: 26). However, carving would lose its prestige.

VANISHING ART

Three centuries later, French gastronomic writer Grimod de La Reynière, who devotes the first third of his *Manuel des Amphitryons* (1808) to the '*Dissection des viandes*', recalls that 'this ingenious art' used to be accorded such aristocratic importance that, in its accomplishment, 'one recognises the possessor of an hereditary fortune'. The last tutor given a young man was the master carver. Even a pupil incapable of construing a verse of Virgil or a sentence of Cicero with the book open 'understood every sinew of a duck, a goose, or even a bustard'. Arguing for the maintenance of this art, he says an amphitryon who knows neither how to serve nor carve is as shameful as the 'owner of a splendid collection of books who has not a clue how to read' (1987: 168).

However, his English contemporary, Launcelot Sturgeon, warns against sitting next to the mistress of the house, 'unless you choose to incur the risk of being forced to waste your most precious moments in carving' (1823: 50). If you 'should, unhappily, be forced to carve', then do not work up a sweat, do not hack (no 'mangling done here!'), do not 'put your neighbours in fear of their lives' and do not apologise for awkwardness. He remembers a man of high fashion depositing a turkey in a lady's lap. With admirable composure, the carver finished telling a story and then quietly said, 'Madam, I'll thank you for that turkey' (39–40).

Another who finds carving a bother, William Kitchiner complains that the meal's purpose is too often lost in ritual.

> Ceremony, does not in any thing, more commonly, and completely triumph over Comfort, than in the administration of '*the Honours of the Table*'.
>
> Those who serve out the Loaves and Fishes, seldom seem to understand, that he fills that situation best – who fills the plates of the greatest number of Guests, in the least portion of time (1821: 49).

In an even nobler rebuff to over-elaboration, Brillat-Savarin provides what his loyal translator M.F.K. Fisher declares to be 'reassuring simplicity' in his instructions (reproduced here in full): 'To carve meat well, care must be taken to have the flesh make a right

angle, as nearly as possible, with the knife blade: the meat thus carved will look nicer, will taste better, and will be more easily chewed' (Meditation 5; 1971: 67, 72 n.2).

These dinners are beginning to sound positively informal and, as an indication of an even mightier social change, in her *Treatise on Domestic Economy*, published in Boston in 1841, Catharine Beecher opens with a few general pointers.

> It is considered more proper to carve sitting than standing; as an expert carver does not need to stand. The carving-knife should be very sharp, and not thick or heavy. All ladies should learn to carve, as it is very difficult, without, and very easy, with, practice. It is considered a genteel accomplishment, for a lady to carve at her own table (356).

That is, the duties were becoming much less formal and shifting from the 'head' of the household to the mistress. A book published in Edinburgh in 1845 advises: 'The young housewife should accustom herself to carve with neatness and activity ... The carving is not to be done with any appearance of exertion, nor by mere strength in wielding or wrenching the knife. It must be done with placidity and neatness, as if by dexterity or skill'. Here, too, the mistress no longer slices according to status: 'Distribute equally among your guests what may be considered the delicacies' ('The Mistress of a Family': 112–13).

The English cook Eliza Acton, who urges that 'a gentlewoman should always, for her own sake, be able to carve well and easily', opens her considerable *Modern Cookery, for private families, reduced to a system of easy practice* (or at least my edition of 1868) with eight delicately etched plates of haunch of venison, quarter of lamb, sucking pig, pigeon, snipe, woodcock, hare, and so on. The accompanying instructions for 'A Turbot' include: 'If the point of the fish-knife be drawn down the centre of the back through to the bone, in the lines *a b c*, and from thence to *d d d*, the flesh may easily be raised upon the blade in handsome portions' (xxxvii–xxxviii).

Where the medieval cook might have sewn roast swans and peacocks back into their feathers, and might majestically have 'frushed' (crushed) chickens and 'unbraced' (loosened) ducks, Acton declares that sending a pheasant to table with the head on is a 'barbarous custom, which has been partially abandoned of late in the best houses, and which it is hoped may soon be altogether superseded by one of better taste'. When partridges are served to ladies, she reports it is customary to take off the heads, to truss the legs short and to 'make them appear (in poulterer's phrase) *all breast*' (xlii–xliv).

The disappearance of public carving was accompanied towards the end of the nineteenth century by the switch from arraying food on tables (*service à la français*) to sending in individual plates (*service à la russe*). The distribution of food moved from the hierarchical to the individualistic (and more on this in Chapter Thirteen).

By the early twentieth century, *Mrs Beeton's* fears that 'carving is an art to a great extent neglected in this country'. The 'modern fashion of serving *à la Russe* has to a large extent relieved the host and hostess from carving at dinner, but the art is still required at breakfasts, lunch-eons, and quiet family repasts'. Skilled carving also survived as a spectacle in public dining-rooms, but *Mrs Beeton's* complains that 'gourmets' turn to their neighbours and discuss the latest news 'while the *maitre d'hôtel* is giving an example of an art the acquisition of which has cost him the study of a lifetime'. Without doubt, the book continues, the foremost carver of recent times had been Monsieur Joseph, proprietor of the Restaurant Marivaux, in Paris, and some-time director of London's Savoy Restaurant. In his restaurant, 'every aid was given to obtain effect; the orchestra stopped dead, and taking his stand at the head of the room the master sliced off joints, one after the other, with vigorous single cuts, holding the bird on a fork in his left hand' (1909: 1258–9). Restaurant reviewer Lieut.-Col. Nathaniel Newnham-Davis describes Joseph in his *Dinners and Diners*, published in 1899.

> In an irreverent moment I was reminded of the Chinese torture of the Ling Chi, in which the executioner slashes at his victim without hitting a vital part in the first fifty cuts, as I watched Joseph calmly, solemnly, with absolute exactitude, cutting a duck to pieces with a long, thin knife; but irreverence faded when the rich sauce had been mixed before our eyes and poured over the slices of the breast – the wings and legs, plain devilled, coming afterwards as a sharp and pleasant contrast (87).

This spectacle, tracing its history back thousands of years, can still be seen in Chinese restaurants offering Peking duck.

CIVILISING PROCESS

The increasing coyness about cutting meat in public might be credited to general refinements in culinary art. French culinary commentator Châtillon-Plessis (pseudonym of Maurice Dancourt) writes in 1894:

> Much could be said on the 'civilising' role of cookery.
> Through concealing by clever decoration or sophisticated cooking techniques the *cruel* appearance of cuts of meat, the art of cookery certainly contributes to the softening of manners.
> Compare what I would call the *bleeding dish nations* [e.g. Britain] with the *sauce nations* [e.g. France], and see whether the character of the latter is not more civilised (Mennell 1985: 309).

A more sophisticated theory of the overall pressure towards refinement, or 'civilising process', has been proposed by sociologist Norbert Elias (Mennell 1989). Even the aristocrat in the medieval period apparently spat and farted in public but 'innumerable prohibitions and taboos' grew up around these actions, just as they have around the knife. 'Certainly the knife is a dangerous instrument in what may be called a rational sense. It is a weapon of attack. It inflicts wounds and cuts up animals that have been killed.' But now it awakens disproportionate fear, distaste and guilt. In medieval times, the chief prohibition was that teeth should not be cleaned with a knife. Elias notes increasing social pressure against holding cutlery, especially knives, 'like a stick' and even 'wherever possible not to use the instrument at all'. In China, where the knife disappeared from the table many centuries ago, the people say: 'The Europeans are barbarians ... they eat with swords' (1978: 122–6).

Along with suppression of the knife, Elias registers the removal of carving from public view. Where entire beasts were divided up in public, the sectioning was transferred, within nineteenth-century European culture, to the sideboard and then the kitchen. The slaughter of animals is left to abattoirs, which are removed from the decent parts of town. There are those for whom the sight of butchers' shops is distasteful and 'others who from more or less rationally disguised feelings of disgust refuse to eat meat altogether'. Elias explains the way that 'the distasteful is *removed behind the scenes of social life*' in terms of interconnected trends in social relationships (120–1). As their connections grow more complex, individuals must become more calculating and self-controlled.

However, beyond strictly sociological factors, I need to point to deeper forces. Compared to (relatively unusual) late medieval abundance, we now eat less meat. Urban populations hunt less. Household units have become smaller, so therefore start with smaller cuts. We demote sacrifice to the meatworks, under government inspection. We mainly leave carving to production lines, where cattle are minced into hamburgers. With various elements of cooking handed to multiple specialists, ceremonial knives have been passed to drab food manufacturers. As sharing has become more complex, the proliferating knife has disappeared among society's folds. We now distribute foods and tasks so widely that we lose sight of the point, which is to divide the catch.

Old-fashioned cookery books disclose what used to be the reality for most housewives. To kill eels instantly, 'without the horrid torture of cutting and skinning them alive', spike the spinal marrow at the back of the skull. 'The humane Executioner does certain criminals the favour to hang them, before he [or she] breaks them on the wheel', Kitchiner jests (1821: 231). The expert known as 'The Mistress of a Family' describes 'Killing Fowls, &c.' in a neat manner so they will retain their appearance: 'A turkey is killed by passing a small pen-knife into the mouth, and cutting it below the tongue, then passing the knife up through the head into the brain. After this, hang it up by the feet to let it bleed freely' (1845: 12). So, a 'neat' result comes from bloody intimacy behind the scenes.

German philosophers have wallowed in the tragedy of alienation – as when tools designed to help in our interaction with the rest of nature get in the road. We are immersed in nature. It is our nest, our larder, our market, our womb, our heaven, our challenge. As acquirers, people clutch knives to extract the marrow from nature's bones. With cutting tools, people have carved a niche. However, wielding knives, we have also cut ourselves from nature. We have become nature's self-negation. Furthermore, in the subdivision of cutting-up tasks we have lost touch with one another. In providing services, specialists remove the altar to the meatworks and commercial kitchen, pushing living nature and human labour behind a screen. Domestic cooks enclose blades within food processors. In such ways, cutters increase our power, and these very same instruments separate us from metabolic realities and one another.

VEGETARIANISM

Some feminist commentators portray the knife as belonging to men. Knives are 'quintessentially "male" weapons, by the way', food essayist Margaret Visser lets slip (1992: 172). When a woman is sacrificed in a sadistic D.H. Lawrence short story, 'The Woman Who Rode Away', feminist writer Kate Millett observes: 'substitute the knife for the penis' (1971: 292). In pornography, Carol J. Adams explains, in her *Sexual Politics of Meat*, the 'camera lens takes the place of the knife, committing implemental violence' (1990: 59). Adams is also sympathetic to the conclusion that 'wars can be avoided if meat eating is avoided' (135). Her argument and its tone are summarised in the chapter heading, 'The rape of animals, the butchering of women'. She argues by metaphor, performing 'cross-mapping between feminism and vegetarianism' (13). One difficulty with this is that the cutter is the quintessential cooks' weapon and so – because women have been general cooks – quite feminine. Certainly, in their specialisations, men have turned blades against people and generated a dangerous macho ideology (which has then turned people against blades), but knives start out sharing. An extension of our teeth and claws, the knife efficiently and cooperatively sustains us. First, it welcomes.

Anthropologist Jack Goody writes that the major contrast between traditional men's and women's roles 'lies between men killing and women bearing, nurturing and cooking' (1982: 71). This stereotype is appealing but sentimental, for women cooks use knives assuredly to kill and chop. 'Killing', for Goody, implies hunting big game, including men. No one denies that both hunting and war have been typically male, but they are distinct activities, which he should not blur. Put it this way, Goody should be more cautious about classing men who kill people together with men who, like women, provide our meals. Admittedly, some forms of war can be regarded as serving culinary interests, but my main thrust remains, that knives are by no means *intrinsically* male, nor inevitably anti-social, but quite the reverse. The archetypically caring and sharing implement is (despite its bad press) the sharpest knife.

Cutting two ways, the knife separates and joins us to nature. It brings people together to divide food and roles. In one action, the knife brings choice. In choosing, let us agree that the use of knives in cooking is essential and good. Importantly, it extends our animal natures. Despite picture-book vegetarian fantasies, nature is eat and be eaten. Watch a nature documentary, or even better the grass, to witness creepy-crawly, unsentimental devouring. In a metabolic universe, lion bounds after gazelle; lizard slips down grasshopper. It is a world of talons, claws, beaks, jaws, tongues and – making the cooking creature – knives.

To conclude this paean, a pair of my favourite gastronomic authors extol the civilising influence of the cooks' knife.

SACRIFICE OF THE LAMB

'If either want of appetite, or want of sense, should lead you into a warm discussion during dinner – don't gesticulate with your knife in your hand, as if you were preparing to cut your antagonist's throat.' Written in the early 1800s, this is one of Launcelot Sturgeon's light-hearted 'hints to grown gentlemen', with which he figuratively turns swords into more convivial implements (1823: 39).

In dedicating his *Essays, Moral, Philosophical, and Stomachical* to the Court of Aldermen of London, Sturgeon speaks of their proud origins as a division of citizen soldiers. However, they have long laid aside their swords and lances and now, he affirms, 'the knife and fork shall yet bear ample witness to your prowess'. He wants his companions to reflect this peaceful change in their coat of arms, which carries a dagger and a griffin. He advocates that the dagger be replaced by a carving knife, and the griffin by a gander and turkey (vii–ix), backing his thesis with a piece of dagger doggerel.

> . . . A serviceable dudgeon
> Either for fighting or for drudging;
> When it had stabb'd, or broke a head,
> It could scrape trenchers, or chip bread;
> Toast cheese or bacon (viii).

Pursuing the parallels between kitchen and battlefield, Sturgeon declares that his father 'died gloriously on the field of honour: – that is to say, of an indigestion after a Lord Mayor's feast' (7). Sustaining the metaphor, he complains that the only value of the *esprit de corps* in the army was to get men 'spitted like larks, and sent out of the world before their time'. Whereas, the 'same spirit infused into a legion of cooks, tends to the preservation of life, instead of its destruction'. He demands, 'who would hesitate between the choice of a bullet or a beef-steak in the thorax, or between having his guts run through with cold steel or filled with a hot dinner?'. And yet, while the spirit of the army is roused by the voice of public approbation, this is denied our cooks (191–2).

In an ecstatic cookery book, *The Supper of the Lamb*, Robert Farrar Capon disputes with ascetics, teetotallers, food fetishists and vegetarians. For this Episcopal minister finds a commandment to love the world and its people through cooking. He joins in the theme as soon as we permit him to 'wipe my hands and introduce myself',

and to declare himself an 'amateur'. He means 'amateur' literally and positively: 'The world may or may not need another cookbook, but it needs all the lovers – amateurs – it can get', he says
(1969: 3).

This theologian, who glorifies physicality rather than meaning
and who first cooks and second writes about it, declares: 'Man not
only dines; he also kills and sacrifices . . . Our home ground remains
what it always has been: bloody ground and holy ground at once'.
Capon uses superseded terms, 'man', 'he', 'Father'. His frequent
assumption is that cooks are women, and he their adviser. But his
contemplation is culinary. 'Blood is not pretty. But no book which
tries to see the whole picture – to speak not only about cooking,
but to say what cooking is about – can afford to let it slide out of
mind' (45). For Capon, this 'universal convulsion of twitching death
insists upon the breadth of our humanity, animal among animals;
breaks the angelic pretence'. Sure, he also admits, men have traditionally done the killing of mammals, but this has been part of the
overall human task, 'each man owning the honest interchange by
which he steals his livelihood; each woman's hand intimate with the
crack of wrung neck and severed spine' (48–50).

Capon shows respect for a 'woman with cleaver in mid-
swing . . . A man who has seen women only as gentle arrangers of
flowers has not seen all that women have to offer. Unsuspected
majesties await him' (61). Towards the end of his long 'poem' on
animal slaughter, Capon wonders aloud how he can return the topic
to 'mere' cooking. First, cooking is never 'mere', he says. But, second,
the 'road from temple to kitchen is quite plain. It lies through the
subject of knives . . . of all tools, the knife reigns supreme . . . the
one tool used by more people, more of the time, than any other'
(53–4).

*   *   *

The essential cooks' tool, even more characteristic than fire, is the
knife. From stone, through bronze to iron, cooks have cut to share.
The knife is the basic instrument of human togetherness, but it also

cuts us off from nature. And in dispersing food and so dispersing jobs, it fragments us. As much as any other artefact, the knife makes us human – it becomes the best, and worst, in us. Using a knife more respectfully might help to bring the world back together. If we use knives imperfectly, then let us do better. When the knife comes between people and the cultural creature carves out too greedy a niche, we need to get *closer* to the knife.

CHAPTER EIGHT

Festivals, Beauty and Love

How sad it is to sit and pine,
The long half-hour *before we dine!*
Upon our watches oft to look,
Then wonder at the clock and cook

Beeton 1861: 12

'Punctuality is an indispensable quality in a cook', urges *Mrs Beeton's Book of Household Management* (echoing Brillat-Savarin's Aphorism XVI); 'therefore, if the kitchen be not provided with a clock, beg your mistress to purchase one. There can be no excuse for dinner being half an hour behind time' (1880: 37). A subsequent edition specifies that 'an eight-day dial, which requires winding up only once a week', should be placed over the mantelpiece, so that cook might consult it without turning away from the fireplace (1909: 47). Expressing this time-honoured concern, sauce philosopher Launcelot Sturgeon rises to an epigrammatic crescendo: 'Punctuality is, in no transaction of life, of such importance as in cookery: three turns too many may spoil a haunch: the *critical minute* is less difficult to be hit in the boudoir than in the kitchen; and every thing may be put into a *stew* – except the cook' (1823: 13).

Reciprocally, diners have an obligation to arrive at the appointed hour. Beeton notes that: 'At some periods it has been considered fashionable to come late to dinner, but lately *nous avons changé tout cela* [we have changed all that]' (1861: 12). Brillat-Savarin accuses hosts who wait for latecomers of being 'careless' with their guests'

158

well-being (Aphorism XVII; 1971: 4). For Sturgeon, a person who arrives after the company has sat down 'commits an irreparable injury'. He or she 'disturbs the arrangement of the table; occasions a useless waste of time in empty compliments and excuses; retards the first course; puts the removes in jeopardy; and occasions many troublesome distractions from the great object at stake'. Such persons should be looked upon as the 'common enemies of society' (1823: 13–14). That has applied through history, too, the ancient Greek cook wanting guests to contribute their part to the culinary arts by not requiring foods to be reheated (Athenaeus 379ab; 4: 215).

In lauding cooks, I now parade clocks and calendars as instruments of sharing. For sharing to occur, people have to synchronise with each other and also with nature. Cooks must time the food and, on another level, work with suppliers and the seasons. For such reasons, cooks have rigged up time-keeping systems (Symons 1991: 175–215; Aymard et al. 1996).

In a second illustration to follow, I argue that sharing lies behind the use of standard combinations known as 'dishes'. Before all else, a successful recipe is tasted as being properly distributed. In a third example, the cooks' commitment to sharing generates an ethic of generosity. This chapter explores a trio of everyday institutions of sharing – namely, clocks and calendars, weights and measures, and table etiquette. Given the compulsion of routine, this chapter speaks of nothing less than festivals, beauty and love.

I   A CULINARY THEORY OF TIME

Many foods are at their best when picked at their peak and hastened to the kitchen. Then they must be 'done to a turn': that is, removed from the spit at the precise rotation. They must be cooked *à point* (French), *al dente* (Italian) and *ts'ui* (Chinese). Anthropologist E.N. Anderson explains: 'Ts'ui implies the texture of something very fresh and at its prime, cooked just enough and no more. In particular, it implies a texture offering resistance to the teeth followed by a burst of succulence' (1988: 190).

Cooks might thus seem to be slaves to clocks. But, as absurd as it might appear, the relationship has to be understood the other way around. Clocks are but culinary instruments. Their prime purpose is to facilitate food distribution.

To return to the Sydney restaurant at the opening of this book, Phillip Searle does not use a clock, despite the textbook importance of timing. 'Either I know intuitively, or have had enough experience.' Instead, he *feels* the chemical changes. 'I use my hands with everything – first of all because I'm sensual about it and also because touch and cooking are inextricably connected. You cook with all your senses.' He observes the natural processes – the browning of the bread, the moment the fish is poached, the gap to be allowed for digestion. These become the basis of his routines.

Likewise, before the 'rational' cookery of *Mrs Beeton's* and others, domestic cooks largely relied on their own touching, watching, listening. E.N. Anderson notices that in Chinese cooking: 'Timing is of the essence. The hissing of boiling shrimp, the crackling of frying pigeons, and other sounds are often used as cues' (1988: 190). We could set clocks by cooks' behaviour, and do.

To grasp what happens requires our visiting angel to imagine changes throughout history. With cooks closely watching natural processes, an interval we might now think of as around 15 minutes might have been termed 'the time to cook rice'. Similarly, stages through the day might be broken up into 'cock-crowing time', 'cow-milking time', 'breakfast time', and so forth. We become so used to having our lives apparently ruled by clocks that we forget that they mechanically mimic cooks.

In his essay of 1910, sociologist Georg Simmel conceives social regulation emerging with the need for regular meals. Without becoming too precise, he supposes that 'very primitive peoples did not eat at definite hours but anarchically, simply when someone was hungry. However, having meals together leads at once to temporal regularity, for a given circle can only gather at a previously fixed hour'. This need to meet on an agreed cue – such as when the sun is sinking – he calls the 'first conquest of the naturalism of eating' (1994: 347). Within complex civilisations, cooks rely more and more on conventional time measurements. They and their guests are lectured on punctuality.

Noticing the obvious, that the 'rhythm of working and eating marks the entire life of each person', theologian Edmond Barbotin writes that a meal is the 'starting point in the morning, the relay station at midday, and in the evening the terminus of the day's efforts and the prelude to a night's rest' (1975: 326). Indeed, the concept of the day grows out of this immediate cycle of meals. Revealingly, the English word 'meal' comes from the same root as the German *mahl*, which suggests a fixed time. We agree to meet for the distribution of food when the sun is at its highest, say. The requirements of town life are then served by bells and, borrowing from the monasteries, mechanical hours. In the era of *Mrs Beeton's*, Swiss and then American manufacturers dispersed cheap watches worldwide.

A commentator on technical culture, Lewis Mumford, is impressed by the ensuing regimentation. 'The first characteristic of modern machine civilisation is its temporal regularity ... Breakfast, lunch, dinner, occur at regular hours and are of definitely limited duration: a million people perform these functions within a very narrow band of time' (1934: 269). In fact, he is persuaded that the 'clock, not the steam-engine, is the key machine of the modern industrial age ... even today no other machine is so ubiquitous' (14).

Seasons

In Mrs Beeton's list of 'Times When Things are in Season', fruit is limited in the English April to just apples, pears, rhubarb and 'forced' cherries for tarts (as well as nuts, dried fruit and crystallised preserves). But then in May, cooks welcome 'Apples, green apricots, cherries, currants for tarts, gooseberries, melons, pears, rhubarb, strawberries'. Conversely, game fades out in April with merely 'Hares', and only resumes in August with 'Leverets, grouse, blackcock' and reaches a crescendo in October with 'Blackcock, grouse, hares, partridges, pheasants, snipes, woodcocks, doe venison' (1861: 33–7).

For every recipe, the manual estimates cost, preparation time, numbers to be served, and season. For example, the three versions of 'Tomato Sauce for Keeping (Excellent)' each end: '*Seasonable* from the middle of September to the end of October'. By way of contrast, 'Boiled Bacon' is '*Seasonable* at any time'. In the era of transnational food corporations, we tend to lose the eager anticipation of summer fruits and the consolations of game (or their geographical equivalents). But cooks generally have been highly attuned to seasonal availability. Indeed, they would once scarcely have needed Beeton's printed calendar: they would have known the foods and their festivals.

Dancing in colourful costumes; overeating and drinking *en masse*; going on fasts; shutting workplaces in memory of religious or political figures – to outsiders, festivals can appear as mad as Monty Python sketches. Why have people feasted? Traditional societies might have had communal holidays to express group identity and reinforce social cohesion. Festivals give relief from the work routine – we take breaks, abandon ourselves, and return refreshed. Along similar lines, festivals have been presented as a release, acting as a safety-valve for pent-up emotions. An entirely different view might be that celebrations remind adherents of the basics of their faith. Related to this, festivals have been seen as an end in themselves – they are simply holy-days. There is some truth in all these accounts, but they do not get to the heart.

The English anthropologist Edmund Leach has asked why people dress up in 'funny hats and false noses', engaging in three types of upsetting behaviour: increased formality (such as Sunday piety), masquerade (New Year revelry) and role-reversal (Mardi Gras, when pauper becomes prince for the day); and we might add festivals marked by abstinence, such as Lent or Ramadan. Why these outbreaks? His answer, which he believes he borrows from a founder of sociology, Emile Durkheim, is that we think of the passage of time as generally 'profane' but with 'sacred' moments. Through their elevated character, festivals give meaning to the rest of the weekly or annual routine. Festivals are like temporal milestones for coordinating social efforts (Leach 1961).

Such an explanation gives credence to the sharing of culture for its own sake. Tying higher aspects of existence to the lower, I make the further point that festivals emphasise culinary routines. Inducing reverence, releasing energy, providing respite – festivals are cultural heartbeats of physical survival. Among Bantu peoples, anthropologist Audrey Richards notes that the chief prays ceremonially for rain, and then blesses the seeds before sowing, 'giving the people confidence to go forward on the next stage of their precarious task' (1932: 101).

In such ways, a set of festivals provides a basic calendar. Before diaries, annual cultural timetables comprised a series of high points of the ilk 'apple-blossom time', 'reappearance of large fish', and so on (Nilsson 1920). These were picked out in much-anticipated meals, featuring relevant foods. The collective exuberance helped organise the cyclical gathering, planting, harvesting, shifting of herds, going to sea.

To say that festivals borrow foods is to see them upside-down. Meals are no mere adjunct. Even in the Latin origin of the word, festivals are 'feasts', which indicates that out of coming together to dance, take drugs, tell stories, and so on the most central activity is to share food, the food particular to that season. While feasts are usually said to be a way of 'expressing' some greater reality, they *are* the greater reality.

To take Christian examples (admittedly easier to explain than lunar calendars, notably the Islamic), with no certain birthday of Jesus, it is usually said that Emperor Constantine set Christmas at the winter solstice to compete with already popular festivals – the merrymaking and exchange of presents of the ancient Roman Saturnalia and New Year. However, the emperor's dictate was presumably not so much trying to 'compete' as finding a good and productive location in the winter break. He borrowed a spot that maximised meaning. Jesus was born, he was saying, at the commencement of the year. Likewise, in the case of the lamb of Easter, which is a Christian borrowing from the Jewish, the lamb is not chosen because Jesus is the 'lamb' of God. Rather, Jesus becomes the 'lamb' because he was sacrificed at that time of year. Lamb becomes available in the northern hemisphere's April, according to the Beeton timetable, preceded by 'House Lamb', which has been reared indoors, 'under the artificial system, so much pursued now to please the appetite of luxury' (1861: 34, 329).

A string of festivals is not precise enough to organise ambitious public irrigation schemes, distant trade, large-scale bureaucracies and military expeditions, however. So, historically, it became necessary to make increasingly exact astronomical calculations to come up with an agreed set of rules that modelled the culinary year with reasonable accuracy. The great irony of formal calendars, as with other culinary institutions, is that they gain a momentum of their own, so that their basis becomes overgrown. As time has become more and more rationalised, festivals have become relatively redundant curiosities. During the beginnings of modern Europe, the reforming churches eradicated numerous religious holidays. In *The Protestant Ethic and the Spirit of Capitalism*, Max Weber writes:

> asceticism descended like a frost on the life of 'Merrie old England' ... The Puritan's ferocious hatred of everything which smacked of superstition, of all survivals of magical or sacramental salvation, applied to the Christmas festivities and the May Pole and all spontaneous religious art (1976: 168).

Such erosion of the festive calendar accompanied the industrialists' regimentation of their workforce.

After the French Revolution, that nation experimented with a secular and again much more industrially oriented calendar, based on ten-day weeks. The Soviet government for some years replaced the seven-day week with rolling five- and then six-day weeks, workers being given different days off. Chinese communists also excised the long list of 'superstitious' and 'enslaving' holidays. Such reforms are but dramatic attempts to achieve what has also been achieved by attrition – the factory stamping God out of kitchens.

The biosphere dances to its own rotation, bringing day and night. It also sways to the moon's circling, which casts varying illumination and affects tides. And it waxes and wanes according to its orbiting of the sun, which produces the annual cycle of heat and light. The earth's spinning and circling thus influence the biological supports of society. Time-keeping systems, then, provide handy models of the energy fluctuations to help with social activities of gathering and hunting, sowing and herding, trading and manufacturing, preparing and serving. Precision becomes important with the increasingly intricate division of roles and ensuing cultural complexity.

To us, time can appear objective, independent and compelling. It is a 'striking example of the way in which a widely used symbol, cut loose from any observable data, in common discourse can assume a life of its own', writes sociologist Norbert Elias (1992: 120–1).

People who have internalised a 'time-conscience find it difficult to imagine that there are others who lack the ever-alert compulsion to know the time' (23). As part of this process, we can lose sight of cooks and their responsibilities. I have left for last the most dramatically culinary time tool, the week.

The Week

Weeks are strange. Unlike days, months and years, they are not numbered or named and can be of any length, as we have seen. This seems to suggest cultural arbitrariness.

A common explanation for our seven-day week is that each day is devoted to one of the visibly circling astronomic bodies, as is indicated in the names (even more obviously in French and Italian): Moon-day, Mars-day, Mercury-day, Jupiter-day, Venus-day, Saturn-day and Sun-day. More mathematically, it has been said that seven days are a handy subdivision of the month. However, the lunar month being approximately 29½ days, the Egyptian and Roman weeks of ten days are a closer fit, and so are weeks of three, five and six days. To understand why seven, we are better advised to look at the Fourth Commandment's instruction to rest on the Sabbath. The Hebrew scriptures supply different reasons: to commemorate the release of the Israelites from Egypt (Deuteronomy 5:12–15) and to recall God's rest after creating the world in six days (Genesis 2:1–3; Exodus 20:8–11).

Purely cultural explanations of this kind seem inadequate to account for weeks in general, given their variable lengths. Better to locate some common, down-to-earth, culinary factor, I suggest. As a clue, the week belongs to the settled, agrarian mode of production, based on villages and craft specialisation. More particularly, a study of the week across cultures shows that it is based on the market round. Gathering at the marketplace needs to be periodic, so that buyers know when to meet sellers doing their circuit.

The West African week, which might be of three, four, five, six, seven or possibly eight days, is basically economic, as many of the day names and some names for 'week' show (Thomas 1924: 193). Anthropologist Jack Goody confirms that the LoDagaa, primarily agricultural people of northern Ghana, designate the six days of their week by the name of the village where that day's market takes place. The very terms for 'day' and 'market' are the same (*daa*), and the weekly cycle is simply *daar*, a 'plurality of markets' (1968: 34). As for the Western cycle, the most generally accepted account is that the Jewish week derived from the Babylonian, and that every seventh day was the Babylonian market day (Nilsson 1920: 333). Like the day and the year, the week is a tool of those insufficiently sung creators, the cooks.

Just as timing systems originate in the cooks' prime chore of sharing, so too do ideas of 'balance', 'proportion' and 'taste', and more profoundly than might at first be expected.

II A Culinary Theory of Beauty

The first kitchen utensil listed in *Mrs Beeton's Book of Household Management* is 'a good set of WEIGHTS and SCALES', without which 'it is not possible to ensure success'. This 'absolutely necessary' contraption is of the type when the cook must bear in mind '*always to put the weights away in their respective places*'. In the 'great laboratory of every household', upon which bodily health depends (1880: 23), cooks apportion and ration as carefully as apothecaries. Selecting little brass weights from their box, cooks ensure everyone a proper serve. Here, then, would appear to be further clear proof of sharing's centrality.

But this idea needs refinement, since Isabella Beeton recommends using scales, it transpires, for the successful following of recipes. Exact measures supplant such references as 'a small piece of that' and 'a handful of the other'. So that cooks may 'reproduce esteemed dishes with certainty, all terms of indecision should be banished', the manual warns (1861: 39–40). Nonetheless, 'esteemed dishes' are themselves ways for ensuring healthy serves.

Initially, it must be said that numerical rigidity in recipes is scarcely two centuries old. In fact, modernity can be typified by the proliferation of written recipes. With the mass production of cookery books at the end of the nineteenth century, enormous treatises easily extended to 1000 pages and, by the early twentieth century, *Mrs Beeton's* exceeded 2000 pages. In 'rational' cooking (and the word is often used), the instructions become dense and precise.

In 1817, in his *Cook's Oracle*, William Kitchiner claimed to introduce scientific precision. Writing for the 'rational Epicure', he rejects vague expressions like 'a dust of flour – a shake of pepper, – a squeeze of lemon'. His recipes are the 'results of experiments carefully made, and accurately and circumstantially related'. The time requisite for dressing (preparation) is stated, and the quantities set down in number, weight and measure. 'This precision has never before been attempted in Cookery books', he boasts (not entirely accurately). To replicate his results, he recommends obtaining glass measures divided into 'Tea' and 'Table Spoons' from Price's glass warehouse, near Exeter 'Change in the Strand. 'No Cook should be without one, who wishes to be regular in her business' (1821: 30–1).

Instructions such as 'do it until it is done' can be unsettling. Certainly, the vagueness of the recipes hampers our recreation of medieval dishes. Rather than assuming that such food was highly spiced, Madeleine Pelner Cosman suggests that the numerous flavourings listed were used in tiny quantities (1976: 47). The omission of quantities and times need not mean they were unmeasured either, she believes. Elite and merchant-class kitchens, pantries and storerooms contained numerous calibrated scales and measuring vessels. Hour-glass timers and early clocks were also part of the kitchen of the fourteenth and fifteenth centuries (55–6), and similarly precise measurements were required in the marketplace (85–91). In fact, measuring equipment is as old as civilisation. Scales were common in the Harappan cities near the Indus Valley, and that already stretches back 4500 years. Nonetheless, despite the measuring apparatus in many kitchens, cooks basically combine ingredients by experience and, ultimately, taste.

In general, too, recipes were rarely recorded. Techniques were handed down from master to apprentice and, even more to the point, from mother to daughter. But what exactly did these cooks know and check? Why do cooks prepare *dishes* in the sense of standardised combinations of foods prepared in standardised ways? Measurements imply recipes, and recipes imply dishes, but why dishes in the first place? A historical sociology of the recipe or dish has rarely (if ever) been attempted, but I can suggest some basic points.

A Brief History of the Dish

In some imaginary golden age before cooking, people shared food naturally, in that they ate casually from their habitat as they moved. Their appetites were stimulated, and satisfied, by the natural environment. Variety was also enforced by the seasons. Then, with the invention of cooking, people introduced definite procedures for sharing. In particular, they needed rules on who should get what part of a large beast. Next, people stashed away agricultural staples, which needed to be supplemented with other ingredients in the pot or accompanied by a sauce. At this point, cooks took charge of 'made dishes' of prescribed elements, the aim of which was still to share around valuable foods.

The relevant concept is the 'made dish'. This is a 'dish composed of several ingredients', the dictionary tells us. Importantly, it is a standardised combination. Even in its English use, 'made dish' goes back a long way. In *The Anatomy of Melancholy* of 1621, Robert Burton complains of 'an infinite number of compound, artificial, made dishes, of which our cooks afford us a great variety, as tailors do fashions in our apparel'. For him, made dishes were the cooks' principal tricks, and included blood puddings, various baked meats, cakes, pies and sauces (1.2.2.1; 1932: 225).

While people have shared plates of simple foods much more than we might assume, made dishes – or 'dishes', for short – still have a long and complicated history. Babylonian scribes impressed complex recipes onto clay tablets in cuneiform 3700 years ago (Bottéro 1985). By 400 BC, the whole of Persia was scoured for something the king might like to drink, and 'countless persons' would devise dishes that might please him (Athenaeus 144b; 2: 159). The historian Herodotus reports that the typical Persian meal consisted of only a few main dishes, 'but they have many sorts of dessert, the various courses being served separately' (1.133; 1972: 97). That is, instead of scattering the banquet table with many different foods, they seemed to have relied on a succession of fancier concoctions.

In his vast miscellany on Greek cuisine, Athenaeus mentions many made dishes, including some as contrived as those to be satirised in the *Satyricon* of Petronius. Greek cookery books contained directions to make a spiced gravy (*karykê*) invented by the Lydians. They also spoke, he writes, of *kandaulos*, or pilaf, 'of which there were three varieties, not one merely; so exquisitely equipped were they for luxurious indulgence'. One version used boiled meat, breadcrumbs, Phrygian cheese, anise and fatty broth (Athenaeus 516cd; 5: 323–5).

François Pierre de La Varenne's book *Le Cuisinier François* of 1651 includes numerous delicately prepared French made dishes, which the English often referred to contemptuously as 'kickshaws', a corruption from *quelques choses* (somethings) (Mennell 1985: 72). Later, the term 'made dish' would seem to have been directed principally at *ragoûts*. While William Kitchiner prides himself in giving exact measurements, not all that many were required in his cookery book two centuries ago. The bulk of the recipes are devoted to explaining each of the main methods of cooking (boiling, baking, roasting, deep-frying and broiling) and when to apply them. He pays some attention to the accompanying sauces, for whose recipes quantities are specified. The category of 'Broths, gravies, and soups' also occasions some precision. But this leaves merely the final one-eighth of the book to cover 'Made Dishes, &c.', prescribing the likes of 'Haricot of Beef', 'Broiled Rump Steak with Onion Gravy', and 'Bread and Butter Pudding'.

More recently British families sat down to a 'proper meal' of 'meat and two veg' cooked by mother (Murcott 1982; Charles and Kerr 1988: 226).

But to return to my theme, assuming a modest but ancient history of standardised recipes (unwritten and written), why have people used dishes? The answer is sharing, and the way to ensure a proper distribution is to balance the flavours.

A Symphony of Flavours

Explaining his cooking for English-speaking readers, Chinese–American author Lin Yutang says that the 'whole culinary art of

China depends on the art of mixture'. No one, for instance, knows how cabbage tastes until it is properly cooked with chicken, and the chicken flavour has gone into the cabbage and the cabbage flavour has gone into the chicken. He then admits that when Chinese people see vegetables such as spinach or carrots cooked separately and then served on the same plate with pork or roast goose at a foreign dinner, 'they smile at the barbarians' (1939: 322). But subtlety has been sought in many cuisines.

In the eighteenth century, as Jean-François Revel recounts in *Culture and Cuisine*, French chefs took balance to a new level, replacing the 'old-style cuisine of superimposition and mixture' (simple additions) with the 'new cuisine of permeation and essences' (subtle combinations) (1982: 171). His authority for this is the sophisticated foreword to chef François Marin's *Les Dons de Comus* (*The Gifts of Comus*, the Roman god of feasts) in 1739. The foreword's author (thought in fact to be two Jesuit priests) claims that the science of the cook is to mix and blend foods:

> so that no ingredient dominates the others and the taste of all of them comes through; and, finally, of giving them that unity that painters give to colours and of rendering them so homogeneous that all that remains of their diverse flavours is a fine and appetising taste and, if I dare say so, an overall harmony of all the tastes thus brought together (187).

Confirming the imperative to balance entrusted materials, an ancient Greek stage cook declares that he is firstly a gourmand, because, as he instructs: 'keep tasting it again until the flavour is right; tighten it, as you would a harp, until it is in tune. Then, when you think that everything is by this time in harmony, bring on your chorus of dishes, singing in unison' (Athenaeus 345f–346a; 4: 67–9).

And what is so good about a well-proportioned *ragoût* that 'tastes of every thing, and tastes of nothing'? This is '*kitchen gibberish*', William Kitchiner writes, for a 'Sauce in which the component parts are well proportioned'. A sagacious cook, instead of 'wantonly wasting the excitability of her Palate', will call in 'the Balance and the Measure' (1821: 62–4). The perfect dish ensures enough to go around. It also ensures a balanced diet. That is, the ceaseless travelling of the index finger 'from saucepan to mouth' fulfills the allocative role of good cooks. As a provocative rule-of-thumb, I suggest that the most sharing dishes become those that taste the most balanced. This relates to Dr Kitchiner's advice that the 'prudent Carver will cut fair; and observe an equitable distribution of the Dainties'. If the servers cut bread, meat and cheese 'fairly' (in the sense of 'pleasing to the eye'), this also becomes 'equitable', and then each 'will go twice as far as if they hack and mangle it' (50).

Forget for a moment their mouth-watering creations and think of cooks as rationing resources. Think of them counting out one artichoke for each guest. Think of them balancing the sweet and sour. Think of them ensuring fat, but not too much, and fibre, but not too much. The older method of tasting and the more 'rational' of prescribed weights and measures exemplify the distribution of the kitchen. Cooks use their eyes, ears, touch, and, especially, nose, teeth and tongue, to share. And the most balanced results become the most satisfying, those we agree are the most pleasing. We like fairness. Not just through the dishes, cooks conjure harmonious blends out of the social, cultural and physical worlds.

The aim of precision so that 'no one particular flavour shall predominate' (Beeton 1880: 23) invites us to put in our spoon once more. But this dish is the result of countless experiments over the generations as cooks work, with often limited ingredients, to balance the diet, both socially and nutritionally. It might appear that precision is demanded aesthetically. But it is the other way around: aesthetic success is determined by taste, and taste is pleased by a proper share of ingredients – formulated as a 'grammar' of sweet with sour, t'sai with fan, utility with grace, and so on. Dishes are well-distributed, seasonal, subtly enticing combinations. Starting with the need to share, we reach a theory of good taste and beauty.

III   A CULINARY THEORY OF LOVE

Strength and honour are her clothing; and she shall rejoice in time to come. She openeth her mouth with wisdom; and in her tongue is the law of kindness. She looketh well to the ways of her household, and eateth not the bread of idleness. Her children arise up, and call her blessed; her husband also, and he praiseth her.

Proverbs 31:25–8

The *Book of Household Management* opens with this passage from the Wisdom literature, extolling the generosity of the ideal mistress. Committed to a caring domesticity, Isabella Beeton approves hospitality as a 'most excellent virtue'. The mistress should remember her duty to 'make her guests feel happy, comfortable, and quite at their ease'. Displaying no agitation, she must 'show her tact in suggesting light and cheerful subjects of conversation'. As to the mistress's wider duties of 'charity and benevolence', the book recommends visiting the houses of the poor, certainly in country towns and rural districts, for it provides 'opportunities for advising and instructing them, in a pleasant and unobtrusive manner, in cleanliness, industry, cookery, and good management' (1861: 1–12).

Community is built around the table. People gather to bring and share their offerings. In pursuing individual needs, they care for others. In Georg Simmel's great paradox, people are brought by brute greed or 'material individualism' into mutually beneficial society. And in this cooperation, they take their lead from cooks. At the well-mannered table, cooks become the exemplars of caring and sharing.

Like Babette in 'Babette's Feast', cooks are typically devoted, working without immediate reward, serving others' interests. They track down the best, urge extra helpings and scorn miserliness. Even when times are tough, as in Laura Ingall Wilder's *Long Winter*, cooks take pains to make attractive repasts. Cooks are patient, cajoling, armed with love. They are the peace-makers and civilisers. They look after the young, the old and incapacitated. They open their hand to the poor and reach out to the needy. Out of the incessant process of sharing arises a conception of (and commitment to) the cooks' great virtue, generosity.

One way of formalising this requirement to look after others is table etiquette. Notoriously, such rules become atrophied and stultifying, but Isabella Beeton discloses their good intentions (1861: 905–8) when quoting Brillat-Savarin's final Aphorism: 'To invite people to dine with us is to make ourselves responsible for their well-being for as long as they are under our roofs' (1971: 4). Etiquette is a practical, rule-based ethical system.

From the Christian ethical tradition, Edmond Barbotin says that, in sharing bread, 'I refuse to consider my own life as the only worth-while life'. Around a table, he treats other people 'as an extension of my body and my entire being. I incorporate my fellows at table into myself and myself into them'. In sum, the sharing of food is a 'sharing of life itself' (1975: 327–8).

While the dominant players in the 'market' economy cultivate an ideology of competitive self-interest, mutual benefits accrue from cooperation. Civilisation is a vast interlinked tradition. Besides, gen-erosity is not as disinterested as it might seem. Giving cements social bonds and mutual obligations. Colloquially, you scratch my back, and I'll scratch yours, or: 'Do to others as you would have them do to you' (Luke 6:31).

Technically, cooks practise a basic form of economic exchange known as reciprocity. Even if repayment is not immediate, things will work out over the long run. This is because pivotal social relation-ships are sustained. Such reciprocity fascinated early anthropologists, including Marcel Mauss, whose book *The Gift*, originally published in France in 1925, analyses institutions such as North American Indian potlatch feasts of seemingly irrational lavishness. Historically, and this is taken up in the second part of this book, reciprocity becomes sup-plemented with what economic historian Karl Polanyi terms redis-tribution, where exchange is not between individuals, but through a central institution, and then with the market, greased by money.

Generosity is the ideal we set for those doing our immediate sharing. The cooking of 'gifts' rather than 'commodities' is probably a primary element in the social construction of femininity (Fürst 1997). The main danger is that it will be abused. In so many instances, men have demanded selfless generosity from women. Employers have kept workers in servitude. Cooks have been publicly ignored, privately humiliated, ordered to eat last, and not paid an income. When I speak of cooks sharing, I repeat that I do not assume that the division is fair. Systems of burdens and rewards have been distorted by powerful interests and therefore rarely well sorted out.

The complementary danger to generosity abused is generosity

overdone, making for absurd saints. It is within the reach of cooks to be ridiculously generous, especially when pushed, and yet perhaps they 'love' to cook for reasons of control? In a brief essay, 'Loving cooks, beware!', food writer M.F.K. Fisher explores her ambivalence (1988). As a girl, her own efforts were praised profusely. Then she found that caterers at her school 'were paid *cash*, not compliments'. She had been a 'fool, a dupe, a complete patsy who had thought for years that she loved to cook, when really all she wanted was to feel powerful, important, essential'. She came to observe how Italian men, for example, would exaggerate their praise of even poor food, to keep Mama serene. Having seen through all the trickery, Fisher nonetheless now practises, she writes, her own 'art of making our loved ones believe that we love to cook, because we love *them*'.

The pressures on professionals, too, can become unbearable. 'The French cook is incited to his work by a point of honour inseparable from the culinary art; witness the death of the great Vatel', records the great Antonin Carême (Kirwan 1864: 408). Vatel was working as comptroller of the Prince de Condé's household at Chantilly in 1671 when the prince invited Louis XIV and his court to a three-day festival. In an on-the-spot letter to her daughter, Madame de Sévigné continues:

> 26 April . . . The king arrived Thursday evening, the hunt, the lanterns, the moonlight, the promenade, the collation in a place carpeted with jonquils, everything was as desired. They supped: there were some tables where the roast was lacking, because there were a number of diners who had been by no means expected. This dumbfounded Vatel; he said several times, 'I have lost my honour. This is a blow which I cannot bear.' He said to Gourville [his assistant and successor], 'My head is spinning; I haven't slept for a dozen nights; help me give the orders.'

The fireworks, costing 16 000 francs, were obscured by cloud. At four in the morning, Vatel was roaming all over the place. He met a purveyor with just two loads of seafood and no further supplies apparently forthcoming. The chef's mind grew feverish. He found Gourville and said: 'Monsieur, I cannot survive this blow. I have honor and reputation to lose'. Vatel went to his room, set his sword against the door, and ran it into his heart. 'The seafood, however, was arriving from all directions . . .' (Wheaton 1983: 146).

More touching is the devotion of the Austrian Consul's cook during the massacre by the Russian fleet at Sinope in the mid-nineteenth century.

> The Muscovite murderers were at the very height of their bloody enjoyment, and sending shots into the town, when the cook attempted to cross a garden, to procure some herbs; for Consuls *must* dine, though half the world be dying. She had performed her mission, and was returning, when a thirty-six pounder shot cut her completely in two. Rather than give up the parsley for her master's soup, she thus encountered death (Doran 1858: 96).

As a final example nearly 4000 years ago during the Shang Dynasty, the Chinese cook I-ya was reputed to have had such a sensitive palate that he could taste the difference between the waters of the Tzu and Sheng rivers. By way of bizarre self-abasement, I-ya is recorded as having prepared for his employer, Duke Huan of Ch'i, the 'ultimate taste', the steamed head of the cook's own son (Knechtges 1986: 57–8).

The unhealthy self-abnegation of cooks complements the eaters' sin of greed. In achieving a better balance, cooks and diners (the generous and the hungry) might learn from one another. Brillat-Savarin decides: 'I cannot see why I, always a stranger to any hateful sentiments, should exclude myself from my own generosity' ('Transition'; 1971: 344–5). Mind you, Brillat-Savarin is sensitive to fake generosity. He tells of the legendary Antoine Beauvilliers, who ran the most elegant restaurant in Paris at the end of the eighteenth century. This host knew personally all the foreign heads of state, and 'ended by speaking all their languages, at least as far as his profession demanded'. His prodigious memory enabled him to recognise, after twenty years, people who had eaten perhaps once or twice at his restaurant. Beauvilliers would shower a group with special attention, advising for and against dishes, and calling for bottles from a cellar to which he alone held the key. '[A]ll these *extra* additions to the total bill seemed so many courtesies', Brillat-Savarin comments. But after the host had taken his bow, the 'swollen bill and the bitterness of paying it were proof enough that the dinner had been enjoyed in a restaurant and not a private home' (Meditation 28; 1971: 315–16).

Love

For Hollywood, romance is finding a sexual partner. When great minds have philosophised about love, they, too, have talked sex. In *The Symposium*, Plato advocates the highest form of love, speaking about reconciliation with the most abstract other – indeed, about something even more idealised than what is now known as 'platonic' love. Yet he models this 'real' love on the crudest desire for a youthful body. Initiation into the mysteries of love begins by engaging with the physical beauty of another person, he writes, and then with the beauty of bodies generally, and then of souls, then moral beauty and next the beauty of knowledge and finally abstract beauty itself. Its origins in animal lust are now apparently transcended. The happiest person finds 'absolute beauty in its essence, pure and unalloyed, who, instead of a beauty tainted by human flesh and colour and a mass of perishable rubbish, is able to apprehend divine beauty where it exists apart and alone' (211de; 1951: 95). Viennese psychiatrist Sigmund Freud reinverted this, reducing the higher love of philosophers and poets to sexual desire, with sexual union its goal. All the variations of love are traceable to the libido and the other forms of creativity are sublimations. The psychical energy man 'employs for cultural aims he to a great extent withdraws from women and sexual life' (1963: 40–1).

A sexual theory of love would thus seem to force a choice between either lust or an onerous and quite mysterious quest for the ineffable. Lovers are expected to separate altruistic love (for children, for example) from physical desire, on which it is nonetheless based. The love grounded in sexual lust can appear like a quest for power and domination. It can seem self-obsessed. It also relies on the idea of the lover passively admiring beauty rather than actively finding it – beauty being 'in the eye of the beholder'. Fortunately, even without seeking a more cooperative sexual model, an alternative is available.

In culinary theory, the source of love is sharing meals. 'Kissing don't last: cookery do!' a young bride is advised in George Meredith's novel *The Ordeal of Richard Feverel* (1909: 280), and there are other benefits.

To the extent that cookery involves generosity rather than desire, this is a giving rather than a taking love. It extends to all at the table, so it is dispensed much more widely. It brings people, nature and cultural forms together, to make a many-layered mingling. Lovers who are like cooks face the world generously, not hungrily. This love is therefore arguably deeper and more universal than sexually-based love. It is also a more realistic model for couples sharing a table through life.

The English word 'commensality' means sharing a table (Latin *mensa*), but also implies the formation of some sort of social unit. 'Company' and 'companionship' derive from sharing bread (*panis*) and bring a sense of 'accompanying'. 'Conviviality' means to live (*vivere*) together and adds joyous connotations. These words confirm that in sharing physical goods, people gain something more – taking bread together leads to fellowship, and so on. This greater partnership has many names, but it belongs to a love based on the cooks' sharing, love founded in generosity.

This culinary theory of love might appear novel, and yet it is confirmed in everyday experience. While sexual bonds cannot be denied, not all family networks and friendships are primarily sexual. Instead, our most valued relationships are clearly determined by

food-sharing. Our 'hearth', 'family', or 'household' eats together. Similarly, we might define our friends as those with whom we comfortably share a meal. Furthermore, sharing bread is at the heart of a world religion, one noted for its emphasis on forgiveness and good works.

Love is generally viewed as the primary requirement and guide for conduct and character in Christian ethics. The 'great commandment' is about loving God, your neighbour and yourself (Mark 12: 28–34 and parallels). It is striking, moreover, that the less usual Greek *agape* is used in the New Testament to refer to love. It predominates to the near-exclusion of *philia* (friendship) and the total exclusion of *eros* (desire, sexual desire) (McDonagh 1983: 341). This is presumably at least partly to avoid the sexual overtones of *eros*. And that love was experienced by Jesus and the early followers at the table is confirmed by the simple observation that they used *agape* not just to describe their love but also their meals, or 'love-feasts' (Symons 1998).

The Sentiments of Sharing

Introducing her groundbreaking study of food and society, anthropologist Audrey Richards sees that, 'while sex is necessarily a disruptive force in any human society, and one which must be checked and regulated to some extent if the community is to survive, man's food-seeking activities not only necessitate cooperation, but definitely foster it'. For such reasons, she begins her book:

> Nutrition as a biological process is more fundamental than sex. In the life of the individual organism it is the more primary and recurrent physical want, while in the wider sphere of human society it determines, more largely than any other physiological function, the nature of social groupings, and the form their activities take (1932: 1–2).

Richards is particularly interested in the development of 'sentiments' or emotional ties, generated in the cooperative satisfaction of the primary drive of hunger. Through a biographical study, she confirms that the southern Bantu child, initially dependent on its mother, gradually learns to join in various cooperative food-getting endeavours. In later childhood, a boy's kinship ties acquire new meaning.

> No longer confined to the narrow life of the household and women's circle, he becomes aware of the wide net of kinship rights and obligations which bind him to other huts and families beside his own. He is conscious of the importance of the laws of property and food ownership; he realises that social status is measured to a large extent by the right to eat or distribute food (76).

In Bantu society, the father is the 'possessor, giver, and controller of food'. The head of a family is respected when never in want and able to distribute food freely from the pots provided by his wives. 'The greatness of an African is before all else a matter of pots' (78).

Richards decides that the 'whole institution of marriage acquires new meaning' when seen in terms of the nutritive system, the Bantu marriage contract a 'regulation of the handing on to the next generation of the control of food supplies' (139). Given that social power tends to accompany the control of food, she views a tribal leader as the 'father' of the wider group, taking control of food resources, receiving tribute, organising economic activities, and making contact with the tribal ancestors, whose blessings are essential for prosperity (144).

The idea of marriage being based in food-sharing is also present in African myths. A typical legend told among the Basuto of southern Africa pictures the first men as living on one side of a great river and subsisting on game, while the first women keep to the other bank and gather grass seeds. One day, when the hunters could not cook their meat because their fires had gone out, one of them crossed the river and met a woman, who took him to her hut, and introduced him to porridge made of grass seeds. He liked it, and said, 'I will stay and sleep here'. His companions followed him one by one, and the institution of marriage was thus founded on the exchange of meat and cooked grain between men and women (202–3). As in this Basuto story, the original domestic unit is cook and hunter, a private–public split whose history becomes momentous in the second half of this book.

Foodie Marriages

In the world of Paul Levy, the London food journalist, gastronomic puck and maintainer of fine philosophical tastiness, marriages are made in kitchens. In a magazine article and then book on the phenomenon of 'foodies', he and collaborators write that, when in search of a mate, foodies do not squander their money and time on the theatre, concerts, cinema or bed.

To a real foodie, love goes hand in hand with food. When they fall in love their first thought is of the meals they will eat, plan or cook with their beloved. As the romance blossoms, the big moment arrives. No, not bed, but the market and then the stove . . . the discovery that you both have memories of the same meal, the same favourite restaurant, or the same recipe will bring you together forever (Woods et al. 1982: 68).

'Plays and concerts are a problem for Foodies', say Levy and Ann Barr in *The Official Foodie Handbook*, 'do you eat before or after? You always discuss it, decide neither would be fair to the food, and skip the performance' (1985: 20). The wedding is gastronomically memorable, and cooking marriages are founded in routines.

Foodies are lucky in that their rituals of shopping, preparation, eating and loading the dishwasher are so repetitive and comforting that anyone married to or living with a foodie soon feels completely trapped, like a patient in a hospital (21).

Like the writers for food-mad Greek audiences nearly 2500 years ago, and London and Parisian wits closer to 200 years ago, Paul Levy and his co-authors match the pleasures of the plate with those of the pen. Yet, like those before, they speak many a truth lightly. Their comic reversals turn established hierarchies and accepted priorities right-way up: cooks make marriages.

*   *   *

Cooks should never be ignored. In quest of them, in this first half of the book, I have thumbed through novels, several gastronomic texts and numerous other items, found clues and appended my own observations. In proposing that the activities of cooks are focussed on the distribution of food, I have caught them red-handed with knives, implicated them in our means of time-keeping, peered into their 'dishes', and accused them of shaping basic partnerships.

In such examples, I have found cooks behind social and cultural institutions, much more than is generally recognised. Cooking is sharing and, spiralling outwards, it sweeps civilisations before it. Ironically, in extending their powers, cooks have created self-aggrandising rivals. In the second part of the book, taking a much more deliberate path through history, I demonstrate how sharing both meals and their preparation has shaped us.

PART TWO

SHARING AND CIVILISATION

CHAPTER NINE

'The Pudding that Took a Thousand
People to Make'

 Children in Victorian England used to read a story entitled 'The Pudding that Took a Thousand People to Make'. It did not tell of a thousand workers clambering over one gargantuan mound of flour and fruit. Instead, the children learned that the familiar plum pudding was a cooperative effort of many people in many trades and many places. As recalled by Cambridge classicist T.R. Glover, the story was 'not an appeal to greed but to imagination, and the child ranged over the world that furnished his parents' cook with the materials that made the Christmas pudding – the seven seas and Natural History, plants and animals, ships and sailors' (1942: 137).

We are far from self-sufficient. We need others to plant and harvest wheat, process and transport flour, tend vines, dry and market fruit, convey brandy. Ships must be built, maintained and provisioned, and clerks must keep records. That surely already covers a 'thousand' people. Beyond immediate debts, countless collaborators have gone before, domesticating plants, refining tools, developing recipes, forming concepts, colonising empires. There is much culture and agriculture, much cooking, behind a plum pudding.

Two centuries ago, foreshadowing 'The Pudding that Took a Thousand People to Make', French food writer Grimod de La Reynière found that those who think seriously about cuisine find themselves roaming widely.

> The gastronomic arts ... embrace all three realms of nature, and the four corners of the globe, all moral considerations and all social relationships. Everything comes within their scope in a more or less direct way and if they may seem superficial it is only to vulgar minds, who see no more to a kitchen than saucepans and no more to dinner than dishes (1987: 185–6).

Once the pudding's network of interdependent makers has captured our imaginations, we can draw instructive inferences. One is that we do not have to go far to find tasks that initially appear to have little to do with cooks. The orchardists, the millers, the road-builders and, indeed, the entire society direct their energies at indulging one child. Another implication to be drawn here is that the making of the pudding makes the world as we know it.

In his cosmological treatise, *Timaeus*, Plato depicts the demiurge (Creator) as a cook with a giant mixing-bowl. Plato's recipe is somewhat arcane, but it would appear that the physical world starts out as a spherical pudding of the four elements of fire, air, water and earth, to which are added pre-existing soul and a measure of the Same and Different (35a; 1971: 47). Coming at last to humans, and explaining why people's destinies are linked to the heavens, Plato says the demiurge:

> turned again to the same bowl in which he had mixed the soul of the universe and poured into it what was left of the former ingredients, mixing them in much the same fashion as before, only not quite so pure, but in a second and third degree. And when he had compounded the whole, he divided it up into as many souls as there are stars (41d; 1971: 58).

God is a great cook, serving an edible universe to itself. An ancient Jewish text declares: 'The Holy One ... causes the winds to blow and clouds to ascend and rain to descend ... and prepares a table before every single person' (Neusner 1975: 33). The idea of the generous and creative server seems to lie behind the request: 'Give us this day our daily bread' (Matthew 6:11).

As demiurges on earth, cooks bring together flour, eggs, fruit and spices. They summon up knowledge and skill. As they offer food, they expect help in return. That is, as they allocate segments of the pudding, they divide up the pudding-making. They call on fuel suppliers and tool-makers. As cooks have mixed their puddings, they have blended wider ingredients – the 'plants and animals, ships and sailors' and everything – into the great pudding of civilisation. The author of another story, 'A Learned Dissertation on a Dumpling', finds: 'The universe itself is but a pudding of elements. Empires, kingdoms, states and republics are but puddings of people differently made up' (Pullar 1971: 164).

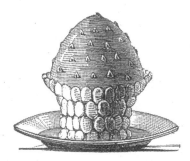

As this book opened, an angel descended into Phillip Searle's Sydney restaurant, seeking, in Laura Esquivel's phrase, 'the secrets of love and life as revealed by the kitchen' (1993: 216). Together, we have poked the coals, stirred the cauldron, spoken of love and frowned over books. In the first part, we have tried to work out what cooks do. With a motif of sharing, I have put forward three broad tasks: acquiring the raw materials and then dividing the spoils, while at the same time nurturing the necessary social and cultural arrangements.

In this second part, I turn more deliberately to history. Now that we have studied what cooks do, let us examine how it came to be that way. How have cooks changed, and how have they changed the world? I well remember my start at first reading cookery writer Elisabeth Rozin's claim that: 'Much of the history of the Western world was determined by a desire for seasoning ingredients' (1982: 197). And yet she merely invokes the schoolbook recital of conquest for the sake of spices. In fact, the increasingly sophisticated satisfaction of our most basic needs, the responsibility of cooks, has shaped our world in all sorts of ways. We are what we eat – cooks have not just made our meals, but have made us.

Sharing food and sharing jobs go together; one demands the other. Over time, cooks have shared cooking more widely, until the sun could never set on pudding helpers. Our own life is so packed that it feels like everything else but a way of dealing with food. But, as roles have split off, specialists have claimed independence for their work. This detachment and aggrandisement has been at the expense of the cooks at the heart of the enterprise.

But we have 'more important' things to do; cooking is merely a means to higher ends. As Socrates declares: 'base men live to eat and drink, and good men eat and drink to live' (Plutarch 21e; 1927: 111–13). This dismisses cooking as mere refuelling, along with much drudgery and occasional entertainment. It relegates cooking to the animal in us, to the toil of former societies, to the 'lesser' activities of women, and, as the icing on the cake, to the refined seductions of decadent sensibilities. Enthusing about human progress in *Man Makes Himself*, prehistorian V. Gordon Childe identifies the main revolutions in history, each marked by an 'upward kink in the population curve' (1965: 14). In each, he stresses the part played by the division of labour, with specialisations 'all withdrawn from the primary task of food-production' (142). People apparently move away from food activities, while magically feeding an expanded population. We have shared food, and so tasks, more and more widely, across bands, tribes, chiefdoms, city-states, empires, globes.

From another quarter, even Isabella Beeton considers that food-getting was once a total preoccupation; now it is a mere refinement. The early stages of human progress were a 'gradual succession of triumphs over the rude materialities of nature'. Through these phases, the great object has been just to live. But, she continues,

> by-and-by, comforts are multiplied, and accumulating riches create new wants. The object, then, is not only to *live*, but to live economically,

agreeably, tastefully, and well. Accordingly, the art of cookery com-
mences; and although the fruits of the earth, the fowls of the air, the
beasts of the field, and the fish of the sea, are still the only food of
mankind, yet these are so prepared, improved, and dressed by skill
and ingenuity, that they are the means of immeasurably extending the
boundaries of human enjoyments (1861: 39).

Do we live to eat or eat to live? In a metabolic universe, eating
is living. It is fantasy to think we ever transcend the 'rude materialities
of nature'. For humans, cooking is the only alternative to death.
Cooks are in charge. Civilisation is a culinary act. It is just that now
the potter provides the bowls, the sailor unloads the tea-chests and
the balladeer adds the conversation. The duties of the cook have
split off, over and over, wondrously reconstituting culture, generating
a public sphere – tragically, to cooking's conceptual diminishment.

The seed drops and grows into a tree, which produces fruit, which
is picked and prepared for eating, leaving the seed to enter the soil
again. Likewise, grains of wheat are planted, harvested, ground into
flour, with some seeds set aside to start the process again. Fowls
peck spilt grain and lay eggs, some eaten and some hatched. Wheat
captures the sun's energy, which rises through chickens, eggs and
Socrates to the pinnacles of civilisation. These cycles are not just
ecological but also social and cultural, circulating across all boundaries of time and place. In this whirl of consume and be consumed,
particular items are transient; but form persists physically, chemically,
genetically and culturally. This is the cooks' great pudding.

Cooks' sharing sustains physical bodies, cooperative endeavour
and ways of life. With the division of labour, the sharing is shared.
Our society shares food and food jobs so comprehensively that it
goes almost unnoticed. But, if we look, we catch pudding-makers
everywhere.

FETCHING WATER

In the delightful booklet *Pots and Pans of Classical Athens* (1964),
Brian A. Sparkes and Lucy Talcott reproduce scenes of the once
universal chore of fetching water. The scenes decorate pottery that was
actually used in handling that water. For example, the painters chose

the inside of one shallow cup for a circular composition showing a naked man hauling the rope at a well. For households without their own well, water was also available at public fountains, and the potters decorated vessels with scenes of women collecting water at such places. In one version, the artist shows streams from the 'mouths' of two 'animals' on the wall being caught in jars with three handles, two on the side for lifting and a higher one for pouring. Two pairs of women pose in elegant profile, one pair filling the jars, and the other carrying them on their heads. 'The girls have stilled their chatter at the artist's bidding', write Sparkes and Talcott. They contrast this idealised scene with a less formal one of a boy jauntily hoisting the water jar to his head. This better fits Aristophanes's impression in *Lysistrata* of the women's crowded and clattering meeting place, the fountain-house.

In the story of the 'Sorcerer's Apprentice', a novice is left to fetch water. Rather than do it himself, he despatches a magic broom. Unhappily, not knowing the command to turn the broom off, the apprentice tries to destroy it by chopping it in two. Now, instead of one broom, two fetch water. As the apprentice panics and chops, the brooms multiply. In the historical division of labour, the mundane chore of fetching water has indeed transformed into a massive infrastructure of reservoirs, pipes, head-offices, engineering schools, capital markets, government regulations, and so on. Where all cooks once carried their own water, many now rely on an industry. Long before Athenian women gathered at fountains, rulers' names were frequently associated with the provision of water, with reservoirs and tunnels.

The archaeological treasures shown in Sparkes and Talcott's booklet also remind us that, alongside the traditional hearth, grindstones and mortars were in incessant use. But the milling of flour, too, moved out of the house. The bakers (and their slaves) took over not just the communal oven, but the preliminary grinding. Then, the miller's trade was increasingly separated until it became the highly rationalised industry we know now.

Cheese-making and brewing, too, started out domestically. Typical of the separation of tasks, as raised in the chapter on the cooks' knife, men have taken over as sacrificing priests, butchers, carvers, warriors. Potters and metalsmiths borrowed the fire, applying cooking skills to earth to contrive objects of elegance and style to help with the cooking. So, too, the sciences can be presented as emerging out of cooking, in their techniques, equipment and interests.

Culinary fecundity did not escape the playful philosopher Brillat-Savarin, who asserts that 'all human industry has concentrated on adding to the duration and the intensity of the pleasures of the table'. So people ornamented their goblets and vases, crowned their guests in flowers, and dined in gardens and the woods. Dancers, jugglers and mimes began their entertainments. Perfumes were sprayed in the air, and 'it even happened that naked beauties acted as servant girls, so that every human sense joined in a complete pleasure' (Meditation 14; 1971: 183–4). The talking and singing around meals became professional with Egyptian harpists, Greek flute-girls, Roman clowns, medieval bards and global television. Such is the specialisation that in the world of learning there is now an expert for virtually every sentence in this book.

As numerous such elements of the cooks' duties have split off and shifted into the public space, they have become relatively autonomous, formalised, male, 'important'. While bakers and brewers might acknowledge their help to cooks, artists might not. Visit a public gallery, and paintings, mosaics and sculptures are labelled 'art'. Meanwhile, useful silverware, ceramics and glass are termed 'decorative art'. However, from the cooks' standpoint, poets and painters do not create culture, but adorn it. Like the scenes on an ancient Greek *kylix* (cup) and *hydria* (water jar), art gives meanings to our lives. The decorators say, this is no ordinary cup but a cup for people of this type, drinking in this manner. Then these signs detach as seemingly

autonomous art, with its own rules, and lift the eye to the walls.

In the ancient comedy *Odysseus* by Anaxandrides, a fisherman casts doubt on the popularity of conventional artworks. 'As for the artists, to be sure, their lovely handiwork is hung up on *plates* to be admired. But this handiwork of ours is ceremoniously wrested from the casserole and quickly disappears from the frying-pan. For, good sir, what other art makes the lips of youngsters burn?' (Athenaeus 227b; 3: 23). The Greek word translated and italicised here as '*plates*' was used for both what cooks and artists display on.

Given the slant of art curators, the ancient peoples who decorated vases, shaped spears, fought wars and buried their rulers might have survived without cooking. Yet, when we look, we see again and again how these achievements fly from the cooks' mixing-bowl. This is not to reduce art, religion, politics and the rest to 'mere' cookery, but the reverse – to confirm their extraordinary range, depth and richness, when linked to life's real struggle.

DIFFERENTIATION

Are we animals, or something different? Is culture part of nature, or is it anti-nature? Anthropologist Louis Dumont provides an interesting discussion of such problems, in which something can appear to be its own negative. He calls it a 'hierarchy' of 'opposites' (1980: 239–45). I employ a similar principle, preferring to speak, however, of a 'dialectic' of 'complements'. This stresses that such apparent contradictions are to be understood historically. Let me explain.

In the culture–nature example, taking an evolutionary viewpoint, it is possible to say that culture emerges within nature, and so belongs to the natural world, while at the same time divorces itself. In turn, 'culture' in the sense of 'high culture' belongs to and stands against 'culture' in the fuller, anthropological sense; public culture emerges from and snubs everyday culture, as I complain.

In another, highly pertinent instance of self-negation already mentioned, the word 'economy' started out referring to the management of the *oikos* (Greek, 'house'). Accordingly, ancient author Xenophon's *Oikonomikos* is not a precursor to Adam Smith's *Wealth of Nations* but to Mrs Beeton's *Household Management*. In the sixteenth and seventeenth centuries, people began to speak of public activity as, by analogy, the 'political economy', shortened to 'economics' from the late eighteenth century. Ironically, we now use the tautology 'home economics' for the original 'economics'. Worse, those activities belonging to the original economy are often divorced by the emergent economy. The public economy thus both derives from and stands against the original.

As aspects of 'cooking' split off, they come to stand against cooking. Since the prototypical eater, Adam, moved away from the prototypical provider, Eve, the cooks' negations have disowned their ancestry. Look at poets now and they appear quite dissociated from cooks. But look back at how bards contributed to feasts and it may not prove so simple. With connections, oppositions, engagements and disengagements, this is not just history but evolution. The 'Art of Cookery' gradually develops, as Isabella Beeton finds, 'from the earliest and simplest modes, to those of the most complicated and refined' (1861: 39). Change is cumulative. We cannot easily abandon new specialisations, but at least we can keep an eye on the big picture, not snub our foundations.

Technically, my argument relies on the rolling cart of social evolution, based on functional differentiation. 'Differentiation' implies both dividing and developing, not unlike the cells in an organism. The division of labour ripples systematically down the production chain from acquisition, through distribution to cultural construction. Not just trade specialisation, but material culture, technology, representational systems and other aspects of culture differentiate in this way. Let me show this in the splitting of the rooms in a house.

THE EVOLUTION OF KITCHENS

The Chinese phrase for breaking up a household translates as 'dividing the stoves' (Anderson 1988: 182). Roman poet Horace mentions a hamlet of five 'hearths' ('*agellus habitatus quinque focis*'), meaning of five 'households'. Around 1100, a hearth tax or *focagium* was introduced in Normandy. When the authorities conducted censuses for taxation purposes in late-medieval France, they generally counted not heads or houses or even heads of households but fires (Contamine 1988: 425).

So much starts from the hearth. The simplest dwelling is just one room, with a fire, to which food is brought for preparation and consumption. People may sleep around the embers and do all manner of things, but, essentially, they work with cooking pots, storage bins, and grinding stones and knives, and focus on food-sharing. The single-roomed structure can thus reasonably be viewed as the kitchen, which then divides and multiplies. As walls adjoin, the circular structure becomes rectilinear.

Historically, the keeping of food is the first settled function, so that the simplest house then divides between a workspace and separate storeroom, which might be a bin, silo, stable, cellar or loft. This key structure is often relegated both physically and conceptually to an outhouse. Among northern European forests, the habit was to bed down on top of the mighty stove. But, after food preparation and storage, the decisive separation is the bedroom, giving the long-standing appearance of the two-part house (plus food storage).

In 1417, the ploughman Jean Petitpas of Jaux (Oise), France, lived with his wife and three small children in a house that consisted of the typical two parts, known as the *foyer* and *chambre*. The English 'foyer', meaning entrance area, comes from the French, for 'hearth, home', and in turn derives from the Latin *focus* for 'hearth'. In Montaillou, a French town in the late Middle Ages for which the inquisitor left comprehensive records, this central portion of the house was the *foganha* (and elsewhere the *chas* or *foconea*). 'One of the tasks of the housekeeper, or *focaria*, was to keep a fire going in the fogaha at all times during the day and to cover it carefully at night for fear of fire', reports historian Philippe Contamine. The women spent most of their time here; the door remained open directly onto the street from morning until evening (1988: 453, 457).

Even the ambitious early medieval building started out as just one large room with lightweight partitions. In 1177, in the palace of the counts of Champagne at Troyes, the prince sat on a dais during banquets, dominating the guests at two large tables down the room. He slept on the other side of the partition behind him (Barthélemy 1988: 420). Even with more rooms, a primary distinction was long retained between the 'hall' (*salle* in French; *sala* in Italian), which included the functions of kitchen, dining space and general living room, and the 'chamber' (*chambre*; *camera*). The hall and its fire was the relatively public gathering point, while the chamber was private. In significant households, the Steward was in charge of the hall ('steward' presumably deriving from Old English for 'house, hall') and the Lord Chamberlain in charge of the chamber.

In the evolution of the kitchen, as activities – including dining – were removed, the hearth became increasingly focussed. It began to be hidden at the back or downstairs, so that it looked tacked on, as if the main purpose of a house were showing off the best furniture or playing cards. So, in the hierarchy of houses in Tuscany on the eve of the Renaissance, for example, one room served all purposes for the poor. If the house had two rooms, they were the familiar *sala* (living room and kitchen) and *camera* (bedroom). As an instance of further sophistication, in 1456 Papino di Piero, head of a peasant family of six, added a second bedroom, as well as a *cella* (storage room). Another farming family of four also had a storage room and a 'bread room', which might have been a bakehouse. Meanwhile, in the city, an increase from two to three rooms usually meant a dedicated kitchen, or another bedroom. For their provisions and share of the crop, even the simplest bourgeois family had a storage room, and the well-to-do built storage vaults, woodsheds, stables, lumber rooms and offices. Besides these, and the kitchen, living rooms and bedrooms, the wealthiest added vestibules, anterooms, arms rooms, studies, courtyards, arcades, and loggias, where they could enjoy the air on hot summer days (Roncière 1988: 179–80).

So, an evolutionary differentiation of the kitchen fans out according to wealth and status. A line runs from the humble rustic abode, all crammed into the kitchen, to the multi-storeyed palace, still, in a real sense, the kitchen, subdivided. As bedrooms, halls, bathrooms and even anterooms are divided off, each room attracts its own expertise and its own grandeur, and denies its parentage. Just as the kitchen splits and grows, so, too, do towns and entire civilisations. The cooks' tasks are subdivided more finely through entire states. Now, in many parts of the world, cars drive to the next meal. Trucks back up to both ends of the sausage factory. Buses take the industrial army to earn its crust. People do not see the kitchen for clouds of smoke, the ancestor for all her offspring. If we peer through the haze, we can nevertheless witness the emergence of this public hearth.

Symbols

In his mighty study of magic and religion, *The Golden Bough*, James George Frazer seeks to explain sacred hearths like that of the south-western African herders, the Herero. Kept alight by the chief's senior unmarried daughter, the holy fire was the ceremonial centre of the village. Beneath ritual and symbolism, however, Frazer finds the desirability of 'some one place in the village where every house-wife could be sure of obtaining fire without having to kindle it by friction' (1911: 260). Nomads would then, he suggests, invest the 'simple old custom with a halo of mystery and romance', attributing efficacy to the fire in repelling evil and maintenance of the flame with the 'majesty or even the life of the king' (266).

Indeed, in customs like the Herero's, Frazer finds the basis of public cults like that of Vesta in ancient Rome, in which six vestal virgins watched over the city's flame. Chosen from upper-class families when young, these women were permitted to marry after thirty years of service, while protecting their virginity under the threat of being buried alive. Vesta started out as a domestic god, along with others called the *lares* and *penates*. Similarly, with a god of the hearth, Hestia, Greek cities had a *prytaneion*, a temple in which the sacred city fire would stay burning and from which Athenians would take fire when leaving to found new colonies. While Frazer fails to peer into Herero cooking as such (based on milk, butter and meat from cattle, sheep and goats), he demonstrates that, in the hands of public specialists, religious ritual and meaning lift conspicuously away from the mundane.

Like breaking bread, sprinkling salt has been regarded as a symbol of union since at least Homer's time. The Bible speaks of 'covenants of salt' (Numbers 18:19). In Leonardo da Vinci's *Last Supper*, Judas is shown upsetting the salt, presumably to symbolise betrayal. In former days, Russians made bread without salt so that it might be sprinkled on as a welcoming sign (Smith and Christian 1984: 127). But make no mistake, the use of salt does not start out as a symbol. Initially, it is actual salt, actually shared. Only through repeated use does salt become a symbol of itself. This is similar to the way that the concept of time gains apparent independence from cooks, as discussed in Chapter Eight, and there is a world of other examples.

This separation of symbols from material items and practices is a crucial form of differentiation. In a 'dialectic of complements', as I have called this evolutionary process, symbols gain a command of their own, which can detract from their basis. For those Bantu of Africa studied by Audrey Richards, cattle could become so important that their primary values came to lose out to their secondary. 'The herd is less important as a source of meat, milk, and leather, than as the object of social ambitions, rivalries and emotions', she marvels (1932: 97).

As a highly pertinent category of cases, as experts develop, they come to find nothing more powerful than their layer of reality. Audrey Richards observes that economists and anthropologists pay lipservice to the necessity of nutrition, and then, 'having granted so much to the biologist', begin their chapter anew. Food-getting is promptly forgotten, she complains, and 'economic organisation is considered as evolving in human society according to its own laws, apart from the physical structure and needs of man' (14). Cultural anthropologists themselves can concentrate upon food as a 'symbol' and ignore its physicality. In like manner, psychologists regard food as 'gratification', biochemists treat it as 'nutrients', engineers as 'public works', and so on. Food and its preparation have priority over the rituals and languages that emerge, and yet cooking certainly also involves languages and recipes. The trick is to keep together and divide at once, through this dialectic of differentiation. Without a knowledge of history, the cooks' world remains fragmented, the jigsaw not even acknowledged.

PROFESSIONALISATION

While agriculture has attracted considerable scientific, economic and even poetic interest, the cooking of those same raw materials has met with a 'shamefaced silence', German cookery reformer Baron von Rumohr recognised almost two centuries ago. He complains that the 'philanthropists' would rather give the 'impression that farming improvements are aimed only at stimulating trade or encouraging the circulation of money. They are loath to admit to themselves or others that there is any importance in trying to improve people's diets' (1993: 41).

If agriculture seems so much more important than cookery, which it serves, this is because it is established as a male, public, 'economic' activity. If hunters are mighty, then it is because they share more grandiosely. If cooks sometimes fail to appear central, this mystification comes from specialists granting themselves and their interests dominance. The chauvinism of knowledge goes hand-in-hand with the sharing of jobs. Eve gives a chore to Adam; Adam puffs up with pride.

To advance their professions, practitioners formalise techniques, compose textbooks, induct apprentices, form guilds, claim special privileges, restrict entry. Inevitably, professional discourses proclaim their own importance, often to the detriment of alternatives. As a striking example, the hero of academic philosophy, Plato, preached a worldview that elevated rational argument (against empirical science) as the one access to true reality. In a subsequent chapter, we will watch how, with temples, priests open the kitchen out in public, festoon it impressively with art, instruction and meaning, and call this great kitchen the home of the gods. Just as priests compose

hymns of praise to the gods, and to their chief agents in this world, palace poets praise the king, and poetry; warriors promote war heroics, and dress accordingly. I can give an amusingly blatant example of self-serving professional propaganda from perhaps 4000 years ago.

In ancient Egypt, privileged schoolboys learned to write by transcribing classics. Modern scholars now have access to abundant papyrus copies of standards such as 'The Satire on the Trades' (perhaps 2150–1750 BC), even if the beginners so 'mangled' the archaic language that 'translation is often uncertain' (Pritchard 1969: 432–4). The lines scorn the barber, who stays shaving after dusk. If he works valiantly, 'his arms will fill his belly, like a bee eating for its work'. The builder must work outdoors in a treacherous wind, his muscles being destroyed and, for all this, 'What he eats is the bread of his fingers, and he washes himself *once a season*'. The gardener carries his produce to town, and has to water his vegetables in the morning and vines in the evening. By contrast, the students recite, the job of the scribe is sweet. No scribe lacks food. The lines promise: 'I shall make thee love writing more than thy mother . . . it is greater than any office; there is not its like in the land'.

MEDICINE

The textbook case of professionalisation has been that of medical practitioners. Their suppression of rivals might even have contributed to the persecution of witches by the Christian Church. In an influential polemic, feminists Barbara Ehrenreich and Deirdre English argue that, with European medicine firmly established as a secular profession by the fourteenth century, doctors campaigned against women healers as witches. The pair draw attention to the 'most fantastic accusation of all: The witch is accused not only of murdering and poisoning, sex crimes and conspiracy – but of *helping and healing*'. The professionals were called in to adjudicate at the witch trials, and so: 'The trial in one stroke established the male physician on a moral and intellectual plane vastly above the female healer he was called to judge'. When witches were systematically assassinated, the 'real issue was control: Male upper class healing under the auspices of the Church was acceptable, female healing as part of a peasant subculture was not'. A major element of the threat was that the woman healer was an empiricist: 'She relied on her senses rather than on faith or doctrine, she believed in trial and error, cause and effect . . . In short, her magic was the science of her time' (1973: 13–14, 19).

To the extent that they were village specialists in herbs, concoctions and diets, these women were cooks who coped with the untoward. However, they were vilified as anti-cooks, toiling and troubling over devilish brews. The sixteenth-century woodcut by Jasper Isaac, *Abomination des sorciers*, illustrates the satanic cookbooks, the open hearth with pots ready for bizarre ingredients, the cauldron of prophecy in which fantastic, symbolic animals were prepared, the cupboard containing philtre (aphrodisiac) and potion pots, and the strainer used in divination. Inverting the ideals of courtly cookery, the banquet consisted of 'no other meats than carrion, and the flesh of hanged men, unbaptised children, and unclean strange animals, all cooked to be savourless and served without salt' (Cosman 1976: 114).

The witches craze is but an extreme example of the devaluation of the womanly, the domestic and the culinary, and was demonstrably infected with specialist rivalry. A century ago, in a text on cookery, Dr J.L.W. Thudichum retails 'jokes' about dangerous women. For example, he writes that, after two French playwrights, Messieurs Brasier and de Demassan, included some negative references to the female cooks, they came to fear having their meals 'mixed with deleterious ingredients'. Or, again, one of Madame du Deffant's cooks was so bad that it was said that the only difference between her and the poisoner Marquise de Brinvilliers was in the intention (1895: 632).

But what are the roots of Western professional medicine? According to classicist Benjamin Farrington, historians have raised three possible ancient Greek sources: the temples of Asclepius, the god of healing; the physiological opinions of the philosophers; and the training provided by the superintendents of gymnasia. But instead of religion, philosophy and athletics, Farrington harkens to an ancient authority who suggests the debt lies with cooks. This was the unknown author of the Hippocratic tract *On Ancient Medicine* dating from the middle of the fifth century BC.

The Greek scientist decides that human beings would not have stayed healthy on the same raw diet as the ox and horse. Fortunately, some benefactors discovered foods that better 'harmonised with their constitution'.

> So from wheat, by winnowing, grinding, sifting, steeping, kneading, and baking it, they produced bread, and from barley they produced cake. Experimenting with food they boiled or baked, they mixed and mingled, putting strong pure foods with weaker, until they adapted them to the power and constitution of man ... To this discovery and research what juster or more appropriate name could be given than medicine, seeing that it has been discovered with a view to the health, well-being and nourishment of man, in place of that mode of living from which came the pain, disease and death?

At the time of the Hippocratic author, Greek medicine was becoming philosophical in a rationalistic sense. 'Observation dwindled, speculation increased', Farrington writes (1953: 66–9). So, the ancient author wanted to accord empirical methods the authority of age. With predecessors in cooks, the art could be called 'ancient'. In so doing, he or she sourced medical advice to the largely women's world of 'folk' or hearth medicine and religion.

THE FLOWERING OF ATHENS

Not just meals, but also chores, tools, arrangements, words and knowledge have flown from cooks' bowls. With time, the offshoots have gained a measure of independence. I have called the overall principle 'dialectical differentiation' to emphasise the apparent contradiction between interdependence and rejection. In feeding us, cooks have made civilisation, including all the subsidiary professions, however ungrateful. My examples have come from everywhere, and so let me give a thumbnail sketch of one particular pudding.

The flowering of Athens around 2500 years ago has been viewed as philosophical (thinkers such as Socrates, Plato, Aristotle), architectural (public buildings such as the Acropolis, Parthenon, Propylaea, Erechtheum), artistic (the epics of Homer; the plays of Aeschylus, Sophocles, Aristophanes), scientific (Pythagoras, Democritus, Hippocrates), economic (the market), political (democracy) and military (the victory at Marathon; Alexander the Great). As mentioned in

Chapter Three, numerous Athenians, preoccupied with good dining, had a wise and witty commitment to cooks. Indeed, culinary enthusiasm and knowledge seem never to have been keener. So, the triumph of Athens was also culinary (Cadmus, Archestratus, Sicon, Athenaeus, and so on).

A cook presented by Athenion in his comedy *The Samothracians* credits his art with raising people from a 'bestial and lawless life' to civilisation. The first step was to replace cannibalism by roasted meat. Then some clever cook added salt. Sauces and seasonings further advanced culinary art. 'Then, with the progress of time someone introduced the stuffed paunch, cooked a kid so that it melted in the mouth, gave it distinction with fine trimmings.' With such delights, the populace eschewed eating one another and consented to live together, so that 'cities became civilised, all through this art, I repeat, of cookery' (Athenaeus 660e–661d; 7: 41–5). It was much more involved than that. In fact, philosophy, architecture, art, science, economics, politics and warfare can be shown to serve cooks. Taken all together, Athens was a fabulous kitchen.

At the time of Homer and Hesiod, the Greeks could be described as backwoods warriors and smallholders, living on the periphery of great civilisations. Then, among other busy bees, Solon, who was elected Athenian leader in 594 BC, instituted sweeping economic, social, political and legal reforms. He faced up to the lack of water, as Plutarch records. Since the country could not rely on rivers, lakes or springs, 'most of it comes from artificial wells'. Solon therefore legislated that people should use any public well within 800 metres; otherwise, they had to dig. Having dug to 20 metres without water, they could fill a vessel of 30 litres twice a day from a neighbour (*Solon* 23; 1960: 66).

'Solon had above all a food problem to solve', T.R. Glover explains. 'To pay for foreign wheat, or – for Solon deliberately appealed to the domestic emotions of common people – to pay for the people's food, Solon headed Athens to industry and opened her doors wide to the skilled man' (1942: 107–8). The discovery of silver at nearby Laurion is said to have paid for the navy, which guaranteed safe passage to the grain ships from the Black Sea.

With success in the Persian wars (500–449 BC), the inheritors of

Aegean culture seized not just riches but also the cultural baton from the east, building on the achievements of such civilisations as the Sumerian, Egyptian, Harappan, Hittite and now Persian. In the age of Pericles (a large part of the fifth century BC), Athens experienced a surge of development rarely equalled in history.

With its port of Piraeus, Athens made the ideal *emporion*, or trading centre. The author (probably Xenophon) of *Athenian Revenues*, a pamphlet dated about 355 BC, declares that Athens lies at the centre of Greece, even of the whole inhabited world, so 'every traveller, who would go from one end of Greece to the other end, passes Athens as if the centre of a circle, whether he goes by sea or land'. And so even foreign merchants should be encouraged to set up there by attractions such as good seats in the theatre, hospitality, and better hotels, shops and exchanges. 'What we want is not an empire, but better hotels', he writes. And not just ship-owners and merchants should be welcomed, but also artisans, poets and philosophers (Glover 1942: 77–8).

The Athenians were not the inventors of the town market, but their vibrant culture grew up around the trading-place, known to them as the Agora. With well-known spots for sellers of specific items, a person might say, 'I went round to the garlic and the onions and the frankincense and the perfume' (Webster 1969: 60). This, too, is where residents could purchase horses and slaves, and hire cooks for the day.

The comic poet Antiphanes lists the superior local products: 'Honey, wheat-bread, figs ... Sheep, wool, myrtle-berries, thyme, wheat, and water. Such water! You'd know in a minute you were drinking the water of Attica' (Athenaeus 43bc; 1: 187). Aristotle reckoned bee-keeping as one division of the true or proper art of money-making (*Politics* 1.11; 1982: 89). It is clear from the references of Aristophanes that a variety of vegetables were grown on Greek farms and marketed (Glover 1942: 67). Athenaeus hails the fig tree as the guide to civilisation (74d; 1: 321–3).

While the Greeks exported wine, oil and manufactures, mainly pottery, the three main imported items were wheat, fish and cheese. Athens had to get food by sea; but in the winter months – from the end of October to April – there was no navigation. With care there was no great difficulty in keeping wheat, stored in pits. Greece colonised the great granaries of Sicily and southern Italy, Egypt and the northern shores of the Black Sea, which also provided the second great staple, salt-dried fish. While Greeks kept sheep and goats for cheese, they also imported it, along with hides and lard, from Sicily (Glover 1942: 86–100).

Perhaps the reasons for the rise of Athens are as intractable as those for Rome's fall. Yet the several possible explanations – enlightened law-making, military triumph, silver-mining, the strategic port location of Piraeus, and so on – come together as an explosion of cooking. Indisputably, with all these developments, the people of Athens improved their tables. And as for a social nucleus pulling it all together, consider the symposium.

THE SYMPOSIUM

Throughout the rise and triumph of Athens, men gathered in little clusters all over town for a meal that dissolved into a drinking party. Ideally eight in number, they reclined on couches, one of the refinements borrowed from Persia. At these symposia (Murray 1990), they admired material refinements, including the host's drinking paraphernalia, perhaps of pottery or, if smarter, metal. They employed entertainers, including *hetairai* (like Japanese geishas). Some gentlemen roved from place to place, gourmet gangs in search of thrills. Out of the symposia came feuds and also male clubs and alliances.

Above all, the symposiasts talked. They gossiped, argued, created, recited. They analysed books and plans for the city. They talked politics and asked riddles, like the following: what is 'the nurse of life, the foe of hunger, the guardian of friendship, the physician of famine . . .'? Answer: 'The table' (Athenaeus 455f; 4: 569). Directly and indirectly, they discussed and planned cooking.

The aristocratic 'sympotic' lifestyle developed in the seventh century BC from the Homeric warrior-feast under the influence of eastern luxury, Oxford classicist Oswyn Murray writes. The warrior group was 'transformed into a leisure group', just as, in turn, the Romans would emphasise eating rather than drinking and allow mixed sex feasting groups, although the equality of participants was no longer observed.

Murray points out the enormous effect of the upper-class symposia on burgeoning Greek culture. He detects the influence of these drinking groups in much of the pottery, poetry, architecture, politics, legislation, military organisation and social customs of the time. The very manufacture of painted pottery reflects a:

> style of life based on the symposion, for which the majority of these vessels were made, with their distinctive shapes adapted to the needs of the symposion, and their decoration reflecting the interests and activities of those who took part. Most of the forms of Greek lyric poetry outside the religious sphere demonstrate that this poetry was composed for the symposion, that its public was conceived of as the sympotic group.

And so on, as Murray runs through the multiple impacts (1983).

Philosophical treatises such as Plato's *Symposium* follow the symposium format, which leaves an unduly ascetic version of gentlemen immersed in lofty debate, pointedly separate from the dining. Through such influences, the symposium has even tended to be seen as an invention of philosophy, rather than the other way around. All the same, the after-dinner discussion, formalised as philosophy, can be viewed as where rich and powerful Athenians organised business, politics and the arts so as to improve their meals.

By what form of combat would an ancient aristocrat conduct a 'Trial of the Suitors'? The answer establishes Athens's credentials as a gastronomic culture. During an Olympic games, the head of a powerful family, Cleisthenes, announced that any Greek who thought himself good enough to marry his daughter, Agarista, should present himself within sixty days. He began by asking each to name his country and parentage, and then, according to historian Herodotus (6.125–31; 1972: 433–5), Cleisthenes kept them in his house for a year, to get to know them well – and the 'most important test of all was their behaviour at the dinner-table'.

Among several distinguished suitors, one came from Sybaris in southern Italy. Even among so many 'sybaritic' citizens, Smindyrides stood out for delicate and luxurious living. Seeking to impress, he brought 1000 slaves – fishermen, fowlers and cooks (Athenaeus 273bc; 3: 227). Despite this, by the prospective father-in-law's final banquet, requiring the sacrifice of 100 oxen and the suitors competing in music and in talking in company, Cleisthenes had reduced the list to two Athenians. Unfortunately, that city's wealthiest and best-looking man, Hippocleides, disgraced himself by dancing on a table and standing on his head, beating time with his legs in the air. So Cleisthenes picked Megacles. And Megacles and Agarista's first son was another and even greater Cleisthenes, who, upon becoming ruler in 506 BC, was one of the founders of Athenian democracy.

In this picture, Athens adds up to a many-tiered project to improve the water supply (Solon's reforms), the food supply (nearby farms and far-flung trade), market distribution (the famed Agora) and material culture (pottery), along with a well-articulated super-structure (democracy, literature, philosophical discourse). Athenian civilisation was focussed on meals through their very own seminars, which were a relatively democratic version of an institution we shall find to be common throughout the pre-modern world. Of course, culinary civilisation was well understood by Brillat-Savarin, who provides the final taste of the spread to come.

A PHILOSOPHICAL HISTORY OF COOKING

'Cooking is the oldest of all arts', Brillat-Savarin petitioned two centuries ago: 'Adam was born hungry and every new child, almost before he is actually in the world, utters cries which only his wet nurse's breast can quiet'. Not just the oldest art, he persists, but the most important: 'Cooking is also of all the arts the one which has done most to advance our civilisation, for the needs of the kitchen were what first taught us to use fire, and it is by fire that man has tamed Nature itself' (Meditation 27; 1971: 279). In this section in *The Physiology of Taste* on the 'philosophical history of cooking', Brillat-Savarin sets out further speculations.

The human race was probably originally fruit-eating, the self-styled 'professor' proposes. We were the clumsiest of beings, our stomachs small and the fruit insufficiently nourishing. The 'very realisation of his [man's] weakness led him to find ways of making weapons . . . Once armed, he made of all the creatures who surrounded him his prey and his nourishment'. The murderous instinct, Brillat-Savarin decides, is still with us (280).

Raw flesh digests easily, seasoned with a little salt, and has but one inconvenience: it sticks to the teeth. Nonetheless, people's instinct for self-improvement led them to subject meat to fire. Since it soon 'became obvious that meat cooked upon live coals is not free from dirt', the morsels of flesh were impaled on sticks above the fire (282). Cooking made further great progress as soon as heat-resistant vessels of brass and clay became common – 'there were soups, gravies, jellies, and all such things'. With respect to metal implements, Brillat-Savarin poses a teaser: metals are worked with other metals (the blacksmiths' hammers and tongs), 'but I have yet to meet anyone who could explain to me how the first tongs were made, or how the first hammer was forged' (284).

Theorising on the pleasures of the table, Brillat-Savarin deduces that people began to gather for meals when they ceased to feed on fruit alone.

> The preparation and distribution of food necessarily brought the whole family together, the fathers apportioning to their children the results of the hunt, and the grown children then doing the same to their aged parents. These gatherings, limited at first to the nearest relatives, little by little were extended to include neighbours and friends.

He continues: 'Later, and when the human race had spread out, the tired traveller came to join in such primitive feasts, and to recount what went on in the far countries of the world. Thus was born hospitality'. Languages 'must have been born and perfected' at meals, from either administrative necessity or the natural loquaciousness of the occasion (Meditation 14; 181). The alphabet was introduced to Europe by Cadmus, once cook to the king of Sidon. Homer's own work is testimony, writes our alert scholar, that poetry and music were well and truly established as part of the delights of feasting.

Brillat-Savarin moves on to the sumptuous banquets of Middle Eastern kings, who possessed lands rich in everything, especially spices and perfumes. It was 'these soft and voluptuous people' who first would lie on couches around the banquet tables. Along with songs of friendship, pleasure and love, Brillat-Savarin hints how philosophy itself arose, since everyone 'strove to give even more worth to the feast by his agreeable conversation, and table talk became a science' (Meditation 27; 284–5).

Brillat-Savarin keeps up the history of cooking through Roman banqueting, the barbarian invasion, the Crusades, the periods of Louis XIV, Louis XV and Louis XVI. At the end of the eighteenth century, and thus reaching his own times, he detects the proliferation of food trades – 'our cooks, caterers, and pastry- and candymakers, our grocery store owners and such'. Physics and chemistry have been called to the aid of alimentary art, and new crafts sprung up, such as that of the *petit-four* bakers, who stand somewhere between the true cake-bakers and the candymakers. Speaking of progress in horticulture, preservation and the importation of dishes, he decides that 'everything that precedes, accompanies, or follows a banquet is treated with an orderliness, a method, and an address which shows a desire to please which should delight any guest' (299–301).

Every time I return to *The Physiology of Taste*, I am impressed by the light but erudite touch. Brillat-Savarin certainly includes the essential ingredients of gastronomic evolution. For him, at base, it is the human appetite that, through ingenuity, drives history. As he argues, the singular suffering of human beings incites them towards pleasures, their enlargement, perfection, complication and finally worship. Social beings are brought together by the 'preparation and the distribution of food'. At meals, languages are born and perfected. The increasing number of trades split off. Over the next six chapters, I try to improve on Brillat-Savarin's history of cooks, drawing on nearly two centuries of subsequent social science.

*　　*　　*

Skimming over palaeolithic Africa, ancient Mesopotamia, courtly China and nineteenth-century England, in the rest of the book we keep a historical look-out on cooking's trio of main tasks: extraction, distribution and organisation. We watch for changes as, in charge of our eating and drinking, cooks draw goodness from forests, gardens, seas and markets. They divide it up and then bring us together at hearth, village square and restaurant to share. Overall, cooks enmesh the tasks in a fine cultural net of recipes, rules and meanings.

Observing the emergence of civilisation, and yet not so minutely that we miss the overall features, we see the work shared and spoils divided ever more widely. Numerous technical trades separate out, male (traditionally) specialists promoting their callings. Between them, they create the public world, its back turned on cooks, each job fleeing the hearth, forgetting. We discover how the cooks' three functions are developed in turn, so that elaborate modes of extraction make room for fancier distribution, and so for more sophisticated organisation. Our story begins when photosynthetic plants and foraging animals make way for humans, who dine. Cooking-beings start as gatherers; the next great innovation is redistribution, and our own times are knowledge-based, although how knowingly we might want to discuss.

CHAPTER TEN

E v e   a n d   A d a m

The evolution from ape to recognisable human demonstrates the principle of the movie-camera. In several strides, the stooped, hairy figure on the left smartens up and stands upright. Stop the frame and we are not certain what we see. On one side, we declare the creature pre-human, and, on the other, we recognise ourselves. The flickering image comes courtesy of the forensic perseverance of archaeologists, whose ground searches, chemical analyses and genetic fingerprints help solve crimes sometimes millions of years old.

Applying the microscope to one rib-bone is not enough. Archaeologists need every scrap of evidence – not just the bodies and the weapons but their precise location. Then, around the material remains, they must weave plausible scenarios. Not just laboratory but also human scientists, they must bring the profile to life, showing actual activities, relationships and grunts. With due caution, they can compare modern shots of chimpanzees and gorillas.

Most of all, in interpreting the drama, they need hunches. Even at the risk of rushed judgements and wishful thinking, they must have a theory. Without broad concepts, they risk distraction. To capture the shadowy creature's movements, these sleuths must communicate intuitions into what makes this creature lift its head and strut.

Waving airily, archaeologists tell us that our forerunner *Australopithecus* scavenged large animals five million years ago – or maybe half that. Human precursors used tools three million years ago – or maybe two. After perhaps *Homo habilis*, *Homo erectus* and early *Homo sapiens*, modern people, known with redoubled wisdom as *Homo sapiens sapiens*, are detectable 130 000 years ago – well, definitely 40 000 years or so.

Despite the uncertainties, digging up Stone Age bones is grimly fascinating, messing with our own evolution, revealing ourselves to ourselves. In this chapter, we close in on the branching-point, the original human act. What, historically, marks our emergence? When do we stop talking about animals and think about us?

In pursuing self-understanding, archaeologists have feared that no feature is sufficient in itself. For example, all kinds of animals use tools, even insects, so it cannot be the use of tools that distinguishes the human being. Chimps hunt cooperatively, which rules out some kind of merciless tribalism. Instead, archaeologists prefer to catalogue a range of physiological changes, such as bipedalism, manual dexterity and bigger brains. With strong but delicate fingers, human ancestors could pick berries, dig roots and remove the tough peel of fruits. But obvious anatomical modifications – within changing ecological conditions – should not distract us from less material developments.

Anthropologist Clifford Geertz urges that, over the long term, changes in culture are so potent that they bring about physical changes.

> Though it is apparently true enough that the invention of the airplane led to no visible bodily changes, no alterations of (innate) mental capacity, this was not necessarily the case for the pebble tool or the crude chopper, in whose wake seems to have come not only more erect stature, reduced dentition, and a more thumb-dominated hand, but the expansion of the human brain to its present size (1973: 67).

So, prehistorians have increasingly also enumerated cultural innovations – such as tools, family structures and language.

Physical features and cultural accomplishments interweave: standing on two feet frees the hands for carrying tools, which uses extra brainpower, which makes for a complex culture, more adaptable to diverse habitats. A similar heap of sticks can fall into different sequences: to learn ideas and skills takes a long childhood, leaving children incapable of looking after themselves until six or seven years of age, and so demanding committed parents, which requires social developments. The long chase requires evaporative cooling, which favours sweat glands and little hair; being relatively hairless means children cannot hang on, and so parents devise some sort of sling for carrying children; the sling also carries food. The large, cooled brain begins to be used for language perhaps only 60 000 years ago (Noble and Davidson 1996).

We go round and round, knotting a bigger ball of factors. It might begin to seem as if we cannot pinpoint anything essentially human, after all. And yet the erect figure on the right looks back and torments itself about the apparent distance from the rest of nature. My suggestion is that prehistory may finally not be like police work at all. What if, rather than having to nab one guilty party, we can blame an entire social problem? In the end, we seek not a simple key, but an overall concept. I pin our humanity on cooks. All the suggested abilities – free hands, nimble fingers, clever brains, extended child-care, domestic partnerships, stone cutters, fire, and so on – can be bundled up as the many talents of cooks.

French prehistorian Catherine Perlès accepts that we share many aspects of feeding with other animals: other animals carry food to their lairs or transform it before consumption. However, she says, we transform food on a different level. The human species prepares its food by heat, for one thing, and combines ingredients, for another. So she proposes that the *culinary act* distinguishes the human species, and is not just a symbol of, but a factor in, that very humanisation (1979: 5).

Perlès also emphasises the sociability of the culinary act; it spells the end of individual self-sufficiency. Just tending the flame, for example, would have involved a division of tasks: certain members would acquire combustible material, while others kept up the fire and others went in search of food. 'The culinary act is from the start a *project*', she writes. Drying, fermenting, mixing and cooking by heat required new levels of skills, especially foresight and reflection. Cooking is highly intentional; ingredients have to be selected, for example (9). And, as I argue, the culinary act is essentially sharing.

Various types of wear on teeth give an indication of diet. A *Homo erectus* specimen from near Heidelberg, Germany, has marks on the six front teeth suggesting that meat was held in the front of the mouth and cut off with a flint tool. In more recent examples, excessive wear on the occlusal (biting) surfaces suggests the presence of grit from cooking in ashes or the stone-grinding of cereals. As a generalisation, less chewing was needed as cooking techniques developed (Renfrew and Bahn 1996: 291). And, in like manner, the prehistory of cooks and the culinary act is to be read in charred grain, middens (garbage heaps), coprolites (fossilised faeces), tells (mounds left by successive settlements), storage pits, bloodstains, pots – and, mostly, kitchen implements.

CUTTING IMPLEMENTS

'[S]ometime between 3 million and 2.5 million years ago, long before Louis Leakey's handy person [*Homo habilis*] was on the scene, the australophithecines achieved a technological breakthrough – as great as any that was ever to occur in human history. They began to make cutting, slicing, and chopping implements out of pieces of rock', lauds anthropologist Marvin Harris. The earliest stone choppers and flakes – such as those found at Gona in the Hadar region and at the Omo Valley, both in Ethiopia – already reveal a trained facility for selecting the best materials to serve as cores and hammers and for delivering well-aimed blows to detach razor-sharp flakes. Nicholas Toth of Indiana University has duplicated these simple implements and used them to butcher elephants and other large, tough-skinned animals. He found that heavy choppers were good for severing straight branches from a tree and with small flakes he could whittle points of spears. Other flakes were useful for scraping meat, fat and hair from hides (Harris 1989: 41, 44–5).

Simple flaked stone tools are so old that the first technological era or 'palaeolithic' (*palaios* 'ancient'; *lithos* 'stone') would appear to have been tripped off by *Australopithecus*, a genus that existed before *Homo*. They had skulls that were bio-mechanically adapted for a diet that required rigorous chewing; the shape and wear of the teeth suggest a diet of coarse or bulky plant foods. But, in search of more nutritious foods, they might also have developed tool-use and upright posture. Marvin Harris speculates that they sharpened sticks to help extract ants and termites from their nests (1989: 32).

The earliest cutting implements appear to be at least 300 000 years older than the earliest specimens attributed to the large-brained *Homo* genus. Nonetheless, *Homo habilis* had been called 'handy' for having the manual dexterity to manufacture the early artefacts necessary to acquire and process foods that were more concentrated sources of nutrients, such as nuts, deeply buried roots, or meat from large animals (Sept 1992: 3–4).

With the first tools, we find the cooks' stamp, and that was well before not just cooking fires but even the earliest 'humans'. Because of their human-like characteristics, the early tool-makers have been called 'hominids', the members of the primate family Hominidae, which includes *Australopithecus* as well as *Homo*.

GLYNN ISAAC AND FOOD-SHARING

In the 1970s, in the Koobi Fora area of Lake Turkana, Kenya, Glynn Isaac, a researcher from the University of California, Berkeley, and his group recovered 119 chipped stones at the site of a hippopotamus carcass perhaps two million years old. Most of the stones were small, sharp flakes that, when held between thumb and fingers, would have made effective cutting implements. Isaac found that the sediments bearing these artefacts included no natural stones larger than a pea. He concluded that the tool-makers had carried their stones from elsewhere, presumably to help obtain meat from the carcass.

In a second useful site, the group found several hundred stone tools scattered over an area 16 metres in diameter. Along with the tools were fragmented bones, which, particularly the teeth, could be identified with several animal species. The site appeared to have been the sandy bed of a stream, where hominids may have sat, perhaps digging in the sand for water, and enjoying the shade and safety of the adjacent trees. This sort of stone only naturally occurred at least 3 kilometres away.

Isaac claims that he had found:

unambiguous evidence that two million years ago some hominids in this part of Africa were carrying things around, for example stones. The same hominids were also making simple but effective cutting tools of stone and were at times active in the vicinity of large animal carcasses, presumably in order to get meat. The studies strongly suggest that the hominids carried animal bones (and meat) around and concentrated this portable food supply at certain places (1979: 32).

There are several possible advantages in postponing some food consumption and bringing it to a central point. One is that the hominids seized food quickly and withdrew to a spot sheltered from their own predators. Another is that they left their young behind at a 'nest' or 'den', in the manner of birds, wild dogs and hyenas. However, looking to human models raises a further possibility. The transport of food is associated with a division of labour. In societies of modern hunter–gatherers, women contribute the majority of *gathered* foods; such foods are mainly plant products, but may include shellfish, small reptiles, eggs, insects and the like. The men usually contribute the *hunted* foodstuffs: mammals, fish and birds. Typically, the women and men roam in separate groups and eventually bring the main haul to a home base.

Accordingly, to explain his archaeological evidence, Isaac proposes a food-sharing model. Both the morphology and the patterns of wear of the hominid teeth suggest the consumption of plant foods. Estimating that they could not have transported a sufficient amount of plant food to be worth sharing without a carrying device, he supposes the use of something like an uncomplicated bark tray. Other tools might also have been possible, such as a digging-stick. He writes:

> the system I visualise would have worked best if the mobile hunter–scavenger contribution of meat to the social group was balanced by the gatherer–carrier collection of high-grade plant foods. What is certain is that at some time during the past several million years just such a division of labour came to be a standard kind of behaviour (33).

Glynn Isaac imagines his hominids living much like other higher primates, the differences apparent only after prolonged observation. Perhaps at the start of each day we would observe a group splitting up as some members went off in one direction and some in another.

These subgroups would feed intermittently as they encountered ubiquitous low-grade plant foods such as berries, but we might observe that 'some of the higher-grade materials – large tubers or the haunch of a scavenged carcass – were being reserved for group consumption when the foraging parties reconvened at their starting point' (34).

The practices might seem familiar, but Isaac stresses that these creatures were not, in fact, human, but proto-human. Their language may have been rudimentary. Some division of labour might require scarcely more communicative abilities than chimpanzees, but the 'hunters' and the 'gatherers' would exchange information on opportunities they encountered. Food-sharing would also be greatly assisted by the ability to 'calculate complex chains of contingencies that reach far into the future'. Such a need must have provided an important biological basis for the evolution of the human intellect. Isaac thus proposes that the increase in the size of the brain and enhanced capacity for communication are a 'consequence of the shift from individual foraging to food-sharing some two million years ago'. Also, he believes that the model helps explain social ties, notably the basic institution of marriage. Chimpanzees enjoy, if that is the word, opportunistic relations between the sexes. However, the sexual division of labour would favour a 'mating system that involved at least one male in "family" food procurement on behalf of each child-rearing female in the group' (34–5).

Isaac's hominids look to me like early cooks. They might have bark trays and certainly primitive knives. The foragers bring acquisitions back to a 'home base', suggestive of a rudimentary kitchen, where gathered foods might need preparation, such as shelling nuts, presumably by females. Equally, we might see the young joining in, learning domestic skills. Greatest success would belong to those groups with the richest and most useful culinary culture. These creatures shared food and, with that, employed a basic division of labour. If they were not cooks, these food-sharers were well on the way.

Admittedly, Isaac's picture is contested. There is doubt, for instance, about the archaeological evidence for home bases – until much later, even hundreds of thousands of years after the appearance of the genus *Homo* (McGuire 1992: 159). Another important archaeologist, Lewis Binford, has argued that hunting animals had in fact killed their prey at the sites. Microscopic examination might settle whether marks were left on bones by teeth or cutters (Renfrew and Bahn 1996: 372). Yet the general direction is convincing. To echo Isaac, it is certain that home bases became standard 'at some time during the past several million years'. This helps shift attention from hunting as the formative factor. As he affirms, studies of human evolution have tended to have a male bias if for no other reason than that bone (hunted by the male) is generally much more durable than plant residues (gathered by the female) (1979: 33).

WOMANLY VIRTUES

The pretty image of ancestors plucking the apples of Paradise was spoiled by nineteenth-century scientists and their 'Man the Hunter' headline. In *The Descent of Man* in 1871, Charles Darwin presents hunting as the behavioural catalyst that selected for an enlarged brain, tool-use, reduced canine teeth and bipedalism, thus splitting the lineages of humans and apes. The scenario became: hominids encroach on the savannah by eking out their vegetarian diet with increasing amounts of hunted flesh. The human characteristics of foresight, dexterity and so forth were selected for fast and wily hunters (Blumenschine and Cavallo 1992: 72). This fitted the self-image of being athletic, dominant and male. It is the stereotype of empire builders who are *naturally* ambitious, polygamous and violent.

However, the physiques of *Australopithecus* and early *Homo* were 'unprepossessing'. Females stood about 1.2 metres tall, with males under 1.5 metres. Their long arms and handily curved fingers suggest they still took refuge in trees, escaping predators such as lions, sabre-toothed cats and hyenas. As for tools, even early *Homo* wielded merely rough-hewn scrapers and unworked hammerstones, which were not true weapons (73). Such creatures might only have left the safety of trees to scavenge animal remains left by more dangerous carnivores, perhaps using stones to break open bones to extract marrow. The advent of flaked stone technology about 2.5 million years ago may then have enabled hominids to remove the meat for transporting back to a home base (76). Our ancestors must have

remained primarily *scavengers*, at least until the appearance of the
first *Homo erectus*, about 1.6 million years ago.

So, why the need to stand upright? Margaret Ehrenberg, a feminist
prehistorian, points out that, while an infant chimpanzee can cling
to its mother's body, leaving her hands free for walking or carrying
food, the young of an early hairless hominid would have needed to
be carried.

> ... this seems a much more likely stimulus both to bipedalism and
> to the invention of tools for carrying the infant as well as food than
> is the need to see prey animals over tall savannah grass and to throw
> simple weapons at them, which has been the traditional explanation
> for these changes (1989: 42).

Papers at an international conference in 1966 became the basis
of Richard B. Lee and Irven DeVore's collection entitled *Man the
Hunter*. The meeting was stimulated by recognition that 'hunting
and gathering, as a way of life, is rapidly disappearing' (1968: vii).
But the noble intention of giving value to such people was subverted
by the unfortunate choice of label, 'Man the Hunter'. For the editors,
'hunters' has become merely a 'convenient shorthand, despite the
fact that the majority of peoples considered subsisted primarily on
sources *other than meat* – mainly wild plants and fish' (4). In his
own paper, Lee shows gathering to be more important than hunting,
except at the coldest latitudes (42–3). However, with 'hunter' as
descriptor and 'man' as subject, the book came to symbolise the
extinction of an idea, arousing vigorous responses entitled 'Woman
the Gatherer'.

The scavenging and food-sharing model denies the hunter his
heroics. Instead, in our origins, people seem vulnerable, omnivorous,
opportunistic homebodies. We are scroungers, sharers and socialisers.
In short, we seem like cooks. We start as cooks and, then, in the
original division of responsibilities, men split off as specialised
scavenger–hunters. We can see why women might keep the housework
(given their greater implication in biological reproduction), and thus
men look less like cooks. But the question then becomes: when and
why has the original role been devalued? Why have hunters (and

other subsidiary male workers) been made more important?

I have just noted the promotion of the predatory self-image. To examine this further, take this quotation from the advocate of sharing, Glynn Isaac.

> Among recent human hunter–gatherers the existence of a division of labour seems clearly related to the females being encumbered with children, a handicap that bars them from hunting or scavenging, activities that require speed afoot or long-range mobility (1979: 32).

Words such as 'encumbered' and 'handicap' betray a hunter's slant. Sure, women might agree that they have worked harder for fewer rewards, but it might also be argued that they kept the key job, the housework, for themselves. Men could not plead the same justification for staying home, and were condemned to the lonely and dangerous frustrations of the hunt and war. The women's sharing role is fundamental but male (public) culture diminishes it and shuts it out.

Babies know on what side their bread is buttered. They cry 'ma, ma' – hence 'mama' in numerous languages. Woman is the direct nourisher through umbilical cord and mammary gland. Relatively, man is the appendage, making this the story of Eve and Adam.

According to Genesis 2:23, 'this one shall be called Woman [Hebrew, *ishshah*], for out of Man [*ish*] this one was taken'. However, the concept of 'humans, the sharers' reverses this precedence, suggesting that Genesis should have declared: 'Man is torn from Woman' (*ish* from *ishshah*). Hunting splits off from cooperative foraging.

Time and again in this story, cooks invent processes, which then gain their own force, to the detriment of the originators. Hunters usually demand the better diet, while women stay at home with the basic duties. This defines the 'female', and the public destination of the sub-tasks defines the 'male'. Whether men are 'sent' or 'take' the jobs, to bolster this external authority, they promote a self-image of quick-witted conqueror rather than thoughtful sharer. They portray cooks as looking after mundanities, giving men time for 'civilisation'. This is Man the Ideologue, and the elevation of the 'hunter' is the prototype.

FIRE

Not everyone will view a gaggle of hominids scavenging 2.5 million years ago with stone cutters and bark carriers as cooks. Not everyone will accept hominid food-sharing as cooking. However, everyone recognises embers and enticing aromas. Tending the fire evokes domestic life, as explored in Chapter Four.

The oldest human use of fire has not been pinpointed persuasively. Bones that appear to have been cooked on a wood fire have been found at the Swartkrans Cave, South Africa, in layers dating up to about 1.5 million years ago. Until this, the earliest evidence of the use of fire, dating back some half a million years, was found in the Zhoukoudian caves near Beijing (Renfrew and Bahn 1996: 240). In both cases, the fires would seem to have been kindled by *Homo erectus*.

Further clouding the issue, it is misleading to suggest that people discovered, let alone invented, fire. Fires had been part of the natural habitat well before any of our ancestors came along and, as sociologist Johan Goudsblom points out, have been exploited by many organisms. Birds of prey catch birds and insects fleeing fire. Predators hunt amid the smouldering remains. Herds of deer and bovines venture back to lick the salted ashes. Many animals seek the warm embers at night (1992: 15). The trick is, of course, to control the flame, to domesticate fire.

Food has long been baked in coals or under heated rocks, steamed inside animal stomachs and leaves, boiled in rockpools by heated stones, and so forth. An oven could be as simple as a hole in the ground, or a covering of heated stones. However, improved textures and flavours may not even have been the reason fire was first controlled. People could have employed fire to keep wild beasts at bay, to trap them, to scare them out or to create open grassland, where tender shoots and leaves would be more accessible. People have long used fire to harden wooden weapons, and to keep warm at night. But even these uses, while not cooking in the narrow sense, improve the cooks' supplies, expanding the human niche.

The conquest of fire – found in every known society – implies self-conquest, a fascinating aspect of Johan Goudsblom's deliberations. While the erect posture and the concomitant aptitude for carrying and manipulating objects endow a capacity for transporting burning matter, keeping fire going implies foresight and care. It means self-control, since fire naturally arouses the flight response. It means being able to learn from and obey elders. 'The technical problem was, at the same time, an intellectual and emotional problem, and a problem of social coordination' (18–19).

We can presume that the requirements of caution and foresight are, in the words of Goudsblom, 'so forbiddingly difficult that it puts them beyond the reach of any species but *Homo*' (21). Additionally, we can speculate that humans prevented other species, such as chimpanzees, from developing the ability. The winning species would use its monopoly to ward off rivals. It is possible that 'exclusion from the use of fire may have blocked further socio-cultural development; at the same time, the exigencies of living *with* fire may well have contributed to the singular development of the human capacity for language and thought' (23). The power exercised through fire was quintessentially social – that is, keeping it burning required cooperation, division of labour and reverence, contributing to the human capacity to engage in ritual (40–1). Overall, Goudsblom portrays it as an exemplar of the 'civilising process' of his sociological mentor, Norbert Elias.

According to Catherine Perlès, the attention people had to pay to their cooking would have supplied them with 'the first subtle and intimate knowledge of matter', thus forming the basis for the further development of the empirical natural sciences (Goudsblom 1992: 35). J.D. Bernal writes similarly in *Science in History*: 'Just as the tool is the basis of physical and mechanical science, so is fire the basis of chemical science' (1969: 70). Until recently, nearly all synthetic materials relied on the control of fire – pyrotechnology – not just cooking as such, but hardening wood, firing pottery, glass-making, and smelting and casting metals. Little wonder that the four elements of which the world was said to be composed in ancient natural philosophies are earth, air, water and fire.

The First Rib

Ape-humans came down out of the rainforests equipped with good colour vision and a sense of smell and taste – we might almost acclaim their gourmet palates. They had fine hand–eye coordination and foraged in groups. Further adaptations such as a two-legged gait, bulkier brain and cooperative ways let inquisitive gourmets with creative appetites spread through a decent proportion of the lands.

Whether we find cooks as many as two or three million years ago depends what we look for. We certainly do not find French farm women whipping up an *omelette aux fines herbes*. But we find evidence of a rudimentary culture of food-sharing, which, in the first half of this book, I was at pains to propose was the essence of cooking. We find precursors to the cooks' knives. Then, when women lost their first rib, so to speak, sending men off as hunters, and gathered around the roasting and baking fire, cooks could scarcely be mistaken.

In defining the human essence, people have tried numerous suggestions including original sin, reason, tool-making, increasing brain size and hunting. To bundle up all such attributes, I promote James Boswell's distinction. In a look at our origins, I find cooking to be the missing link.

Developing the still quite animal facility of foraging, these long-lost predecessors were essentially food-finders. They remained within nineteenth-century anthropologist Lewis Morgan's stage of 'savagery', the 'period in which the appropriation of natural products, ready for use, predominated' (Engels 1948: 28–9). In terms of my three elements of cooking – acquisition, distribution and organisation – these earliest ancestors essentially developed the first. It is with the so-called Neolithic Revolution that the next responsibility – distribution – was entrusted to specialists. The means of gathering were brought under greater control with agriculture and stock-rearing, and, along with this, cooks took sharing to a new, urban level.

The complex developments can be encapsulated in one concept: storage. Morgan distinguished the emergence of this state of 'barbarism' by the use of pots (Engels 1948: 25). In these, food could be kept, and boiled. With kitchens, stoves, gadgets and recipes, this became the sort of cooking about which we become nostalgic. It is the farmhouse *omelette* that we consider next.

CHAPTER ELEVEN

The Settled Hearth

Historian J.H. Breasted invented the term 'Fertile Crescent' in 1914 for the sweep of territory flanked by the Tigris and Euphrates in the east and the Nile in the west, the 'cradle' of farming and civilisation. Perhaps the name was overly romantic, but archaeologists have tended to abandon it in favour of compass-based (and misleading) options such as 'Ancient Near East', 'South-West Asia' and 'Middle East'. They also chase all sorts of fascinating developments elsewhere, especially in China, South-East Asia and Central America.

In 1941 prehistorian V. Gordon Childe introduced the idea of the 'Neolithic Revolution' – the time when people stopped gathering and hunting just that day's food, and settled down and grew it. They domesticated grasses, initially where they were plentiful in the wild, and then other crops and animals. They built durable houses. They adopted new social relationships, and came to 'own' land more possessively. Certainly, compared to biological evolution, people moved abruptly from food *procurement* to food *production*. However, under scrutiny, the 'Neolithic Revolution' has proved another overly neat concept. People were not foragers one day and farmers the next. Indeed, agriculture and animal husbandry took many millennia to establish, and in innumerable sites. The prime cause is debated, whether improved climate, population pressure or cultural innovation.

And yet something glorious happened around 10 000 years ago in the fertile arc stringing modern Iran, Iraq, Turkey, Syria, Lebanon, Palestine, Jordan and Israel together.

THE NATUFIANS

The 'Natufians' is the scholars' name – borrowed from a cave in Palestine – for people living from 12 500 to 10 000 years ago at the eastern end of the Mediterranean. The Natufians had a sophisticated range of stone implements, including flint sickles on bone handles and pounding and grinding equipment. For, as well as hunting gazelle, they obtained much of their food from stands of wild grasses. Their environment was so rich in cereals that they were a virtually sedentary people. Experiment has shown that enough wild einkorn (a type of wheat) can be harvested with their flint-edged reaping-knives over three weeks to produce cereal food for a year (Clark 1977: 50). Over the generations, Natufian reapers dug storage pits and established semi-permanent villages. By about 10 000 years ago, they had also begun cultivation, leading the archaeologist Robert J. Braidwood to call them 'incipient agriculturalists' (Redman 1978: 71). They had done the groundwork for the 'neolithics'.

Many sites in the Fertile Crescent are known as 'tells' (from the Arabic for 'hill'), mounds created by the accumulated layers of disintegrated mudbrick walls and cultural debris as new occupants built on the ruins of predecessors. Slicing into ancient villages and towns, archaeologists find that, at the bottom, the earliest structures were small and circular. The strains of grain were wild. Then, in higher layers, the dwelling became rectangular, the grains gained genetic 'improvements' and animals show signs of domestication. The layers let us watch the long 'revolution', a great innovation initially viewed in terms of farming.

Braidwood was drawn to the modest settlement of Jarmo near the Zagros mountains in modern Iraq in the 1950s because the 'hilly flanks' supported the very plants and animals that were later to be domesticated by farmers in the Western tradition. Nowhere else could be found together wild wheat, barley, sheep, goats, pigs, cattle and horses. Nearly 9000 years old, Jarmo consisted of about twenty-five houses huddled together, each with several small rectangular rooms. Clay ovens and the bases for silos were built into each house. The villagers cultivated two-rowed barley, emmer and spelt (two more types of wheat), and peas, and herded and maintained sheep and goats. In such sites, the students of old crop varieties, the palaeoethnobotanists, observe various modifications as grain was domesticated. When wild wheats ripen, the ears 'shatter' so that the seeds fall to the ground, whereas the cultivated versions hold together. Perhaps the fact that non-shattering ears better survived the trip back to the base, where they were spilled and grew, meant they selected themselves for cultivation.

Excavations at Jericho, billed as the world's oldest town, have yielded traces of emmer, einkorn and two-rowed barley, as well as legumes (peas, lentils and horse-beans). Similar species were found at another Natufian settlement, Beidha, further to the south in modern Jordan, with pistachio nuts rounding off the picture. The growing of both cereals and pulses would have provided a balanced diet and continued soil fertility. Animals appear to have been domesticated in a wide area, dogs at least as early as plants, and then perhaps goats and, over the next couple of millennia, sheep, pigs and cattle.

A contributing factor to the rise of early towns was trade. The perhaps 2000 inhabitants of Jericho, which was already fortified around 9500 years ago, apparently extracted salt from the Dead Sea. By about 8000 years ago, Çatal Hüyük on the Konya Plain in southern Anatolia (within Turkey) was unusually prosperous, apparently assisted by trade in obsidian (volcanic glass) from nearby quarries. Obsidian makes very sharp instruments, including sickles.

While neolithic innovations may have spread from the Fertile Crescent through Europe, the Indus basin and Egypt, a separate development, based at first on the cultivation of millet, seems to have taken place in China. Excavators at a site of neolithic millet farmers at Cishan (formerly Tz'u-shan) in northern China have found pit-houses, storage pits, serrated ground-stone sickles, querns (hand-mills) and early ceramic examples of the three-legged cauldron, the *ting*, that can be dated to around 8000 years old. Pigs and dogs were kept, and chickens perhaps first domesticated (Bahn 1992: 104). Roughly simultaneously, another focus in South-East Asia exploited rice. Later, but distinctively, Mesoamerican agricultural life was under way by 4000 years ago with corn and several bean species.

So far in this narrative (compiled from such sources as Braidwood 1960; Leonard 1974; Clark 1977; Bender 1978; Redman 1978; Fagan

1980; Moore 1985; Ehrenberg 1989; McGuire 1992; Bahn 1992; Crabtree 1993; and Renfrew and Bahn 1996), we have not seen the distinct hand of cooks. This cannot happen until we usher women in.

*   *   *

Das Mutterrecht or 'mother right' was the supposed association of the family with the mother, before the invention of monogamy meant paternity could be determined. In the nineteenth century, Swiss historian J.J. Bachofen explained the origin of agriculture in terms of these matriarchs first protecting and then learning to cultivate plants. Early in the twentieth century, in *The Golden Bough*, James George Frazer held that the use of digging-sticks by women, the gatherers, in search of root crops would have increased yields.

Further gains would have come from winnowing seeds on the same ground. The extra numbers being attracted to the productive spot would, inadvertently, have led to permanent settlement. He therefore supposed that 'women have contributed more than men towards the greatest advance in economic history, namely, the transition from a nomadic to a settled life, from a natural to an artificial basis of subsistence' (1912: 128–9).

Women are still recognised as inventing horticultural society. Whatever the precise details, as foragers became semi-sedentary and more intensive in their activities, the gatherers plausibly tended specialised crops. With depleted local game reserves, women might also have kept the first domestic animals, perhaps the young of a mother killed by hunters (the men). Only later, when animals were used to pull ploughs, would men appear to have taken over both agriculture and stock-breeding. However, while women should still be seen as the revolutionaries, cooks settled down *before* cultivating crops, and for a profound reason.

THE NEOLITHIC KITCHEN

Frazer, Childe, Braidwood and others have depicted the gradual settling down of the neolithic in terms of food production. But this emphasis on farming, like the emphasis on 'man, the hunter', proves too male-oriented. We can view this diorama differently. Instead, we can watch cooks at work. We can observe that the key feature of this new fixed hearth is storage. The 'home base' and 'hearth' became a definite kitchen, sheltering foods. The basic neolithic advantage was, not too anachronistically, the cupboard, which opened a Pandora's box of food-sharing opportunities.

Cooks invented food storage, and only then, as support for this, surrounded the kitchen with garden plots and farmyards. Intensive farming was, in a real sense, an adjunct to kitchen containers and appliances, therefore explaining why people settled down before starting to farm. In this culinary revision, primary production becomes part of the activities clustering around the kitchen table.

Prehistoric foragers undoubtedly preserved and stored food, but on a limited, exceptional scale. While women might have used bark trays, skin pouches, woven baskets and string bags to carry plant foods back to base, at the transitional stage, cooks began to make storage the cornerstone of their labours. Initially, they collected wild species, and later grew them. Cropping annually, cereals needed to be stockpiled. Livestock eventually became a form of storage, too, the animals fattened in good times to help survive bad.

In explaining social development in terms of ecology, biologist Jared Diamond sticks to the conventional emphasis on food production. Nevertheless, he finds that the Fertile Crescent offered another great advantage for the domestication of species beyond the large, readily harvested stands of wild ancestors. This was the Mediterranean climate. Many plants, especially cereals and pulses, had adapted to the long, hot, dry summers in a way that made them useful to humans. They were annuals, meaning that they died off in the dry season. Their survival depended on large seeds, which were highly suited to storage (1997: 136).

We are used to thinking of houses as primarily sheltering bodies. However, the originals were scarcely more than stockpiles of staples and processing facilities. My archaeological sources mention semi-subterranean pits, rock-hewn hollows, plastered niches, baskets, bins, basins, troughs, storerooms, silos, granaries. In these, cooks kept seeds, beans, roots, tubers, nuts, dried fruits and so on. This is universal, so that in the first millennium the quite distant lowland Mayan settlements (in Mesoamerica) relied heavily on tree culture, noticeably that of the ramon tree (*Brosimum alicastrum*). Requiring little care, the highly nutritious ramon nuts were stored for up to eighteen months in an underground chamber called a *chultun* (Fagan 1980: 339).

This presentation of storage as central accords with archaeological talk of a number of 'pre-adaptations' for agriculture, such as storage pits and ground-stone tools (Moore 1985: 45). The neolithic shift has also been depicted as part of the long-term technological move from 'implements' to 'facilities'. The former are tools, such as a hand-axe or knife, that transmit kinetic energy. 'Facilities', such as pits and pottery, store potential energy. Reliance on new facilities and heavy artefacts would have encouraged the users to remain in one place (Redman 1978: 86). I go so far as to say that this shift from implements to facilities belongs to the cooks' transference of attention from food acquisition to food storage.

We no longer went to food; it came to us. With storage facilities, we were not just the focussed animal (Latin: *focus*, hearth), but became the arcane animal (*arca*, chest).

THE ARCANE COOK

Once cooks began to store staples, diet became simplified. The preferred species had to be storable, for a start. Seeds and nuts keep themselves, so long as they are safe from vermin. Then, as an increasingly dense population tended to strip the local area clean, the chosen foods had to be reliably cultivated, and so variety was further reduced.

The stockpiled foods generally required tedious preparation. For one thing, cooks had to preserve some by drying, boiling, parching or fermenting. Then, as a rule-of-thumb, kept food needed more work. Seed had to be separated from the chaff. Even after threshing and winnowing, some of the husks remained and these had to be removed by pounding the grain between stones. But while tools used by foragers had to be either light enough to carry or simple enough to be made on the spot, once people were domiciled, grinding and other equipment become much more ambitious and physical. By the beginning of the neolithic era, stone hand-mills, or querns, were standard (Moore 1985: 17).

Cooking (in the sense of heating) was a precondition for agrarianisation. Owing to their high nutritional value and ability to be stored for long periods, grains were appropriate staples; however, they had to be made more digestible. Foods were therefore cooked more, using the basic methods already known.

Sophie D. Coe, a culinary researcher, has complained in exasperation: 'Archaeologists know an immense amount about cooking pots. Unfortunately most of them know little or nothing about cooking. When they find pieces of cooking pots they usually toss them aside as "utilitarian ware", or indulge in typological system-building so involved that no sane cook could possibly recognise her *batterie de cuisine*' (1989: 15). While fascinated by food production and glancing at social nutrition, archaeologists have tended to skim over the actual cooking of the Natufians and early neolithics. Presumably, though, the techniques were basic: many plant species were consumed with little preparation other than peeling, and the catch was still roasted. But it was the preparation of grains that these storing cooks moved to centre-stage.

These cooks could prepare cereals in a number of ways, including germinating, soaking, boiling, steaming, parching and baking. Reay Tannahill draws attention to an old technique in which the cook would set fire to ears of corn and then beat off the kernels so that in one action, the corn was dressed, winnowed, ground and baked (1988: 24). In the Fertile Crescent, I assume that the cooking led principally to varieties of bread and porridge, in scenes not too distant from conditions disclosed in the Latin poem *Moretum* mentioned in Chapter Four.

The inhabitants of Australia are reported to have used seed-grinding stones more than 30 000 years ago. Such an innovation in the exploitation of natural species (part of the so-called 'broad spectrum revolution' thought to precede the neolithic and only going back perhaps 12 800 years in the Fertile Crescent) is said to imply that they made bread (Beale 1996; Fullagar and Field 1997). Such bread could have been baked on the heated ground between parted coals. One modification would be to bake bread in a hole, and another would be to enclose it under a small cover. Settling down with kitchen 'facilities' also includes the possibility of permanent ovens. As already mentioned in Chapter Four, the tannur (tandoor) oven is traced back to the Fertile Crescent over thousands of years.

Writing about *The First Farmers* for a popular audience would seem to have encouraged Jonathan Norton Leonard to notice kitchens, and even that they were 'in many ways the focal point of the agricultural revolution' (1974: 28). He describes an impressive clay oven constructed nearly 9000 years ago at Robert J. Braidwood's site of Jarmo. It consisted of a dome of *tauf* (a coarse mixture of mud and straw, applied in layers) built inside one of the storage spaces. Its fire door opened onto the courtyard and its flue ran up the wall and presumably ended in a chimney above the roof. The cook stoked fuel through the fire door and, after obtaining the desired temperature, raked out the coals and ashes to put in food, and closed the door. The Jarmo oven may also have been used to parch grain to loosen the husks and make the seeds easier to grind (106).

Gastronomic writers (not the least Brillat-Savarin) dilate upon the distinction between roasting and boiling, as epitomised in Homer's spits and Esau's 'mess of pottage'. The not entirely unrealistic simplification is that hunters roast meats, while peasants boil (and bake) grains, beans and roots. According to historian of science J.D. Bernal, relative to the ease of roasting on sticks and baking in ashes, 'boiling represents a real problem'. The first ingenious idea was to heat water in leather buckets or waterproofed baskets by dropping in hot stones. Such stones, cracked by heating and chilling, have been found at prehistoric camp-sites. 'The crucial discovery, however, was that by coating a basket with thick clay it could be put on the fire and actually improved in the process' (1969: 70). This, in fact, is pottery.

Palaeolithic people knew how to make pottery: every fire on a cave floor would have hardened the clay around it. The oldest known intentionally baked clay, in the form of figurines, dates from at least 26 000 years ago (Renfrew and Bahn 1996: 319–20). The Jomon hunter–gatherers of Japan, who were making simple ceramic vessels at least 12 700 years ago (Bahn 1992: 174), lived a more or less sedentary life, stewing their dinner long before they took up agriculture. For Jericho and other digs in the Near East, archaeologists speak of the 'Pre-Pottery Neolithic A, B and C', because neolithic innovations did not rely on pots and, for storage, stone vessels and white plaster sufficed.

Nevertheless, in common use in the Fertile Crescent about 8000 years ago, pottery further standardised the cooks' tasks. Fired-clay jars could hold liquid and also protect from pests (in fact, the arrival of pests presumably hastened pottery). A regular supply of fireproof and watertight containers, easily breakable but as easily replaceable, also made it possible to boil or stew, and there were other uses. Once containers that could hold liquid for long periods were in use, the slower chemical changes of fermentation could be noted and exploited, Bernal argues (1969: 70). Analysis of a red stain inside a 30-litre Sumerian jar from Godin Tepe, western Iran, and dating around 3500 BC is taken as evidence of the world's earliest wine (Renfrew and Bahn 1996: 261).

*   *   *

In summary, then, in their Rousseauean paradise, people just roamed about, plucking nourishment directly from trees. However, neolithic kitchens were the citadels of a culinary revolution based on food storage. Cooks provided a radical change in diet, increasingly replacing the wild with the cultivated and processed.

Where gatherers employed a mental map, showing where to find food in the natural world, storers used recipes to navigate the kitchen repository. While foragers were at the mercy of the natural bounty, settlers adopted the restrictions and the possibilities of the domesticated menu.

In Chapter Six, I outlined the basics of the traditional agrarian meal of staple and sauce. As well as the carbohydrate – bread, porridge, rice, potatoes, yams, and so on – cooks collect and send out for supplements: the ancient Greeks enjoyed *opson* with their *sitos*, and the Chinese combine *fan* and *ts'ai*. With stored staple and varied extras, this was now the cooks' formula. They processed cereals and made breads and porridges. They supplemented these with chopped meats, roots, leaves, fruits, salt and spices. The neolithic era can thus be conceived as the shift to dishes, as cooks transferred their attention from wild foods to ingredients.

After thousands of years fixing the hearth's place within the ecology, prehistoric cooks bequeathed pretty much the legacy of culinary ingredients in use today. Broadly speaking, the main centres of domestication were the Ancient Near East, China and Central and South America. The swag of Fertile Crescent ingredients included barley, wheat, onions, garlic, leeks, coriander, fennel, cabbage, mustard, radish, lentils, peas, chickpeas, dates, goats, sheep, pigs, cattle, geese and ducks (Oppenheim 1977: 42–6, 312–13). In Asia, millet, wheat, rice, coconuts and bananas were important early, along with the mung bean and soybean. In Central American villages, winter squash, tomatoes, avocadoes, beans and corn were staples by around 3500 BC, while Peruvian settlements relied heavily on the potato, and contributed the kidney bean, lima bean and peanut.

THE DISTRIBUTION REVOLUTION

The previous chapter examined cooperative culture and food-sharing at the service of improved gathering. The Neolithic Revolution was accompanied by radically different ways of obtaining food – those that would provide long-lasting staples. Nonetheless, everywhere we look, we see the development of my second 'moment' of cooking, distribution. This was not just hoarding for the immediate household. When food is accumulated, it is readily exchanged for other goods; it can be paid as tax, and so on. This mode of life created all kinds of social and cultural potential, too, as was recognised nearly two centuries ago by that historically literate old authority, Baron von Rumohr. He saw that once people were dependent upon grains and thus settlements, they had the opportunity of preserving the experience of many generations in buildings, works of art and books, and so, he says, of developing abstract ideas (1993: 121).

There was wider sharing, although not equally: far from it. Foragers 'own' very little, and 'own' everything under the sun. When settled, people 'owned' more definitely and selfishly – individual food stores, plots of land, livestock, buildings and equipment. It is possessive capital. Stored foods could be distributed in more formal ways, backing functional divisions and social classes.

Domestic cooks stirred the neolithic pot, which turned on the preparation of stored ingredients. The kitchen was the birthplace of equipment and techniques such as milling, baking, alcoholic fermentation and extraction of oil. Such tasks could become more efficient when taken over by specialists. And, of course, the flip-side of more sophisticated food distribution was the division of labour. Town and country exchanged crafted goods and services, on one part, with raw materials, on the other. One rib after another was now torn from (or given up by) Eve – horticulture, baking, brewing, potting, catering, trading . . . Furthermore, among this differentiation of culinary chores, priests took on many 'reproductive' tasks that ensured the cultural maintenance of society. Soldiers ensured its violent containment. And so, in sharing through storing, cooks constructed civilisation.

THE RISE OF CIVILISATION

Around 3500 BC, settlements in the Fertile Crescent took a serious step in size and ambitiousness, such that prehistorians have spoken glowingly of the emergence of 'civilisation'. Other parts of the world had adopted, or were adopting, permanent hearths, but here was an explosion of truly public facilities – with urbanisation, marked division of labour, distinct social classes, a differentiated political system and a redistributive economy. This initially occurred around the Tigris and Euphrates, otherwise known as Mesopotamia (Greek, 'between the rivers').

British archaeologist Andrew Sherratt has spoken of a 'secondary products revolution' in the middle and late fourth millennium BC. It indicates a shift from floodplain horticulture to a greater reliance on livestock. Instead of domestic animals (goats, sheep, cattle) being exploited just for their meat and hides, they were now also used for secondary products such as milk and cheese, wool and traction (pulling). Sherratt argues that the revolution responded to population growth and territorial expansion of agriculture, which required the penetration of more marginal environments. American archaeologist Peter Bogucki has shown that the age and sex of the cattle and the use of ceramic strainers (interpreted as cheese sieves) indicate dairying as early as 5400 BC, making the 'revolution' another intensification rather than an abrupt dislocation (Renfrew and Bahn 1996: 287).

The plough was a more difficult tool than might be supposed, since it had to be adapted to the nature and condition of the soil. Cattle were used to draw it, and a seeding attachment dropped the seeds into the furrow (Oppenheim 1977: 314). Childe heralds the plough's agricultural revolution.

With two oxen and a plough a man can cultivate in a day a far larger area than can a woman with a hoe. The plot gives place to the field, and agriculture (from Latin *ager*, 'a field') really begins. And all that means larger crops, more food, and expanding population. And incidentally men replace women as principals in cultivation (1965: 122–3).

Food production changed from a small-scale task, which one woman or a group of women could have performed with comparatively little equipment, to a series of complex operations that could be spread among specialists. Turning from hunting, men tended to be more involved in ploughing and herding, leaving women to process milk into cheese and yoghurt.

The wheel was applied in manufacturing industry about 5000 years ago. As Childe explains, with a lump of clay spinning on a horizontal wheel, the potter could shape in a couple of minutes a vessel that would take several days to build up by hand. Given that women were engaged in pottery as a domestic craft, the wheel was another step in culinary outsourcing: 'the potters are now specialists, withdrawn from the primary task of food-production and exchanging their wares for a share in the communal surplus', he writes (124–5).

Another specialist use of the cooks' fire was metal-smithing. The Bronze Age, conventionally taken to span from 2000 to about 700 BC, was when metals were first used for tools and weapons, although casting was well established in the Middle East by 3500 BC. Since tin and copper (the alloy's main ingredients) do not usually occur in proximity, their demand boosted trade significantly. Likewise, in China, the period of bronze use coincided with the stratification of society and state development in the Shang and Chou dynasties of the second to first millennia BC (Bahn 1992: 71). While metallurgy was not essential for the formation of states (as proved by its absence from the early American civilisations), not only did it add to the range of objects worth hoarding, but it also supplied superior weapons for protecting or appropriating these objects. Weapons came to be monopolised by one specialised trade, the warriors.

*   *   *

V. Gordon Childe coined the terms 'Neolithic Revolution' and 'Urban Revolution' as earlier parallels to the Industrial Revolution. Using the less-sensational expression of 'transformation', prehistorian Charles L. Redman embraces both steps towards the full agrarian economy under the rubric *The Rise of Civilisation*. He speaks of an 'Agricultural Transformation' (*c.* 8500–6500 BC), the harbinger of 'subsistence and settlement', and an 'Urban Transformation' (*c.* 4000–2000 BC), representing a 'change in scale and the complexity of societal organisation', such that we might truly speak of cities (1978: 3–5).

The introduction of farming has been described in this chapter, and the subsequent massive innovation of cities will be pursued in the next. Recast in culinary terms, however, they both involve food storage and distribution, and so might be spoken of together. Storage is initially at the level of the household and then the city-state. Rather than each peasant household retaining stores near its own hearth, a more complex social sharing was evolving, based on public storage and distribution. Food-sharing remains an underlying concern in the next chapter, but on a convincingly public scale, directed by temple officials poised on grain stockpiles.

While kin could rely, essentially, on communism – on gift exchange in which any repayment was left open – a city of specialists relies on more formal exchange, initially on what is known as 'redistribution', which leads to money. Among other results, societies became much more socially and politically stratified. Friedrich Engels was alert to the revolutionary implications, and in his study of the *Origin of the Family, Private Property and the State*, published in 1884, he notes that, previously: 'Food had to be won anew day by day'. But when people began keeping livestock (and other stored wealth), they introduced a fatal distinction – private property. The same applies to artistic products, metal utensils, articles of luxury and, 'finally, human cattle – the slaves'. Given that men made themselves the owners of the new sources of foodstuffs, this phase marked, he thought, the *'world-historic defeat of the female sex'*. With the reins of the house seized, the 'woman was degraded, enthralled, the slave of the man's lust, a mere instrument for breeding children' (1948: 54–7). Also, with the first cities – and their accompanying agriculture, mining, transport, deforestation, soil degradation and population explosion – men exploited the natural world with renewed vigour.

Is this always to be the way – that we must remain ambivalent about human success? Some advances in cooking bring social or ecological gains, but often costs, which we might call the culinary tragedy. Anyway, the circumstances were ripe for fine public cooking, with dedicated professionals, extensive recipe collections, and banquets so fabulous that we could scarcely re-stage them today. And we are still speaking of 5000 years ago.

CHAPTER TWELVE

The Temple as Kitchen

The ancient city of Ur in Mesopotamia grew in size and importance during the third millennium BC, becoming briefly the ceremonial centre of an empire, and remaining a key centre of Persian Gulf trade. The city has been thought to be the home of Abraham, the legendary founder of Judaism and also revered by Christianity and Islam. Between 1922 and 1934, British archaeologist Sir Leonard Woolley revived Ur's fame with a joint team of excavators from the British Museum and University Museum of Pennsylvania.

The city of Ur might have had a population of 200 000. The average Sumerian house was a small, single-storey, mudbrick construction around an open court. The well-to-do house of two storeys had a dozen rooms, the ground floor consisting of reception room, kitchen, lavatory, servants' quarters and sometimes even a private chapel. There were low tables, high-backed chairs and beds with wooden frames. People had household vessels of clay, stone, copper and bronze; and baskets and chests made of reeds and wood. Ur had avenues and a public square for promenading as well as feasts. A tumble of large and small houses on narrow lanes surrounded the sacred centre, with temples and ziggurat (Kramer 1963: 88–9).

The ziggurat, towering over Ur as all Mesopotamian cities, was a structure of the same general shape as the pyramids in Egypt, Central America and elsewhere. One of the highlights of Woolley's twelve years of work was finding the ziggurat, built by the Sumerians around 2500–2400 BC and buried inside a later one. The original ziggurat measured about 50 metres by 40 metres at its base and stood well back on a raised terrace, which accommodated religious buildings, and all was enclosed by a highly buttressed wall. Sir Leonard takes us on a guided tour.

Once through the surrounding 12-metre-thick wall and a foyer, with doors leading off to storerooms or service chambers, we face the staircase up the stepped side of the ziggurat. Crossing to the right, we enter a building and come to what must have been an unroofed central court. Its floor is only clay and against a wall stands a raised brick-and-bitumen tank reminiscent of a scullery sink that was probably used for the preparation of food or the washing of utensils. Off the court are two square chambers, each entirely taken up by a great fireplace, square in one and circular in the other, and showing signs of constant use. There are also three large presumed storerooms.

Woolley tells us that this is the temple of Nanna, the eldest son of the chief god, Enlil, and the patron deity of Ur. Yet the archaeologist confesses, 'There is nothing here that suggests a temple; the obvious term to apply to such a building is "kitchen"'. He explains that sacrifices were offered to the god, and:

> the flesh of the votive animal had to be cooked, whether it was roast with fire or seethed in the pot, and the cakes and the show-bread had to be baked, so that a kitchen was an important part of the temple . . . In the present instance we have a kitchen and no temple.

He suggests that the actual house of the god was atop the awe-inspiring ziggurat. It was more convenient for the kitchen to be at the base, and 'only the prepared food would be carried up to be laid before the god' (1954: 104).

This is not the end to it. The building to the left, as one enters the terrace, is similar. Facing us as we go through its central court are two rooms entirely taken up by big furnaces or fireplaces. 'Here then we have a second "kitchen"', Woolley announces (105). This would have been the temple dedicated to Nin-gal, the wife of Nanna, as well as to some minor deities.

Among later structures at Ur described by Woolley is the temple of Enannatum, Nanna's High Priestess, occupying 80 by 80 metres, alongside the wall of the ziggurat *temenos*, or sacred area. The maze of rooms includes service chambers, magazines and a set of rooms comprising the kitchen. In an open court was a well, and by it a bitumen-proofed tank. Against one wall are two fireplaces for boiling water, and against another the brick 'cutting-up table', the marks of the butcher's knife still clearly visible. In a side room is a beehive-shaped bread oven, and in another room the cooking-range, which has two furnaces and circular flues, and rings into which the cauldrons were set. Using local actors, Woolley photographed the kitchen in use. He declares that 'after thirty-eight centuries one could yet light the fires and reconstruct with all its activities . . . just such a kitchen as there was at Shiloh when the Ark of the Covenant was there and the sons of Eli quarrelled with the Israelites over their share of the sacrificial meat' (170–1).

Finding that thieves have left only scattered fragments of decoration at the ziggurat, Woolley remarks: 'Where nothing more survives than a few tattered mud-brick foundations it is not easy to conjure up anything of splendour' (105). He excavated, photographed, measured and lifted the remaining souvenirs and did not find the gods. The superstructure had long since evaporated. But, just as Woolley found, these temples were fundamentally kitchens, out of which emerged the trappings. He gives the impression that the kitchens had been directed at feeding the gods. This is not what really happened at all, of course. The food was really for the people. Despite himself, the excavator of legendary Ur has uncovered an embarrassing truth. In this chapter, I show that, at least in origin, temples are public kitchens.

COOKING FOR THE GOD

In a section titled 'The Care and Feeding of the Gods', cultural anthropologist A. Leo Oppenheim explains that a Mesopotamian god was an image, statue, ikon. It lived in the sanctuary of the ziggurat with its family and was looked after like royalty, being fed, washed and maintained. While usually kept from public view, the image could be seen when carried in solemn procession through the temple compound or certain streets (1977: 186–7).

Oppenheim presumes that the image was believed to consume

the food and drink merely by looking at it. In his reconstruction (based on a later period than Ur), linen curtains were drawn (192), a table was placed before the image, then water for washing was offered in a bowl. A number of liquid and semi-liquid dishes were arrayed on the table, along with beverages. Next, specific cuts of meat were served. Finally, fruit came in what one text describes as a beautiful arrangement. Musicians performed and the *cella* (body of the temple) was fumigated. The table was cleared and more water offered for cleansing the image's fingers. 'Having been presented to the image, the dishes from the god's meal were sent to the king for his consumption', Oppenheim finds. Records remain of the Assyrian kings' pride at having received 'leftovers' from the sacrificial meal (188–9).

The feeding of the god 'presents itself as the very *raison d'être* of the entire institution', Oppenheim notes (188). Beyond that, however, he describes the Mesopotamian temple and (when it emerged along-side) palace as a great household, 'the household of the deity or that of the king'. Each derived its income primarily from agricultural holdings, either directly or through rent and taxes; secondarily from what its own workshops produced; and lastly from the offerings of worshippers of the god, and gifts prompted by the respect for or fear of the king. 'A central administration received all income and disposed of it by redistributing what was not set aside for storage.' King and god alike were surrounded by personnel 'we call courtiers and – quite inappropriately – priests'. The menial work was performed by slaves or, to a much larger extent, serfs (95–6).

The temple typically employed many hundreds of people, sharply differentiated according to occupation, and many working in food production, transport, storage and administration. One long list includes ploughmen, plough-leaders and ox-drivers, herders for various animals and their supervisors, gardeners and their assistants, a striking number of fishermen, several classes of storehouse administrators and subordinates, scribes (each keeping up the paperwork on particular commodities), 'master' and 'ordinary' craftsmen, messengers, teamsters, boatmen, merchants and traders. The processing of primary products was done by bakers and cooks, butchers, brewers and leatherworkers. The preparation of flour (along with the spinning

and weaving) was the task of female slaves (Falkenstein 1974: 8). Each of these, including the scribes, took part of the cooks' larger responsibilities.

The dictionary accepts a temple as a 'building devoted to the worship, or regarded as the dwelling-place, of a god or gods or other objects of religious reverence'. Such a definition – relating to the gods rather than people and their world – tends to marginalise, even disconnect, the temple. Scarcely able to put ourselves into the worshippers' shoes, we experience the temple as an exotic art collection superimposed upon daily activities long buried in dust. But these were not just monuments to inspire citizens; they were political, economic and artistic centres, necessary to the organisation of this more ambitious level of physical sustenance.

The best products of the agricultural holdings, fields and gardens and of the immense herds of cattle, sheep and goats were sent to the temple. These large quantities of beer, bread, meat and sweets, served to the image as required by the daily ceremonial of the sanctuary, became income or rations for the administrators and workers who supervised and prepared the food for the god's table, were distributed to the needy and were stored for future use or trade. Vast numbers of cheap 'bevelled rim' bowls have been interpreted as ration or perhaps, conversely, offering containers (Beale 1978).

To bring the temple back to life, think of it as a kitchen. Consider the priests as elevated cooks, feeding an extended household. Rather than some isolated monastery, the early Mesopotamian temple (and later palace) administered food throughout the society. Imprinting the cooks' duties on a public domain, the temple played a key role in the emergence of civilisation. This narrative does not dismiss the gods. Quite the contrary, it calls them back in.

THE EMERGENCE OF THE STATE

Modern Iraq can lay claim to being the site of the earliest civilisations. Here, in the area of the Tigris and Euphrates, as many as five millennia ago, flourished the Sumerians, followed by the Akkadians, Babylonians, nearby Assyrians, Hittites, and so on. Beyond Mesopotamia, civilisation erupted in Egypt and the Indus valley, and elsewhere in China and, eventually, Mesoamerica.

In seeking the roots of civilisation in and around Ur, prehistorians and historians (as written records become increasingly available) have again come up with a tempting set of explanations, some as simple as the plough (and so agriculture), the wheel and writing itself. At a more sophisticated level, it is only mildly discourteous to quip that German scholars have found public works, British authorities monumental art, the French public ceremonies, Russians class struggle and Americans early business.

V. Gordon Childe has retained a hearing for a 'road to civilisation' interlinking such factors as the aggregation of a significant fraction of the population in cities; the differentiation of full-time specialists; the concentration of economic and political power; the use of writing; and standard weights and time-keeping, and so some science (1951: 161). The idea is that a range of new specialists, contributing at one-step-removed to agriculture, were fed by surpluses raised from primary producers. Irrigation increased productivity, leading to centralised control of food supplies, production and distribution. Taxation and tribute (tax-like contribution to a central authority) led to the accumulation of capital.

In the 1950s, historian Karl Wittfogel made much of the observation that the 'hydraulic states' grew up in fairly hot major river valleys – not only the Tigris–Euphrates, but also the Nile, Indus and Huang He (Yellow River). The rivers provided the means of irrigation, which more than compensated for any lack of rainfall, and of navigation, which enabled the importation of missing resources and the central delivery of foods. The great alluvial plains also provided high yields, thus supporting denser populations but requiring strong management. Canals had to be dug and kept in repair. The water had to be divided according to agreed formulas. 'To ensure this, a power stronger than the individual landowner or even the single community was mandatory: hence, the growth of governmental institutions', explains Sumerian scholar Samuel Noah Kramer. Bolstering this, since Sumer produced a surplus of grain but had practically no metals and little stone and timber, the state needed to obtain these either through trade or force (1963: 5).

Already in 4000 BC, Mesopotamia was a fully agricultural society, with people grouped into villages of perhaps several hundred individuals. Wheat and barley remained the staple crops, now supplemented by dates that yielded not only prodigious supplies of fruit but also wood. Marshes and estuaries teemed with fish, and reeds provided other building materials. Fired clay served for tools until trade was established with surrounding areas. The large herds of sheep, goats, donkeys, cattle and pigs required to feed the masses were now harder to keep, which helps explain why the herds became the responsibility of the expanding temples, and temple officials assumed broader control of the economy, culminating in the Sumerian city-states of tens of thousands of inhabitants. This is described by anthropologist Robert Adams, who made pioneering use of aerial surveys in charting the growth of Mesopotamian cities. With the cities as the setting for storage, exchange and redistribution, the small shrines in the early villages developed into temples, which became a 'complex of workshops and storehouses surrounding a greatly enlarged but rigidly traditional arrangement of cult chambers'. At some point, specialised 'priests' appeared, assuming the role of economic administrators, as attested by ration or wage lists found among the earliest known writing (1994: 13–16).

All in all, as a collective focus of food acquisition, distribution and organisation in the world's earliest cities, the temple took the cooks' responsibilities into the public domain. With great storehouses and dining facilities, the organisation had aspects of agribusiness corporation, bank, marketplace, taxation department, standards bureau, welfare body ... As a focus for sustenance, the temple was at once like a kitchen and like a state, before many institutions had broken off. The Ur ziggurat represented a kitchen elevated over a community, helping to hold it together – a magnified kitchen at the beginning of what came to be termed 'civilisation'.

With the assistance of public gods, the officials encouraged recognition of the temple's importance and authority. They lifted their responsibilities out of the ordinary into a transcendent realm, in which they were experts. To follow sociologist Emile Durkheim, the gods can be interpreted as the priestly deification of social demands. So, when temple officials declare that 'Enlil says ...', it can be translated without much loss of meaning as 'the common good dictates ...', although sometimes it is a sectional interest. Claiming the authority of the great god Marduk, the ruler might equate the 'national interest' with his own.

Kramer provides a translation of a hymn to Enlil, his temple (the Ekur) and his city (Nippur) that can appear as propaganda in favour of priestly food-sharing. The hymn glorifies the god Enlil, 'whose command is far-reaching, whose word is holy'. Like heaven, the temple cannot be overturned. 'Its feasts flow with fat and milk ... Its storehouses bring happiness and rejoicing ... Enlil's house, it is a mountain of plenty.' All the lords and princes bring their gifts to the temple. The king, whom Enlil has called and made high in the land, has directed his offerings, including foreign booty, into the storehouse and lofty courtyards. Without Enlil, the hymn declares, no cities would be constructed, no cattle stalls would be built, no king would be raised, no high priest born, the clouds not yield their moisture, the fish lay no eggs, plants and herbs would fail to grow, the trees not yield their fruit (1963: 120–1).

Anthropologist Audrey Richards observed the same association of chieftains with food supplies among the Bemba of Zambia. She found the big chiefs using food gifts, and the culinary labour of women, to feed an impressive number of officials, workers and visitors. A special granary steward handed out baskets of grain each morning to the senior wives in charge of cooking and brewing. The importance of food distribution to political organisation was epitomised by the institution of *kamitembo*, the sacred kitchen. The new settlement of a chief started with the building and consecration of this kitchen, and the chief's fire burned there and in two other sacred houses perpetually. The institution of the *kamitembo*, the capital's ceremonial centre, illustrates the close association between power and the distribution of provisions. 'The chief owns the food and receives tribute, and the chief provides for his subjects and distributes cooked food to them', Richards concludes (1939: 150). The male, political domain seems so much more important than the humble, female kitchen.

ROYAL STANDARD OF UR

The temples were soon rivalled by palaces, the dominant noble households among those with large staffs and holdings. After the early role of temples in the formation of the state, the palaces took over many functions. And yet, A. Leo Oppenheim writes, nothing is known of any stress between them. 'Apparently the temple organisation was on a steady decline after the Sumerian period, and the palace organisation, grown rich and complex in a territorial state, overshadowed it increasingly.' Now the king was looked after as a god. The palace included a spacious hall, 'perhaps used for official banquets, a purpose suggested by an Assyrian text which contains instructions for such a feast, to be attended by the king and his nobles' (1977: 105).

During his excavations, Leonard Woolley souvenired the so-called 'Royal Standard' of Ur, a pair of mosaic inlays in lapis lazuli and shell. Given that one side portrays the royal chariot with prisoners and three grades of troops, and the other side what appears to be the victory feast, Woolley took it to be a military standard, held aloft before soldiers. 'We actually found it lying against the shoulder of a man who may have been the king's standard-bearer', he adds (1954: 87).

Others have gone along with his military emphasis, perhaps mentioning that the other, so-called 'Side B', shows a royal banquet. However, this explanation has been challenged and the 'standard' is now often said to have been a sound-box for a musical instrument, and at least as much attention paid to the 'Peace' as the 'War' side. The rise of the palace was associated with warfare, and the rise of warfare was linked with the accumulation of wealth, which might have attracted marauding pastoralists, and certainly stimulated the need to secure more raw materials from hostile territory and rival cities. In Sumerian times, political power lay in the hands of free citizens and a religio-economic city-governor known as the *en*. As the threats from other city-states and barbarians became more violent, the war leader known as the *lugal* or 'great householder' came to hold a superior place. Perhaps originally selected from major landowners, the position came to be hereditary (Kramer 1963: 74; Jacobsen 1987: 448–9).

'Agrarian society is doomed to violence. It stores valuable concentrations of wealth, which must needs be defended, and the distribution of which has to be enforced.' This is the dismal depiction by anthropologist Ernest Gellner (1988: 154). In Sumerian, as in many other languages, the word for slave derives from the term for foreigner. They were prisoners taken in war, impoverished nomads or marginal farmers who sold themselves and families into bondage (Hamblin 1973: 94). Taking hostages was pointless to hunter–gatherers, but they provided cheap labour for domestic work in mansions and on agricultural estates in settled societies. To some degree, armies make life safe for cooks, maintaining order across and between the lands – even if pacification readily becomes errant, adopting the internal logic of warfare. In any case, the so-called 'Royal Standard' was originally interpreted back-to-front. The feast was the central activity, supported by military forces.

The king 'pacified' or brought order to territory in many more than military ways, attending to the physical infrastructure and cultural superstructure. 'The King of the Road' proclaims itself to be a self-laudatory hymn by King Shulgi, who ruled in Sumer around 2094–2047 BC. Shulgi regarded himself as a runner, and the hymn describes his marathon from Nippur to Ur, about 160 kilometres, and back, so that he could celebrate two banquets in one day. The king was truly blessed by all the gods, and describes himself as 'the all bountiful' or 'he who multiplies all things'. The hymn also records his transport successes, not just keeping the roads in good repair, but also establishing a network of shady resting spots and inns, where he installed 'friendly folk', so that the wayfarer might find refuge 'like in a well-built city'. Kramer finds in these the 'earliest known prototypes of the Near Eastern caravanserais and the modern motels' (Pritchard 1969: 585). Centrally, however, the monarch took control of food distribution among a stately 'household' based on storage.

STORAGE

As we have seen, the earliest permanent dwellings grew up around food stores, and the village chief gained the biggest herds and silos. Now city-states made storage a political enterprise. Men took the kitchen pantry into the public, decorated it with art, instruction and meaning, and called it a temple (and then palace). With civilisation a miracle of storage-based distribution of all kinds, the secret of kitchen-states was the ability to commandeer, squirrel away and share vast public stockpiles of staples. With the storage-centred town, the tasks could be dispersed to increasing numbers of specialists, starting with ploughman, soldier and scribe. And, at base, the gods' bureaucrats maintained vast granaries, warehouses, flocks and herds.

In the Tigris–Euphrates valley, cities possessed granaries of considerable size. Some were attached to temples, others were situated on the banks of canals or elsewhere. A text from Ur around 2130–2000 BC implies that the commandant of a granary is responsible for 10 930 person-days' payment (presumably of barley) to scribes, overseers, shepherds and irrigators; another text refers to the royal barley, to be returned with interest, received by Lulamu from the canal-bank granary (Wheeler 1968: 35).

Another literate valley system (that is, one having writing) lasted from around 2500 to 1700 BC in what would become West Pakistan and which is known as the Indus (after the river) or Harappan (after the site of its first rediscovery). Harappa was a highly organised city of bricks (many subsequently stolen for purposes such as railroad building). A set of barracks within a walled compound suggests the public employment of workers of some kind. They probably laboured on platforms holding large wooden mortars and long wooden pestles for pounding wheat and barley. This is confirmed by a remarkable group of granaries, each 15 metres by 6 metres and ranged in two rows of six, and all within easy reach of the (former) river. Here, archaeologist Mortimer Wheeler imagines, the 'flow of grain, doubtless the principal source of civic wealth, was regulated and distributed by government officials with their clerks and labourers' (1968: 32–5).

In 1950, Wheeler showed that a structure at Mohenjo-daro, previously thought to have been baths, was in fact the massive base of a huge granary. The podium, originally 50 metres long and 25 metres wide and then enlarged, had criss-crossing passages in the brickwork foundations to ensure ventilation beneath what would have been a massive timber superstructure (43). In both Harappa and Mohenjo-daro, Wheeler supposes, the granaries were replenished by a system of state tribute, and that in some measure they fulfilled the 'function of the modern state-bank or treasury' (35). Incidentally, he also reports that the Harappans kept cats to protect the grain from rodents. The proof is a brick in which the footprint of a cat is slightly overlapped by those of a dog; the depth and spread of the impressions 'indicate the speed of both animals' (85).

Tourists make a pilgrimage to Minoan Crete to marvel at the palace of Knossos and its neighbours. Built around storehouses, the palaces served as the economic, religious and socio-political centres of the most productive territories of the island. The western magazine at Knossos held 420 big jars or *pithoi*, each estimated to have a capacity of 586 litres. They would have held a large part of the area's wine, cereals and olive oil, important for cooking, lighting, cleaning and export (Warren 1994).

In China, excavations at Luoyang, the eastern capital of the T'ang Dynasty (618–906), have uncovered more than 200 subterranean granaries, some containing decomposed millet seeds, and on their walls inscriptions recording the location of the granary, the source of the stored grain, its variety and quantity, and the date of storage (Renfrew and Bahn 1996: 266).

To conclude this 'cook's tour' of the storage foundation of civilisation, the city of Huánuco Pampa was a provincial capital in the Andes on the royal road to the Inca capital, Cuzco. We are speaking of the decades before the Spanish conquistadors landed in Peru in 1532. Inca rulers exacted taxation in the form of labour on state lands and construction projects, including building Huánuco Pampa itself. This city with a floating population of up to 15 000 looked after more than 500 warehouses for the storage of the state's potatoes and maize at an altitude ideal for keeping (but not growing) tubers. The city's enormous plaza (550 by 350 metres) was the 'setting for hospitality raised to the state level'. For archaeologists Craig Morris and Donald E. Thompson, the ceremonial feasting helped 'establish the notion that participation in the state was something more than working in the state's fields or fighting a distant war' (1981: 91). More than that: eating and drinking together was not just a reward but the whole point of the labouring, warring and maintaining the imperial cold store at Huánuco Pampa.

REDISTRIBUTION

Viennese-born economic historian Karl Polanyi speaks of three basic historical modes of economic distribution: reciprocity, redistribution and market exchange (1957: 250–6). Since sharing is the cooks' core responsibility, his categories help our understanding, especially of the magnification of the kitchen into the state, with its specialised labour supplied through public storehouses surmounted by temples and then palaces.

Reciprocity is between roughly equal individuals. It is a gift exchange in that immediate repayment is not expected. It is the fundamental way of sharing sustenance, with appealing overtones of personal obligations and generosity, and limited hierarchy. It continues today within households. Early economies operated entirely at this level; at the same time, through a network of giving, goods such as stone axes and jewellery could be traded over remarkable distances. The modes are by no means mutually exclusive, and reciprocity also continued at the temple and palace level, according to Polanyi, since foreign trade was still largely organised on the principle of reciprocity of gift and counter-gift.

The next mode, *redistribution*, implies a central organisation that appropriates and then redistributes goods. This method – generally through some form of government supported through tribute – enables and generates a greater division of labour and more complex social relationships. 'Redistribution occurs for many reasons, on all civilisational levels, from the primitive hunting tribe to the vast storage systems of ancient Egypt, Sumeria, Babylonia or Peru',

Polanyi writes. The principal mode explored in this chapter, it is also 'demanded by social ideals as in the modern welfare state. The principle remains the same – collecting into, and distributing from, a centre'.

The third type, *market exchange*, implies a marketplace and bargaining relationships. It places a premium on price (often to the detriment of more important qualities). Polanyi argues that the true market economy only began in nineteenth-century England (1944). However, depending on the definition, others have found markets going back perhaps 4000 years (Renfrew and Bahn 1996: 338), and I would presume all sorts of food exchange went on alongside redistribution at Ur and earlier.

Indicative of the complex realities, the typical Sumerian city consisted of three parts. First was the city proper – the walled area containing the temple or temples, the palace with the residences of the royal officials and the houses of the citizens. Next came the 'suburb' or 'outer city' of houses, farms, cattle folds, fields and gardens, all of which provided the city with food and raw materials. Then there was the harbour, the centre of commercial activity, especially that concerned with overland trade. Foreign traders lived in the 'port'; there they kept their stores and were provided for by the tavern-keeper (Oppenheim 1977: 115–16). The chief god in the Sumerian pantheon, Enlil, bore the epithet 'trader of the wide world' and his spouse 'merchant of the world' (Falkenstein 1974: 9).

In a book published in 1959, Russian Assyriologist I.M. Diakon-off demonstrated that the temple was not the only early economic organisation. Free citizens owned a large proportion of the land alongside the temple estates. The free members were organised in large patriarchal families or family communities, these uniting through clans and villages into 'nomes' or 'city-states' (1974: 8). The aristocratic households presumably paralleled temple distribution.

At another level, A. Leo Oppenheim has discussed early evidence for food pedlars in Sumerian texts that speak of persons of low esteem selling roasted barley and of the beer-maker offering harvesters beer for their thirst. Early dynastic lists mention other pedlars selling salt and alkali (used for soap) (1977: 356 n.13). But this still does not seem to account fully for the feeding of the city. 'The

important problem of how the inhabitants of such cities were supplied with food and consumer goods is difficult to solve', Oppenheim
admits. In Mesopotamia, references to markets are rare, and they
seem to have been a late development, stimulated by the extraordinary
size of the cities. The impression is that markets were more at home
outside Mesopotamia, in Elam and Anatolia. Indeed, the Hittite word
for city, *ḫappira*, is etymologically connected with that for market
(128–9). And even a 'free' market needs the support of a central
administration.

LEARNING

In Chapter Eight, I used time-keeping as an example of a tool whose
origins are often forgotten and yet are essentially culinary. As public
'cooks', priests were particularly concerned with seasonal coordination. With highly climatic gods, priests became dab hands at annual
production calendars, their supporting round of festivities, and
astronomy. With festivals, the home of the gods could be seen as a
sanctified place where the common people were guaranteed seasonal
renewal and where splendour symbolised the common well-being.
When the Mesopotamian market square came into being, it set the
seven-day week going.

Another standard-setting role of a central administration is establishing fixed weights and measures. Fragments remain of later copies
of the laws of Ur-Nammu, the founding ruler (2112–2095 BC) of
the Third Dynasty of Ur. Among other achievements, he is credited
with calibrating measurements. 'He fashioned the bronze *silá*-measure,
he standardised the one *mina* weight, [and] standardised the

stone-weight of a shekel of silver *in relation
to* one mina' (Pritchard 1969: 523–4). In
Harappa, distribution relied on standard
weights made of various kinds of usually
cube-shaped stone. They ranged from those
minute enough for a jeweller to use to those
so large that they had to be lifted by a rope
or metal ring. When excavating, Mortimer
Wheeler found the remains of scales to be
disproportionately rare, possibly because

wood was generally used and had long since decayed. The 'constant accuracy' of the weights is an 'illustration of civic discipline' (1968: 83).

Along with such innovations, the first civilisations brought literacy and numeracy, and the emergence of both was associated with the food distribution by the temple. The invention of writing around 3000 BC enabled the keeping of administrative records and the passing of messages over long distances. It also added to the means for transmitting knowledge from generation to generation. Writing, in fact, is a form of storage.

From the overwhelming preponderance of lists of goods, historical sociologist Michael Mann recognises that the world's first writers were not so much interested in epic history as a proper accounting system for gazelles and lambs. 'From this evidence, their temples were merely decorated stores; the inscribers less priests than clerks. But these were important stores, being at the centre of the production-redistribution cycle' (1986: 89).

The 'loving detail and passion for exactitude' of the tens of thousands of tablets uncovered from around 2100 BC 'must qualify the Ur III empire for the title of the first bureaucracy', says British archaeologist Nicholas Postgate. A text from Drehem discloses that during the three years of the reign of Shulgi one department handled '28 601 cattle, 404 deer, 236 wild sheep, 38 horses, 360 onagers [wild asses], 2931 donkeys, 347 394 sheep, 3880 gazelles, 457 bears, 13 monkeys and 1 [unidentified animal]' (1977: 81). Clay tablets were the characteristic writing material of Mesopotamia, and the Sumerians took to impressing their signs with a triangular stylus, leaving a wedge-shaped (cuneiform) mark. Egyptians wrote with reed pen and ink on papyrus and their hieroglyphics (Greek, 'sacred carving') were already perfected in the First Dynasty (3110–2884 BC).

The gods, as guardians of Mesopotamian cities, gave laws to humankind through representatives and these, too, were written down. The lengthy Code of Laws is attributed to Hammurabi, king of Babylon who flourished between 1792 and 1750 BC, and who may have begun the temple often now identified as the tower of Babel. A prologue explains that Hammurabi has brought peace to an extended territory, where he has multiplied the water, cultivation, grain stores and splendid banquets. And his laws were an 'etiquette' for a mighty, society-wide 'table'.

Among numerous matters, including prices for hiring a long list of equipment and tradespersons, the laws decree that if a private soldier or commissary is carried off while on armed service, and his field and orchard are then given to another, his property shall be restored should he return. If an artisan has taken a son as foster child and taught him his handicraft, the child 'may never be reclaimed'. If a landholder has opened his canal for irrigation but has let the water ravage an adjoining field, he shall replace lost grain. When a gentleman has hired a boatman and boat, then the boatman shall make good any freight that he might lose.

A tavern was a place of disrepute. According to Laws 108 and 109, if it is proved that a woman wine merchant has failed to supply the full value in wine, then she is to be thrown into the water. If outlaws have congregated at her establishment 'and she has not arrested those outlaws and did not take them to the palace, that wine seller shall be put to death'. The code sets interest rates, so that if one farmer stores grain in another's house, 'he shall pay five *qu* of grain per *kur* of grain as the storage-charge per year' (Pritchard 1969: 163–78).

THE CUISINES OF ANCIENT SUMER AND BABYLON

Countless ordinary cooks continued their womanly, domestic, peasant-like activities throughout all this, the necessary supports of the loftiest institutions. This is to think of the state as the meeting-point of the society's kitchens, where they come together to produce, store and share on a highly differentiated scale. The temple (with its offshoots) is a socialised kitchen. While the people's cooking might have left few records, we can get some idea from the oldest known recipes.

During the Third Dynasty of Ur around 2000 BC the Sumerians were very conscious of the superiority of their cuisine, French Assyriologist Henri Limet writes. They said that the bedouin of the western desert did not know what civilised life was: they ate their food raw. If you gave them flour, eggs and honey for a cake, they would not know what to do with them. The Sumerian cuisine shared the later Arabic tendency to use spices in large quantities, Limet contends. Our word for cumin comes from theirs. They also shared a taste for garlic and other kinds of onion. Fruits were frequently dried in an oven or the open air to facilitate their transport (1987: 137–9).

Precise methods were used to prepare food, with the general word 'to cook by heating' being *bašālu*. When meat or fish was placed in direct contact with fire (a grill or *ki.ne* was used over the flames), it was described as being 'touched by fire'. Stews and soups were simmered in pots and kettles of various shapes and sizes. Some breads seem to have been cooked in the coals and the Sumerians also used several types of oven. A *du.ru.un* or *di.li.na* was a clay oven, which was preheated before baking bread, as is still done today. If the opening at the top was closed off, cakes and other dishes could be baked (139–40).

Eighteen or twenty types of cheese are among the 800 food and drink terms inscribed in Sumerian and Akkadian on two Babylonian tablets. This number might already seem impressive, but a historian from the Sorbonne, Jean Bottéro, estimates that these are only half the food terms used by the Babylonians, whose civilisation succeeded that of the Sumerians (1985). The vocabulary includes 300 kinds of bread, depending on the choice of flours, spices and fruit fillings, and the addition of oil, milk, beer or sweetener (fruit juice and honey). The breads ranged from 'tiny' to 'very large' and were shaped as a heart, a head, a hand, an ear and a woman's breast.

Unleavened bread was baked on the inside wall of a small upright clay oven or *tinūru*, and also leavened bread in dome ovens. The Babylonians also appear to have refined cooking in liquid. The tablets mentioned above name more than 100 dishes prepared by cooking in water. They are known generically as TU_7 in Sumerian, *ummaru* in Akkadian – soup in English. As well as water, various oils and fats were used as a medium. Two important vessels were invented for boiling: the covered pot, usually made of fired clay, and the open kettle, made of bronze.

The Mesopotamians used several methods for storing and preserving foods, especially drying some fruits and vegetables. The texts mention 'salt beef', 'salt gazelle' and 'salt fish'. They preserved fruits in honey. They made beer and wine, and knew about lactic fermentation. And they prepared a fermented sauce for both kitchen and table use out of fish, shellfish or grasshoppers, like the Vietnamese *nuoc mam*.

Possibly the oldest surviving written recipes belong to the Mesopotamians, dating to approximately 1700 BC. These are three Akkadian tablets in the Yale University cuneiform collection, originally thought to be pharmaceutical formulae, and one so poorly preserved it is not much help. The tablets have revealed a 'cuisine of striking richness, refinement, sophistication and artistry, which is surprising from such an early period. Previously we would not have dared to think a cuisine four thousand years old was so advanced', Jean Bottéro comments.

> All of the features of Mesopotamian cookery point to a serious interest
> in food ... which we are entitled to call gastronomy. They reveal a
> level of technical skill, a professional dedication, actually a complex
> and detailed art practised by the cooks and other kitchen workers.

Assuredly, the recipes belonged to the male cooks of the temple and palace, the *nuḫatimmu*, who existed for the benefit of and under the patronage of the elite. Bottéro presumes that domestic cooks (women) also turned out dishes that, although not quite so complex or varied, were tasty and imaginative.

The best-preserved tablet – YBC 4644 (for 'Yale Babylonian Collection') – takes just seventy-five lines to give twenty-five recipes. Each recipe simply lists the ingredients, the basic steps and the name, which is derived from the chief ingredient or the appearance of the dish. The compressed style makes the recipes seem like *aides-mémoirs* for professional chefs, Bottéro writes, although they would actually have been kept by scribes. The name of each dish is preceded by the generic term *mê*. This literally means 'water', but presumably signifies 'bouillon', 'stew' or possibly 'sauce'. The dishes are usually simmered for a long time in water and fats in a covered pot. In two, however, a type of braising is used in an open kettle. Above all, variety is assured through the many seasonings, frequently garlic, onion and leeks, and possibly mint, juniper berries, mustard, cumin, coriander and others that remain untranslated. Various meals, flours and possibly malted barley are used to thicken the liquids, as sometimes are milk, beer and blood. Salt is mentioned. Twenty-one recipes feature meat as their chief ingredient, and four vegetables. The meat stews include stag, gazelle, kid, lamb, mutton, squab and a bird called *tarru*. There is also a boiled leg of lamb, and spleen stew. Another is thought to be 'mustard stew', as well as 'a stew with salt', 'a red stew', 'a clear stew' and 'a tart stew'. One name, 'Assyrian stew', suggests it has come from the northern part of the country, and another, 'Elamite stew', ascribes it to neighbouring people.

In contrast, the other well-preserved tablet – YBC 8958 – devotes 200 lines to just ten recipes for various kinds of bird, both domestic and game. The recipes indicate many steps, numerous utensils, complex combinations and sometimes as many as ten different seasonings. Translation of the broken and worn tablet is made even more speculative by the complications of the directions, and our unfamiliarity, but one reconstructed recipe, the name of which has been lost, seems to be a way of serving small birds on bread, as some kind of pie (1985: 43–4).

EGYPTIAN PYRAMIDS

'Hail to thee, O Nile, that issues from the earth and comes to keep Egypt alive!' As an exercise, schoolboys in ancient Egypt copied the many verses of the 'Hymn to the Nile', composed maybe 4000 years ago. Supplying birds, fish, trees and so on, the river is 'bringer of food, rich in provisions, creator of all good, lord of majesty, sweet of fragrance'. It is the maker of barley and emmer wheat, so that the temples might be festive, and it 'fills the magazines, makes the granaries wide, and gives things to the poor'. The river provides food, clothing, lighting and the means of trade. It is little wonder that when the Nile rises 'then the land is in jubilation, then every belly is in joy, every backbone takes on laughter, and every [grinning] tooth is exposed' (Pritchard 1969: 372).

In Egypt, by 3000 BC, a singularly impressive ruler, the pharaoh, and his regional governors controlled a series of small city-states, geared to exploit the Nile valley through highly organised irrigation and river transport. The state skimmed off surplus produce from subsistence farmers to pay its officials, soldiers, necropolis workers, and so on. Prominent among the arms of the state were the Granary, which collected and redistributed the 'taxes' of grain, and the Treasury, which handled most other products, such as metals, cattle and perhaps flax.

With their daily ritual, festivals, building activities and estates, Egyptian temples required not so much theologians as administrators. The rituals were centred on offerings and, behind these, lay the 'complex economic organisation of the sanctuaries, with their own domains, transport-ships, store-houses, workshops, and so forth' (Janssen 1979: 508). As I have argued, such institutions hoist the branches of domestic cooking activities into the glare of the public. There is a deal of trumpeting and other carrying on, with the jobs divided up, professionalised, and given higher authority. But the temple – along with the ruling class – is still conducting the three main functions of the cook: getting in the food, sharing it and maintaining its culture.

On the south wall of the Medīnet Habu temple at Thebes, Ramesses III (c. 1197–1165 BC) inscribed what is known as the Offering Calendar, listing the loaves, cakes, jars of beer and at least apparently some cattle to be provided for daily offerings, as well as the monthly feasts and annual festivals. Jacob J. Janssen, an Egyptologist specialising in the New Kingdom, estimates that the daily offerings would be enough to feed 600 families of six to eight adults. A small proportion was presented to the gods on the offering tables in front of the sanctuary, and then consumed by the priests. The bulk was distributed directly to the community (1979: 511–12). At festivals, apart from the actual priests and other temple personnel, a considerable number of people from outside received a share. Janssen has proof that 'part of the population of the West Bank at Thebes was incidentally provided with food by the temples; that is, the temples played a part not unlike the parish-relief boards of the Christian Churches' (515).

The pyramids are 25 million tonnes of quarried limestone laying to rest just three pharaohs in relatively insignificant and claustrophobic burial chambers, along with outbuildings, walls and an impressive track for hauling vast blocks of stone up from the Nile. As Kurt Mendelssohn puts it: 'The pyramids of Egypt are immensely large, immensely ancient and, by general consensus, extremely useless' (1986: 9, 196). They might be explained as the burial places of tyrannical rulers whose obsession for immortality compelled them to whip human ants to exhaustion. However, as a physicist who came late to Egyptology, Mendelssohn believes the exertion must be explicable, and his *Riddle of the Pyramids* leads the way to a more culinary explanation. While the pyramids might not be described as 'kitchens', they played a part in the construction of the public 'household'.

Herodotus was told (admittedly 2000 years after the project) that 100 000 men laboured for three months annually, presumably during the flooding of the Nile when no agricultural work could be done. Employing simple assumptions, Mendelssohn confirms the need for a seasonal and essentially unskilled workforce of 70 000, on top of about 10 000 permanent artisans. The feeding, clothing and upkeep of this colossal army for part of each year must have revolutionised the pattern of life of the whole country. A large section of the working population came under the jurisdiction of the central administration, instead of their tribal council and village elders (142–5).

Mendelssohn assumes that work was essentially voluntary. Tally marks give the teams names as 'Boat Gang', 'Craftsmen Crew', 'The Powerful White Crown of Khufu' and the like. Some, such as 'Vigorous Gang' and 'Enduring Gang', seem to imply pride and competition. Even beyond religious and nationalistic motives, Mendelssohn points out that 'even 5000 years ago the provision of food by a central authority may have given villagers a new and much-needed sense of security'. Large government grain stores protected against fluctuations in the Nile inundation. 'Altogether one begins to wonder whether esoteric religious concepts were really more important in bringing about the Pyramid Age than such down-to-earth issues as assured food supply and a new dimension in neighbourliness' (148). 'What mattered was not the pyramid – it was *building* the pyramid', Mendelssohn decides. But it was shortlived, the main work occupying little more than a century because the centralised state had been attained (196–8). The business of state-formation would not have been as deliberate as that. Still, to twist Mendelssohn's argument into another shape, the massive task of building pyramids erected a public kitchen over the private ones.

*   *   *

Like the previous one, this chapter has jumped upon an important platform in the cooks' history, the opening-up of food-sharing based on storage. This was done in the household and then in the extended 'household' of larger groupings. It is the level from which the great cooking traditions of the world would grow. I have attempted to make a provocative point, that the numerous professionals around the early temples and courts were, in a manner of speaking, specialist cooks. The effort of feeding the state administration might be disregarded as 'merely' supportive, while priests, warriors, aristocrats and artists set about their more 'important' activities. However, I treat those higher tasks as, in fact, subsidiary to the central push, cooking – public cooking. The officials extracted food from peasants and dependants and redistributed it on an exalted scale. This was still the work of cooks, fancy cooks. As is now to be canvassed, the regal banquet remained the very heart and soul of the state, at least until recent times.

The earliest cooks, as gatherers, were preoccupied with food acquisition. These last two chapters have seen the cooks' central task, food distribution, extended essentially through storage. The temple/palace, towering over the earliest city-states, with formalised rituals, social hierarchy and male bias, is an expanded household that endeavours to incorporate the rest of society. There is one comparable revolution remaining, the intense differentiation of the cooks' third responsibility, food organisation. Traditional methods, which are essentially followed for their own sake, have been replaced over the past couple of centuries by the scientific. Both food and jobs are now shared so widely that we are directly dependent upon the entire world. It might seem paradoxical, but this is also the backdrop to the creation of the individual palate, as each person becomes a sovereign cook. We can, potentially, eat like kings and queens, which is enough said to lead into the next chapter.

CHAPTER THIRTEEN

Sovereign Consumers

Trimalchio is the fictional host of the notoriously misjudged feast in the *Satyricon*, the ancient Roman prose and verse romance by Petronius. In the long 'Dinner with Trimalchio' section, the impossibly wealthy landowner comperes a parade of spectacularly silly dishes, loudly interspersed with entertainment.

To show knives as centrepieces of society in Chapter Seven, I described Trimalchio's exuberant carvers 'slashing' at a great platter of meats and then a whole boiled calf. In another of the production numbers, a circular tray matches foods to the signs of the Zodiac – over the Heavenly Twins, testicles and kidneys; over Libra, a balance with a tart in one pan and a cake in the other, and so on (Petronius 1977: 51). Attendants let dogs loose to announce a huge wild boar surrounded by little piglets of cake. A hunter pulls out a knife, lunges at the boar's side and out flies a flock of thrushes. Fowlers catch the birds (54–5). In the early hours a cock crows; Trimalchio has it fetched and popped in a pan (84).

While the *Satyricon* has sometimes been quoted as if it is a straight depiction of Roman decadence, Petronius has set out to satirise *nouveau riche* vulgarity. Trimalchio yearns to 'add Sicily to my little bit of land' so that he can then sail to Africa without leaving his own property (62). Combining coarseness and cunning, this billionaire produces scales just to show he had not lied about the weight of a bracelet (78). He boasts that his monument is to be inscribed: 'HE LEFT AN ESTATE OF 30 000 000 AND HE NEVER HEARD A PHILOSOPHER' (83).

Trimalchio desperately wants to 'display some culture at our dinner' (53). But this philistine prefers his art in the form of acrobats and horn-players. With troupes of servants, and numerous entertainers, it was 'more like a musical comedy than a respectable dinner party' (48). The host drunkenly humiliates his wife, abuses unknown servants, tells weak jokes, plays pranks, and shames great shifts of cooks. My visiting angel should take a closer look at the *Satyricon* – it's a great read. Even more intriguing than the fictional party, however, is the real-life story behind it.

The satirist is thought to be Titus Petronius Arbiter, who died stylishly in 66 AD. After the increasingly decadent Emperor Nero ordered his arrest, Petronius got in first, severing his own veins. Nonetheless, according to Roman historian Tacitus, he had his wounds bound so that he might chat and listen to friends recite light lyrics and frivolous poems. Then, 'he appeared at dinner, and dozed, so that his death, even if compulsory, might look natural'.

After an early government career, Petronius had turned to his chief talent, the pursuit of pleasure.

> He spent his days sleeping, his nights working and enjoying himself. Others achieve fame by energy, Petronius by laziness. Yet he was not, like others who waste their resources, regarded as dissipated or extravagant, but as a refined voluptuary. People liked the apparent freshness of his unconventional and unselfconscious sayings and doings.

When admitted into Nero's intimate circle, he earned the unofficial title of *arbiter elegantiae* – 'arbiter of taste'. Tacitus explains that 'to the blasé emperor nothing was smart and elegant unless Petronius had given it his approval' (1971: 389–90).

In 59 AD, Nero established a literary circle, which went into session after dinner. More than one future emperor belonged, as did the poet Lucan and other writers. 'To philosophers, too, he devoted some of his time after dinner, enjoying their quarrelsome assertions of contradictory views. There were enough of such people willing to display their glum features and expressions for the amusement of the court', snipes Tacitus (321). Scholars suspect the *Satyricon*'s comic sketches, racy poems and occasional reflections on philosophy and art were written for this group.

But why ridicule banquets for a group devoted to some of history's biggest? Not offended by great culinary extravaganzas, Petronius objected, I presume, to them done badly. His crass fictional host – whose wealth and power almost matched Nero's – misunderstood his responsibilities. And do not dismiss the responsibilities: an *arbiter elegantiae* such as Petronius played a pivotal role in government, as did such banquets.

In this chapter, I place fancy dining at the heart of the regal enterprise until recent times. As a little boy at a magnificent parade, I expose the emperor as a kind of over-arching cook, whose assistants are numerous and household is estate-wide, even imperial. A tyrant such as Nero was not just a spoilt individual, but at the apex of the state as extended kitchen. As landowner, tax-collector, trader, defender, law-maker, social worker, patron of the arts, and factory chief, the ruler was a courtly cook who expanded the acquisition of food, its distribution and maintenance to a higher level.

Nero became a self-parody, but the ancient Roman emperor was the *chef* (French, 'head' or 'chief') of a vast military–agrarian kitchen based on oil, wine, grain and salt and legions at the frontiers. The sophisticated administration, long-distance trade and cosmopolitan mobility brought spices from China, South-East Asia, India, Persia, Arabia and East Africa. Keeping in touch with culinary opportunities, he retained a small circle of culinary experts, who gathered in a less democratic version of the Athenian symposia, sampling, in one banquet reported by Tacitus, marine animals from the ends of the earth (1971: 362). Nero was even said to have been served the last stalk of an extinct Libyan spice, silphium (Dalby 1996: 140).

MORE BANQUETS

King Solomon's wealth and wisdom attracted the Queen of Sheba, who came with a great retinue, camels bearing spices and gold and precious stones. Her reaction to what she found? 'Not even half had been told me' (1 Kings 10:1–7). The ruler of ancient Israel from approximately 961–922 BC, Solomon was the patriarch of a vast household, the palace's normal daily provisions being 'thirty cors of choice flour [a cor being a volume equivalent to 229.7 litres], and sixty cors of meal, ten fat oxen, and twenty pasture-fed cattle, one hundred sheep, besides deer, gazelles, roebucks, and fatted fowl' (1 Kings 4:22–3). Twelve officials across Israel, presumably from the twelve tribes, sent supplies – 'each one had to make provision for one month in the year' (1 Kings 4:7). To support this vast household, Solomon built storage towns, chariot towns and cavalry towns (2 Chronicles 8:4–6).

On a sandstone block outside his throne-room, the Assyrian King Ashurnasirpal II (883–859 BC) proclaims: 'I organised the abandoned towns which during the rule of my fathers had become hills of rubble, and had many people settle therein; I rebuilt the old palaces across my entire country in due splendour; I stored in them barley and straw'. He built many temples, a canal through the mountains for irrigation, and fabulous orchards. During his conquests of many countries, he made comprehensive botanical collections that included the date, olive, pistachio, pomegranate, fig and grape.

Most spectacularly, Ashurnasirpal built his palace in Calah (modern Nimrud). The inaugural banquet required vast quantities of food (the sheep, doves, various fish, eggs, loaves, jars of beer, skins of wine and much more were listed in lots of 10 000). For ten days, the king feasted 47 074 men and women from his own lands, 5000 delegates from neighbouring territories, 16 000 inhabitants of Calah and 1500 officials from his palaces, sending them home 'healthy and happy' (Pritchard 1969: 558–60). Ashurnasirpal might be viewed as a tyrant going on a binge, or as a high-level cook.

Such extravagant banquets were widespread in the ancient world. Athenaeus reports on a wedding feast in Macedonia in the third century BC that could have been a model for Trimalchio 300 years or so later. Taking their places, the guests were presented with silver cups to keep as their own. Mountains of food were pressed upon them, sufficient to distribute to their slaves standing behind. After musicians, dancing girls and drinking, a large pig was carried in, its belly disclosing numerous birds and fishes. After more drinking, guests were presented with a piping-hot kid, with another silver platter to keep, as well as spoons of gold. Naked women tumbled among swords and blew fire from their mouths. One of the guests, Hippolochus, discloses that they left 'quite sober – the gods be my witness! – because we were apprehensive for the safety of the wealth we took with us' (Athenaeus 128a–130e; 2: 91–101). We need a clearer understanding of what such lavishness means.

WHY BANQUETS?

Ascetics have a ready response to such shows of wanton affluence: they are a sign of moral deterioration. With more sociological sophistication, in *The Theory of the Leisure Class*, Thorstein Veblen draws attention to 'conspicuous consumption'. At costly entertainments, competitors are not only brought in as witnesses, but also to help consume the excess of good things (1899: 75). At banquets coming to a peak at the Versailles palace of Louis XIV and lasting until Charles X, French monarchs ate in state – that is, 'with all due ceremony' and watched by their subjects. Yet with hunger widespread outside the palace walls, for a monarch to eat lavishly was a sign of dominion. 'Banquets were designed to impress subjects' eyes as much as to fill royal mouths', historian Philip Mansel finds (1994). Or, as Reay Tannahill puts it, the royal banquet was an 'important item in the public relations budget ... a political and social statement that had only the most incidental connection with gastronomy' (1988: 80).

As well as impressing guests, banquets are said to appease the gods, express social alliances and develop visual aesthetics. But deferring to 'important' things such as religion, art, politics and economics scrapes cooks' concerns to the edges. Monarchs were *chefs* at the heart of a redistributive economy. Nothing is more basic than being well fed, and so power is directed at that task. When monarchs organised irrigation works, opened trade routes, maintained internal order, they had an eye to the menu. When their armies marched on foreign fields, they recruited new ingredients, recipes and cooks. When their artists and artisans constructed sumptuous palaces, they set off the tables. When courts wove an intricate etiquette of wit and delicacy, they engaged in the most central of activities, improving the meal in its endless artistic, organisational and tasteful refinements. These were culinary empires, cooking courts, charismatic kitchens.

Norbert Elias points to court society's double face.

On the one hand it has the function of our own private life, to provide relaxation, amusement, conversation. At the same time it has the function of our professional life, to be the direct instrument of one's career, the medium of one's rise or fall, the fulfilment of social demands and pressures which are experienced as duties (1983: 53).

Even more profoundly than Elias suggests, the courtiers made private life public. They extended the *oikos*, admittedly to a privileged hierarchy, by tying together new acquisitive, distributional and organisational shapes. Changes to high culture no doubt had an influence on time-honoured practices at more humble hearths. But the dependency still went largely the other way: the courts exploited everyday activities, common knowledge and ordinary women cooks and men labourers. Like the temple-states before them, the palaces made up their grand or 'political' households from the mass of little households beneath them.

This is not to deny that many rulers actually fell for their own pomp and ceremony, over-reached their military ambitions, and attained genuine heights of decadence, but the effective prince kept in touch. The ruler cultivated a lively circle of intimates who ordered luxuries from the known world, rewarded the innovative cooks and scolded failures. They set the agenda for law-making, cultural collecting and chic. This was gastronomic government.

'History has not failed to record, one by one, the battles, victories, and defeats of nations which no longer exist', chides nineteenth-century chef Alexis Soyer. 'But, after all, neither heroes, soldiers, nor people, can be always at war.' Mainly, people have been active with the 'prose of life . . . the business of life – eating and drinking' (1853: 4). Conventionally, historians have shown more attachment to the insanities of warfare than to the 'waste' of fine feasts. If history is to be told in kings, battles, architectural styles and technological triumphs, this ought to be within a culinary context.

THE PERSIANS

The ancient Greeks were scandalised by the luxury of the Persians, whose kings wintered in Susa, summered in Ecbatana, spent autumn in Persepolis, and the rest of the year in Babylon. The 'golden' or exceptionally pure water of seventy bubbling pools of the Choaspes river was reserved for the king and his eldest son; anyone else drank it on penalty of death. The country was scoured for something the king might like to drink, and 'countless persons devise dishes which he may like to eat'. As well as providing foods done in the traditional ways, slaves worked on both new edibles and methods. According to more than one source, the king offered a large reward for anyone who invented a delicacy (Athenaeus 144bf, 513ef, 515ac, 539b; 2: 159–61; 5: 311, 317, 437–9).

One thousand animals were slaughtered daily for the Persian king's breakfast – horses, camels, oxen, asses and deer among them. The many birds included giant Arabian ostriches, geese and cocks. The so-called 'king's dinner' might thus appear prodigal. However, he treated a vast number of guests, who spent half a day in washing and getting dressed beforehand. At festivals, everyone dined in the great hall, although usually some guests dined outdoors in public view. Even those indoors were housed separately from the king, who could observe them through a curtain. After dinner, eunuchs would summon about a dozen drinking companions for the king, but even they would have to sit on the floor and could not enjoy his wine. Only moderate portions were served to guests, who took leftovers home to their households – Persians of high rank typically kept their slaves this way. In fact, the elite preferred to go to court for breakfast, so that they might entertain their own guests afterwards (Athenaeus 145a–6a; 2: 161–5).

A visiting Persian king would expect a town to put on a punishingly expensive dinner, as a form of taxation, in proportion to its population. Herodotus records that when King Xerxes, who was marching through Greece around 480 BC, was to spend a night in a town, the people distributed stores of grain and worked for months making flour. They bought and fattened the best cattle, fed up their fowl, and ordered gold and silver cups and mixing-bowls. This was just for one dinner, with the table adornments going to the king's immediate circle, and much of the food to Xerxes's army. The royal party 'pulled up the tent next morning, seized the cups and table-gear and everything else it contained, and marched off without leaving a single thing behind'. With towns being bankrupted like this, a citizen of Abdera urged his compatriots to visit the temples and give thanks that they had been spared half their troubles, because Xerxes was not in the habit of taking a morning meal and therefore *two* dinners a day (7.118; 1972: 480–1).

On his retreat from Greece, Xerxes is said to have abandoned both the battle and his tent. When his Spartan vanquisher, Pausanias, saw the embroidered hangings and decorations in silver and gold, he ordered the Persian bakers and cooks to prepare a meal. He also had his own servants do a Spartan dinner. Laughing at the difference, Pausanias invited the Greek commanding officers to examine the two tables, saying, 'Gentlemen, I asked you here in order to show you the folly of the Persians, who, living in this style, came to Greece to rob us of our poverty' (9.82; 609).

When Alexander the Great captured Darius III's household at Damascus in 330 BC, Parmenion recorded the following: 'I discovered concubines of the king who played musical instruments, to the number of 329; men employed to weave chaplets [garlands], 46; caterers, 277; kettle-tenders, 29; pudding-makers, 13; bar-tenders, 17; wine-clarifiers, 70; perfume-makers, 14' (Athenaeus 607f–608a; 6: 277). 'Flute-girls and harp-girls' are the largest single category, but when caterers are supplemented by the kettle-tenders and so on, the food specialists total 406. All in all, from Greek reports, the Persian kings were prodigious exponents of the three core culinary functions: acquisition, distribution, organisation. They gathered from far and wide through plunder, tax and tribute. Then they allocated provisions among tiers of dependants and guests. Throughout, they set standards both for the court and the wider culture. In league with their big domestic staffs, the aristocrats tried new dishes, invented new desires and planned further triumphs.

From a Greek philosopher's viewpoint, according to Plato, an autocrat is actually a slave to base and never-ending appetites. The search for satisfaction becomes an obsession, leading to crime. This makes the tyrant the unhappiest man of all (*Republic* 562a–580c; 1974: 381–403). Nicknamed the 'High-Liver', Polyarchus responds that, as the most powerful people, kings are the most free of all to do what is natural, and they can be seen to follow bodily pleasures. We, too, should go along with nature's bidding, and not subjugate the appetites. 'But lawgivers, in their desire to reduce the human race to one level and to bar every citizen from luxury, have caused a class of things called virtues to bob up', he complains (Athenaeus 545a–546c; 5: 469–75).

'Magnificence' (*megaloprepeia*) is one of the 'virtues' at the basis of Aristotle's *Ethics*. Taking the middle ground, he declares that magnificence is the mean between pettiness and vulgarity. The petty man will spoil the beauty of an effect by skimping and fretting; the vulgar man directs an 'ostentatious outlay in wrong circumstances and in a wrong manner'. Magnificence requires style. 'The magnificent man is a sort of connoisseur ... his outlay will be large, and appropriate ... he will spend gladly and generously, because precise reckoning of the cost is petty.' We do not speak, he says, of the excellence of a possession, such as gold, but the excellence of an achievement, such as entertaining the whole city at a banquet. Magnificence need not be public; it is also displayed in 'private' occasions such as a unique wedding (1122a–3a; 1976: 149–52). Ancient cities and estates relied on redistribution through temples and courts and the 'euergetism' (good deeds) and charity of wealthy employers (Veyne 1990). Magnificence lifts generosity – a core quality of cooks – to a high art.

THE ABBASID COURT

Situated in the cradle of civilisation, Baghdad became a great city under the Abbasid line, which held sway in the years 749–1258. The caliph or ruler was surrounded by several *nadims*, or 'boon companions', *nadim* relating to 'to drink with'. Under the early Abbasids, the *nadims* were kept at a distance from the caliph, with a curtain separating them at meals (as with ancient Mesopotamian gods and Persian kings). However, caliphs increasingly joined in literary and drinking sessions (alcoholic drinks originally being favoured within Islam).

In medieval Islam, people of artistic and intellectual talent depended on the court. From the gaggle of tutors, literateurs, astrologers, physicians, singers, dancing girls, and so forth, a group of *nadims* were given a permanent court position, a salary often higher than that of judges and theologians, and additional rewards, including territory to administer and exploit, writes historian Anwar G. Chejne (1965). With officials as rivals, one of them, a secretary, boasted to a *nadim*: 'I am a help and you are a hindrance; I am for eagerness and you are for jest; I am for hard work and you are for leisure; I am for war and you are for peace'. The *nadim* retorted: 'I am for well-being and you are for trouble; I am for companionship and you are for service; when you get up I sit down; and when you are angry I am friendly'. The eleventh-century ruler Ibn Iskandar wrote in a guide to his son: 'But if you regard the purpose of such companionship to be no more than eating, drinking, and jesting . . . that is the conduct of worthless people'. In fact, they did not merely eat, drink and make merry; they planned it. These were serious diners with a detailed knowledge of cooking and its requirements. In the ninth century, Al-Mutawakkil awarded a *nadim* 100 000 dinars for the preparation of a meal he liked, but, to avoid criticism, ordered that the sum be paid in instalments.

The first Arab cookery book, *Kitab al-Tabikh*, was written by a *nadim*, Abu Ishaq Ibrahim b. al-Mahdi (779–839), a renowned poet and musician as well as caliph briefly. The names are known of ten of his contemporaries, including later caliphs, who also compiled recipe collections. Furthermore, writes historian David Waines, each work represented 'no mere court cuisine . . . It was rather the collective possession of a cosmopolitan leisure class . . . In a word, the cultural revolution of 9th century Iraq . . . spawned a gastronomic "new wave" whose influences were soon felt throughout the Abbasid empire' (1984).

Baghdad's gourmands were blessed by a remarkable 'green revolution', which followed the rapid spread of Islam in the seventh and eighth centuries (Watson 1974). This 'revolution' was based on the arrival of new crops (such as rice, hard wheat, sugar cane, watermelons, eggplants, spinach and lemons), increased cropping (four times or more over a two-year period when there had previously probably been only one harvest), vastly developed irrigation, the strength of one language and a sophisticated culture with footholds in three continents, and impressive libraries and botanic collections. Baghdad became, in the words of a contemporary, 'the market to which the wares of the sciences and the arts were brought, where wisdom was sought as a man seeks after his stray camels, and whose judgement of values was accepted by the whole world' (Waines 1984). In such a context, we ought not sideline gastronomic fascination as some fringe benefit of a literate elite amid abundance, because it belongs to and helps drive that entire process. The Abbasid *nadims* executed government from the table for the table.

*   *   *

In pre-industrial societies, powerful people knew and cared about cooking. While departmental officials no doubt belittled culinary affairs to serve their own interests, rulers were yet supreme cooks, *chefs de cuisine*. Certainly, they took on the organisation rather than the labour, but think of courts as the centres of the redistribution of food, tasks, wealth and ideas. Far from irrelevant indulgence, palatial dining created a thriving state. As an example of this, the *Ain-I-Akbari*, the classic manual of the statecraft of the Mughals, who arrived in northern India in the first half of the sixteenth century, includes a recipe section (Appadurai 1988: 13).

The separation between eater and cook is, on the face of it, nowhere wider than between ruler and culinary minions. But stark differences in social status tend to obscure close working links. The most exalted monarchs were still only two or three steps from the soil – through officials, cooks and peasants. In spite of the social divide, many top cooks tended to come from the lower ranks. Innumerable peasant boys took the whiffs and wisdoms of village life to the cities. Humble cooks rose to the highest positions. Relying on the wider horticulture and food crafts, as well as the genius of the people, courtly banquets arrived through the 'tradesmen's entrance'. All this can be confirmed from the Chinese experience.

CHINESE CULINARY COURTS

In terms of antiquity and richness, the Chinese culinary tradition must come close to being the world's greatest (another broad contender is the Middle Eastern). Indicative of a consistent appreciation of the links between good cooking and good government, the first text of Taoism, the *Tao Te Ching* of Lao-tzu, contains the famous line: 'Governing a large state is like cooking a small fish'. In other words, excessive handling will ruin the fish or state. But the necessary culinary skills of governors go well beyond that.

The first documented Chinese civilisation was the Shang Dynasty more than three millennia ago. Cultivation was primarily by digging-sticks and hoes, and yet it was a complex agricultural society calling for an urban capital, a literate bureaucracy, the first Chinese calendar, and great bronze castings. The famous cook I Yin, or the Governor of I, was discovered and appointed prime minister by the founder of the Shang Dynasty, Emperor T'ang. His reputation is demonstrated by a long passage in the *Annals of Master Lü*, in which I Yin discourses at length on 'perfect flavours'. He begins by classifying animals that provide meat into three categories: denizens of the water that smell fishy, predators of flesh that smell gamey, and grass-eaters that smell goaty. The cook corrects these with the five flavours (salty, bitter, sour, hot and sweet) and the three materials (water, wood and fire). The food is cooked for a long time but is not ruined. It is sweet but not sugary. It is fat but not lardy. 'The transformations in the cauldron are so utterly marvellous and of such subtle delicacy, the mouth cannot put them into words, and the mind cannot comprehend them', the great cook concedes (Knechtges 1986: 53).

I Yin recites an enormous list of delicacies from all parts of the kingdom, including orangutan lips, yak and elephant tails, flying fish, oranges from the banks of the Yang-tzu, pomelos from Yün-meng, and water from the springs of the K'un-lun. He tells T'ang that the only one qualified to obtain these things, which would have to come as tribute, is a Son of Heaven (emperor). However, one cannot become a Son of Heaven by force. One must first understand the Way and perfect one's moral character. 'Once the Son of Heaven is created, the perfect flavours will all be supplied' (53–4).

Through his prime minister, the emperor unites the whole of creation, drawing the culinary strings together, tuning them in perfect harmony to satisfy not just physical hunger but an aesthetic sensibility nonetheless tied directly to the peasants and the land. The emperor is at the peak of a hierarchy of perfected dishes, professional chefs, finely adjusted trading networks, exact gardening, careful cultural practices. As with I Yin, who arrived at court with cooking tripods and meat stands on his back, top professional cooks were often 'of the people'. Their genius recognised, they brought with them village experience. They kept contact with merchants and the daily market. Typically male, they had studied at their mother's table.

The next dynasty, the Chou (*c.* 1027–256 BC), was the classical age of Confucius, Lao-tzu and Mencius. Since the most ancient Chinese literature, the art of good government has been compared to the perfectly blended stew, and two Chou texts, *Tso chuan* and *Mo Tzu*, refer to the *ting*, or cauldron, as the prime symbol of the state (Chang 1977: 11). In a passage in the *Tso chuan*, the statesman Yen-tzu declares:

Harmony may be compared to a stew. Water, fire, vinegar, meat pickles, salt, and plums are used to cook the fish fillets. It is heated by means of the firewood. The cook blends the ingredients and equalises them by taste, adding whatever is deficient and decreasing whatever is excessive. His master then eats it and thereby composes his mind. The relationship between lord and vassal also is like this ... when the administration is composed and unobtrusive, there are no contentious hearts among the people (Knechtges 1986: 51).

The *Rites of Chou*, an idealised prescription for the administrative system, compiled perhaps around the third or fourth century BC, lists the following officers of the royal household involved with food and drink: 152 masters of viands, who supervised the planning and prep-aration of meals for the king, the consorts and the crown prince; 70 butchers; 128 court cooks; 128 outer cooks, charged with preparing the sacrificial offerings and food for the military guard and guests; 62 assistant cooks, who did the actual cooking on the stoves; 335 masters of the royal domain, who provided all the grains, vegetables and fruits for the royal table; 62 game hunters; 342 fishermen; 24 turtle catchers, who provided all the shellfish; 28 meat-driers; 2 food doctors, who supervised the proper preparation of food and drink; 110 regulators of the wines, who supervised the officials who made wines and other drinks; 340 winemakers; 170 beverage makers; 94 ice-house atten-dants; 31 bamboo-basket attendants, charged with serving food in them; 61 meat-pickle makers; 62 picklers; and 62 salt makers. Of the 4133 officers of the royal household, 2263 (55 per cent) were reputedly involved in the preparation of food and drink (Knechtges 1986: 49).

Tombs of the Han Dynasty (206 BC–220 AD) are richly decorated with kitchen scenes cut in stone, impressed in brick or modelled in clay. In one stone engraving dating from the second century AD, and analysed by a French student of Chinese culture Michèle Pirazzoli-t'Serstevens (1985), a man draws water from a well with a pulley. Another cuts a piece of meat hanging in a larder alongside a turtle, birds, a dried hare, various offal, a pig's head, and legs or shoulders of pork. Further men clean a fish and slaughter sheep, steer, pig and dog. A man plucks a fowl, while a dog watches a basket holding others, still alive. A woman stirs a vast pot on a stove; another stokes the fire; a man chops wood; and smoke blows from the chimney. Men put food on skewers and cook them over a fanned brazier. Three cooks work with rolling pins at a low, narrow table. Two women may be fermenting beer and another perhaps watches over its filtering.

In this busy scene, Pirazzoli-t'Serstevens counts forty-three work-ers. Of these, eight are women, who were responsible for cooking cereals, keeping the stove going and preparing fermented foods. The men's work includes slaughtering, preparing and cooking meat, and making pasta and/or dough. Neither the costumes nor the hairstyles or hats immediately betray someone directing the activity. Only one man might be a head chef since he is not carrying or holding anything and seems to be overseeing the three with rolling pins.

SUNG CUISINE

'Thoughts of food occupied the minds of many men of Sung [960–1279]', marvels historian Michael Freeman. 'Poets celebrate it, writers of memoirs list it, even philosophers thought it worth their consideration.' Formulating 'conscious and rational attitudes about food', these citizens objectified cuisine as a relatively self-contained art, engaging professional cooks and a specialised discourse. And he proposes three historical prerequisites for such a 'cuisine'. Firstly, he finds the use of many ingredients, both familiar and exotic. Along with this, a cuisine derives from cultural pluralism: a 'cuisine historically . . . organises the best of several traditions'. Secondly, these are available to a large elite of critical, adventurous eaters. They must exceed a critical mass larger than an individual court, which may command superlative cooking, but not a cuisine. Finally, this cosmopolitan elite shares hedonistic attitudes towards eating, rather than ritualistic. 'Food meant primarily for ritual, while perhaps wonderfully rich and sophisticated, is imprisoned by concerns other than gustatory' (1977: 143–5).

This combination of factors only occurs in large cities. But Freeman then appends a further 'important element, perhaps the decisive one': the changes in agriculture that produced abundance and variety. The citizens of the two Sung capitals especially, as the 'beneficiaries of twin revolutions, in agriculture and in commerce', became probably the 'best-fed mass population in world history to that time'. Marco Polo was overwhelmed by the huge variety and quantity at the ten principal markets at Hangchow and its 'infinite' number of street markets. Two agricultural innovations that appear particularly significant to Freeman are the appearance of new strains of rice and the concomitant commercialisation of agriculture (143–9).

Freeman seems to be describing a vibrant, bourgeois, individualistic cuisine of collaborative cooks and diners. In Sung society, the wealthy households had at least one cook (153). However, further to his statement that material abundance led to refined ideas, the gourmets and professionals did not just react to, but also organised and inspired the wider changes. A self-conscious 'cuisine' was presumably not merely the result of a 'happy coincidence of developments in agriculture and commerce', as Freeman writes (144–5), but helps drive the entire historical process.

Another contributor to the important survey *Food in Chinese Culture*, edited by K. C. Chang, credits the 'preoccupation of the civilisation with good food' to its relative 'openness'. Without castes (and with clan structures that cut across the social strata), without hereditary professions and with few closed social groups, special skills were readily diffused through society. Writing about the Yüan (1271–1368) and Ming (1368–1644) dynasties, professor of East Asian studies Frederick W. Mote gives the instance of a woman of the common people, who might be famous for a soup while having one son a cook in a great household and another the governor of the province. Since cooking skills were not sex-specific and the interest in food deep and widespread, 'no skilled practitioner was likely to remain undiscovered', he adds. In fact, from another source, we learn that the Ming imperial kitchens were dominated by cooks from Shantung, who yielded to Manchu cooks, then to those from Chekiang, and some from Su-chou, with successive cooks attaching their names to dishes (Mote 1977: 238–9; Spence 1977: 292).

Like the Abbasid 'new wave', the Chinese gastronomic fascination was not some fortuitous side effect of a thriving economy, but belonged to and helped drive the whole enterprise. Gourmets and their cooks should be regarded as a calculating group of active consumers, not indolently stuffing themselves, but creating their world, commissioning the Christopher Columbuses of their time.

ROYAL ENGLAND

In medieval Europe, the imperial household collapsed from Nero's heights to loose networks of monasteries and feudal manors. The monasteries were highly organised households, which helped establish time-keeping and other templates of modernity (Weber 1976: 118–19). The manorial system was a way of allocating land ('feuds' or 'fiefs') under the king in return for services, especially military. Viewed from the base, each little pyramid was built on the hardworking, and often wronged, peasants supplying 'surplus' to those higher up the line. Each manor and abbey was relatively self-sufficient, with its brewer, potter, serfs and gardeners. The lord (the 'loaf-keeper') sat at the top table in the hall with the lady ('loaf-kneader').

The royal entertainments of Richard II, who ruled England 1377–99, transport us 'into the fabled regions of romance, or the enchanted land of fairy revelry', to quote the study done more than two centuries ago by the Reverend Richard Warner (1791: xxxi). The prodigality of King Richard was enormous.

> Two thousand cooks, and three hundred servitors were employed in his kitchen. Ten thousand visitors daily attended his court, and went satisfied from his table. To furnish food for this numerous company, twenty-eight oxen, three hundred sheep, an incredible number of fowls, and all kinds of game, were slaughtered every morning (xxxii).

For Warner, testimony that 'our young monarch was an egregious epicure, as well as sumptuous entertainer' is provided by *The Forme of Cury*, the recipe collection of the master cook or cooks of his kitchen, wherein he is called the 'best and ryallest vyand of alle csten

ynges' ('best and most royal eater of all Christian kings') (1). It was only fitting that, once imprisoned, Richard is thought to have starved himself to death. But the English recipes were similar to those in Taillevent's *Viandier*, which repeated those in older French and Italian works – proving that the recipes were 'common property across the continent' (Mennell 1985: 49–51).

Based in one of the massive palaces at Whitehall, Richmond, Hampton Court, Nonsuch or Greenwich, the court in Tudor England catered for 1500 or more diners every day. Mansions such as Burghley, Hardwick, Longleat, Wollaton and Cowdray could deal with their own everyday requirements and those of the court on its annual progression through the country. The complex administration is illustrated in the *Booke of the Household of Queene Elizabeth* of 1600. Working under the direction of the Lord Chamberlain, the Clerk to the Kitchen controlled a total staff of 160, his eleven chief officers – either 'serjeants', chief clerks or master cooks – each running a specialist department. The Serjeant of the Accatry, for example, was responsible for gathering beef and mutton from the queen's pastures, as well as veal, pork, lard, sea fish, freshwater fish and salt. These were passed to the Serjeant of the Larder and his Yeoman of the Boyling House. Poultry, game birds and lambs were the responsibility of the Serjeant of the Poultry, whose Yeoman of the Scalding House prepared them for the cooks. The Serjeant of the Bakehouse had a Yeoman Garnetor to maintain supplies of grain and flour, Yeomen Pervayers who carried supplies into the bake-houses, and further yeomen and grooms who baked bread for the entire household (Brears et al. 1993: 145–6). The Serjeant of the Pastry prepared all the baked meats, pastries and pies. In the Spicery, the Chief Clarke controlled the finer aspects of bakery, with yeomen to beat the spice into powder, using pestle and mortar, others to make wafers for festivals, and further yeomen to run the Confectionery, which supplied pears, wardens (an old species of cooking pear), figs, raisins and other fruit. The master cooks worked at a long masonry bench in which were set firebaskets lined with sheet iron and fuelled with charcoal (148–9).

With so many administrators and aristocratic servers, the person actually called 'cook' was relatively behind the scenes. There seem to be no famous names. Yet the craft was highly skilled, which suggests that either the rulers knew their stuff, or the cooks deserved more credit – probably both.

Tsarist Russia

The Tsar of Russia dined at a raised table with officials of church and state on either side. A procession through the streets might deliver a meal to a foreign ambassador. In their social and economic history of food and drink in Russia, R.E.F. Smith and David Christian warn that the ostentation even in time of famine 'should not deflect us from considering some of the wider implications'. Provisioning the court had an impact on the whole country and economy (1984: 121). Tsars wore chefs' hats.

Over the centuries, the tsars' feasts were distributed from four sideboards or cupboards, representing four of the government departments. The Department of the Great Palace, or central administration, which was represented by the central serving station, laden with precious plate, raised taxes, and spent a great proportion on provisions. According to a book published in the 1660s, the Drinks Office had more than thirty cellars, 'apart from the cellar with overseas drinks', requiring a staff of at least 300. The Bread Office included fifty master bakers and, backing them, the Grain Office had some 300 granaries in which to store the receipts from the tsar's crown villages, the towns down the Volga and the fields sown for the tsar. The Food Office had three high officials, twenty clerks, fifteen junior cellarers, and more than 150 master cooks, under-masters and apprentices, dishwashers, water-carriers and watchmen. Their dishes were all recorded and distributed 'according to the registers and the annual lists'. As well as its dry stores, the Food Office had provisions of meat and fish, both fresh and salt, in fifteen ice-cellars. Close to Moscow, and in some nearby villages, dairy farms supplied sour cream, milk, cheese and butter. The tsars had fisheries along the Volga. Deficiencies were made up for from the markets.

Overall, then, the palace organisation concerned with food and drink had a staff of a dozen or so officers, some of very high rank, and 600 underlings. These figures do not include hundreds of servants, guards and others who were used as extras on ceremonial occasions. With supplies coming from all parts of Russia and imports from as far away as Central Asia, India and the Canary Islands (circumnavigating Scandinavia to reach Moscow), Smith and Christian find that the palace 'generated a demand which had an impact . . . both at home and abroad' (121–8).

When Peter the Great (1672–1725) replaced Moscow with a court and capital in the Western style at St Petersburg, the port was the entry for not only a range of luxury foodstuffs and equipment, but also a sizeable community of Western Europeans and their cooks. At first these newcomers were mainly Dutch and German, in particular, Saxon and Austrian; later they were Swedish and, predominantly, French. Peter also sent many Russians abroad to learn various skills, visited Western Europe himself and recruited many foreigners. In 1704, he acquired Johann Velten, the Saxon cook to the Danish ambassador to Russia. As a measure of Peter's legacy, an English governess recorded in the mid-1730s that the 'Diet of Russia is excellently good, and, in my Opinion, this Place is very fit for an Epicure'. Her explanation was that 'Eating and Drinking take up a third Part of their Time'. In the second half of the eighteenth century, cooks were so regularly recruited from abroad that they almost completely replaced Russians in the households of the higher gentry. When an early Russian cookery book appeared in 1816, its author claimed that Russian cooking was a thing of memory (1984: 173–6).

THE BOURGEOISIE

Throughout history, the palace has been a kitchen writ large – accessing the best raw materials and supplying a mixed and interesting diet to a hierarchy of aristocrats, staff, artisans and, often, the needy. A court has been an overstated household, an 'artificial' *oikos*, at the pinnacle of other relatively self-contained households. With its departments and estates, it provided an essentially centralised, redistributive mechanism, straddling both town and country. But the mode of food distribution promoted inequality; the centripetal forces of wealth separated rich from poor.

We have seen earlier signs of bourgeois consumerism, but decisively in Europe around the close of the eighteenth century, albeit in slow motion, the old order shattered. Royal departments were rivalled by a network of commercial and industrial bureaucracies. Another kind of 'household', the market-city, grew up, based not on redistribution but on the more anonymous flux of money. With the aggressiveness of capitalist firms, the *oikos* became global.

Within the world household, the modern capitalist enterprise relies on calculation and presupposes a predictable legal and administrative system. In place of intuitive justice, according to sociologist Max Weber, the new state operates with the 'expected performance of a machine' (1968: 1394). Modern administration does not seem to be focussed upon cooking, except in the most diffused sense. Bureaucrats are meant to leave their mouths at home or at lunch, put aside their sensual selves. Only very indirectly concerned about the pleasures of the stomach, agribusiness shapes individual tastes according to the aims of efficiency and the 'bottom line'. Fortunately, the system retains savouriness through the survival of gastronomically more appropriate small businesses, domestic kitchens and healthy appetites. All in all, as newly created bourgeois palates, we now share a mass court, which vastly surpasses Solomon's in its sacrifices. French cuisine is an example of this culinary revolution.

The arrival of distinctively 'French' cuisine, which used to be credited to Catherine de' Medici's chefs from Florence, is now usually delayed at least until the middle of the seventeenth century. Sociologist Stephen Mennell pronounces that '[i]ndisputable literary evidence' is not found until the publication in 1651 of La Varenne's *Le Cuisinier françois* (Mennell 1985: 71). In his cookery book *Les Dons de Comus* (1739), François Marin makes the point: 'We have in France several great Lords who, for their own diversion, do not disdain sometimes to talk about cookery, and whose exquisite taste contributes greatly to training excellent chefs'.

In dedicating *Le Cuisinier gascon* (1740) to his employer, the Prince de Dombes, the anonymous author bursts forth so enthusiastically that some readers (for example, Revel 1982: 188–9) think it must be the prince himself:

I can no longer keep silent: to the glory of an art which since You have exercised it has become as noble as it was already essential to the needs and pleasures of life, I shout from the rooftops that You are, Monseigneur, one of the best cooks in France ... I have seen you a hundred times busy in the kitchen, a hundred times have I had the honour of working under your orders. If I have acquired any reputation in my craft, I owe it even more to the emulation to which you have inspired me than to the desire I have always had of meeting your taste (Mennell 1985: 81).

However, if the cookery writers of this period still looked to the courtly nobility for their standards, Mennell says they 'found their readership among the bourgeoisie as well'. In the expanded *Suite des dons de Comus* (1742), Marin includes a section directed at the 'Bourgeois of modest fortune, Artisans, and other people of the Third Estate' (1985: 81–2).

Another prolific, groundbreaking author, Menon, about whom we know nothing but the name, broadened his audience with the immensely successful *La Cuisinière bourgeoise* (1746). The sex of '*la cuisinière*' gives it, according to Mennell, a quite unambiguous social meaning – 'only the less well-to-do members of the middle class would, by that date, make do with a woman cook in charge of their kitchen' (82). Many town households, struggling to become like little

courts, accepted not a proud male specialist but a female all-rounder.

For historian Theodore Zeldin, it was not until the nineteenth century that 'what is now known as the French style of cooking' was largely created (1977: 732). At the top, Zeldin puts Antonin Carême, the supreme name on many lists. Later called the 'Cook of kings and King of cooks' (Montagné 1961: 211), Carême worked in private households, but now the diners were not all aristocratic. French dishes were often named in honour of individuals of taste and judgement; in the seventeenth and eighteenth centuries, the names came from the court, with a thick white sauce commemorating the Marquis de Béchamel (d. 1703) and an onion sauce Charles de Rohan Soubise (1715–87). However, by the time of Carême, the names of dishes tended to be bourgeois. In one gourmand's list, 'Carême bestowed fine names on his soups:– *Potages Condé*, *Boïeldieu, Broussais, Roques, Ségalas* (the three last learned and agreeable doctors); *Lamartine, Dumesnil* (the historian); *Buffon, Girodet*; and ... *Victor Hugo*' (Kirwan 1864: 409). When Carême was working in the house of Madame Rothschild, there was talk of the composer Rossini, whose name is borrowed for several dishes, going to the United States. He was good enough to say, the chef reports, 'I'll start at once if Carême will but accompany me' (Kirwan 1864: 406).

The French Revolution treated gently the vast population of relatively independent peasants on their tiny plots (Lefebvre 1977), in contrast to the brutal dispossession in the United Kingdom by means of enclosures and clearances, so that French farms and gardens were a key contributor to the now definite superiority of that cooking. Yet these were years of turmoil at many levels – from the pursuit of the political ideals of *egalité* and *liberté* to a long list of new technology, starting with iron stoves – during which gastronomy again became self-conscious. According to Athenaeus, *Gastronomy* (*gaster*, Greek for stomach; *nomos*, law) was one of the titles given for Archestratus's ancient work (4e; 1: 19). In 1801, an otherwise undistinguished contributor, Joseph Berchoux, reintroduced the word *gastronomie* with an eponymous poem. Publishing copiously on behalf of the new breed of well-to-do Parisian consumers, by 1810, Grimod de La Reynière, one of history's greatest gastronomers, revelled in the many innovations, hailing Nicolas Appert's 'admirable discovery [of bottling] ... His bottled peas, runner beans, broad beans, haricot beans, cherries, peaches, gooseberries, apricots, plums, etc, are even more succulent, more exquisite this winter than they were last' (Aron 1975: 108).

Until the second half of the nineteenth century, the grand French (and so European) meal followed so-called *service à la française*. The typical dinner consisted of three services: soups, removes (dishes 'exchanging' with others) and entrées (dishes making an 'entrance') belonged to the first; roasts and *entremets* ('between' or side dishes) to the second; desserts to the third. Within those services, many dishes were arrayed together on the table, and selections served by servants. A less formal echo of this procedure survives in modern buffets (158). This was replaced by *service à la russe*, in which courses are plated individually for each diner, a system borrowed, as the name suggests, from Russia.

A visitor to the court of False Dmitri I in 1606 recorded that the 'dishes were not served all at once, but one at a time: there were very many of them, but all tasteless' (Smith and Christian 1984: 115). When Carême was at the court of Alexander I in 1818, he admired *service à la russe*, but considered it unsuitable for French cooking. Then, in the mid-nineteenth century, Urbain Dubois spent some years in Russia as chef to Prince Orloff and, upon his return, helped popularise the new system (Wheaton 1983: 291 n.30).

According to social historian Jean-Paul Aron, *service à la russe* is 'defined by three principal clauses: the carving is done in the kitchen, or on the sideboard in the dining-room; the waiters offer the dishes to each guest, from the left, in turn, according to protocol; all the courses in each sequence are destined for all present'. The change is both simple and profound – from a 'spatio-temporal configuration' (a table arrayed with food) to a 'linear progression' (successive plates).

For Aron, 'qualitative diversity' (your selection from a table of food) is replaced by the 'simplified arithmetic of identity' (the same plate as your neighbour). This 'impoverishes' choice, fulfilling the 'wish of a Jacobin society in revolt against individual differences; it realises that egalitarian ideal which is invading more and more aspects of life. By 1890 the cause is finally won. There is a ravishing new simplicity' (1975: 160–1). Georg Simmel accepts that, in *service à la russe*, plates 'must all be identical, they cannot tolerate any individuality'. But, at the same time, he finds that, as opposed to the shared bowl, the 'plate is an individualistic form. It indicates that this portion of food is exclusively divided off for this one person' (1994: 348). This therefore promoted possessive individualism, further underscored by the free choice offered by *à la carte* (ordering 'from the menu' of priced items).

During the rise of French cuisine, the court 'household' was steadily replaced by the pluralistic city of individuals. Supplanting the monarch and immediate court, the privileged bourgeoisie now shaped the instruments of trade, technology and taste. Of all innovations, none was more revealing of modern, urban individuals than the restaurant. The rise of restaurants will be given an alternative slant next chapter. For the present, the point is that cuisine was no longer directed by tyrants, but by the 'invisible hand' (Adam Smith) of innumerable gastronomically-informed players. Mennell speaks to the agreed wisdom when he calls Auguste Escoffier's *La Guide culinaire* of 1903 'biblical' or 'paradigmatic' (1985: 157). With individualised dishes, to be served in courses, and from kitchens reorganised as production lines, this book defined international bourgeois cooking. Where celebrated chefs up to and including Carême worked for private households, Escoffier belonged to the new era of grand commercial dining.

THE RESTAURANT REVOLUTION

An eye-witness, Grimod de La Reynière advances three reasons why restaurants emerged in France with the French Revolution: the rage for English fashions, including the taking of meals in taverns; the influx of large numbers of revolutionary deputies from the provinces;

and cooks seeking re-employment after the break-up of the aristocratic households. In *The Art of Dining*, based on articles in London's *Quarterly Review* in 1835 and 1836, essayist and lawyer Abraham Hayward adds a fourth hypothesis: cautious of displaying their plunder in opulent homes, the new *millionaires* 'preferred gratifying their Epicurean inclinations at an eating-house' (1853: 23–4). The political upheaval no doubt had an enormous impact on dining, but Stephen Mennell raises a distinct problem: restaurants pre-date the Revolution (1985: 135–44). Equally, I suggest that it is more illuminating to reverse the question and ask why the Revolution arose at the same time as restaurants, and no one helps here better than Brillat-Savarin in his Meditation 28, 'On Restaurateurs'.

In Brillat-Savarin's philosophical history of cooking, the restaurant is the final of the *'Dernier perfectionnements'* (finishing touches) (Meditation 27; 1971: 301–2). But few who throng to them bother to unravel the 'maze of ideas which [has] finally resulted in this highly useful and popular institution'. The inventor must have been a 'genius and a profound observer' of people.

He starts with a concise definition.

> A restaurateur is anyone whose business consists in offering to the public a repast which is always ready, and whose dishes are served in set portions at set prices, on the order of those people who wish to eat them (Meditation 28; 1971: 309).

We need to remember that the near universal way to serve meals until this time (1825) was to place the pot or pots on the table for all to share. The grander the meal, the more dishes. In fancy dining, the artistic creation was the table; in fact, Carême viewed cooking as a branch of architecture. Hotels served limited ranges at fixed times, Brillat-Savarin explains. The caterers (*traiteurs*) did not provide portions, but 'whole courses' – an entire joint, say – and 'anyone who wished to entertain a few friends must order from them well in advance'. With the restaurant, artistic creation became the individual plate. In one blow, high quality became publicly available; even more significantly, cooking/sharing was individualised.

The restaurant inventor realised, according to Brillat-Savarin, that:

if he should cut off a chicken wing to please the first comer, there would not fail to be another arrival who would gladly accept the leg; that the carving of a slice of roast meat in the obscurity of the kitchen would not ruin the rest of the joint; that nobody minded a slight increase in cost when he had been served well, and promptly, and properly . . . that a wide choice of dishes and a set price for each one would have the advantage of being adaptable to every purse (310).

Restaurants hastened the emergence of the sovereign consumer. At the table of a first-class restaurateur, any person could dine as well as a prince, 'or more so, for the feast at his command is quite as splendid, and since he can order any dish he wishes, he is not bothered by personal considerations or scruples'. And this dining, potentially at the level of the wealthy household, was offered in the marketplace.

Brillat-Savarin observes that two pieces of paper open and close the occasion. The first is the *carte*, menu or bill of fare, which is necessary to list the various dishes on offer and to disclose their prices. At the conclusion, the *carte à payer* (the bill) lists the dishes actually taken and their cost (309). The bond of money introduces a relative distance, so that the host and eater need not even know one another. No longer bound by master–servant obligations, the cook and diner gain flexibility, a freedom of a kind.

The flexibility of restaurants stimulated culinary art, he suggests. Through competition, as soon as a 'highly worthy recipe for ragout can make the fortune of its inventor, cupidity, that power of powers, fires all the imaginations and puts every cook to work'. New edible substances are found, old ones are bettered, and 'both new and old combined in a thousand ways. Foreign inventions have been imported;

the world itself has been put to use, and contributes so much to our daily fare that in one meal we can trace a complete course of alimentary geography' (313–14). Despite 'Babette's Feast', the creative, 'individual' chefs were still predominantly male. Brillat-Savarin lists some of the great Parisian places and their specialities: the Veau Qui Tette owed its celebrity to sheep's trotters, the Frères Provençeaux to cod with garlic, Véry to truffled entrées, Baleine to the great care taken to serve fine fish, and Henneveu to the mysterious little private rooms on the fourth floor (315).

Jean-Paul Aron speaks of the 'strange trading' that went on after 1765 at Boulanger's and Lamy's, 'where food was served, sometimes at all hours of the day, sometimes at set times only, and served at individual tables' (1975: 15). While Brillat-Savarin leaves this distinctive use of separate tables implicit, he describes the various types of customers seated at them – the solitary diner, the lovers immersed in their meal, the married couple who have long lost anything to say, and, in the middle of the room, the regulars, most of whom dine at reduced rates and from a set list of dishes. 'They know by name all the waiters, who tip them off secretly to what is best and freshest.' In return, they attract other customers 'like the tame ducks which hunters in Brittany use to lure in the wild ones' (Meditation 28; 1971: 312).

Overall, the restaurant is an open 'household' virtually only restricted to those who have the ability to pay, and where chefs and their staff take over as hosts. In theory at least, the diner has the chance to flit between establishments. Such circumstances generate the modern consuming person, who peruses menus with taste and education, we hope.

Such restaurant individualism gave Brillat-Savarin cause to worry, however. He witnessed diners 'serve themselves from any plate of food, already cut up, which is being passed, and then they put it down in front of them instead of handing it to their neighbours, whom they are not used to considering'. He also viewed the solitary diner with some concern, claiming such behaviour promoted egotism (313 and footnote). Indeed, a favourite scene of nineteenth-century writers and illustrators became the isolated glutton, with knife and fork in mid-flight and plates and bottles already emptied under the table. Solo enjoyment may be intense, but we are sharing only the basic need for fuel (Simmel 1994: 348).

The clever restaurateur played a leading part in shaping the modern individual, and with this, the French Revolution planted the banner of '*Liberté! Egalité! Fraternité!*'. Indeed, the complete individual might be defined as the eater with preferences, who chooses from the world of foods, theories and practices.

MODERN ARBITER OF TASTE

An aunt complained that the late nineteenth-century restaurant reviewer Lieut.-Col. Nathaniel Newnham-Davis had been the 'worst conducted small boy that ever was' and was now 'getting unpleasantly fat' (1899: 22). The plump critic admits this in his racy collection of articles from the *Pall Mall Gazette*, chronicling belle époque dining at the then centre of civilisation, London, where César Ritz took personal charge at the Savoy, with the kitchen under Escoffier. Badly conducted he might have started out, but the adult Newnham-Davis became a modern *arbiter elegantiae*, promoting, on the one hand, great chefs and their practices and, on the other, informed consumers.

Early on the appointed day, he would head off to the chosen restaurant to interview the manager or, failing him, the *maître d'hôtel*. The higher up the scale of responsibility, 'the more intelligent help you will get in ordering your dinner, the more certain you are to have an artistic meal, and not to be spending money unworthily'. With friendly assistance, composing a menu for a small dinner is a pleasure, in which a suggestion on one side is amended by a better idea from the other. Newnham-Davis declares in favour of a dinner *à la carte* rather than *table d'hôte*. Although it is now 'cooked to the minute', he compares eating *table d'hôte* to 'landing a fish which has been hooked and played by someone else' (xix–xx).

To give an idea of this critic's smart style, here is a snippet from his review of a restaurant in The Strand, Romano's, which advertised Parisian cuisine, lighting by electricity and 'Service at separate Tables'.

A little too much onion with the *perdreau en casserole* we both thought, otherwise admirable. Salad good, artichokes good, though we preferred plain vinegar as a dressing to the *hollandais* one, and the ice delicious.

Then Miss Dainty trifled with cherries cased in pink sweetness and sections of oranges sealed in transparent sugar, and our two friends from the table at the far end came across and took coffee and liqueurs with us, and talked of the old days when Romano's was but a quarter of the size it is now, when it was far more Bohemian than it is now, when there was a little aquarium in the front window into which the sons of Belial used to try and force each other late at night, much to the consternation of the gold-fish (26–7).

When Newnham-Davis chaperones 'Miss Brighteyes', the debutante daughter of an old friend, she babbles on about her cousin's wedding decorations, about Miss Mary Moore's black and white dress at the supper a week gone by, about the respective merits of Princes' and the Niagara skating-rinks, and other chit-chat – neglecting the 'serious responsibility' of appreciating a good dinner. 'I tried in vain to make Miss Brighteyes understand that the caviar she was eating deserved some attention . . .' (241).

Summoned to a dinner with the Editor, he chooses the impeccable Berkeley Hotel, being rewarded with the very best corner table, overlooking Green Park, and being overlooked by the attentive partners.

'Very good soup indeed', said the Editor, as he laid down his spoon, and Jules, who was within hearing, smiled as if the wish of his life had been accomplished, while Emile beamed as if he had come in for a fortune.

However, a faultless dinner for the gourmet is flawed for the journalist: 'nowhere in England or abroad could we have been given a better dinner. Indeed, from my point of view, it was too good a dinner, for there was no weak spot in it to fasten a criticism on' (165).

The actual cooks are no neglected hands, but forceful presences in the conspiracy of delight. Newnham-Davis knows them and, on more than one occasion, tours the kitchen. Concerned about the freshness of the fish and the origin of the raw materials, he is disconcerted to learn from Joseph that the 'vegetables and all the poultry for the Savoy come from France, and I was beginning to feel quite ashamed of England as a food-producing country, when a handsome compliment to the English mutton restored my confidence'. Joseph explains that though English beef is good for roasting, only French beef is used for *bouillon* (86).

Newnham-Davis's relationship with managers, *maîtres d'* and chefs might appear one-sided, with exaggeratedly attentive service, which appears indirectly on the bill. However, he listens to advice, and in his 'Foreword' complains that, faced with names which mean nothing to them, hundreds of customers have fallen back upon the harmlessly homely soups, *petite marmite* or *croûte au pot*. As an educator of the new classes, he encourages them to be brave, and inquire: 'What is that?' (xvii–xviii).

*   *   *

The consumer holds fabulous court. In many ways, he or she has taken charge of the meal, thereby conducting the third of my 'moments' of cooking. For us industrial masses, the shelves are stocked with a thousand and one delights. We dine at different corners of the world. Choosing whatever we want, we are knowledgeable, or should be. The modern person wanders the city picking from the stalls, grazing in a megalopolis of distraction. And we can be extremely picky. We can demand an alternative even in a family meal, and request when eating out. We seek untried pleasures, confirm old favourites, choose vegetarian options, develop allergies, slim, or suppress our appetites altogether.

As sovereign consumers, we have everyone working for us. The trick, of course, is that we too are part of that system. Shamefully, this cooperation is distorted so that some dine as 'kings', many as paupers. Pursuing the greedy logic of capital accumulation, large, well-disciplined teams determine, delimit or degrade our menus. Amid the seething distribution, hyper-specialisation, and the industrialisation of culture, we lose our grip on metabolic realities.

The magnificent banquets of former rulers have usually been written off as hollow shows of status. But this should not get in the road of seeing them as centrepieces of culinary organisation. Truly regal cooks maintained close connection with the roots of good food – well-managed gardens, hand-picked orchards, comfortable exchanges, wise workers. Wealthy households enjoyed a kind of hand-made modernity. Courts were early consumers, reflected in their calculating hedonism, rational reflection and adventurousness. Such palace banquets have gradually been popularised, although trans-national food corporations can scarcely claim to market *haute cuisine*.

In this chapter, cooks have worked largely anonymously in courts and privileged households. As the splendour has collapsed, the art-istry has been professionalised and many practitioners lionised – the cooks have become chefs. Meanwhile, the feeding of the ordinary people has occasioned an even more vibrant and anonymous street industry. In the next chapter, the alternative view of the rise of the professional cook is from the bottom up.

CHAPTER FOURTEEN

The Sons of Mama Camous

A self-promoting chef in Victorian England, Alexis Soyer, yearns: 'Somebody will, perhaps, one day publish a chronological history of celebrated cooks'. He starts with the mythical ancient Greek hero Cadmus, described in Athenaeus (658e; 7: 33) as the cook to the King of Sidon (1853: 253–4). But from more recent scholarship, we might start much earlier and more concretely than that.

In ancient Sumer, a list of artisans from the Early Dynastic period (2900–2330 BC) begins with 'cooks' (along with basket-weavers, jewellers and so forth), although no individual is identified. Another text lists 'the great cook' and 'chief cook', and one of these chefs even left an imprint of his seal bestowed by King Ibbi-Sin (Limet 1987: 140). An Egyptian papyrus from the Thirteenth Dynasty (around 1750 BC) lists the eighty servants of a single Theban household. Probably slaves, more than half are 'Asiatics' (foreigners from the 'near East'). Most are women, mainly labouring in the weaving rooms, but among the male workers are cooks. The far from complete text names two Asiatics: Sene-Res-seneb and 'Su . . . he is called Ankhu-seneb' (Pritchard 1969: 553).

Starting with Sene-Res-seneb and Ankhu-seneb, it might seem possible to trace a clear lineage of professional cooks from the earliest temples, through palaces and wealthy households to hotel dining-rooms and restaurants, climaxing with Escoffier and Fernand Point. In proposing a chronicle of chefs, Soyer marvels: 'how many glorious names will not culinary annals have to register!' (1853: 254). But a complete list would hardly be realisable; the much messier reality is that even professional cooks have been everywhere. Cooks have laboured not just at great tables, but also in monasteries, hospitals, galleys, canteens, colleges, barracks, taverns, street stalls and cook-shops.

Fine professional chefs can trace their heritage back and back. But that could be misleading because, characteristically, they have not only inherited the traditions of a distinct trade, but they have also remained close to the domestic cooking bubbling around them. Professional cooks compete with and negate, but also emerge from and depend upon, home cooks.

It is not even easy to decide whom to call a professional cook. On one side, when does a domestic cook selling her excess shade over into commerce? On the other, compounding the difficulties, specialists of all kinds serve culinary duties. Out of the numerous callings cooking beyond the family hearth, only some actually term themselves 'cook'; bakers do cooks' jobs, but are thought of as separate. But what about pastry-cooks? Some of the complexities in sorting out the origins of professionals are illustrated by the Athenians.

COOKS IN THE MARKETPLACE

A potential host is hiring a cook in the special section of the Athenian marketplace. He hails the freelancer as 'Daedalus', proverbially ingenious, and declares that his intelligence is next only to another cook called Perfection. 'So', he says, 'I have come to pay the price you demanded' (Athenaeus 293a; 3: 313–15). But the host secretly considers him to be one of the 'disreputable' type who would commit theft and let his mother starve (Theophrastus 1973: 37).

For his part, an experienced cook guards against being hired by a stingy host. Youths who have pooled their savings and come to market with their tell-tale cry, 'Who's willing to get up a cheap little dinner?' are bound to complain about the food; but a young man gobbling up his patrimony in a love affair is a carefree spender (Athenaeus 292c; 3: 311–13). The deal done, the cook trundles his assistants off to the appointed dining place: 'Bring a soup ladle, a dozen skewers, a meat hook, mortar, small cheese scraper, skillet, three bowls, a skinning knife, four cleavers ... the small kettle and the things from the soda-shop [grocery stall]. Late again, are you?

Bring also the axe and the rack of frying-pans' (169bc; 2: 267–9).

In the last chapter, we found professional cooks in courts. With this market scene, largely reconstructed out of lines from the stage recorded by the ancient scholar Athenaeus, we take to the streets to observe professional cooks feed cities. Villagers work local land, fetch water and firewood, milk goats and trap game, satisfying most of their own needs. But once a town reaches a certain size, its people are no longer self-reliant. In any case, they congregate as non-farm specialists. Lacking the home comforts of garden, livestock and larder, city-dwellers depend on a communal water supply, public stoves and wide-scale food-sharing. Take-away food proves to be a very, very old invention.

Cooks could have entered the Athenian market from several directions. Theirs was a 'great man' theory, crediting an inspiring teacher – Sicon, for example – as the 'founder' of the art (Athenaeus 378ab; 4: 211), but there are more sociological possibilities. While commercially minded and raffish, cooks (*mageiroi*) might have descended from the sacrificing priests responsible for the dispersal of meat, as we have seen. Tellingly, the cook, the butcher and the priest shared the name *mageiros*. In Homer's *Iliad* and *Odyssey*, King Agamemnon and King Nestor's son sacrifice animals – 'So reputable and important, then, was the dignity pertaining to the cook's art', Athenaeus deduces (660ac; 7: 39). Once in the marketplace, cooks were still employed to carry out sacrifices at festivals and weddings (659d; 7: 35). While the household's women and slaves laboured over the everyday barley-cake, male professionals dealt with special occasions revolving around meat. But there is another possibility.

In completing nothing less than the twentieth century's third PhD on ancient Greek cooks, classicist Guy Berthiaume finds that the word *mageiros* arose around 450 BC, when commercial expansion filled tables with wheaten bread (rather than barley), much fish and abundant vegetables and spices (1982: 12–14). The tragic poet Sophocles wrote at that time: 'I, being the cook [*mageiros*], will season skilfully' (Athenaeus 68a; 1: 295). Certainly, Greek culinary life appears to have been galvanised with the capture around Sophocles's time of Persian banquet cooks and their accoutrements. Perhaps this helped push sacrificers away from religious values to those of gourmandise, getting up smart dinners for suitors and successful sea-captains.

This suggests another line of development: from the elaborate cooking of mansions and palaces, with their phalanxes of dependants, came marketplace cooks, no longer slaves. Athenaeus could not find a cook spoken of as a slave in comedy, except by Poseidippus; the profession belonged to the free-born (658f; 7: 33). Heracleides and Glaucus of Locris, compilers of cookery books, held the cooks' art inappropriate 'to slaves, or even to merely ordinary freemen' (661e; 7: 45–7).

Further complicating our understanding of hired cooks' origins, as in so many other times and places, the most exciting cooks were foreigners. When Antiphanes catalogues the special products of each city, he declares that cooks come from Elis, part of the Peloponnesus (27d; 1: 119). This is perhaps because the first man to 'tie on the wreath of victory at the Olympic contest' was a cook, Coroebus of Elis (382b; 4: 229). From modern Scio, a large and fertile island off the coast of Ionia, the Chians 'have been by far the best in inventing dainty dishes' (25f; 1: 113). Antiphanes confirms fine cooking as the 'Sicilian arts' and, in another play, a character responds to fragrant steam issuing from the earth: 'Some seller of frankincense dwells in the chasm, or else a Sicilian cook' (661f; 7: 47).

Why were (and are) cooks so often foreigners? Perhaps their methods were seductively unlike home cooking. They could have emigrated because they were financially ambitious. While they might not have set out as cooks, that might have offered a ready living. While Athenaeus and his sources provide a vibrant snapshot, they are sociologically hazy. Did smart cooks at the Agora descend from wealthy households? From Persian courts? From charismatic chefs? From temples? From Sicily? I suggest that each of these traditions contributed.

And there is a further element to be considered: that cooks belonged to the general ruck of street traders. Throughout history, professional cooking of the highest order has often emerged from street food, and that from ordinary households. As possible evidence, while the word *mageiros* – 'cook', 'butcher' and 'priest' – was associated with meat distribution, it is also, confusingly, said to relate to bakery as it derives from *masso* (to work with the hands, and so to knead dough) and *maza* (barley-cake). This is 'because the baking of bread was originally the chief business of the cook' (Liddell and Scott 1909: 422). This implies that the cooks emerged from what might generically be termed 'cookshops', in the all-embracing sense of street businesses scarcely distinguishable from domestic kitchens. It seems we ought to attend to the tumult.

COOKSHOPS

The cookshop relies on specialisation and economies of scale to run an oven or stoves, with which to supply ready-cooked meats, pies, pastries, sauces and so on. It is also where people have often sent their own foods to be baked. In recent times, a labourer in China, as in many other parts of the world, would take a choice piece of meat to a 'street kitchen', giving precise instructions on how to cook it (Cheng 1954: 23).

The concept of the cookshop encourages us to think in terms of an incremental model of commercial cooking. The earliest city-states grew up around a temple, palace or grand household, providing a nucleus of distribution. Together with their own estates, patriarchal rulers appropriated foodstuffs to feed officials, artisans, slaves and the needy. In addition to such 'redistribution', however, cities have enjoyed more chaotic forms of exchange, a clamour of catering. Household kitchens have spilled out across countless front steps as domestic cooks supplemented the household income, supplying meals to neighbours, boarders and travellers. They began to specialise in bread, alcohol, soup, the meal of the day, pig butchery, some delicacy or other. Street vendors took the domestic kitchen further into the public. Hawkers have cried their wares; the smell of baking bread has attracted customers; tavern-keepers have built reputations. People have had to eat, meet, improvise; and this has meant people's cooks. A touch more specialised than domestic sharers, street food has often been supplied by 'professed' cooks (those claiming quali-fications). They have often had retail premises – cookshops. Their addresses became well known. Elegances were multiplied. They became regulated trades.

As a rule-of-thumb, the more tasks moved outward, the more

'male' they became. This is why this chapter is called 'The Sons of Mama Camous', emphasising both the masculinity of the public domain and its dependence on the feminine or domestic. We can see the initial step into the street taken in a village outside Dakar in Senegal, where an 'enormous amount' of 'petty selling' goes on between women. They might sell part of their market purchases (raw vegetables and fish), partially prepared foods (couscous needing only final steaming) and cooked foods (fried doughnuts, grilled peanuts). The proceeds provide the small sums needed for purchasing relish or medical supplies (Mackintosh 1979: 184).

Even before the earliest states were formed in Mesopotamia, sharing a village oven made sense. Ovens found at Çatal Hüyük on the Konya Plain in southern central Anatolia and dated around 8000 years ago are so big that their owners could be called professional cooks or, in this case, bakers. The writer of a letter probably from Sippar nearly 4000 years ago complains: 'I have no hired man who would grind the barley (for me) so we have been eating bought bread' (Oppenheim 1977: 385 n.13). Under house arrest in Jerusalem, around 600 BC, the prophet Jeremiah was given a loaf of bread daily from the bakers' street while the city's supplies lasted (Jeremiah 37:21).

Also peeling off from the domestic kitchen was the specialist brewer. The alehouse and wine tavern would often offer meals, accommodation, gambling and prostitution, the latter being frequently mentioned as why innkeepers were often women, as if they might not be expected to be running enlarged households. One such Mesopotamian innkeeper became Queen Ku-Baba, founder of the Third Dynasty of Kish (Oppenheim 1977: 151).

Travellers in the ancient world took rations, especially when it was necessary to camp in the open air. However, it was unthinkable to carry victuals more than a few days. While respectable people endeavoured to rely on the hospitality of members of their own class, the caravan routes had networks of inns. We have already heard that, 4000 years ago, King Shulgi set up hostels along the roads of Sumer operated by 'friendly folk'. The stopover in ancient China was provided by a Buddhist or Taoist monastery. By the time of the T'ang Dynasty (around 1400 years ago), *kuan* (hostels) dotted

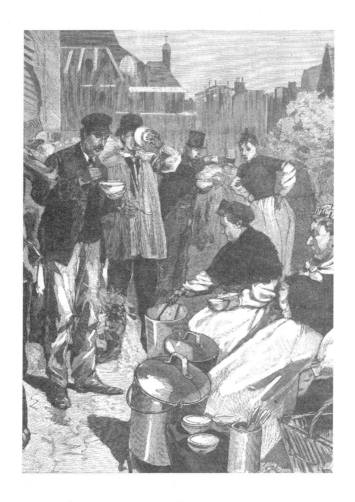

well-travelled roads. Their name means something like 'official', signifying that these originated as lodging places for official travellers (Schafer 1977: 136–7).

The ultimate variation on what I have generically termed cookshops is the dedicated eating-house, which archaeologists have termed (somewhat loosely) a 'restaurant'. A 4000-year-old building uncovered in the ancient Harappan city of Mohenjo-daro includes residential quarters around a typical courtyard and, in archaeologist Mortimer Wheeler's words, 'towards the street, industrial or commercial premises of some note'. Of three rooms neatly paved with bricks set on their edge, one room contains a well and five conical holes in the floor lined with wedge-shaped bricks, apparently to hold the pointed bases of large jars. Although they might have been dyeing vats, the premises may well have been a 'public restaurant' (1968: 51).

In the busy trading city of Ur around 3800 years ago, buildings were unquestionably used for food service, such as the one to which Leonard Woolley gave the fanciful address of 'No. 14 Paternoster Row'. This 'restaurant' – 'exactly like the cookshops of a modern bazaar' – had a wide window opening onto the street and a brick counter immediately inside, presumably to display cooked dishes. The kitchen contained a circular bread oven and a solid brick range, with troughs for charcoal meat braziers (1954: 186). In the Hebrew Song of Solomon, written in the third century BC or earlier, a 'rose of Sharon' is taken by her beloved to a 'banqueting house', where, swooning, she calls: 'Sustain me with raisins,/refresh me with apples' (2:4–5).

The Chinese, who invented just about everything else, have long been adept at city-living. And nowhere has the whole range of cookshops been more brilliantly displayed than in China. The jam-packed history edited by K.C. Chang, *Food in Chinese Culture* (1977), reveals that much of the finest cooking during the Sung Dynasty (around 1000 years ago) was available in the street; even Emperor Hsiao-tsung was said to enjoy visiting the market districts to dine, one of the contributors, Michael Freeman, records.

Vendors swarmed the streets, even carrying their barbecued chicken, lamb shanks and dried fruits into restaurants. Some of their

items came from large workshops, which also manufactured dumplings, roast goose, sugared or honeyed jujubes, stuffed lungs and
bean soup. As well as noodle shops, we read about numerous dives
selling 'rough food', the lists at working-men's places demonstrating
that every scrap of an animal was used. In Kaifeng, heavy soups or
pottages were common – such as blood soup, flour soup and dishes
made of heart, kidneys and lungs. In Hangchow, these were joined
by various kinds of buns.

In terms of fine restaurants, the Sung writers reveal where to eat
food of every region of China and how to feast while afloat on the
West Lake or throw a catered banquet in a rented palace. At elegant
establishments, the silver serving pieces weighed a 'hundred ounces'.
Places quickly went in and out of fashion: in Kaifeng, the best for a
while was the White Kitchen on An-chou Alley in the Western
Precinct, followed by the House of Li's Blessing on Chick's Alley.
Early in the twelfth century, pre-eminence moved to the Pavilion of
Lengthy Blessings, under the east wall of the Ching-ying Palace.
Importantly for historians of true (*à la carte*) restaurants, the men
of Kaifeng would extravagantly shout orders – each person ordering
differently. The waiters, called 'gong heads' or 'callers', would remember these instructions. In an instant, they returned with three dishes

in the left hand and twenty bowls up the right arm, distributing them precisely as ordered (Freeman 1977: 151–3, 156–63).

Jumping the centuries, in 1795, Li Tou published *Yang-chou hua-fang lu*, a tour of public dining of the old city of Yang-chou, where cooks could be remembered for particular dishes. Tea shops attracted tourists with their famous snacks; a restaurant cooked lamb so well that people started queuing at dawn; bars stocked wines from all over the country and special wines for every season; other restaurants were famous for frogs' legs or for food served in a beautiful setting by beautiful girls and where scholars settled in for an evening and wrote poems. Most especially, Yang-chou was famous for numerous floating restaurants. Diners ordered in advance, and once the food had been prepared, it was ferried to the host and his guests and servants, eating, relaxing and ordering wines from other boats near by. Historian Jonathan Spence finds that many floating restaurants were exceptionally fine, though others served for dalliance (1977: 289, 292).

* * *

The American 'diner' is a cheap roadside dining-place resembling a railroad dining-car. Its history is usually dated to 1872, when Walter Scott, a street vendor in the industrial area in Providence, Rhode Island, moved up from a basket to a horse-drawn wagon. Through a window, he served shift workers boiled eggs with buttered bread, frankfurters, sandwiches and sliced chicken. The idea was copied: in 1883 Ruel Jones, a competitor in Providence, was the first to order a specifically designed lunch-wagon. His cousin, Samuel Messer Jones, moving to Worcester, Massachusetts, went further: patrons could sit in his wagon. By 1898, the 'king' of wagon-building, T.H. Buckley, employed fifty-five craftsmen in Worcester. The fancier models came tile-lined, with marble counters and brass cash registers. With local regulators seeking to control these multiplying 'eyesores', many operators rented off-street parking, and covered the wheels with skirts. Lunch-wagons evolved into diners during the first decades of the twentieth century (Pillsbury 1990: 37–8).

The people's street food has been fiercely challenged by authority, with religious strictures, guild restraints, political clean-ups, hygiene panics and now the market distortions of large, cult-like corporations such as McDonald's and Pizza Hut bent on global domination (Vidal 1997). But the unstoppable undergrowth of public cooks can still be observed.

STREET FOOD

Balut is a boiled, fertilised duck's egg. You crack open the wide end, sprinkling in a little salt, sipping the broth, and then breaking the rest to savour the red yolk and tiny chick inside. According to Manila food scholar Doreen G. Fernandez, the perfect Filipino *balut* is seventeen days old. At that stage, the duck is still wrapped in white and does not show beak or feathers. Vietnamese and Chinese like their equivalent of the *balut* even older, whereas, in the United States, it is usually sold at a less threatening sixteen days. Not that vendors at bus terminals in the Philippines jib at selling nineteen-day holdovers to customers they will never see again. The *balut* is practical, inexpensive, nutritious, available in all seasons and described by poet Tom Agulto as 'the national street food of the Philippines'. It is sold, Fernandez says, 'on streets, at stalls, outside movie houses, outside nightclubs and discos, in markets; by vendors walking, sitting or squatting; at midnight and early dawn, at breakfast, lunch, merienda and dinner time' (1991: 101–2).

Honouring the abundance and variety of street food in the Philippines, Fernandez speaks of green-mango sellers on the back roads and fruit and peanut sellers pedalling through the traffic. In residential streets, *taho* vendors carry soy-bean curd, sliced and flavoured, from house to house. Those parking carts outside schools manage to keep their corn warm and show it off at the same time. Vendors gather at transport hubs, including long-distance bus-stops, selling:

> vari-coloured iced drinks faintly flavoured with pineapple, coconut and strawberry; green mangoes fresh-peeled per customer, to dip in salt or *bagoong* [fermented fish sauce]; peanuts boiled or fried; whole peeled, or sliced fresh pineapple in plastic bags; and especially *balut* and barbecue.

Many make their own rice cakes or ice-cream, but contribute only the *sawsawan* dipping sauce for fishballs made in workshops in Chinatown and the markets (99–100).

Off a main artery in Manila, Aurora Boulevard, couples preside over large pots of chicken or tripe porridge (*arroz caldo*; *goto*). This is a makeshift restaurant (*carinderia*) on a large-wheeled cart as a table, with a row of from perhaps just two to even more than a dozen covered pots (*calderos*). The customers peer in, choose and sit with their backs to the traffic, while dishes are washed in buckets and basins on the pavement. Many stands are lined with dipping sauces and piled with half-cooked skewered pig and chicken parts, ready to be grilled. Every part is used, and given 'pop' names: *Walkman* for pigs' ears, *Adidas* for chicken feet, *PAL* for wings, *IUD* for intestines (for similarity in appearance). A man or a woman cooks, fans the coals, sells and gives change, 'all in a haze of smoke that wafts the flavours along the street and entices customers' (100–1).

Fernandez reports the economic pressures behind a street food business, a 'small, fast, cash operation' at the lower rungs of capitalism. Virtually no outlay is needed, no credit given, the employees can all be in the family, their 'only' skills cooking and selling. She says that a rice-cake seller in Hagonoy, Bulacan, invests perhaps 250 or 300 pesos in the day's materials and makes it back by the afternoon, with about 100 pesos profit and the family fed with the wares. A two-*caldero carinderia* in front of a Davao home supplies the family meals, enough cash for the next day's capital and a little extra (102).

The operators have taken a very small step from the traditional Filipino meal eaten in the open in the market, street or field. In the basic agricultural and riverine communities, people are dependent upon each other, so that they extend home to the street, to chat, play games, mend fishing nets, work on pots and baskets, eat and celebrate. At fiestas, tables are set up in the streets. Street food in the Philippines, Fernandez concludes, is not only a convenience for busy working people, or an economic phenomenon of hard times. 'It is also and especially a communal gathering rooted in a sense of the street as communal space, in an understanding of meals as movable in time, as flexible feasts that make their own spaces and shape their own meanings – in home or village or street' (102–3).

The Filipino street vendors are relatively unconstrained by government regulations, strong guilds and hygiene goals. But this 'unruliness' of the hawkers is a vibrant demonstration of the age-old method of feeding cities. With the retreat to the suburbs throughout much of the twentieth century, advanced industrial cities lost some of this time-honoured street culture. They gave an impression that households cooked alone. But many present-day Asian and other cities indicate some of the hubbub of urban centres since the beginning. The complex mix of urban food distribution through centralised redistribution, market economy and street cooks is well illustrated by ancient Rome.

'BREAD AND CIRCUSES'

The poet Juvenal complains that the public of ancient Rome was only concerned with two things: *panem et circenses* – 'Bread and the Games' (*Satire* X: 80; 1974: 207). As a modern scholar, Jérôme Carcopino, adds: 'The Caesars had in fact shouldered the dual task of feeding and amusing Rome. Their monthly distributions at the Portico of Minucius assured the populace its daily bread' (1956: 223). On the stated day, a proletarian husband (not his wife) knocked at the portico to receive the little wooden tablet (*tessera*) entitling him to a ration of grain (202).

In ancient political economies, the rich owners of grain stores could purchase position and prestige through both generosity and profiteering (Garnsey 1988). Adding to this, the bedrock of feeding Rome – which already exceeded a million mouths two millennia ago – was the distribution of cheap or free grain and later bread by the public service called the Annona (after the word for 'annual crop'). When Pompey took charge in September 57 BC, he had to obtain grain for a minimum of 486 000 people. Rome's grain supply required a vast rural workforce. Expensive to transport over land, huge quantities of grain were shipped from the southern shores of the Mediterranean. Carcopino records that the Annona annually stored 20 million *modii* (4 669 000 bushels) from Egypt and twice that from Africa (1956: 28). This gave added importance to Roman ports, especially Ostia, where vast warehouses, or *horrea*, stretched out of sight.

In the middle of the Forum of Ostia rose the temple of Annona Augusta – that is to say, the Divinity of Imperial Supplies. Sixty-one small rooms around three edges of the square were dedicated to professional associations (195). More than 150 such associations were recognised in Rome, and included the wholesalers of corn, wine and oil; the retailers of lupins, of fruits and melons; the market gardeners, who also operated as greengrocers; those who brought their own fish to sell; the vintners, who carried wine on their carts in the skin of a large animal; the bakers, who were assisted by a miller; and then there were pastry-cooks and confectioners, and many more (198–9).

In his long *History of Rome*, written around the turn of the millennium, Livy recalls the magnificent victory of the Roman Army in 187 BC, after which the soldiers' importations from the east included more elaborate and expensive banquets. It was then that the cook, who had to the ancient Romans been the most worthless of slaves, 'began to have value, and what had been merely a necessary service came to be regarded as an art' (39.6.3–9; 1936: 237). The wealthy householder employed slave cooks in his mansion, or *domus*, which was connected to heating, water and sewerage. This is where diners ate in luxury, three reclining on each couch, arranged on three sides of, and giving their name also to, the *triclinium* or dining-room. Silver table services were common, leaving earthenware for the poor.

While fourth-century Rome had around 1800 mansions, the bulk of the population lived in 46 600 *insulae* (Carcopino 1956: 29). An *insula* was a large tenement block, an interest-bearing piece of real estate. As early as the third century BC, *insulae* of three storeys ceased to excite remark, but with their frequent collapse, one emperor forbade building more than 20 metres high, although they still often burned down (35–6). The apartments had undifferentiated rooms, without services or fireplace. This suggests that the inhabitants either cooked simply on a portable brazier, or that they hardly cooked at all, relying instead on the street.

Carts were banned during daylight hours. Instead, the streets were filled with people, sitting, standing, walking and, for the most part, talking, eating and preparing to eat. Those receiving payment in grain would have taken it to numerous millers and bakers. The *insula* dwellers obtained other food from vendors carrying trays, from market stalls and from groundfloor booths and shops called *tabernae*. Opening onto the street with wooden shutters, a *taberna* might be the storehouse of a merchant, the workshop of an artisan or the counter of a retailer, baker or cook.

The ancient equivalent of a bar had an L-shaped marble-topped counter that faced the street and ran back inside, where round holes in it held wine jars and a charcoal-burning furnace for hot water. The customer stood in the street and wine was ladled from one of the jugs, and served with bread, a cut of sausage, and the like (Casson 1974: 211–12). Extolling country living, poet Horace derides the city attractions of 'brothel and greasy café' (*Epistle* I.14; 1979: 156). While praising farm fare, Juvenal deplores gluttons who would hock the family silver to satisfy their greed off earthenware and decries ditch diggers who dream of the 'smell of tripe in some hot and crowded cookshop' (*Satire* XI: 81; 1974: 229). Roman cookshops were thought deceitful by Macrobius because they displayed eggs, liver and onions under water so that they looked larger (7.14.1; 1969: 502).

From her studies of Pompeii and Herculaneum, Helen H. Tanzer finds four distinct types of shop supplying cooked meals. The *popinae* were places of bad repute, where the *popa* or butcher, having assisted the priests at sacrifices, sold the leftovers. The *thermopolia* were hot drink shops for snacks and light meals (probably stews kept hot in bain-maries in a counter of marble or cement). Some cubicles could be rented, and stairs led up to the dining-room. The *cauponae* were taverns – that is, wine shops that were also eating-houses. People in a hurry could also pick up a bite, and, again, it would be something cooked by the proprietor (1939: 41–3).

To find a professional cook, a *coctor* but more likely a *coquus*, one looked for a *hospitium*, an inn, which included a dining-room. It might be made by combining houses, or even purpose-built. The innkeeper was called the *hospes*. Important people stayed at a friend's villa, but the inns near the city gates had stables and were frequented by merchants, gladiators and the homesick (47–8). Such inns were named after animals (The Elephant, The Camel, The Cock), things

(The Wheel, The Sword), and deities (The Diana, The Apollo) (Casson 1974: 205–6). At the better-class restaurants, customers could recline rather than sit (213).

MEDIEVAL COOKSHOPS

The self-sufficiency of the typical peasant family in medieval Britain should not be over-emphasised, warns economic historian M.M. Postan. Labourers were often fed at work, and made small purchases such as salt. Most villagers were compelled, by the lord's monopoly, to take their grain to the village mill to be ground into flour or gruel meal (and often to use the lord's ovens, grape press, and so on). However, the expense of fuel (owned by the lord) added to the demand for bread baked by outsiders, beer provided by ale-wives and food cooked by professionals. 'In weekly markets and above all in larger fairs, cooks and sellers of every kind of cooked or baked food were as conspicuous as they are nowadays in market places in India or in the Middle East, and for the same reasons', writes Postan (1975: 223–5). This reliance on outside cooks is further illustrated by Geoffrey Chaucer's Reeve's Tale. When unexpected company arrives at the mill, the miller sends his daughter out shopping while he roasts a goose: 'This millere into toun his doghter sende/For ale and breed, and rosted hem a goos'.

Partly because of the difficulty of keeping meat fresh, but also because only the larger houses had adequate means for cooking, the people of medieval European cities relied on cookshops for a selection of sauces, pies, puddings and baked meats. A customer could either buy a hot dish ready for eating or bring a joint to be cooked. In *A Description of London*, written about 1183, William Fitz Stephen describes a public cookshop: 'There daily, according to the season, you may find viands, dishes roast, fried and boiled, fish great and

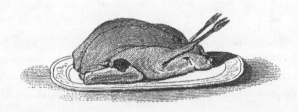

small, the coarser flesh for the poor, the more delicate for the rich, such as venison, and birds both big and little'. If friends should arrive unexpectedly and weary with travel, everyone can 'hasten to the river bank, and there all things desirable are ready to their hand'. All the dainties are 'set forth before their eyes. Now this is a public cookshop, appropriate to a city and pertaining to the art of civic life', he writes. An ordinance of the guild of Cooks, Pastelers (pastry-cooks) and Piebakers in England, dated 1378, sets out prices: 'The best roast pig, for 8d. Three roast thrushes, 2d. Ten eggs, one penny. For the paste, fire and trouble upon a goose, 2d. [In this case the customer provided the goose.] The best capon baked in a pasty, 8d' (Drummond and Wilbraham 1939: 32–3).

A cook employed to prepare meals for medieval pilgrims on the road from Southwark to Canterbury would know how to roast, boil, broil, fry, make stews and bake pies. More specifically, in his General Prologue, Chaucer says his 'Cook of London' could boil chickens with marrowbones, prepare a tart with 'powder merchant' (a mixed spice) and 'galingale' (an aromatic like ginger), and also make the best 'blankmanger' ('white food', being a kind of pudding of shredded chicken breast or other meat stewed with imported rice, almonds and sugar). This cook is named Roger of Ware, and apparently a contemporary cook of that name was well known (Hieatt 1996).

The midday meal for the townsman was roast meats, pies, stews or soups, bread, cheese, ale or beer. At the Westminster Gate, poet John Lydgate reports that the cooks 'proferred me bread, with ale and wyne,/Rybbs of befe, both fat and ful fyne', while at London Stone, he could buy 'hot shepes feete', 'makerell' and 'ryster [oyster] grene' (Drummond and Wilbraham 1939: 62–3). The London Brewers, for their dinner in 1423, not only paid to have one goose and two rabbits cooked by a baker, but they hired spits, pewter vessels and other equipment, plus 'a minstrel', two turnspits, a laundress, a man for 'cariage of donge' (dung), and a cook, Thomas Bourne. The cook would have brought his own assistants, included in his price (Henisch 1976: 84–5).

In seventeenth-century London, a good deal of meat was still distributed through the cookshops, many remaining near the river in 'Cooks row'. Impressed by the large amount eaten even by the poor, French visitor Monsieur Misson found that at a cookshop:

> Generally, four Spits, one over another, carry round each five or six Pieces of Butcher's Meat, Beef, Mutton, Veal, Pork and Lamb; you have what Quantity you please cut off, fat, lean, much or little done; with this, a little Salt and Mustard upon the Side of a Plate, a Bottle of Beer and a Roll; and there is your whole Feast (Drummond and Wilbraham 1939: 128).

During the first half of the eighteenth century, the artisans and labourers in English towns again lived well. They breakfasted early on bread, butter, cold meats, enormous quantities of cheese, and beer (gradually being replaced by tea). The principal meal, served at noon, was often eaten (at least by the men) at a tavern or bought at a cookshop, and usually consisted of meat and now vegetables, followed by cheese (258). In *The Adventures of Roderick Random*, published in 1748, Tobias Smollett describes a 'dive', or cookshop in a cellar, 'almost suffocated with the steams of boil'd beef, and surrounded by a company consisting chiefly of hackney-coachmen, chairmen, draymen, and few footmen ... who sat eating shin of beef, tripe, cow-heel [like pigs' trotters, only cattle] or sausages, at separate boards, covered with cloths, which turned my stomach' (1979: 65).

In London, as in Paris, from the later seventeenth century, men of the upper classes began to frequent coffee-houses or *cafés*. The coffee-houses of Restoration London were centres of political intrigue and commercial intelligence and, primarily, dining-rooms. But the eighteenth century's closest approximations to the later restaurants, both in their social and culinary position, were the taverns. They had started offering wine, as opposed to beer at ale-houses, and became noted eating places. John Farley was Principal Cook at the London Tavern, Collingwood and Woollams were at the equally famous Crown and Anchor Tavern, and Richard Briggs served at The Globe in Fleet Street and White Hart in Holborn (Jeaffreson 1875, 2: 241–55; Mennell 1985: 137).

While cooks of acclaim were typically male, women were employed in moderately sized English households (and a long line of female cookery teachers published recipe books, starting with Hannah Woolley, whose *The Queen-Like Closet* appeared in 1670). But in the *Mrs Beeton's* era, even women cooks became harder to get. Why should they dedicate their lives to others' households for token, and deteriorating, pay? In the novelist Saki's oft-quoted line from *Reginald on Besetting Sins* (1904), 'The cook was a good cook, as cooks go; and as cooks go she went'.

Commenting in 1864, A.V. Kirwan assumes that 'men cooks' provide a more professional and refined style of cooking than the typically female domestic, and that some hosts can only afford to bring in a proper *chef de cuisine* to supervise special dinners.

> In the case of men of moderate fortune, it is very likely a first-rate man cook, French or English, will be introduced for the occasion, and come the day before the dinner to make preliminary arrangements, and to give directions to, and to aid the ordinary woman cook of the household.

If a person 'cannot fully rely on their own English female cook', the alternative would be to 'contract with some renowned undertaker or *entrepreneur* of dinners, such as Gunter, Staples, Bathe and Breach, &c.' (1864: 75–6). Even in the most moderate establishments, the 'ordinary cook, with the aid of a first-rate man cook, has quite enough to do in preparing the soup, fish, meats, fowl, and game', and so he suggests that 'patties, and all kinds of pastry, jellies, ices, &c., should be procured from the confectioner' (193). Additionally, Kirwan reveals that it is often better to purchase a quart or gallon of turtle soup from a 'professional artist' in a first-rate hotel (132–3).

RESTAURATEURS VS TRAITEURS

While competing in the marketplace, cooks have, since ancient times, formed guilds. A little booklet of *Notes on the History of the Company of the Mistery of Cooks of London*, published by the Cooks' Company perhaps in the early 1960s, dates the Fraternity's formation to 1311–12. The trades regulated themselves and were regulated in terms of fair trading and health, were taxed and given some protection by the City and crown. That is, they operated as a profession, with its mutual promotion and restrictive trade practices – limiting entry through (often exploited) apprenticeships, sharing tricks of the trade, and fixing prices.

Giving away some of the hard-won knowledge in *The Whole Body of Cookery Dissected* in 1661, William Rabisha recognised:

> that divers Brethren of my own Fraternity may open their mouths against me, for publishing this treatise, pretending that thereby it may teach every kitchen-wench, and such as never served their times, and so be prejudicial to the Fraternity of cooks . . . (Mennell 1985: 91).

Although apprentices were exploited, they could look to an eventual position in society. One London merchant in the fifteenth century left a sum of money 'to lytell Jak of my kechyn, he to serve oute his termes' (Henisch 1976: 86). The 1433 will of Walter Mangeard, 'Citesen and koke [cook] of London', shows him able to provide for his wife and 'Litill Watkyn, my Godsone and my servant', and also to leave money to his church and to the London Fraternity of Cooks (72).

In Paris in 1268, in the *Livre des métiers* [*Book of Trades*], Etienne Boileau includes those statutes that defined the Cooks' Guild. To keep a lid on numbers, they restrict each member to one apprentice at a time; cooked meat can be kept only three days, unless adequately salted, and so on (Scully 1995: 236–7). The guild of cook–caterers, the *cuisiniers*, paralleled the hierarchy in the court kitchens, and the regulations of the guild permitted lateral movement at the same level of proficiency (Wheaton 1983: 72–3).

Do not forget we are talking about public cooks: *cuisiniers* are not to be confused with *queues*, master cooks employed in noble households and convents. Furthermore, the guild of *cuisiniers* was forever splitting and being challenged by new specialisations. The Tax Book for Paris in 1292 lists twenty-one *cuisiniers*, or cookshop keepers, and three *oiers*, or 'goose-cooks', from whom it was possible to buy boiled or roast meats of many kinds. Sauce or gravy was furnished by the *sauciers*, of whom the same tax roll enumerates seven, and who belonged to the corporation of vinegar-vendors (Andrieu 1956: 3–4, 6). For a wedding, a well-to-do host might send out to the sauce-maker for a 'quart of cameline for the dinner and for the supper two quarts of mustard' ('Goodman' 1928: 246). The name 'cameline' might come either from the herb *Camelina sativa* or from its dominant spice, cinnamon, or *cannella* in Italian (Santich 1995: 61).

Another corporation was made up of the *pâtissiers*, who sold pork-pies, poultry and eels, as well as tarts and flans of soft cheese and new-laid eggs. In 1292, Paris had sixty-eight of these, along with related tradespeople: two bakers of 'canary-bread' of fine white flour; three *fouaciers*, who made cakes of butter and eggs; seven *gasteliers*, who made cakes but not pastry; and nineteen *oubliers* or makers of wafers and light pastry (Andrieu 1956: 6). A great household might rely for luxurious trifles on its own waferer and confectioner, or follow more modest establishments and buy them ready-made. The wafer could be savoury, with a cheese filling, or spicy with ginger, but the classic one was sweetened with sugar or honey. Its pet names were *nebula* (cloud) and angel's bread. In Paris, his basket covered with a fresh white napkin, the waferer confidently offered free samples (Henisch 1976: 75–7). To accompany spiced wine after a wedding feast of twenty covers (forty people), the *Goodman of Paris* recommends ordering from the wafer-maker 'a dozen and a half of cheese *gauffres* . . . a dozen and a half of *gros batons* . . . a dozen and a half of *portes* . . . a dozen and a half of *estriers* . . . a hundred sugared *galettes*' ('Goodman' 1928: 240).

In 1467, the guild of *cuisiniers* split into *rôtisseurs*, who retained the character of the original cookshops, and *chaircuitiers-saulcissiers* or specialist cooked-meat and sausage vendors, and the antecedents of the *charcutiers* (Andrieu 1956: 4). In 1557, the Venetian ambassador Lippomano could write: 'The roasters [*rôtisseurs*] and the pastrycooks [*pâtissiers*], in less than an hour, will arrange a dinner for you, or a supper, for ten, twenty, or a hundred people; the roaster will give you the meats, the pastrycook the tarts, the meat pies, the little cooked dishes, and sweets; the cook will give you aspics, sauces, stews' (Wheaton 1983: 76).

These tradesmen sold goods to be carried away, but a further offshoot of the *cuisiniers* was the *traiteurs* – eating-house keepers or caterers. They were popular with the modest people, for they sold small quantities at low prices. From statutes in 1599, they specialised in weddings and banquets, held on their own premises or elsewhere. Meanwhile, food was still sold in taverns. To be more precise, the vintner sold wine to take away, the tavern-keeper sold wine by the jug, consumed on the premises, and the *cabaretier* provided food on a table properly laid with cloth and cutlery (Andrieu 1956: 7).

When Antoine Beauvilliers opened the first great restaurant, La Grande Taverne de Londres – in 1782, according to Brillat-Savarin, and in 1786 according to others – a new trade, deriving partly from English taverns, had broken away from the *traiteurs* (Mennell 1985: 138–9). The caterers had an exclusive right to sell cooked meat dishes, but limited themselves to selling whole cuts of meat, not an individual helping. That monopoly was contested in 1765 by Boulanger, a seller of *bouillons*. While the *traiteurs* claimed the exclusive right to sell *ragoût*, stock fell outside their monopoly and was sold under the name *restaurant*, in the sense of 'restorative'. Boulanger extended this and sold sheep's feet to which he added a white sauce. The *traiteurs* saw this as a *ragoût*, took the matter to court, and lost. As food historian Barbara Santich explains, the reasoning was that *pieds du mouton* were not actually cooked in the sauce (1987: 201). The title of *restaurateur*, which has on occasion been aptly translated as 'restorator', began to supplant that of *traiteur* (caterer) in prestige.

At the point of the creation of the individualistic and often elaborate restaurant, Brillat-Savarin's 'finishing touch' in the gastronomic pageant, the history of cookshops intersects with that of the culinary courts. But I warned in the previous chapter that the grandest and lowest cooking retained links. The top French chefs both came from the grand households and rose from the streets. With restaurants, a regal banqueting style descended to the marketplace, so that commoners might become sovereign consumers, while vigorous street food rose to a closeted, fine setting, meeting the knowledgeable, sentient connoisseur.

Overall, the lesson is not to fret over historical lineage, when the important point is the closeness of high to low cooking. Heritage – that is, roots into the past – is perhaps not as determinative as authenticity, which reaches into the soil as well. We meet again the housewives providing behind-the-scenes support for even the most glittering cuisines.

PEASANTS AND PRINCES

As a servant of high society, Henri Charpentier looked after Baron Rothschild, Sarah Bernhardt, Theodore Roosevelt and 'Diamond' Jim Brady. He invented 'Crêpes Suzette' for the prince who became Edward VII of England. After moving to the United States, this French *maître d'hôtel* opened a restaurant on Long Island in the Gatsby era, and Prohibition agents eventually trucked away his fabulous – and by then clandestine – cellar. However, like so many great food providers, he had a peasant upbringing.

Charpentier's sentimental autobiography, *Those Rich and Great Ones: Or life à la Henri*, is piled with timely kindnesses, debts repaid and just deserts, and confirms the close connections of great restaurateurs with the soil, that 'professed' cooks have never been far from domestic. Henri Charpentier was abandoned in the south of France in 1880 by his upper-crust and teenage mother, who left him to be brought up by peasants. His greatest fondness is reserved for these earliest teachers, especially his foster-mother, Mama Camous, whom he amply recompensed with support in her old age, and his older step-brother, Jean Camous, who worked under Escoffier and became a top chef himself.

'All our food came to us by processes that to city people would seem extraordinary', Charpentier reminisces. For example, the household's solitary nanny-goat went up the slope in the morning with a withered, empty bag. At sundown, she returned with the other village goats, prepared to defend with her horns her filled udder – 'but to me, Henri, who was her friend, she would surrender it to the last drop. So you see, I grew up in a family which had milk but no milk bill'. Mama Camous made all kinds of excellent breads and pies of a kind called *tarte de blé*, which came from the oven beautifully brown and with a rim puffed high (1935: 16–18). She produced all sorts of wondrous dishes from 'cooking pots suspended in the blackened fireplace'.

One day it would be a rabbit they had sacrificed; another time the victim would be some hen that had retired from egg-laying. My Mama Camous would prepare even an old hen so that it would be saluted by Escoffier (43).

For a picnic, the men of the village gathered in a grove of chestnuts around the magnificent oak table – its patina 'a history of French wines' – piled with half a dozen hams, numerous roasted rabbits, great loaves of bread and sausages of many varieties. The village butcher took pride in slicing the ham in transparent sheets, the *mortadella* of pig's head and gelatine even thinner, and the salami like paper. At four in the afternoon, the women arrived, bringing baskets of *beignets*, apple fritters cooked with currant jelly (18–19).

By the age of ten, Henri was apprenticed. If that sounds early, 'I would remind you that the admirals of the English began as young and did not have so much to learn' (24). He joined his foster-brother, a kitchen tyrant, called a 'no-return' chef because 'Not one course was taken from the kitchen until Camous had tasted and approved; but when he had approved you had adventure in a tureen! Romance in a casserole! Paradise in the sweet!' (45). Maintaining contact at the market with the source of good cooking, Jean Camous would pick out the farm woman's least desirable head of lettuce, complaining: 'See how its centre is yellow and cut by a worm. A worm, Madam!'. She would turn her head in disdain, because she had, always, wonderful merchandise. But he clucked like a disturbed rooster, until she selected her finest lettuce. The chef would concede that this was an exception, and so on, until she had picked out the eyes of her own stock (57–8). Do not get the idea that, with such behaviour, this chef took advantage. No, it was important for him to keep the goodwill of all those who brought him produce. For the same reason, he spread his business among several stall-keepers.

On the other hand, he dared not allow one of them to take advantage of him (59–60).

Charpentier describes how Jean Camous gradually accumulated sufficient *fraises des bois*, and tested if the peas were fresh, the mushrooms were the right species and the eggplant suitable: 'How do I know that? Camous told me but he did

more than tell me. He demonstrated . . . Tomatoes? Ask your nose!'
(65). Charpentier learned to understand fresh produce 'as any country
boy knows it'. An actual odour of wild watercress or of a ripe tomato
from his own garden in the United States was sufficient to bring
back the old market memories of Le Havre, which also included the
'tight spheres of cabbages', the 'wide haunch of a seated market-
woman' and the 'scrape of baskets along the stones' (60–1).

If circumstances ever compelled him and his wife to live on a
small income, Charpentier considers he would still eat excellent food.
'But that is not remarkable when you think how many times I watched
my dear foster-mother make one egg impart its flavour to pancakes
for a big family' (69). On a 'very small piece of land on this broad
continent I could build a paradise'. As well as rabbits, hens and goats,
he would keep a pig. 'Eventually he would weigh enough to provide
me with a pound of pork for every day in the year.' But Henri would
deprive himself of some, trading a ham for another small pig, just
as they used to do in Contes (71).

Henri often wondered what chef Camous would have thought if
he were 'compelled to buy vegetables three thousand miles from the
gardens which produced them'. Why, Camous was so set upon having
fresh fish that he bought, not from a dealer, but from a fisherman,
whom he once scolded: 'I want my fish from you tide by tide!' (68).

*   *   *

Scratch a society restaurateur, and sniff the ample stew. In the
modern restaurant, one secret has been the continuous links between
kitchens high and low, between career cooks *à la Henri* and their
bounteous mothers. In supplementing (and thereby diminishing)
women in the home, street cooks of all kinds have contributed to
the shape and vigour of cities. As shown in previous chapters,
professional cooks have, in turn, been exploited and regulated from
above. For civilisation has also been produced by the grand, parasitic
households of high priests, kings and emperors. Sharing food and
jobs, our ambitious, inventive and plain hardworking ancestors have
cooked up a steaming pudding. These have been some of the finest

adventures of the cooking animal, and the results can still be admired around the world.

But the civilisation of village, street and courtly kitchen is passing, as all levels of the culinary economy, society and culture are now being reshaped by the modern, mass-marketing food industry. For just over two centuries, starting in Europe, industrialists have deposed priests and princes, supplanted peasants on their plots, cleared forests, dragged oceans and laden the lands with factories. Developers have regimented public spaces and called them malls. No longer an overflow of the maternal kitchen, all food belongs increasingly to the vaulting corporation.

So, next, we monitor modernity as it breaks through with institutional science, petro-chemical industry, agribusiness, supermarketing, magazine recipes and ever-loud television. We experience the single-minded ravages of aggressively laissez-faire reorganisation. Food emerges from electronic banks, legal offices and advertising agencies, and the public street is taken over by fastfood franchisers. We have entrusted cooking to big boys in suits.

CHAPTER FIFTEEN

Freedom from Cooks?

Once upon a time there were two sisters, Laura and Lizzie. Every morning and evening, they heard the goblins cry:

Come buy our orchard fruits,
Come buy, come buy:
Apples and quinces,
Lemons and oranges,
Plump unpecked cherries,
Melons and raspberries,
Bloom-down-cheeked peaches,
Swart-headed mulberries,
Wild free-born cranberries . . .

The young women knew not to heed the call – their friend Jeanie had once tasted the fruit, only to waste away and die.

'No,' said Lizzie: 'No, no, no;
Their offers should not charm us,
Their evil gifts would harm us.'

After repeated blandishments, Lizzie remained resolute, but Laura eventually succumbed. She visited the goblin market and feasted on the fruit, paying with a lock of her golden hair. Now that she had been tempted, she pined for more. But, having tasted, she could no longer hear the cries of the goblin men. In her distress, she no longer ate, slept, or did her chores. She grew thin. Her eyes were shrunken.

Lizzie made up her mind to take a silver penny to get fruit for her sister. The goblins refused to sell on these terms. Instead, they tried unsuccessfully to force their new victim to eat, squashing fruit against her clenched teeth. Lizzie returned home, covered in flesh and juice, and invited Laura to lick her body.

> *Hug me, kiss me, suck my juices*
> *Squeezed from goblin fruits for you,*
> *Goblin pulp and goblin dew.*
> *Eat me, drink me, love me;*
> *Laura, make much of me;*
> *For your sake I have braved the glen*
> *And had to do with goblin merchant men.*

Laura ate, and returned to good health. Years later, the sisters would tell their children the story, warning against the goblin market, praising Lizzie's strength, and drawing the moral: 'There is no friend like a sister'.

This is a condensation of Christina Rossetti's 567-line poem *Goblin Market*. Written in 1859 in England, it could have come from a beautifully illustrated book of children's tales. It could be dismissed as naive, brightly coloured, dated. But its strong images cry out to be pondered.

The poem has usually been taken to be almost embarrassingly allegorical. In feminist and lesbian interpretations, for example, the abundant fruits are often seen as symbols of knowledge, sexuality or female creativity. However, let us not get carried away with symbolism. Crucially, let us assume that it is real food, that an apple is an apple. Let us accept that the long and vivid lists of unblemished fruits come from an actual market, and that the seducers and rapists are real sellers, real 'merchant men'.

Christina Rossetti lived at a time when many people were still relatively self-sufficient. The sisters had many chores. In their rural idyll, they:

Fetched in honey, milked the cows,
Aired and set to rights the house,
Kneaded cakes of whitest wheat,
Cakes for dainty mouths to eat,
Next churned butter, whipped up cream,
Fed their poultry, sat and sewed . . .

These are the jobs of the traditional kitchen, reliant on immediate resources – the local physical environment and household labour. The sisters would have obtained fruit from their own orchard. Nevertheless, at the time of writing, the impersonal food industry, 'that unknown orchard', was taking over. The new businesses were beginning to advertise with an 'iterated jingle/Of sugar-baited words'.

Christina Rossetti sets her story in a dreamy place. It could seem purely imaginary. However, Laura can be taken to have really been tempted by the fabulous food from the mysterious new market. Even if Rossetti might not have given this blunt explanation, she conveys glimpses of the surrounding revolution.

A critique of the brave new food industry gaining ground in the mid-1800s was published under the initials 'M.M.' in the London literary magazine *Fraser's*, apparently by a contemporary of Rossetti's, Mary Ellen Meredith.

We have let the beer of the people disappear, and have grown ashamed of roast beef ... Draught ale has vanished, and all the bottled compounds that go by that name are but unwholesome concoctions of drugs and camomile. We have brought chemistry into our kitchens, not as a handmaid but as a poisoner (1851: 607).

This makes Rossetti's poem a study of contradictory pressures. While the goblins are really only interested in their pound of flesh, Laura is seduced: 'You cannot think what figs/My teeth have met in'. Alienated, she goes on a hunger strike. Having eaten of the foreign fruit, Laura 'sat down listless in the chimneynook/And would not eat'.

At the same time as Laura is tempted by perfect-seeming fruit, the sisters are aware of their bodies as beautiful objects. The poem is imprecise about the ages of these 'maidens', and yet gives the impression that they are girls becoming women. They have long golden hair. They later have children.

Rossetti's brother Dante Gabriel was a leader of the Pre-Raphaelite brotherhood of painters and poets, who rejected industrial England for a medieval romance. Many of their paintings were of beautiful women. In a much shorter poem entitled 'In an Artist's Studio', Christina Rossetti describes her brother's various portraits of his future wife: 'He feeds upon her face by day and night'. Moreover, he 'feeds' not on her actual face, but as he wants it to be: 'Not as she is, but as she fills his dream'.

Just as the *Goblin Market* dramatises Victorian women's emergence as purchasers of commodities, it shows them as commodities themselves. Deborah Ann Thompson, a scholar of English literature, finds this in Rossetti's 'lingering on the gold hair of these women', gold also being a feature of the goblin market. In total, critics such as Thompson have located an insider's account of anorexia nervosa. As well as symptoms of obsessive–compulsive eating within the poem, they have extracted biographical evidence of Rossetti's anxieties about food and body size.

Without many traditional supports, young women are torn by divergent demands. On the one hand, they are meant to be the sustainers. On the other, they have to be wary of food, since it is associated with weight gain. They are to show enthusiasm for cooking for others, but not necessarily themselves. In introducing such interpretations of the *Goblin Market*, Thompson writes: 'Bourgeois women experienced the confusions and anxieties of changing social roles through the production and consumption of food' (1991: 99–100).

I, too, present the *Goblin Market* as a nostalgic reverie responding to dislocation, counterpointed by the sisters' closeness. The sisters and the merchants might as well live in separate lands. The women are torn between their homely past and the dream of a chore-free utopia. They are tugged by illusions of perfection in fruit, on one side, and figure, on the other. They cannot understand the new nature, in which food seems unrelated to production. They are both lured and repelled by show without substance.

In pain, Christina Rossetti confronts the invasion by the (male)

food industry into the domestic world and the promise and trauma for young women torn between traditional chores and the emerging market. Where women had been productive household labourers, toiling together as 'sisters', they have become consumers and public figures. This reading of her poem suggests that Christina Rossetti sought to come to terms with the contradictions of modernity.

TRADITION INTO MODERNITY

Women offered conflicting criticisms of the first edition of *Geist der Kochkunst* (*The Spirit of Cookery*) in 1822, author Baron von Rumohr admits in a revised edition a decade later. As a man writing a cookery book, he was accused both of encroaching on women's traditional domain, and of keeping them trapped there.

> Is it then an encroachment? This would mean that women fully accept that it is their duty to run the household. If, on the other hand, it is a reminder of hated duties which were cast off long ago, then it cannot simultaneously be seen as an encroachment. What more can I do? (1993: 59).

While Rumohr certainly still assumes that it is women in the kitchen, a more recent commentator, sociologist Victor Hell (1982), defends the Baron as addressing himself particularly to women 'not to confine them to the domain of the three Ks, but to open them up to the economic life'. According to Hell, Rumohr connects *Kinder, Kirche, Küche* to 'grander' questions – as if 'children, church, kitchen' are not mighty issues, and that again is the paradox.

327

Rumohr seeks to address the decline in traditional cooking, already observable in Germany early in the nineteenth century. He values what he calls 'national and provincial dishes', which had their 'foundations in the local characteristics, both of people and country, and are almost always tasty and nutritious'. However, these trusted items were being undermined by a rash of inappropriate cookery books, by 'these haphazard accumulations of recipes of all kinds, many of which are quite absurd' (1993: 49). He does not rate the mounting numbers of recipe collections 'great intellectual works'. They are either 'products of flat, unreflecting experience', or they are 'straight compilations . . . devoid of any scientific ideals' (43).

Not inheriting a 'traditional' cookery based upon the sensible preparation of local products and so resorting to 'soul-destroying' books, the 'respectable virtuous wife' no longer knows how to prepare meals. This results in household discontent, says Rumohr. Instead of the meal being the gathering point of family members, a formerly diligent man will 'be off to the market, the drug store or to any other purveyor of witches' brews. Thus the bad habit begins and the family's health and contentment, and even its common livelihood, will rapidly descend the path to total ruin'. Rumohr wants to play his part in alleviating the evils by taking the art of cookery 'right back to basics' (52–4).

Rumohr prefers to replace age-old recipes with general information about methods and ingredients, leaving nuances and shades of culinary invention to the imagination of the individual cook (54). Rather than a succession of recipes, the greater part of *Geist der Kochkunst* is devoted to methodically setting out principles and important tips. Book One, aimed at 'animal foodstuffs', explains topics such as roasting, boiling, stocks, soups and deep-frying. Book Two explores the handling of 'foodstuffs and seasonings from the plant world', including bread, porridge and nutritious vegetables.

Nonetheless, Rumohr compounds his sin of being yet another man telling women what to do by blaming the decline in traditional expertise upon the wrong attitudes of the cooks – 'housewives have grown too lazy, too ignorant and too falsely refined to keep proper storecupboards', he scolds (171). Instead, his complaints can be more properly laid at the feet of industrialisation. The goblin merchant men were already luring good housewives.

Where a noble lady was, in Rumohr's eyes, no less noble for having spearheaded the making each autumn of countless sausages, hams, bacons and so forth, even in Italy such practices were being 'sacrificed'. With a theme of the need to 'mix usefulness with grace' (as in Horace's *miscuit utile dulci*), Rumohr remonstrates that 'their advancing state of refinement is also daily rendering German women less capable of attending to the ordinary necessities of life, to the long-term provision, maintenance and distribution of stores' (115). However, with the new industry taking over processing, households were already preserving less of their own food. 'In many German towns, pastry and cake "factories" have risen from the ruins of the art of true housekeeping' (131). He is even translated as deploring 'fast food shops', which had so far established in a few provinces only, but notably Upper Saxony (52).

Even earlier, Mary Wollstonecraft analysed the situation in her *Vindication of the Rights of Woman* (1792), which has been called the first great document of feminism. In it, she blames wealth, male expectations and the denial of education for making women lazy and decadent, taking them away from healthy and family-oriented cooking and child-rearing. Her solution is universal female education and the redistribution of wealth. When women are educated, men will find them more attractive and simple home life more fulfilling, and so will no longer expect idleness and coquetry.

MODERNITY

Two centuries ago, by far the great majority of the world population were peasants, sharing their flame, pot and bed of straw with pigs and fowls. Even in grander households, people repeated the actions of their parents. Most food was obtained locally by the eaters themselves. Hunting was often still possible (or poaching). Cooking was done on a wood fire, perhaps for the majority of people with just one cauldron, gridiron, pot or wok. Flora Thompson's *Lark Rise* describes how even in the 1880s in some parts of England every house had a productive garden or allotment. Vegetables were eaten in their season. Each cottage kept a pig, whose death meant bacon for winter, or longer (Drummond and Wilbraham 1957: 281). Even if I have spoken of ungendered 'cooks', traditionally they were women.

Then, Rossetti's sisters, Rumohr's housewives and Wollstonecraft's emancipists were invaded. Their kitchens were blasted by revolutions: the scientific, the agricultural, the industrial and the capitalist. It took some decades, but their gardens were stripped, their kitchens sterilised and their golden locks demanded. The gnomes substituted the market economy (Polanyi 1944) and factory kitchen (Symons 1982).

Sampling from dictionaries and encyclopaedias provides clues to the morally complicated recipe. Take traditional kitchens and subject them to the commercialisation of production, steam power, mechanisation, the rise of capitalist corporations, cohesive nation-states and urbanisation. Mix these with mass literacy, the enfranchisement of the population and mass political parties, the application of science to all spheres of life, the reliance on fossil fuels, power utilities, time and motion studies, flexible capital markets, trade unions, and social mobility. Then throw in, for good measure, artificial flavours, public health, the welfare state, meritocracy, unemployment, the maturation of social services, secularisation, the segmentation of knowledge, plastics, agribusiness, supermarketing, planned obsolescence, globalisation, mass media, marketing, Rachel Carson's *Silent Spring*, Hollywood, pop art, hippies, nuclear power, greenhouse effect, cyberspace, downsizing, spin doctors. And serve!

Laura and Lizzie's kitchen exploded into myriad fragments, strung together with railtracks, cables, highways, container ports, wires, trucks, jets and optical fibres. Once relatively self-sufficient, people now divided up food and labour so intricately that they lost sight of the connections. Specialist workers were too caught up to recognise their part in the global *oikos*. Yet farmers, engineers and school teachers all cooked the same, shared pudding. The cook is dead; long live the cook!

While it is commonplace to state that technology has shifted employment from agriculture to manufacturing, and from manufacturing to services, we can now interpret this in terms of industry sweeping up the cooks' three core duties in turn. Over the past two centuries or so, food industrialisation has progressed through these main moments (acquisition, distribution and organisation), each platform successively building on the other.

The Industrialisation of Acquisition

The so-called Agricultural Revolution required land, and Jack Drummond and Anne Wilbraham, food historians, describe the brutal effects of the clearances and Enclosure Acts in Britain, which had started in the twelfth and continued into the nineteenth century. Previously largely self-sufficient peasants were turned into agricultural labourers, who drifted into the cities, where they became a pool of dispossessed proletarians available for factories. 'The small farms were being swallowed up by the big estates and many a cottage and its little garden plot was ruthlessly "liquidated" ', they write (1957: 280). Meanwhile, setting the pace, the British Empire commanded commodities from around the world, including from plantations reliant on the forced labour of African and other slaves (Mintz 1985). Revelling in the benefits of 'Empire', agricultural educator J.F. Ainsworth-Davis lists the 'obvious examples' – 'Spices, cane sugar, rice, tea, chocolate, coffee, oranges, lemons, and turtles' (1928: 169).

The fundamental questions of agriculture – soil fertility and manuring – became a scientific problem at the end of the eighteenth century. With *Chemistry in its Applications to Agriculture and Physiology* in 1840, the hero of organic chemistry, Justus, Baron von Liebig, shattered the assumption that plants derived their organic substance from the humus of the soil and showed the chief source at least of carbon was the atmosphere. Nitrogen was absorbed by the roots as ammonia and lime regulated the acidity of soils. Such knowledge laid the foundation for artificial manuring. Liebig, whom Drummond and Wilbraham see as possessing 'strongly developed commercial instincts', attempted to sell a fertiliser, as well as foods for use in animal husbandry. He was connected at various times with the marketing of a highly successful meat-extract, as well as infant and invalid food, a baking powder and similar ventures (1957: 284–6).

The social and technological reorganisation of primary production represented a kind of Stone Age for modern industry, in that the main action, as with our scavenging forebears, was directed at food acquisition. Based on this, the next step was forging a system of food storage and distribution (analogous to city-state civilisations), which gained momentum during the late 1800s.

The Industrialisation of Distribution

One of the nineteenth-century food industry's 'great achievements' was the development of canning. In 1806, the French Navy sampled meat, fruit, vegetables and even milk bottled by French pioneer Nicolas Appert. A partner in an English iron-works realised the value of Appert's discovery if tinned iron could replace glass, and by about 1812 got a factory going. A government inquiry in England in the 1850s traced food-poisoning to Stephen Goldner's company, where the size of cans of meat had been increased beyond 6 lb (2.7 kg), so that the internal bulk was insufficiently heated to kill micro-organisms. When tinned beef moved from being an item used at sea into the domestic market, the importation into England leaped from about 7 tonnes in 1866 to 10 000 tonnes five years later (Drummond and Wilbraham 1957: 317–22).

The development of refrigeration took thirty years of often costly experiment in several countries, with shiploads of meat going bad on long voyages. But a major step was made in Australia by James Harrison, who in 1850 designed the first ice-making machine. At the Melbourne Exhibition in 1872, Harrison exhibited an 'ice-house' – the precursor of the freezer – that kept sides of beef and carcasses of sheep until the next year, when some of the meat was eaten at a public luncheon (323–5).

'Roller' flour mills attracted attention from the 1870s. They were quicker, easier to use and, last but by no means least, produced whiter flour than grinding between flat stones. While consumers have been said to want whiter flour, the most telling advantage is that, without the germ, the danger of rancidity is almost eliminated (297). The bacteriological knowledge that resulted from Pasteur's studies led to milk pasteurisation from about 1890, again more as a means to increase the 'life' of the milk than to kill germs that might harm the drinker (301). Nestlé started making condensed milk at a Swiss factory in 1866, margarine was produced in experiments for the French Navy and in 1902 a patent to make powdered milk was taken out (303–4).

Such processing techniques formed the basis of distribution through grocery chains. The primitive advertising industry matched early brand names, such as Excelsior and Peerless, with equally corny slogans: 'Smith's self-raising flour – Never surpassed'. In the last decades of the century, Dr John Harvey Kellogg transformed a Seventh Day Adventist sanatorium in Battle Creek, Michigan, into a fountainhead of patent foods, especially Kellogg's 'Toasted Corn Flakes', the artificiality of 'scientific' products being considered somehow more hygienic than raw ingredients. The 'Elijah's Manna' of nearby producer Dr Charles Post was the breakfast cereal that grew into the enormous General Foods corporation (Root and de Rochement 1976: 228–9). Essential in food distribution, by 1845, fifty railway lines covered more than 1000 kilometres in England (Drummond and Wilbraham 1957: 288), while the railroad spanned the United States from east to west by 10 May 1869.

THE INDUSTRIALISATION OF ORGANISATION

The idea of all-electric, labour-saving convenience would have appealed to the ancient Greeks. About 2500 years ago, playwright Crates in his comedy *Wild Animals* foresees a time when a person, even without slaves, would not have to lift a finger to manage the household. Each article of furniture would come when called:

> Place yourself here, table! You, I mean, get yourself ready! Knead, my little troughy [kneading-trough]. Fill up, my ladle! Where's the cup? Go and wash yourself. Walk this way, my barley-cake. The pot should disgorge the beets. Fish, get up! 'But I'm not yet done on the other side!' Well, turn yourself over, won't you? and baste yourself with oil and salt (Athenaeus 267ef; 3: 203–5).

Utopian feminists have also anticipated the abolition of household drudgery. Writing in 1848 in the United States, one such reformer, Jane Sophia Appleton, visualises centralised food manufacture. She prophesies that:

> Quiet, order, prudence, certainty of success, govern the process of turning out a ton of bread, or roasting an ox! – as much as the weaving of a yard of cloth in one of your factories. No fuming, no fretting over the cooking stove, as of old! No 'roasted lady' at the head of the dinner! Steam machinery, division of labor, economy of

material, make the whole as agreeable as any other toil, while the expense to pocket is as much less to man as the wear of patience, time, bone and muscle to woman (Hayden 1981: 52).

Communitarian socialists have designed cities without domestic work. After living for a year in the 1860s in the Familistère (Social Palace) established in France by followers of Charles Fourier, Marie Stevens Howland returned to the United States with plans for mass housing with communal facilities. People would live in hotels, or in clusters of four large houses, sharing one service building, combining kitchen and servants' quarters (Hayden 1981: 91–113). In other words, domestic work would be eliminated by being done as part of the public economy.

For Alice Constance Austin, an early twentieth-century publicist of 'The Socialist City', traditional houses demanded the 'hatefully monotonous' drudgery of preparing 1095 meals in the year and cleaning up after each one. Her kitchenless houses would be connected to a central kitchen through a network of tunnels, through which railway cars carried cooked food, laundry and other goods to 'hubs', from where small electric cars delivered to every basement (242–3).

Contributing to the *Ladies' Home Journal* in 1919, playwright and feminist Zona Gale advocates a centralised cooked food supply and distribution. She concedes that abolishing the private kitchen sounds revolutionary. But it must also have once seemed outrageous to suggest abolishing private wells, private kerosene lamps, and 'home spinning, home weaving, home stitching of shirts, home soft-soap making'. For her, the 'private kitchen must go the way of the spinning wheel, of which it is the contemporary' (17).

Writing in 1884, Friedrich Engels is also optimistic:

the emancipation of women becomes possible only when women are enabled to take part in production on a large, social scale, and when domestic duties require their attention only to a minor degree. And this has become possible only as a result of modern large-scale industry, which not only permits of the participation of women in production in large numbers, but actually calls for it and, moreover, strives to convert private domestic work also into a public industry (1948: 158).

Then, in the 1970s, a billboard for Kentucky Fried Chicken said it brazenly and said it all: 'Women's liberation'.

Laura and Lizzie had already been relieved of self-sufficiency in growing and tending raw materials, and, secondly, of preserving them. These are two of what I have presented as the three responsibilities of cooks. The final stage, under way by the second half of the twentieth century, was the centralisation of final assembly and, implied by that, the entire culinary culture. That is, the industrialisation of the garden and then storage made way for the total de-domestication of the kitchen. The balance of actual cooking was relocating to the factory. Altogether, this is the Kitchen Revolution, with the transfer of the last tasks from the domestic to the public economy.

The division of tasks is now, at least theoretically, global. Producers are hyper-specialised, leading fractional lives. I could not begin to count the number of trades. Together with this, the distribution of food is also global, at least theoretically. Since the most primitive division of labour, women have conducted whatever remained of domestic production, while men constructed the 'political' economy. With commercialisation of the entire chain, women, too, achieve public status. Cooks no longer work within the private household, but without. They no longer run the sharing, but play a miniscule part.

The emblematic 'convenience' food became the 'TV Dinner', a complete meal frozen in a foil tray and marketed in the United States under that brand name in 1953 by C.A. Swanson & Sons of Omaha, Nebraska. Their patent the following year featured 'frozen Turkey Dinner, Including Turkey, Dressing, Giblet Gravy, Sweet Potatoes, and Green Peas' (Jerome 1981). Vast bureaucratic organisations are now programmed to produce, distribute, design and popularise a range of pre-mixed cakes, frozen pizzas, carbonated beverages and complete fastfood dinners. There are fewer local dishes and more global icons, such as soda-pop, a beef patty in a bun, and gaudy pizza. With concentration of ownership and vertical integration, the *Harvard Business School Bulletin* used the term 'agribusiness' in 1955 – it encompasses the manufacture and marketing of sprays, fertilisers and feedstuffs for mechanised petro-chemical farms, the production on farms, and the storage, processing and distribution of commodities produced on farms and items made from them. Through loans, contracts and technological dependence, and even direct ownership, family farms have been more closely incorporated into the corporate structure.

The beef comes by freight-wagon, the pasta by container, the snow-peas by jet. As never before, we share completely across communities and oceans, and we share less equally. World hunger has been blamed on over-population, the climate and 'primitive' technology, when the causes can be found within the distortions imposed by affluent nations (George 1977). The more finely we share tasks, the more completely we become dependent for our food – that is, the more completely we become consumers.

After the Second World War, arms manufacturers turned to motor-cars and refrigerators, which together hastened the privately owned '*super*-market'. The household car is needed to reach the carpark and carry a week's load, which can then be kept in the refrigerator. The sophisticated distribution network now includes freezing, road-transport and electronic data-processing via the bar-code. With supermarkets slashing prices, and service, food manufacturers reach consumers through marketing. The corporations 'cook' in the sense that they organise what is on our plate.

With 'iterated jingle' and 'sugar-baited words', the elfin cooks lurk in gaps in soap and crime operas, slip between leaves of colour magazines, and break through sports excitement. In the surreal landscape of television, new husbands surprise with smart shopping, and bright kids want to be fed a short drive away. As French intellectual Roland Barthes points out, myth-making is now almost entirely commercial, the new sacred moment being the 'situation' (1979). Exciting, youthful escapades are promised by an acid-sweet former patent medicine (coca and cola are both traditional stimulants). Cooking theologian Robert Farrar Capon's 'heretical' fear is that the 'world is engaged in a vast missionary effort (spearheaded by zealous Madison Avenue Fathers) to convince us that it is our gastronomic destiny to eat like kings while practising nothing but the most minimal kind of cooking' (1969: 144). Through razzle-dazzle, commerce becomes a very 'visible hand'.

The goblins have cleaved us into producers and consumers. We sell our labour as producers, and buy our meals as shoppers, accumulators, fantasisers. We become entirely specialised producers, commanding vast quantities of technical information, and highly individual consumers – gourmets, dieters, vegetarians, faddists, chocaholics. One half of me is meant to engage in frenzied work (if I am in paid employment at all), and the other in isolated fantasy spending. Sociologist Daniel Bell points out this 'cultural contradiction' between the 'Protestant ethic in the area of production' and the 'demand for pleasure and play in the area of consumption' (1976: 75). The successful person is meant to both 'work hard and play hard', to seek 'best practice' and 'lifestyle'.

Given that we think like we cook, edible profusion means cultural profusion, which scholars in the 1980s called 'postmodernity'. Roland Barthes has been tempted to say that the ' "polysemia" [multiple meanings] of food characterises modernity' (1979: 172). Or, in his *The Postmodern Condition*, Jean-François Lyotard pronounces: 'Eclecticism is the degree zero of contemporary general culture: one listens to reggae, watches a western, eats McDonald's food for lunch and local cuisine for dinner, wears Paris perfume in Tokyo and "retro" clothes in Hong Kong' (1984: 76). We sense the philosophers' frustration at the multiplicity of voices. Yet numerous discourses serve hyper-specialised production and hyper-active selling.

'Mexican? ... Chinese? ... Pasta? ... Italian? ... Indian? ... Pizza? ... French? ... Thai? ... Salad? ... Chicken? ...' The character in the *Cathy* comic strip of Cathy Guisewite is overwhelmed by the choice of 'take-out' menus. In desperation, she picks up the phone and screams: 'Just send some food! I don't even care what it is!! Just send some food!!' But the listener hangs up. And so, in the fourth frame, Cathy stirs a pot on the stove, musing: 'Incredible ... It's become easier to cook dinner than to order' (1995).

* * *

With the hunter–gatherer, the full might of culture was applied to food-collecting. Then, following the neolithic changes, the settled agrarians took the step of storage. Seeds were kept for planting. Livestock was herded. Temples were built on grain silos. The division of labour was moderate, with many farmers, and limited numbers of specialist tool-makers, priests and warriors. Finally, the touchstone of modernity is rationalisation, organisation through accountancy, science and bureaucracy, control that reaches our individual plate.

To think that three million years of human development, all that experiment, all that risk, all those dreams, all that heartbreak, all that repetition, have led to this. We have nibbled. We have stirred the pudding. We have ended with McDonald's. To think that the sum total is Coke clutter – dispensers, billboards, television slots, athletic sponsorships, cities draped in neon. Profit-minded zealots, with a standardised 'formula' and global reach, devalue the human enterprise. We end it smothered in cost-cutting corporate cooking, our mouths agape before a thin, anorexic screen. We have sold our birthright for a mess of globally marketed pottage. We have participated in the complete manufacture of choice. We have the power only to decide our baked potato topping. But is that all? There is resistance. For one thing, cooking has become chic.

THE EXAMINED MEAL

'Foodies' were formally christened by *Harpers & Queen* in August 1982 in an article ('Cuisine Poseur') by three staff writers and several freelancers. The London *Observer*'s food writer, Paul Levy, edited the article anonymously, having signed an agreement, he says, not to sue for the libellous things written about him, the greedy 'King Foodie' (Barr and Levy 1985: 25). The team identified 'foodies' well in time to make the mighty second edition of the *Oxford English Dictionary* and eighteen months before the naming of their cousins, the yuppies. Levy and Ann Barr then armed them with *The Official Foodie Handbook.*

> A Foodie is a person who is very very very interested in food. Foodies are the ones talking about food in any gathering – salivating over restaurants, recipes, radicchio. They don't think they are being trivial – Foodies consider food to be an art, on a level with painting or drama (6).

Barr and Levy explain the rise of 'Mass Foodism' in the 1980s this way: 'the food industry needed Foodies to create new tastes for others to follow'. For twenty years, there had been plenty of signs that 'food was heating up – cookery book sales soaring, television programmers putting gimmicky television cooks into the schedule, travel agencies concocting gastronomic tours, new restaurant guides challenging fat Mich[elin]'. For British cooks, the 'door to joy' had been opened again by Elizabeth David, who issued *A Book of Mediterranean Food* in 1950, followed in 1951 by *French Country Cooking*. 'Their impact was extraordinary, even for a literary nation like the English, who learn everything through reading' (24–6).

The spread of supermarkets and the start of food advertising on television took foodism to the masses (commercial television began in 1954 in both Britain and America). Television channels had cookery programs – Julia Child in America and Philip Harben on the BBC. British newspapers launched colour supplements to catch the food, furniture and fashion advertisements. The *Sunday Times* launched its supplement in 1962, the *Daily Telegraph* and *Observer* in 1964. The *New York Times* Sunday Magazine has carried archfoodie Craig Claiborne's recipes since 1975, a formula now imitated by every American Sunday newspaper, Barr and Levy state (29–30). Gastronomically informed practice arose again with the re-emergence of a simplifying 'nouvelle cuisine', recognised by French restaurant critics Henri Gault and Christian Millau in their *Nouveau Guide* for October 1973 (62–5).

'You are what you eat' is the foodie's 'favourite metaphysical maxim', Barr and Levy (a former academic philosopher) note (33). The foodie knows a great secret: 'The Purpose of Life is Eating Well. But pigs can eat well. The Foodie *thinks* about eating. The Foodie *talks* about eating. The *unexamined meal* is not worth eating' (7).

Writing on English food, Philippa Pullar observes that, like gardening, cooking has become a hobby.

Never has there been so little need to cook. One can simply open tins, unwrap polythene, thaw pies and prepare powdered potatoes – no need even to add milk, butter, salt or pepper – and hey presto! there's a meal. Paradoxically never has there been such an interest in cooking, so many articles in magazines and newspapers, so many books (1971: 229).

As the plethora of cookery books indicates, the original, domestic mode of production offers resistance. Foodies go to great pains to return to traditional cooking, baking, pickling and growing, purchasing handmade butters, cheeses and smoked delicacies, and offering social dining in the shape of the 'dinner party'. They might use public kitchens, but preferably restaurants, that belong to a more traditional craft industry, and to that extent compete with the corporate. On tour, they frequent local markets and kerbside braziers.

The bureaucratic kitchen cannot suck the domestic completely dry. It messily leaves scraps of work at home, residual cooking. A frozen chicken suits the logic of manufacturing and marketing, not ease of cooking. The factories pick the eyes out of the housework, leaving some of the drabbest bits. We still need to shop, store, open packets and wash up. We also find it hard to slip out of the informal jacket of everyday interactions. We still have private lives. 'Private' comes from the same root as 'deprived', which is a negative derivation, given that daily life is highly social, highly cultural. The private is where we meet, at the kitchen table, café corner, laundromat and bar. It is the headquarters, rather than the outpost. This is the basic *oikonomikos*.

The hobgoblins have spun a worldwide web of fantasy. In their attempts to commercialise the entire culture, business corporations mythologise both work and play. To believe the goblin merchant men, we might seem free as never before, to have transcended everyday imperatives. But screen freedom is illusory; to start with, television provides someone else's slant. Worse, fantasies do not satisfy real bellies. There is no restaurant at the end of cyberspace, its believers eating sadly at the windows of virtual 'communities'. Unfortunately for the communication industries (and cultural theorists), we are incompletely cultural creatures – we can never be liberated from the metabolic world. As earthly beings, we are bound by natural laws; they support our only powers. We must still eat, drink, breathe and die.

Similarly, we are enmeshed in social imperatives. We must

cooperate in households and over actual marketplaces. Through sharing, we both constrain and empower one another. We must share to receive; it multiplies our capabilities and options. Through interdependence, we gain the collective power of science, machines, wisdom, poetry, books. In fact, the more sophisticated the economy, the narrower we are as specialists, and so the more we depend on others. We ought to share more fairly.

Having to cook is the price we pay for being human. If we choose freedom *from* the world, we no longer cook. But freedom *within* the world is to cook better. Liberation becomes the power to operate in a complex cuisine. The examined meal is here and now, convivial and culturally responsive. Sharing labour, we each might know more about less, but, as picky eaters roaming a very long menu, we have to grasp an overall picture, a complex gastronomy, as imaginative and fully informed as possible. With the complete socialisation of cooking, we are free to forget, or to recognise ourselves more fully as cooks. Cooks made us, and cooks we remain. We can cook a better world.

THE GATEKEEPER

Working in the 1940s on a program to influence women's shopping, American researcher Kurt Lewin described the housewife as the nutritional 'gatekeeper'. Food gets to the table through 'channels', such as the grocery store, the garden and the refrigerator. Interviewing midwestern housewives, Lewin found that women control all channels except gardening, and even there husbands seldom act alone. Although wives did not mention children controlling any channels, he presumed they had influence through 'rejection of food put before them'. Quoting this, Wm Alex McIntosh and Mary Zey argue that women have been other people's agents. '*Responsibility* is not equivalent to *control*.' They give the analogy of secretaries, who process information, but 'others make and enforce the policies' (1989: 318–19). Women are under an obligation to maintain a harmonious family life, to defer to men, who tend to control economic resources. While women might make day-to-day decisions, pleasing family members is paramount (321). When women provide favourite foods, we might view them as running around at their consumers' beck and call, or as emotionally manipulative.

Once hidden downstairs or out the back and in the charge of servants, the kitchen crept back inside during the twentieth century until it became a central command post. It was made smaller to house the solitary worker, but then the 'open plan' removed walls. This could work both ways: the cook could monitor the rest of the family, and they could help themselves to the refrigerator.

Modern labour-saving machines, prepared food and even restaurant and take-away meals have de-skilled domestic cooking, leaving mindless chores. Or technology might be said to increase power in the kitchen. Food conglomerates provide choice, or distractions. This is the chestnut of consumer sovereignty – whether production is geared to satisfying appetites or to manipulating them. And this raises complex issues of wealth, power and status within our own society, which, needless to say, have to be analysed within the overall picture of cooking.

If the kitchen is the powerhouse of history, then home cooks are important; the hand that stirs the bowl makes the civilisation. For the cultists of domesticity, housework is saintly. Yet, throughout history, women have been publicly accorded low status. No one can deny the drabness; yet we can also promote a more active version, of the cook challenging and collaborating with the natural world, extracting nourishment, guarding the main pleasures, sustaining a sharing society.

We are always slaves to eating and so depend on cooks. But cooks *serve* eaters and, even worse, the eaters' dictatorial bellies! It would seem to make cooks intrinsically subordinate, slaves to appetites. Herein would seem to lie the source of their menial status ('menial' coming from Old French *meinee* for 'household'). Many aristocratic women have had to dine separately, peasant women to serve the men first, and millions of girl babies gone 'missing'. This is not just material dependence, but social and cultural. Collectively, we empower, and disempower, one another. The denial of cooks has been systematic. Housework is notoriously unwaged; the true economy does not appear in national accounts (Waring 1988). On my analysis, cooks are downgraded not because they are women, but because they remain domestics. Men have left for the high ground, literally distributing the meat.

343

In praising cooks, I might seem to favour the traditional role of women in the home. Like Baron von Rumohr, I might be thought to both encroach and trap. However, with the fusion of the domestic hearths, one big kitchen mushrooms over us. This is where all persons move, feeding within a many-roomed city, a one-kitchen world, with access to numerous private and public spaces. As women claim the public, foodie men return to the *oikos*. Throughout, I have kept in view the tension between the cook and the eater. Emerging from the kitchen, women find places at the table (opposite men who ought to rediscover food-sharing). We need to reintegrate as cooks and eaters. The aim of a modern 'material life' must be to share both food and its cooking as fairly as we can. A cook pure and simple or an eater pure and simple is only half a person. Eaters gain by becoming cooks, and vice versa.

None of these debates are new to feminist thinkers, although more likely under the heading 'housework' than 'cooking'. Should housewives be paid? Does the 'working' woman's workload simply double? Does capitalism rely on patriarchy? Is male power or the division of labour to blame? Recent contributions by Carol Johnson, Carol Pateman, Lois Bryson and Chris Kynaston are to be found in an issue of *Women's Studies International Forum* (1996, 19 (3): 193–237). For now, the debates are exemplified by two divergent twentieth-century classics, Virginia Woolf's *A Room of One's Own* and Simone de Beauvoir's *The Second Sex*.

SIMONE DE BEAUVOIR

In *Le Deuxième Sexe*, published in 1949, existentialist philosopher Simone de Beauvoir (1908–86) calls on women to rise above the humdrum through engaging in freely chosen exploits and projects. Rather than 'immanence', which is confinement to a narrow round of uncreative and repetitive duties, she advocates 'transcendence', of which her writing is a model.

In traditional marriage, the male is called to action – 'his vocation is to produce, fight, create, progress, to transcend himself', de Beauvoir writes. He can 'find self-expression in projects' (1988: 466, 469). Meanwhile, woman is condemned as child-bearer, cook and housekeeper to a 'sordid materialism'. Thus 'utility reigns in the housekeeper's heaven, above truth, beauty, liberty ... This is why she adopts the Aristotelian morality of the golden mean – that is, of mediocrity ... Her wings are clipped' (615–16).

The material manifestation of this ideal of happiness is the house; 'it stands for permanence and separation from the world', de Beauvoir writes. The woman decorates this cell: 'Because she *does* nothing, she eagerly seeks self-realisation in what she *has*' (467, 469). She busies herself with 'shining stoves, fresh, clean clothes, bright copper, polished furniture'. The work is only negative – getting rid of dirt, eliminating disorder. 'Few tasks are more like the torture of Sisyphus ... The housewife wears herself out marking time: she makes nothing, simply perpetuates the present.' When any living being enters her house, the maniac orders: 'Wipe your feet, don't tear the place apart, leave that alone!'. The once healthy young woman exhibits nervousness, spitefulness and frustration. 'Severe, preoccupied, always on the watch, she loses *joie de vivre*, she becomes overprudent and avaricious ... bitter and disagreeable ... In this insanity the house becomes so neat and clean that one hardly dares live in it; the woman is so busy she forgets her own existence' (470–1).

Simone de Beauvoir finds the preparation of food fractionally more positive. For one thing, it means going to the market, 'often the bright spot of the day'. It can take the woman out where she might gossip, and even feel part of a group, opposed in that instant to men as a group. Winning a solid cabbage or ripe Camembert from an unwilling storekeeper, she is 'pleased with her passing triumph'. With her fire going, 'woman becomes a sorceress; by a simple movement, as in beating eggs, or through the magic of fire, she effects the transmutation of substances: matter becomes food'. She finds 'enchantment in these alchemies ... Cooking is revelation and creation; and a woman can find special satisfaction in a successful cake or a flaky pastry, for not everyone can do it: one must have the gift' (471–2). All the same, the woman is the victim of natural laws.

> Each day the kitchen also teaches her patience and passivity; here is alchemy; one must obey the fire, the water, wait for the sugar to melt, for the dough to rise, and also for the wash to dry, for the fruit to ripen on the shelf.

The natural cycles condemn her to repetition. They fill her religion with 'primitive superstition'. Men make the gods, she quotes Frazer, 'women worship them' (609–11). While the domestic cook might glimpse profound satisfaction, 'as with other housework, repetition soon spoils these pleasures. The magic of the oven can hardly appeal to Mexican Indian women who spend half their lives preparing tortillas, identical from day to day, from century to century'. The writers, both male and female, who 'lyrically exalt such triumphs' seldom or never engage in actual housework. 'It is tiresome, empty, monotonous, as a career' (472).

Roasts burn, preserves go mouldy and, worse, her products are necessarily consumed: 'a continual renunciation is required of the woman whose operations are completed only in their destruction'. Even if the successful dish is devoured gleefully, the validity of the cook's work is found only in others' mouths; 'she needs their approbation, demands that they appreciate her dishes and call for second helpings'. The matron is subordinate, secondary, parasitic. 'Man marries today to obtain an anchorage in immanence', she writes; 'he wants to have hearth and home while being free to escape therefrom'. Even more for the children, life lies elsewhere. 'Woman tries to set up a universe of permanence and continuity; husband and children wish to transcend the situation she creates' (474–5).

Simone de Beauvoir analyses 'immanence' forcefully. However, she indulges in mystification, in worldly denial. Like Plato, she writes as if food were merely fuel for some indefinable higher purpose. 'Dwelling-place and food are useful for life but give it no significance: the immediate goals of the housekeeper are only means, not true ends' (473). But eating *is* living. Cooking is where real power and real poetry ultimately lie. Culture *is* repetition, and art its self-negation. Cook, eat and be merry!

VIRGINIA WOOLF

English novelist and critic Virginia Woolf (1882–1941) demands an 'anchorage in immanence' in her feminist classic of 1929, *A Room of One's Own*.

It is a curious fact that novelists have a way of making us believe that luncheon parties are invariably memorable for something very witty that was said, or for something very wise that was done. But they seldom spare a word for what was eaten. It is part of the novelist's convention not to mention soup and salmon and ducklings, as if soup and salmon and ducklings were of no importance . . .

Woolf reflects on this, she tells us, after a delectable lunch at an unnamed (male) Oxbridge college. The repast consisted of sole, partridge and a confection, while the 'wineglasses had flushed yellow and flushed crimson; had been emptied; had been filled' (1945: 12–13).

She contrasts this with the dreary evening meal at a much poorer (female) college, flushed down with water. 'Here was the soup . . . a plain gravy soup.' One could have seen through the transparent liquid to the pattern on the plate, if there had been a pattern. Next came beef with its 'attendant greens and potatoes – a homely trinity'. Prunes and custard followed, and, finally, biscuits and cheese. This mind-numbing fare puts the women at a disadvantage. 'The human frame being what it is, heart, body, and brain all mixed together . . . a good dinner is of great importance to good talk. One cannot think well, love well, sleep well, if one has not dined well' (19–20).

With scarcely suppressed rage, she reflects on 'the urbanity, the geniality, the dignity which are the offspring of luxury and privacy and space' (25). If women are to write too, they need these comforts. To put a figure on it, in her experience, women are unlikely to become creative without a modest annual income of £500 and 'a room of one's own'. So, the immanent existence is not merely impossible to forsake, but it is also an essential platform from which to reach much higher. 'Intellectual freedom depends on material things' (106).

Woolf compares fiction to a spider's web, 'attached ever so lightly perhaps, but still attached to life at all four corners'. It may appear a wondrous creation, alive to ethereal breezes. Nonetheless, when the web is snagged, we remember that 'these webs are not spun in mid-air by incorporeal creatures, but are the work of suffering human beings, and are attached to grossly material things, like health and money and the houses we live in' (43).

Where de Beauvoir's wondrously spun work hangs abstractly somewhere in philosophical analysis, hitherto mainly masculine, Woolf deliberately locates her narrative in the everyday world of strolling a university town, measuring the breeze – 'from the south-west to be exact' (18), enjoying specific meals, visiting the British Museum, taking books she quotes from the shelves, looking out a window onto a London street. She reports empirical proof of sexual inequality. 'The history of men's opposition to women's emancipation is more interesting perhaps than the story of that emancipation itself', she finds (57). And, in England in the 1920s, this oppression continues: 'the male is still the voluble sex' (79).

Trying to comprehend, she decides that men have diminished women to make themselves appear bigger. 'How is he to go on giving judgement, civilising natives, making laws, writing books, dressing up and speechifying at banquets, unless he can see himself at breakfast and at dinner at least twice the size he really is?' (37–8). Wondering whether women should become more like men, she speaks about 'that extremely complex force of femininity . . . For women have sat indoors all these millions of years, so that by this time the very walls are permeated by their creative force'. It would be a pity to waste its artistic potential, 'for it was won by centuries of the most drastic discipline' (87). Imagining the uniting of the two forces, she concludes: 'It is fatal to be a man or a woman pure and simple; one must be woman-manly or man-womanly' (102).

That is the answer – we need to be both domestic and public cooks. We need to be both practitioner-cooks and philosopher-cooks. We need to be both cooks and eaters. Even Simone de Beauvoir's dualism admits a similar possibility. If the person doing household work is also a 'producer, a creative worker, it is as naturally integrated in life as are the organic functions', she suggests. 'What makes the lot of the wife-servant ungrateful is the division of labour which dooms her completely to the general and the inessential' (1988: 472–3).

*   *   *

As earthbound eaters, we have tormented ourselves with the question of where to fly. We have yearned for peace, for illumination. We have sought more power, even through daily denial. But, from a study of cooks, we learn that we only soar when we pay attention to the here and now.

NOURISHING WISDOM

In a book entitled *Nourishing Wisdom*, North American psychologist and nutritionist Marc David paints in miniature the importance of the meal. He recalls returning home for Thanksgiving dinner during his first semester away at college. His family were proud of their first university student, but he brought a surprise lecture. 'I had entered school a meat eater and was returning home a hard-core vegetarian', he writes. As the turkey was being served, he discoursed on the evils of meat, speaking with new-found authority on the poisonous effects of cholesterol, saturated animal fats and hormone-injected turkeys. 'To my surprise the air of festivity I anticipated at the unveiling of these nutritional revelations was absent.' Even more to the point, his grandmother was heartbroken that he did not eat her turkey. It was Marc David's worst Thanksgiving.

For the next decade, Thanksgiving followed the same dreadful pattern. His family thought him a lost soul, and he believed they lived in the dark. 'Somehow, though, time changed my attitude toward food and toward life', he admits. So, with hard-earned wisdom, he sat at the table and watched his grandmother carve the Thanksgiving turkey. 'I saw the love she poured into it and instantly knew that for her, eating the turkey meant I loved her – and not eating it meant I didn't. In that moment the choice for me was obvious. I wanted turkey.' Watching him eat, his grandmother saw him 'return from the dead'. The tension at the table melted for the first time in all those years. The 'turkey felt great in my body, and the look of joy in my grandmother's eyes was worth eating all the turkey in the world' (1991: 47–8).

Such legendary grandmothers used to smother us in good things, as much as we could eat, and then a warm drink to accompany more later. Respect was perhaps the main payment their generosity demanded. If we refused the centrepiece of their art, we refused them. If we refused a second helping, we turned them down. This great love might have been limited to the immediate family and confirmed friends. This thrusting of maternal goodness may have loved us almost to death. This dedication may have trapped the cooks at the hearth. But the generosity was genuine. Without cooks, what happens to generosity? What happens to sharing? What can we do for love? Where are grandmothers to show how? If we are no longer cooks, we do not last.

As people who embody the human virtues of warmth and generosity, cooks warrant our gratitude. As people who command an enormous range of knowledge and skills, they demand to be admired. As people committed to our pleasures, cultural development and survival, they are to be worshipped. So many books have been written *for* cooks and so few *about* them. The irony is that when cooks *are* studied they turn out to be pivotal to our self-interest. If 'we are what we eat', then in making our meals, cooks make us.

Now that the myriad tasks have become distractingly specialised, we share one big kitchen, too prodigal almost to take in. As individualistic eaters, we share too anonymously across the world. Distracted by industrialised culture, we are in danger of locking ourselves out of the kitchen. We risk cutting ourselves off from nature, society and culture. Yet to be truly human, we need to become *better cooks*, cooks of erudition and taste, practical and generous.

CHAPTER SIXTEEN

Angels Must Eat

We were welcomed into the grounds of Carclew, a mansion once belonging to a newspaper baron and now a centre for young people's performing arts, by the bounding and signalling figure of a clown. Inside, others in billowing black and white costumes served sparkling red wine, while a quintet played on the stairs. A clown announced dinner. We filed into the ballroom to tables strewn with nothing but rose-petals and arranged in a ring, so that forty-eight of us sat on the outside looking in.

The banging of drums drew attention to the first six dishes, which the clowns paraded out of the makeshift kitchen, set down at various points around the ring, and served. We marvelled, we ate and the musicians played, then the clowns swapped the dishes around, served the nearest diners, and so on, until we had sampled most offerings. The tables were cleared; we drank, admired and chatted; some people exchanged seats, and the process was repeated with a second parade of six dishes. Then came the finale of the desserts.

Everyone knew that this was fabulous food: fish floating in jelly and spooned out of an aquarium; quails breaking out of pigs' bladders and smelling like milk. We immediately agreed that the chef had presented some of the best dishes we had eaten: suckling pig with raisin-filled brioches; a woven-bread basket of ginger-flavoured goose and venison. This banquet combined French and Asian flavours; it interpreted past glories in its own style. None of us had eaten more inspirationally. A transforming meal, it was cooked by Phillip Searle in March 1984 after all the talk at the First

Symposium of Australian Gastronomy, held in Adelaide.

Phillip has said that the very night he agreed to undertake the banquet, assisted by others including Trish Veitch and Cheong Liew, he watched Italian director Federico Fellini's television documentary *The Clowns* (1971). He saw how the use of clowns as waiters could both provide elegant solutions to technical difficulties and convey a statement. Clowns added much merriment, but also carried the inner meaning of the age-old tradition of fools. Of the several levels on which this feast worked, let us start with the practical.

The usual restaurant meal these days employs *service à la russe*, in which successive plates are individually presented to each diner. But a banquet might be expected, again in culinary French, to follow *service à la française*, where several large dishes are displayed and then served, as in the much humbler buffet. As handled two centuries ago by Carême, the first service involved an architectural construction of perhaps thirty-two or forty-eight dishes, which would be admired and then sampled, before a second service of an equal number of dishes, followed by frivolity. Phillip Searle's immediate question of how to display the food was solved by seating the diners as if around a circus ring, with dishes shown off in a grand parade to applause.

In a restaurant, service is from behind, but we were served from the front. Consequently, Phillip was prepared to tread on a few toes by not hiring waiters, but rather six actors and dancers, listed on the menu as 'servers' (and including Geoffrey Rush – well before his Academy Award). They had to look good, but this could create a dilemma. During the symposium, one of the speakers had described perfect service as 'invisible'. How could actors exaggeratedly juggling wine bottles and staggering under heavy platters be anonymous? They could be mimes with painted faces.

Clowns had other advantages. They could make mistakes (drop a fork), lose their dignity (dodge under the table to get out of the ring) and improvise (hold up a toppling tower of ice-cream). They could also play magic tricks. Do you remember how a battered car would arrive in a circus ring and an almost impossible number of clowns would tumble out? In the same way, Phillip made a virtue of his tiny, box-like, makeshift kitchen by having his clowns emerge with an amazing procession of elaborate dishes.

Beyond these practical abilities, the clowns could also make a political statement. Clowns are upstarts, as much at home telling unpalatable truths in the monarch's court as expressing foolish wisdom in popular entertainment. Furthermore, the Fellini documentary showed two main types of clown, the Auguste and the white-face. While the former is the loud, baggy-trousered buffoon, Phillip chose the beautifully dressed, arrogant aristocrat. These white-faced sophisticates were thus more than a match for those they served. One clown stole food from my plate. When a neighbour asked for a doggy-bag, another jester nodded vigorously and pointed at her tummy. The traditional class relationship had been inverted – these waiters were assertive.

We are approaching the central point, which can be regarded as the clown's universal message: 'Who is the fool?'. No one takes food more seriously than Phillip Searle, but he prefers not to intellectualise his passions, and so his clowns mocked the food conference's scholarly pretensions. Take his most amazing-looking dish, disguised under the modest title 'Goose Liverwurst'. After the original procession, applauded with delight, a clown dashed into the ring with disgust on his face and holding at arm's length a shiny black mass with a glistening pink entrail draped over it. When served, the 'liverwurst' was disclosed to be so thickly coated with black truffles that they could be scraped off as a meal on their own. The most revolting-looking dish turned out to be the most extravagant.

The most satisfying account of clowns is still regarded as the book written in 1509 by the Dutch humanist Desiderius Erasmus. *Praise of Folly* is non-stop irony, so sophisticated that it is difficult to know when he mocks his enemy and when he mocks himself. While remaining with the Roman Catholic Church, he was a liberalising Renaissance writer. He was the best-trained classicist of his day, yet he argued the message of Christian simplicity. He lampooned the excessive scholasticism of medieval theologians such as John Duns Scotus. Indeed, the followers of Erasmus came to abuse the hair-splitting followers of Duns Scotus as 'dunsmen' or 'dunces'. Like Erasmus, Phillip Searle told those who theorised so earnestly about food to balance the head with the belly.

With the desserts, Phillip summed up his case. The key dish was described as 'Raspberry and Vanilla Icecream'. Just as he had done away with normal waiters, he had approached this new set of culinary challenges by supplementing some of his usual kitchen staff with friends with talents such as engineering. They had adapted as a mould a large, orange roadside 'witch's hat'. Not only was the ice-cream superb to eat, but it arrived spectacularly as a towering red and white barbershop spiral – a simple pattern presumably not simple to achieve. The cone shape of the ice-cream was repeated in the dozens of wafer cones upside-down around a generous pile of raspberries.

Now think about it a moment. Phillip had thrown himself into sleepless nights constructing a banquet that was now all but demolished – surely an act of magnificent folly. It was also deliberate irony that a chef so keen to communicate his artistry should finish with 'mere' ice-cream, and then to trump that with untouched raspberries. Beyond that, the effect of simple flavours, colours and shapes was innocent and clownish, to at last reduce the mighty banquet to a children's party. And, to top the Erasmus-like message, the cones crowned the earnest gastronomers with dunces' caps.

At that banquet Phillip Searle made it clear that we eat not just with our minds but with our eyes, nose, palate, fingers, teeth and bowels. Our hearts, too. And not just with our bodies, but with our companions and histories and gods. At the time, his 'Clowns' banquet sent me scurrying to the library. Already impressed by what our eating tells us, and having organised this conference on Australian cuisine, I was nonetheless galvanised by the excitement surrounding Phillip's banquet into really trying to understand phil-osophically, no, gastronomically. While, for more than a dozen years, Phillip continued to cut, snip, dissolve and brown, I studied, and this book is a result.

Having eaten at Phillip's resounding table, I come championing cooks. Not just professionals, but cooks domestic, folkloric and prehistoric. They are the nur-turers, sharers, minders. They are the practitioners, creators, observers, thinkers. They are the food-getters, distributors and story-tellers. Cooks are gods on earth. Cooks made us. Cooks are us.

THE WORLD UPSIDE-DOWN

While politicians push and shove from right and left, philosophers tug from above and below. Plato and his successors take the higher, spiritual, ideal ground of truth and goodness. Questing onwards and upwards, we might just glimpse the greater, more real world, they urge. The danger is that we forget our bodies, our companions and natural realities. Others, and perhaps most famously Marx, respond that we must look to everyday solidity. They deny that reality can be finally thought, but instead must be experienced and re-made. And they conceive the sparkling edifice of civilisation as rising upwards from humdrum social activities.

Under the inspiration of Phillip Searle's carnivalesque banquet, I became convinced that the defenders of cooks, too, must invert the world. For us, the force lies in the little things, the unglamorous and the nitty-gritty. Rather than look up to those who demand power, we must accept that, somehow, cooks – seemingly so meek and enchained – nevertheless run things. This extended inquiry into Phillip's genius certainly acknowledges the strength in cooperative effort and the mightiness of ideas. However, they are launched from the here and now. Our finest moments, our greatest banquets, our most wondrous ices only develop from the social struggle to dine. For, to echo Brillat-Savarin, beasts feed, people eat, the wise dine.

Simone de Beauvoir, who observes that housewives become 'severe, preoccupied ... bitter and disagreeable' (1988: 471), favours outgoing activities, which she terms transcendence. We know what she means: women have been bound down in drudgery. 'Home is the girl's prison and the woman's workhouse', writes social reformer George Bernard Shaw (1931: 222). But, in devising solutions, de Beauvoir has to remember that it is not desirable, let alone possible, to exit personal bodies and private worlds; the only final release is death. At the same time, she should be wary of decrying the kitchen, out of which greatness ultimately arises. By contrast, as we have also found, Virginia Woolf argues that material well-being comes first, and then women writers can bring another sensibility, borne of domesticity, to the depiction of reality.

If we are to appreciate cooks more fully, then the conventional world must be turned upside-down. Instead of the usual value hierarchies, which proclaim the higher realms ('high' art, 'high' mathematics, 'finer' instincts, and so on), we must believe that cooks inherit the earth, that cooks have nothing to lose but their ignominy. Likewise, we must join cooks in chopping, grinding and pummelling the world. Only then, having appreciated the traditional, domestic and hands-on within an unrepentantly metabolic universe, we can propose a new balance, one in which everyone has the potential for a truly human kind of transcendence. What counts is cooking. Somehow get that right and all else follows.

THE ANGEL IS GRANTED FALLIBLE FORM

A visiting angel opens this book. A traveller after knowledge, catching the breezes around Sydney's opera house, spiralling between corporate towers and descending into the metropolis, this angel might have gazed at art gallery walls, sauntered down parliamentary corridors, eavesdropped on celebrity chat shows, sought prophets in cathedrals or down dirty streets ... But this angel in quest of humanity landed beside a stove. Starting in Phillip Searle's restaurant, the angel has peered into the 'empire of smoke'. It has sought 'the secrets of love and life through the kitchen'.

If still with me, this angel has now visited a dinner many years ago, a banquet that I have wanted to understand, that has led me throughout time and place, but that can only be recreated in words and memory. An angel disengaged from physical reality might again sit among the clowns. But actual physical beings can never return. However exclusive then, it is now out of reach.

Likewise, in the first chapter, we discovered Phillip Searle alone in his kitchen at Oasis Seros restaurant in Sydney. But even that is deceptive. It is no longer possible even to go to that restaurant. We visited way back in early 1994, and much has changed. When Phillip and partner Barry Ross stepped gamely into the address, the Oxford Street manse had already been Le Café and Perry's. It has since become a café called Eden, run by entirely different people, and then a retail shop, and who knows what by now.

After Oasis Seros opened in February 1987, this cooks' cook was journalistically lionised and initially flourished. 'However, not even Sydney was quite prepared for his highly eclectic mélange of French and Oriental culinary styles', a critic reported in the local *Good Food Guide* for 1988. That Phillip Searle presents neither familiar dishes nor old favourites leads unavoidably to 'confrontation for diners', warns the same guide two years later, even if this is 'arguably the most exciting fare in Australia' (Schofield and Dowe 1989: 106). Having announced the food as the nation's 'most consistently exciting and original', another reviewer, Stephen Downes, goes on: 'At the same time, many dishes are subtle and rely for their appreciation on considerable gastronomic experience' (1990: 26).

Phillip dreamed of going out with a bang. As a couturier in the age of off-the-grill fashion, he would hold a funeral service for high cooking. The mourners would enjoy his final ice-cream. Then, over a few days in December 1994, he and Barry Ross suddenly sold Oasis. In March 1996, they opened a café called Vulcan's, which exploited the wood-fired oven in a former local bakery near their home at Blackheath in the Blue Mountains, two hours' drive from Sydney. By November 1997, Phillip was also a partner in Infinity Sourdough Bakery in Victoria Street in the city.

*   *   *

Angels exist. They flit around this world, equipped to listen to reason, to share the wildest imaginings. As forgiving guardians of human welfare, angels share the kinder qualities of cooks. But pure angels are without practical exigencies of their own to fret about. They exist with no use for senses, hearts or hands. Such angels are raised, whether they admit it or not, on wings of desire. Ideas arise, lightly. But ethereal angels pay a price – the inability to live physically. And so I have tried to capture one's attention, hopefully to persuade it to appreciate the materiality of cooks and cookery.

Even a book, while part of the high culture, can be smelled, touched, admired. Like some favourite object, it can be held in a sensuous way and the knowledge 'owned'. Out of the libraries of knowledge, one book is patently limited. But even that can be seen as a positive attribute. A book contains crafted knowledge. It has a definite history and message. There is a finitude and so ardour in a book. It can also be 'devoured' in manageable chunks and carefully 'digested'. I can sum up a book as a way of actually *possessing* knowledge.

Knowledge of and for itself can become detached, dangerously so, if we are to believe the message of the Erasmus banquet. This book is written for an angel, who inhabits such spaces. It is meant as a tempting morsel, part way between the purely ideal and the real. I want this angel to weary of its passionless detachment, its miraculous abilities of hopping time and place, and to rejoice instead in the human form. So that it might truly appreciate cooks, I must seduce this angel into preferring rude finitude. An angel stuck in the clouds can only appreciate cooks intellectually. I want the seeker to share real meals, real pleasures, real loves, real cooks.

The reality is, of course, that I have guided the angel around. I have relayed some of the many things I have found about cooks, along with some proposals to make sense of human trials and tribulations. It has been my framework, formed with the more than able companionship of generations upon generations. Accordingly, in one final task, one last piece of authorial duty, I must grant this angel mortality. I must give this angel taste and pleasure; I must permit it conviviality, with all that these abilities add to the full appreciation of real, fallible cooks. It might seem an unlikely achievement to be able to release an angel from its vaporous sphere to let it truly dine. Yet I can bring this angel to the real joys of cooking.

For this angel, this angel looking over my shoulder, is you.

ACKNOWLEDGEMENTS

Authors have to be forgiven excessive gratitude to those who have helped with their otherwise solitary labour.

My thinking has been stimulated by many who have joined the Symposiums of Australian Gastronomy and our Adelaide 'symposiettes', including Anthony Corones, Graham Pont, Gay Bilson, Phillip Searle, Gabriel Gaté, Jennifer Hillier, John Fitzpatrick, Barbara Santich, Cath Kerry, Rich Burford, Matthew Hardy, Susan Parham, John Coveney, Jean Duruz, Marion Maddox, David Dale, Alan Saunders, the late Christopher Driver, Alan Davidson, Paul Levy and Tom Jaine.

I take my hat off to those professors who welcomed me to sociology, especially Bryan S. Turner, Bob Holton, Anna Yeatman, Stephen Mennell and Sidney Mintz.

Various kinds of specific assistance came from Rachel Hurst, Sharyn Clarke, Paul Bunney, the late David Rindos and my agent, Margaret Connolly. Penguin's publisher, Julie Gibbs, would seem to have busily backed the project; Julia Cain, Caroline Pizzey, Katie Purvis and Jane Drury were reassuringly conscientious editors and proofreaders; and Sandy Cull contributed a handsome design. The manuscript was generously read in full or in part by Marion Maddox (who had already made numerous suggestions, including a chapter topic), Barbara Santich, Lynn Martin, Robert Dare, John Coveney, Jean Duruz, Jonathan Nicholls, Darryl Thompson, Jennifer Hillier, John Fitzpatrick, Lenna Symons, Robert Crotty, Michael O'Donoghue, Colin Pardoe, Betty Meehan and Rhys Jones.

Many of the above have also been treasured cooks, convives and companions.

And that's before listing some of my favourite authors, from whom I have taken so much – this pudding needed 'a thousand people to make', and then some. Reliant on the products of others and with helpers to stone fruit and lick the spoon, I nevertheless accept responsibility for the stirring.

BIBLIOGRAPHY

This bibliography includes but a tiny sample of the books and articles that speak about cooks. Yet not one is devoted to the general anthropological enigma of what cooks do in relation to other human activities. This is the basis of my claim in the Preface about the uniqueness of this book.

As introduced in Chapter Three, the gastronomic classics of Athenaeus, Grimod de La Reynière, Brillat-Savarin and others include much on cooks, but mainly from the diners' viewpoint. Useful historical surveys like that of Reay Tannahill (1988) veer towards food or diet. Among academics, anthropologist Jack Goody offers a global vision in *Cooking, Cuisine and Class* (1982), but asks a relatively limited question: why do certain societies support a 'high' (elite) as well as a 'low' cuisine? In *All Manners of Food* (1985), sociologist Stephen Mennell brings a wealth of knowledge to English and French cooking since the Middle Ages. Another sociologist, Gary Alan Fine, observes modern professionals in *Kitchens* (1996). From numerous studies of housewives, two different starting places might be Christine Delphy's *Close to Home* (1984) and Ruth Schwartz Cowan's *More Work for Mother* (1989). Barbara Ketcham Wheaton's lovingly crafted *Savouring the Past* includes cooks at work in Paris in the early modern period (1983: 95–112). I thought the big questions might be raised when 'cooks' was promised as the topic for the Oxford Symposium on Food and Cookery in 1995. However, the paper-givers concentrated on a fairly eccentric assortment of, in the words of one suggested title, 'heroes and villains' (Walker 1996: 184).

As to popular accounts, the major part of J.L.W. Thudichum's portentously titled *The Spirit of Cookery: A popular treatise on the history, science, practice, and ethical and medical import of culinary art* turns out to be a 'systematic attempt' to form 'general rules' of how to cook (1895: v–vi). *Cooking Through the Centuries* by agricultural scientist J.R. Ainsworth-Davis is an 'outline of the many changes which have taken place in the character of British food, drink, and cookery, for the last five or six thousand years' (1931: ix). Inspired by a copy of Athenaeus, and not being able to find a history of cookery, Betty Wason wrote her own, appending nearly a gross of recipes; but *Cooks, Gluttons and Gourmets: A history of cookery* (1962) is not especially cogitative. A grand Parisian chef, Raymond Oliver, promises to 'tell the story of . . . the cook' (1967: 14), but his title, *The French at Table*, more accurately announces the amiable ramble. Among this general category, the likeliest contender is L. Lamprey's *The Story of Cookery* (1940), which is a more thoughtful and knowledgeable study than its style, projected audience (presumably young adults) and bibliography might suggest.

For surveys of the literature on food in anthropology, sociology and cultural studies, see especially Murcott (1988), Mennell et al. (1992) and Bell and Valentine (1997).

Basic reference books not necessarily acknowledged in the text include the *Oxford English Dictionary* (1989), *Concise Oxford Dictionary* (1990), *Columbia Encyclopedia* (1967), *Penguin Concise Columbia Encyclopedia* (1987), *Penguin Dictionary of Quotations* (Cohen and Cohen 1960) and the New Revised Standard Version of the Bible (1989).

The date in square brackets is that of original publication.

Acton, Eliza (1868), *Modern Cookery, for private families, reduced to a system of easy practice*, London: Longmans, Green, Reader & Dyer [1845].

Adams, Carol J. (1990), *The Sexual Politics of Meat: A feminist-vegetarian critical theory*, Cambridge: Polity.

Adams, Robert M. (1994), 'The origin of cities', in *Ancient Cities*, special issue of *Scientific American*: 12–19 [Sept. 1960].

Ainsworth-Davis, J.R. (1931), *Cooking Through the Centuries*, London: J.M. Dent.

Alcott, Louisa M. (1954), *Little Women; Good Wives*, London: Collins [2 vols, 1868–69].

Anderson, E.N. (1988), *The Food of China*, New Haven: Yale University Press.

Anderson E.N. & Marja L. Anderson (1977), 'Modern China: South', in Chang 1977: 317–82.

Andrieu, Pierre (1956), *Fine Bouche: A history of the restaurant in France*, trans. Arthur L. Hayward, London: Cassell.

Appadurai, Arjun (1988), 'How to make a national cuisine: Cookbooks in contemporary India', *Comparative Studies in Society & History*, 30(1): 3–24.

Archestratus (1994), *The Life of Luxury: Europe's oldest cookery book*, trans. and ed. John Wilkins & Shaun Hill, Blackawton, Totnes (Devon): Prospect Books.

Aristotle (1962), *Politics*, trans. T.A. Sinclair, Harmondsworth: Penguin.

Aristotle (1976), *The Ethics of Aristotle: The Nicomachean ethics*, trans. J.A.K. Thomson, Harmondsworth: Penguin.

Aron, Jean-Paul (1975), *The Art of Eating in France: Manners and menus in the nineteenth century*, trans. Nina Rootes, New York: Harper & Row.

Athenaeus (1927–41), *The Deipnosophists*, 7 vols, trans. Charles Burton Gulick, Cambridge (Mass.): Harvard University Press (Loeb) [vol. 1, 1927; vol. 2, 1928; vol. 3, 1929; vol. 4, 1930; vol. 5, 1933; vol. 6, 1937; vol. 7, 1941].

Austen, Jane (1972), *Pride and Prejudice*, Harmondsworth: Penguin [1813].

Aymard, Maurice, Claude Grignon & Françoise Sabban (1996), eds, *Food Allocation of Time and Social Rhythms*, special issue of *Food & Foodways*, 6(3–4).

Bachelard, Gaston (1987), *The Psychoanalysis of Fire*, trans. Alan C.M. Ross, London: Quartet Encounters [1938].

Bahn, Paul (1992), ed., *Collins Dictionary of Archaeology*, Glasgow: HarperCollins.

Bailey, C.T.P. (1927), *Knives and Forks*, London: Medici Society.

Barber, Benjamin R. (1996), *Jihad vs. McWorld*, New York: Ballantine Books.

Barbotin, Edmond (1975), *The Humanity of Man*, trans. Matthew J. O'Connell, Maryknoll (New York): Orbis.

Barr, Ann & Paul Levy (1985), *The Official Foodie Handbook*, Australian edn, Sydney: Doubleday.

Barthélemy, Dominique (1988), 'The use of private space: Civilising the fortress, eleventh to thirteenth century', in Duby 1988: 397–423.

Barthes, Roland (1973), *Mythologies*, trans. Annette Lavers, Frogmore (St Albans): Paladin.

Barthes, Roland (1979), 'Towards a psychosociology of contemporary food consumption', in Forster & Ranum, 1979: 166–73.

Beale, Bob (1996), 'Found here: The world's oldest bakers', *Sydney Morning Herald*, Saturday 9 March: 1, 11.

Beale, Thomas Wight (1978), 'Bevelled rim bowls and their implications for change and economic organisation in the later fourth millennium BC', *Journal of Near Eastern Studies*, 37(4): 289–313.

Beauvoir, Simone de (1988), *The Second Sex*, trans. H.M. Parshley, London: Picador [*Le Deuxième Sexe*, 1949].

Beecher, Catharine E. (1841), *Treatise on Domestic Economy, for the use of young ladies at home and at school*, Boston: Marsh, Capen, Lyon & Webb.

Beeton, Mrs Isabella (1861), *The Book of Household Management*, London: S.O. Beeton.

[Beeton, Mrs] (1880, 1909), *Mrs Beeton's Book of Household Management*, London: Ward, Lock.

Bell, Daniel (1976), *The Cultural Contradictions of Capitalism*, London: Heinemann.

Bell, David & Gill Valentine (1997), *Consuming Geographies: We are where we eat*, London: Routledge.

Bender, Barbara (1978), 'Gatherer-hunter to farmer: A social perspective', *World Archaeology*, 10(2): 204–22.

[Berchoux, Joseph de] J.B . . . (1804), *La Gastronomie, ou l'homme des champs à table: Poème didactique en iv chants*, Paris: Giguet et Michaud [1801].

Berdyaev, Nicolas (1939), *Spirit and Reality*, London: Geoffrey Bles: The Centenary Press.

Bernal, J.D. (1969), *Science in History*, vol. 1, *The Emergence of Science*, Harmondsworth: Penguin.

Berthiaume, Guy (1982), *Les Rôles du mágeiros: Étude sur la boucherie, la cuisine et le sacrifice dans la Grèce ancienne*, Leiden: E.J. Brill [*Mnemosyne* Supp. 70].

Blumenschine, Robert J. & John A. Cavallo (1992), 'Scavenging and human evolution', *Scientific American*, 267(4): 70–7.

Bonnet, Jean-Claude (1979), 'The culinary system in the *Encyclopédie*', in Forster & Ranum, 1979: 139–65.

Boswell, James (1924), *Boswell's Journal of a Tour to the Hebrides with Samuel Johnson, LL.D.* [together with *Johnson's Journey to the Western Islands of Scotland*], ed. R.W. Chapman, London: Oxford University Press [1785].

Boswell, James (1970), *Life of Johnson*, ed. R.W. Chapman, London: Oxford University Press [1791].

Bottéro, Jean (1985), 'The cuisine of Ancient Mesopotamia', *Biblical Archaeologist*, 48(1): 36–47 [*L'histoire*, 49, Oct. 1982].

Bourdieu, Pierre (1984), *Distinction: A social critique of the judgement of taste*, trans. Richard Nice, London: Routledge & Kegan Paul.

Braidwood, Robert J. (1960), 'The Agricultural Revolution', *Scientific American*, 203(3): 130–48.

Braudel, Fernand (1982), *Civilization and Capitalism: 15th–18th Century*, vol. 2, *The Wheels of Commerce*, trans. Siân Reynolds, London: Collins.

Brears, Peter, Maggie Black, Gill Corbishley, Jane Renfrew & Jennifer Stead (1993), *A Taste of History: 10 000 years of food in Britain*, London: English Heritage.

Brillat-Savarin, Jean-Anthelme (1970), *The Philosopher in the Kitchen*, trans. Anne Drayton, Harmondsworth: Penguin [1825, dated 1826].

Brillat-Savarin, Jean-Anthelme (1971), *The Physiology of Taste: Or meditations on transcendental gastronomy*, trans. M.F.K. Fisher, New York: Alfred A. Knopf [1825, dated 1826].

Burton, Robert (1932), *The Anatomy of Melancholy*, ed. Holbrook Jackson, London: J.M. Dent & Sons [1621].

Capon, Robert Farrar (1969), *The Supper of the Lamb: A culinary reflection*, Garden City (New York): Doubleday [UK title: *Angels Must Eat*].

Carcopino, Jérôme (1956), *Daily Life in Ancient Rome: The people and the city at the height of the empire*, trans. E.O. Lorimer, Harmondsworth: Penguin.

Casson, Lionel (1974), *Travel in the Ancient World*, London: George Allen & Unwin.

Chang, K.C. (1977), ed., *Food in Chinese Culture: Anthropological and historical perspectives*, New Haven: Yale University Press.

Charles, Nickie & Marion Kerr (1988), *Women, Food and Families*, Manchester: Manchester University Press.

Charpentier, Henri & Boyden Sparkes (1935), *Those Rich and Great Ones: Or life à la Henri, being the memoirs of Henri Charpentier*, London: Victor Gollancz.

Chaucer, Geoffrey (1957), *The Works of Geoffrey Chaucer*, ed. F.N. Robinson, Oxford: Oxford University Press.

Chejne, Anwar G. (1965), 'The boon-companion in early Abbasid times', *Journal of the American Oriental Society*, 85: 327–35.

Cheng, F.T. (1954), *Musings of a Chinese Gourmet: Food has its place in culture*, London: Hutchinson.

Childe, V. Gordon (1951), *Social Evolution*, London: Watts.

Childe, V. Gordon (1965), *Man Makes Himself*, London: Watts [1936].

Clark, Grahame (1977), *World Prehistory in New Perspective*, 3rd edn, Cambridge: Cambridge University Press.

Coe, Sophie D. (1989), 'The Maya chocolate pot and its descendants', in Jaine 1989: 15–21.

Contamine, Philippe (1988), 'The use of private space: Peasant hearth to papal palace, the fourteenth and fifteenth centuries', in Duby 1988: 425–505.

[Cooks Company, London] (nd), *Notes on the History of the Company of the Mistery of Cooks of London*, [London].

Coolidge, Susan [Sarah Chauncey Woolsey] (1957), *All That Katy Did* [incl. *What Katy Did*, 1872], London: Blackie.

Coon, Carleton S. (1955), *The History of Man: From the first human to primitive culture and beyond*, London: Jonathan Cape.

Cosman, Madeleine Pelner (1976), *Fabulous Feasts: Medieval cookery and ceremony*, New York: George Braziller.

Coveney, John (1996), The government and ethics of nutrition, PhD thesis, Murdoch University (Western Australia).

Cowan, Ruth Schwartz (1989), *More Work for Mother: The ironies of household technology from the open hearth to the microwave*, London: Free Association [1983].

Crabtree, Pam J. (1993), 'Early animal domestication in the Middle East and Europe', *Archaeological Method and Theory*, 5: 201–46.

Dalby, Andrew (1966), *Siren Feasts: A history of food and gastronomy in Greece*, London: Routledge.

David, Marc (1991), *Nourishing Wisdom: A new understanding of eating*, New York: Bell Tower.

Davidson, Alan (1988), ed., *On Fasting and Feasting: A personal collection of favourite writings on food and eating*, London: Macdonald Orbis.

Davidson, Alan (1991a), ed., *The Cook's Room: A celebration of the heart of the home*, London: Macdonald Illustrated [Davidson has denied taking the editor's role; see *Petits Propos Culinaires*, 41: 61].

Davidson, Alan (1991b), book review of Edilberto N. Alegre & Doreen G. Fernandez, *Kinilaw: A Philippine cuisine of freshness* (1991), in *Petits Propos Culinaires*, 39: 58–9.

Davis, Norman (1971), *Paston Letters and Papers of the Fifteenth Century*, Part 1, Oxford: Clarendon.

Delphy, Christine (1984), *Close to Home: A materialist analysis of women's oppression*, trans. Diana Leonard, London: Hutchinson.

Department of the Environment (UK) (1972), *Spaces in the Home: Kitchens and laundering spaces* (Design Bulletin 24, part 2), London: Her Majesty's Stationery Office.

Detienne, Marcel & Jean-Pierre Vernant (1989), *The Cuisine of Sacrifice Among the Greeks*, Chicago: University of Chicago Press [1979].

Diakonoff, I.M. (1974), *Structure of Society and State in Early Dynastic Sumer*, Los Angeles: Undena [1959].

Diamond, Jared (1997), *Guns, Germs and Steel: The fates of human societies*, London: Jonathan Cape.

Dinesen, Isak [Karen Blixen] (1986), 'Babette's Feast', in *Anecdotes of Destiny*, London: Penguin: 21–68.

Diogenes Laertius (1925), *Lives of Eminent Philosophers*, 2 vols, trans. R.D. Hicks, Cambridge (Mass.): Harvard University Press (Loeb).

Doran, Dr [John] (1859), *Table Traits with Something on Them*, New York: Redfield.

Douglas, Mary (1972), 'Deciphering a meal', *Daedalus*, 101: 61–81.

Downes, Stephen (1990), *Stephen Downes' Top Fifty Restaurants in Australia*, Ringwood (Victoria): Viking O'Neil.

Drummond, J.C. & Anne Wilbraham (1939), *The Englishman's Food: A history of five centuries of English diet*, London: Jonathan Cape.

Drummond, J.C. & Anne Wilbraham (1957), *The Englishman's Food: A history of five centuries of English diet*, rev. Dorothy Hollingsworth, London: Jonathan Cape.

Duby, Georges (1988), ed., *A History of Private Life*, vol. 2, *Revelations of the Medieval World*, trans. Arthur Goldhammer, Cambridge (Mass.): Belknap Press [series eds P. Ariès & Georges Duby 1987–91].

Dumas, Alexandre (1979), *Dumas on Food: Selections from 'Le Grand Dictionnaire de Cuisine'*, trans. Alan & Jane Davidson, London: Michael Joseph [1873].

Dumont, Louis (1980), *Homo hierarchicus: The caste system and its implications*, Chicago: University of Chicago Press.

Durkheim, Emile (1960), 'The dualism of human nature and its social conditions', in Kurt H. Wolff, ed., *Emile Durkheim, 1858–1917*, Columbus: Ohio State University Press: 325–40.

Ehrenberg, Margaret (1989), *Women in Prehistory*, London: British Museum.

Ehrenreich, Barbara & Deirdre English (1973), *Witches, Midwives, and Nurses: A history of women healers*, Old Westbury (New York): The Feminist Press.

Elias, Norbert (1978), *The Civilising Process*, vol. 1, *The History of Manners*, trans. Edmund Jephcott, Oxford: Basil Blackwell.

Elias, Norbert (1983), *The Court Society*, trans. Edmund Jephcott, Oxford: Basil Blackwell.

Elias, Norbert (1992), *Time: An essay*, Oxford: Blackwell.

Ellwanger, George H. (1902), *The Pleasures of the Table: An account of gastronomy from ancient days to present times*, New York: Doubleday Page.

Engels, Friedrich (1948), *The Origin of the Family, Private Property and the State in the light of the researches of Lewis H. Morgan*, Moscow: Progress [1884].

Ephron, Nora (1985), 'Private lives', *Harper's*, 271(1624): 18–22.

Ephron, Nora (1986), *Heartburn*, rev. edn, London: Pavanne.

Erasmus (1971), *Praise of Folly*, trans. Betty Radice, Harmondsworth: Penguin [1509].

Esquivel, Laura (1993), *Like Water for Chocolate*, trans. Carol Christensen & Thomas Christensen, London: Black Swan [original title: *Like Water for Hot Chocolate*].

Evans, Ivor H. (1990), *Brewer's Dictionary of Phrase and Fable*, London: Cassell.

Fagan, Brian M. (1980), *People of the Earth: An introduction to world prehistory*, 3rd edn, Boston: Little, Brown.

Falkenstein, Adam (1974), *The Sumerian Temple City*, trans. Maria DeJ. Ellis, Los Angeles: Undena [1954].

Farb, Peter & George Armelagos (1980), *Consuming Passions: The anthropology of eating*, Boston: Houghton Mifflin.

Farrington, Benjamin (1953), *Greek Science: Its meaning for us*, London: Penguin [part 1, 1944; part 2, 1949].

Feild, Rachael (1984), *Irons in the Fire: A history of cooking equipment*, Ramsbury, Marlborough (Wiltshire): Crowood Press.

Fellman, Anita Clair (1990), 'Laura Ingalls Wilder and Rose Wilder Lane: The politics of a mother–daughter relationship', *Signs: Journal of women in culture and society*, 15(3): 535–61.

Fenton, Alexander & Trefor M. Owen (1981), eds, *Food in Perspective: Proceedings of the Third International Conference on Ethnological Food Research, Cardiff, Wales, 1977*, Edinburgh: John Donald.

Fernandez, Doreen G. (1991), 'Balut to barbecue: Philippine street food', in Walker, 1991: 98–104.

Fine, Gary Alan (1996), *Kitchens: The culture of restaurant work*, Berkeley: University of California.

Finkelstein, Joanne (1989), *Dining Out: A sociology of modern manners*, Cambridge: Polity.

Fischler, Claude (1990), *L'Homnivore: Le goût, la cuisine et le corps*, Paris: Odile Jacob.

Fisher, M.F.K. (1988), 'Loving cooks, beware!', in Davidson 1988: 12–15.

Fisher, M.F.K. (1990), *The Gastronomical Me*, in *The Art of Eating*, New York: Collier: 351–572 [1943].

The Forme of Cury (1791), in Warner 1791: 1–35 [c. 1390].

Forster Robert & Orest Ranum (1979), eds, *Food and Drink in History: Selections from the 'Annales'*, vol. 5, Baltimore: Johns Hopkins University Press.

Foucault, Michel (1986), *The History of Sexuality*, vol. 2, *The Use of Pleasure*, trans. Robert Hurley, New York: Vintage Books.

Frayn, Joan (1995), 'The Roman meat trade', in Wilkins et al. 1995: 107–14.

Frazer, James George (1911), *The Golden Bough: A study in magic and religion*, part 1, *The Magic Art and the Evolution of Kings*, vol. 2, London: Macmillan.

Frazer, James George (1912), *The Golden Bough: A study in magic and religion*, part 5, *Spirits of the Corn and of the Wild*, vol. 1, London: Macmillan.

Freeman, Michael (1977), 'Sung', in Chang 1977: 141–76.

Freud, Sigmund (1963), *Civilization and its Discontents*, trans. Joan Riviere, London: Hogarth Press.

Fullagar, Richard & Judith Field (1997), 'Pleistocene seed-grinding implements from the Australian arid zone', *Antiquity*, 71: 300–7.

Fürst, Elisabeth L'orange (1997), 'Cooking and femininity', *Women's Studies International Forum*, 20(3): 441–9.

Garnsey, Peter (1988), *Famine and Food Supply in the Graeco-Roman World: Responses to risk and crisis*, Cambridge: Cambridge University Press.

Geertz, Clifford (1973), *The Interpretation of Cultures: Selected essays*, New York: Basic Books.

Gellner, Ernest (1988), *Plough, Sword and Book: The structure of human history*, London: Collins Harvill.

George, Susan (1977), *How the Other Half Dies: The real reasons for world hunger*, Harmondsworth: Penguin.

Giles, Herbert A. (1965), *Gems of Chinese Literature*, New York: Paragon [1883].

Glover, T.R. (1942), *The Challenge of the Greek and Other Essays*, Cambridge: Cambridge University Press.

[Goodman] 'A Citizen of Paris' [Guy de Montigny] (1928), *The Goodman of Paris (Le Ménagier de Paris)*, trans. Eileen Power, London: George Routledge & Sons [c. 1393].

Goody, Jack (1968), 'Time: Social organisation', in David L. Sills, ed., *International Encyclopedia of the Social Sciences*, vol. 16, [USA]: Macmillan & Free Press: 30–42.

Goody, Jack (1982), *Cooking, Cuisine and Class: A study in comparative sociology*, Cambridge: Cambridge University Press.

Gordon, Bertram M. & Lisa Jacobs-McCusker (1989), 'One pot cookery and some comments on its iconography', in Jaine 1989: 55–67.

Goudsblom, Johan (1992), *Fire and Civilization*, Harmondsworth: Allen Lane.

Grimod de La Reynière, Alexandre-Balthazar-Laurent (1983), *Manuel des Amphitryons*, Paris: A.M. Métailié [1808].

Grimod de La Reynière, Alexandre-Balthazar-Laurent (1987), 'A Gourmand Miscellany', in Giles MacDonogh, *A Palate in Revolution: Grimod de La Reynière and the 'Almanach des Gourmands'*, London: Robin Clark: 159–223.

Guisewite, Cathy (1995), 'Cathy', comic strip, *Sydney Morning Herald*, Friday 18 Aug.: 25.

Hahn, Emily (1969), *Foods of the World: The Cooking of China*, n.p.: Time-Life.

Halici, Nevin (1991), 'A kitchen in Sille: Remnants of Turkey's past', in Davidson 1991a: 176–81.

Hall, Catherine (1979), 'The early formation of Victorian domestic ideology', in Sandra Burman, ed., *Fit Work for Women*, London: Croom Helm: 15–32.

Hamblin, Dora Jane (1973), *The First Cities*, n.p.: Time-Life.

Harris, Marvin (1989), *Our Kind: Who we are, where we came from and where we are going*, New York: Harper & Row.

Hartley, Dorothy (1996), *Food in England*, London: Little, Brown [1954].

Hayden, Dolores (1981), *The Grand Domestic Revolution: A history of feminist designs for American homes, neighbourhoods, and cities*, Cambridge (Mass.): MIT.

[Hayward, Abraham] (1853), *The Art of Dining: Or, gastronomy and gastronomers*, London: John Murray.

Hell, Victor (1982), 'Avènement de la gastronomie, goût culinaire, esthéthique des philosophes (Friedrich von Rumohr et Hegel)', *Recherches Sociologiques* [Belgium], 13(1–2): 49–52.

Henisch, Bridget Ann (1976), *Fast and Feast: Food in medieval society*, University Park: Pennsylvania State University Press.

Herodotus (1972), *The Histories*, trans. Aubrey de Sélincourt, Harmondsworth: Penguin.

Hieatt, Constance B. (1996), 'A cook of fourteenth-century London: Chaucer's Hogge of Ware', in Walker 1996: 138–43.

Horace (1974), *Satires and Epistles* [together with Persius, *Satires*], trans. Niall Rudd, Harmondsworth: Penguin.

Howitt, A.W. (1904), *The Native Tribes of South-East Australia*, London: Macmillan.

Hsu, Vera Y.N. & Francis L.K. Hsu (1977), 'Modern China: North', in Chang 1977: 295–316.

Hutchinson, R.W. (1962), *Prehistoric Crete*, Harmondsworth: Penguin.

Isaac, Glynn (1979), 'The food-sharing behavior of protohuman hominids', in [C.C. Lamberg-Karlovsky], *Hunters, Farmers, and Civilizations: Old World archaeology*, San Francisco: W.H. Freeman: 22–35.

Jacobsen, Thorkild (1987), 'Mesopotamian religions', in Mircea Eliade, ed., *The Encyclopedia of Religion*, vol. 9, New York: Macmillan: 447–69.

Jaine, Tom (1989), ed., *Proceedings of the Oxford Symposium on Food & Cookery 1988: The cooking pot*, London: Prospect Books.

Janssen, Jacob J. (1979), 'The role of the temple in the Egyptian economy during the New Kingdom', in Edward Lipiński, ed., *State and Temple Economy in the Ancient Near East*, vol. 2, Leuven (Belgium): Departement Oriëntalistiek: 505–15.

Jeaffreson, John Cordy (1875), *A Book about the Table*, 2 vols, London: Hurst & Blackett.

Jerome, Norge W. (1981), 'Frozen (TV) dinners: The staple emergency meals of a changing modern society', in Fenton & Owen 1981: 145–56.

Jones, Philip E. (1976), *The Butchers of London: A history of the Worshipful Company of Butchers of the City of London*, London: Secker & Warburg.

Juvenal (1974), *The Sixteen Satires*, trans. Peter Green, Harmondsworth: Penguin.

Kenney, E.J. (1984), *The Ploughman's Lunch: Moretum, a poem ascribed to Virgil*, Bristol: Bristol Classical Press.

Kirwan, A.V. (1864), *Host and Guest: A book about dinners, wines, and desserts*, London: Bell & Daldy.

[Kitchiner, Dr William] (1821), *The Cook's Oracle: Containing receipts for plain cookery on the most economical plan for private families*, 3rd edn, London: Hurst, Robinson.

Kitto, H.D.F. (1957), *The Greeks*, Harmondsworth: Penguin.

Knechtges, David R. (1986), 'A literary feast: Food in early Chinese literature', *Journal of the American Oriental Society*, 106(1): 49–63.

Kramer, Samuel Noah (1963), *The Sumerians: Their history, culture, and character*, Chicago: University of Chicago Press.

Kurath, Hans & Sherman M. Kuhn (1959), eds, *Middle English Dictionary*, Ann Arbor: University of Michigan Press.

Kurti, Nicholas (1996), 'Rumford and culinary science', in Walker 1996: 170–84.

Lai, T.C. (1984), *At the Chinese Table*, Hong Kong: Oxford University Press.

Lamb, Charles (1909), *The Essays of Elia*, first series, London: George G. Harrap [1823].

Lamprey, L. (1940), *The Story of Cookery*, New York: Frederick A. Stokes.

Larkin, Jack (1988), *The Reshaping of Everyday Life, 1790–1840*, New York: Harper & Row.

Leach, Edmund (1961), 'Two essays concerning the symbolic representation of time: (I) Cronus and Chronos (II) Time and false noses', *Rethinking Anthropology*, London: Athlone Press: 124–36.

Leach, Edmund (1970), *Lévi-Strauss*, London: Fontana.

Leach, Maria (1972), *Funk & Wagnall's Standard Dictionary of Folklore, Mythology and Legend*, New York: Funk & Wagnall.

Lee, Richard B. & Irven DeVore (1968), eds, *Man the Hunter*, Chicago: Aldine.

Lefebvre, Georges (1977), 'The place of the Revolution in the agrarian history of France', in Robert Forster & Orest Ranum, eds, *Rural Society in France: Selections from the 'Annales'*, vol. 3, Baltimore: John Hopkins University Press: 31–49.

Leonard, Jonathan Norton (1974), *The First Farmers*, n.p.: Time-Life.

Lerche, Grith (1981), 'Khubz tannur: Freshly consumed flat bread in the Near East', in Fenton & Owen 1981: 179–95.

Lévi-Strauss, Claude (1963), *Totemism*, trans. Rodney Needham, Boston: Beacon.

Lévi-Strauss, Claude (1966), 'The culinary triangle', *New Society*, 22 Dec.: 937–40.

Lévi-Strauss, Claude (1970), *Introduction to a Science of Mythology*, vol. 1, *The Raw and the Cooked*, trans. John & Doreen Weightman, London: Jonathan Cape.

Lévi-Strauss, Claude (1978), *Introduction to a Science of Mythology*, vol. 3, *The Origin of Table Manners*, trans. John & Doreen Weightman, New York: Harper & Row.

Liddell, Henry George & Robert Scott (1909), *A Lexicon Abridged from Liddell and Scott's Greek–English Lexicon*, Oxford: Clarendon Press.

Limet, Henri (1987), 'The cuisine of ancient Sumer', *Biblical Archaeologist*, 50(3): 132–47.

Lin Yutang (1939), *My Country and My People*, London: William Heinemann.

Livy (1936), [*History of Rome*], vol. 11, trans. Evan T. Sage, London: William Heinemann (Loeb).

Lovejoy, Arthur O. (1964), *The Great Chain of Being: A study of the history of an idea*, Cambridge (Mass.): Harvard University Press.

Lyotard, Jean-François (1984), *The Postmodern Condition: A report on knowledge*, trans. Geoff Bennington & Brian Massumi, Manchester: Manchester University Press.

M.M. [initials of Mary Ellen Meredith, according to Henisch 1976: 248 n.98] (1851), 'Gastronomy and civilisation', *Fraser's Magazine*, 44(264): 591–609.

MacDonogh, Giles (1992), *Brillat-Savarin: The judge and his stomach*, Chicago: Ivan R. Dee.

McGee, Harold (1986), *On Food and Cooking: The science and lore of the kitchen*, London: Unwin Hyman.

McGee, Harold (1990), *The Curious Cook: More kitchen science and lore*, San Francisco: North Point.

McGuire, Randall H. (1992), *A Marxist Archaeology*, San Diego: Academic.

McIntosh, Wm Alex & Mary Zey (1989), 'Women as gatekeepers of food consumption: A sociological critique', *Food & Foodways*, 3(4): 317–32.

Mackintosh, Maureen M. (1979), 'Domestic labour and the household', in Sandra Burman, ed., *Fit Work for Women*, London: Croom Helm: 173–91.

McKirdy, Michael (1988), 'Who wrote Soyer's *Pantropheon*?', *Petits Propos Culinaires*, 29: 18–21.

Macrobius (1969), *The Saturnalia*, trans. Percival Vaughan Davies, New York: Columbia University Press.

Maddox, Marion (forthcoming), 'Food on the face', *Food & Foodways*.

Mann, Michael (1986), *The Sources of Social Power*, vol. 1, *A History of Power from the Beginning to AD 1760*, Cambridge: Cambridge University Press.

Mansel, Philip (1994), 'The meaning of eating', *Petits Propos Culinaires*, 46: 32–5.

Marx, Karl (1973), *Grundrisse: Foundations of the critique of political economy (rough draft)*, trans. Martin Nicolaus, Harmondsworth: Penguin.

Marx, Karl (1977), *Economic and Philosophic Manuscripts of 1844*, Moscow: Progress.

Marx, Karl & Friedrich Engels (1976), *The German Ideology*, Moscow: Progress.

Medeiros, Carlos Laranjo (1981), *Vakwandu: History, kinship and systems of production of an Herero people of south-west Angola*, Lisboa: Junta de Investigaçòes Científicas do Ultramar.

Mendelssohn, Kurt (1974), *The Riddle of the Pyramids*, London: Thames & Hudson.

Mennell, Stephen (1985), *All Manners of Food: Eating and taste in England and France from the Middle Ages to the present*, Oxford: Basil Blackwell.

Mennell, Stephen (1989), *Norbert Elias: Civilization and the human self-image*, Oxford: Basil Blackwell.

Mennell, Stephen, Anne Murcott & Anneke H. van Otterloo (1992), *The Sociology of Food: Eating, diet and culture*, complete issue of *Current Sociology*, 40(2) [also published as book, London: Sage, 1992].

Meredith, George (1909) *The Ordeal of Richard Feverel: A history of father and son*, London: Constable [1859].

Meredith, Owen [Edward Robert Bulmer-Lytton] (n.d.), *Lucile*, New York: Thomas Y. Crowell [1860].

Millett, Kate (1971), *Sexual Politics*, London: Rupert Hart-Davis.

Mintz, Sidney W. (1985), *Sweetness and Power: The place of sugar in modern history*, New York: Viking.

Mistress of a Family, The (1845), *Cookery and Domestic Economy, for Young Housewives: Including Directions for Servants*, Edinburgh: William & Robert Chambers.

Montagné, Prosper (1961), *Larousse Gastronomique: The encyclopedia of food, wine & cooking*, London: Hamlyn.

Moore, Andrew M.T. (1985), 'The development of neolithic societies in the Near East', in Fred Wendorf & Angela E. Close, eds, *Advances in World Archaeology*, vol. 4, Orlando: Academic: 1–69.

Morris, Craig & Donald E. Thompson (1985), *Huánuco Pampa: An Inca city and its hinterland*, London: Thames & Hudson.

Mote, Frederick W. (1977), 'Yüan and Ming', in Chang 1977: 193–257.

Mountford, Charles P. (1976), *Nomads of the Australian Desert*, Adelaide: Rigby.

Multhauf, Robert P. (1978), *Neptune's Gift: A history of common salt*, Baltimore: Johns Hopkins University Press.

Mulvaney, D.J. (1975), *The Prehistory of Australia*, Ringwood: Penguin.

Mumford, Lewis (1934), *Technics and Civilization*, New York: Harcourt, Brace.

Murcott, Anne (1982), 'On the social significance of the "cooked dinner" in South Wales', *Social Science Information*, 21(4–5): 677–95.

Murcott, Anne (1988), 'Sociological and social anthropological approaches to food and eating', *World Review of Nutrition and Dietetics*, 55: 1–40.

Murray, Oswyn (1983), 'Symposion and Männerbund', in Pavel Oliva & Alena Frolíková, eds, *Concilium Eirene XVI*, (Proceedings of the 16th International Eirene Conference, Prague, 31 Aug.–4 Sept. 1982), vol. 1, Prague: 47–52.

Murray, Oswyn (1990), ed., *Sympotica: A symposium of the 'symposion'*, Oxford: Clarendon.

Neusner, Jacob (1975), 'The study of religion as the study of tradition in Judaism', in Robert D. Baird, ed., *Methodological Issues in Religious Studies*, Chico (California): New Horizons Press.

Newnham-Davis, Lieutenant-Colonel Nathaniel (1899), *Dinners and Diners: Where and how to dine in London*, London: Grant Richards.

Nilsson, Martin P. (1920), *Primitive Time-reckoning: A study in the origins and first development of the art of counting time among the primitive and early culture peoples*, Lund: C.W.K. Gleerup.

Noble, William & Iain Davidson (1996), *Human Evolution, Language and Mind: A psychological and archaeological inquiry*, Cambridge: Cambridge University Press.

Norwood, Gilbert (1931), *Greek Comedy*, London: Methuen.

Oliver, Raymond (1967), *The French at Table*, trans. Claude Durrell, London: Wine and Food Society/Michael Joseph.

Oppenheim, A. Leo (1977), *Ancient Mesopotamia: Portrait of a dead civilization*, rev. Erica Reiner, Chicago: University of Chicago Press.

Perlès, Catherine (1979), 'Les origines de la cuisine: l'acte alimentaire dans l'histoire de l'homme', *Communications*, 31: 4–14.

Petronius (1977), *The Satyricon*, trans. J.P. Sullivan, Harmondsworth: Penguin.

Pillsbury, Richard (1990), *From Boarding House to Bistro: The American restaurant then and now*, Boston: Unwin Hyman.

Pirazzoli-t'Serstevens, Michèle (1985), 'A second-century Chinese kitchen scene', *Food and Foodways*, 1(1): 95–103.

Plato (1951), *The Symposium*, trans. Walter Hamilton, Harmondsworth: Penguin.

Plato (1960), *Gorgias*, trans. Walter Hamilton, Harmondsworth: Penguin.

Plato (1971), *Timaeus and Critias*, trans. Desmond Lee, Harmondsworth: Penguin.

Plato (1973), *Phaedrus and the Seventh and Eighth Letters*, trans. Walter Hamilton, Harmondsworth: Penguin.

Plato (1974), *The Republic*, trans, Desmond Lee, Harmondsworth: Penguin.

Plautus (1965), *The Pot of Gold; The Prisoners; The Brothers Menaechmus; The Swaggering Soldier; Pseudolus*, trans. E.F. Watling, Harmondsworth: Penguin.

Plutarch (1927), 'How to study poetry', *Moralia*, vol. 1, trans. Frank Cole Babbitt, London: William Heinemann (Loeb).

Plutarch (1957), 'On the eating of flesh', *Moralia*, vol. 12, trans. William Helmbold, London: William Heinemann (Loeb): 540–79.

Plutarch (1960), *The Rise and Fall of Athens: Nine Greek lives*, trans. Ian Scott-Kilvert, Harmondsworth: Penguin.

Polanyi, Karl (1944), *The Great Transformation*, New York: Farrar & Rinehart.

Polanyi, Karl (1957), 'The economy as instituted process', in Karl Polanyi, Conrad M. Arensberg & Harry W. Pearson, *Trade and Market in the Early Empires: Economies in history and theory*, Glencoe (Illinois): The Free Press: 243–70.

Porphyry (1965), *On Abstinence from Animal Food* [*De Abstinentia*], trans. Thomas Taylor, n.p.: Barnes & Noble.

Postan, M.M. (1975), *The Medieval Economy and Society: An economic history of Britain in the Middle Ages*, Harmondsworth: Penguin.

Postgate, Nicholas (1977), *The First Empires*, Oxford: Elsevier/Phaidon.

Pritchard, James B. (1969), ed., *Ancient Near Eastern Texts Relating to the Old Testament*, 3rd edn, Princeton: Princeton University Press.

Prizeman, John (1970), *Kitchens* (a Design Centre publication), n.p.: Macdonald.

Pullar, Philippa (1971), *Consuming Passions: A history of English food and appetite*, London: Hamish Hamilton.

Rau, Santha Rama (1969), *Foods of the World: The Cooking of India*, n.p.: Time-Life.

Redman, Charles (1978), *The Rise of Civilization: From early farmers to urban society in the Ancient Near East*, San Francisco: W.H. Freeman.

Renfrew, Colin & Paul Bahn (1996), *Archaeology: Theories, methods and practice*, 2nd edn, London: Thames & Hudson.

Renner, H.D. (1944), *The Origin of Food Habits*, London: Faber & Faber.

Revel, Jean-François (1982), *Culture and Cuisine: A journey through the history of food*, trans. Helen R. Lane, New York: Da Capo.

Richards, Audrey I. (1932), *Hunger and Work in a Savage Tribe: A functional study of nutrition among the Southern Bantu*, London: George Routledge & Sons.

Richards, Audrey I. (1939), *Land, Labour and Diet in Northern Rhodesia: An economic study of the Bemba tribe*, London: International Institute of African Languages & Cultures.

Rombauer, Irma S. & Marion Rombauer Becker (1953), *The Joy of Cooking*, Indianapolis: Bobbs-Merrill.

Roncière, Charles de La (1988), 'Portraits: Tuscan notables on the eve of the Renaissance', in Duby 1988: 157–309.

Root, Waverley (1980), *Food: An authoritative and visual history and dictionary of the foods of the world*, New York: Simon & Schuster.

Root, Waverley & Richard de Rochemont (1976), *Eating in America: A history*, New York: William Morrow.

Rossetti, Christina (1979), 'In an Artist's Studio' & 'Goblin Market', in M.H. Abrams et al., eds, *Norton Anthology of English Literature*, vol. 2, New York: W.W. Norton: 1521, 1523–35 [*Goblin Market and Other Poems*, 1862].

Rozin, Elisabeth (1982), 'The structure of cuisine', in Lewis M. Barker, ed., *The Psychobiology of Human Food Selection*, Westport, Connecticut: AVI: 189–203.

Rozin, Elisabeth (1983), *Ethnic Cuisine: The flavor-principle cookbook*, Brattleboro (Vermont):

Stephen Greene [rev. edn of *The Flavor-principle Cookbook*, 1973].

Rozin, Elisabeth & Paul Rozin (1981), 'Some surprisingly unique characteristics of human food preferences', in Fenton & Owen 1981: 243–52.

Rumford, Count [Benjamin Thompson] (1969), *Collected Works of Count Rumford*, vol. 3, ed. S.C. Brown, Cambridge (Mass.): Harvard University Press.

Rumohr, Baron von (1993), *The Essence of Cookery: Geist der Kochkunst*, trans. Barbara Yeomans, London: Prospect Books [originally under his cook's name, Joseph König, 1822].

Ruskin, John (1877), *The Ethics of the Dust: Ten lectures to little housewives on the elements of crystallization*, Sunnyside, Orpington (Kent): George Allen [1866].

Salaman, Redcliffe N. (1949), *The History and Social Influence of the Potato*, Cambridge: Cambridge University Press.

Sanday, Peggy Reeves (1981), *Female Power and Male Dominance: On the origins of sexual inequality*, Cambridge: Cambridge University Press.

Santich, Barbara (1987), Two Languages, Two Cultures, Two Cuisines: A comparative study of the culinary cultures of northern and southern France, Italy and Catalonia in the fourteenth and fifteenth centuries, PhD thesis: Flinders University of South Australia.

Santich, Barbara (1995), *The Original Mediterranean Cuisine: Medieval recipes for today*, Kent Town, South Australia: Wakefield.

Schafer, Edward H. (1977), 'T'ang', in Chang 1977: 85–140.

Schmidt, Alfred (1971), *The Concept of Nature in Marx*, trans. Ben Fowkes, London: NLB.

Schofield, Leo & Michael Dowe (1989), *Good Food Guide to eating well in and around Sydney [1990]*, South Yarra (Victoria): Anne O'Donovan.

Scully, Terence (1987), '"Aucune science d'art de cuysinerie et de cuysine": Chiquart's *Du fait de cuisine*', *Food & Foodways*, 2(2): 199–214.

Scully, Terence (1995), *The Art of Cookery in the Middle Ages*, Woodbridge (Suffolk): Boydell.

Seneca (1925), *Ad Lucilium: Epistulae morales*, vol. 3, London: William Heinemann (Loeb).

Sept, Jeanne (1992), 'Archaeological evidence and ecological perspectives for reconstructing early hominid subsistence behaviour', in Michael B. Schiffer, ed., *Archaeological Method and Theory*, Tucson: University of Arizona Press: 4: 1–56.

Shaw, George Bernard (1931), 'Maxims for revolutionists', in *Man and Superman: A comedy and a philosophy*, London: Constable [1903].

Simmel, Georg (1994), 'The sociology of the meal', trans. Michael Symons, *Food & Foodways*, 5(4): 345–50 [1910].

Smith, R.E.F. & David Christian (1984), *Bread and Salt: A social and economic history of food and drink in Russia*, Cambridge: Cambridge University Press.

Smith, W. Ramsay (1910), 'The Aborigines of Australia', *Official Year Book of the Commonwealth of Australia*, Melbourne: Commonwealth Bureau of Census and Statistics: 158–76.

Smollett, Tobias (1979), *The Adventures of Roderick Random*, Oxford: Oxford University Press [1748].

Soyer, Alexis [Adolphe Duhart-Fauvet – see McKirdy 1988] (1853), *The Pantropheon: Or a history of food and its preparation in ancient times*, London: Simpkin, Marshall.

Sparkes, Brian A. & Lucy Talcott (1964), *Pots and Pans of Classical Athens* (Excavations of the Athenian Agora Picture Book Number 1), Princeton (New Jersey): American School of Classical Studies at Athens.

Spence, Jonathan (1977), 'Ch'ing' in Chang 1977: 259–94.

Spencer, Edward (1900), *Cakes & Ale: A memory of many meals*, London: Grant Richards.

Steen, Eveline J. van der (1992), 'Fiery furnaces: Bread ovens in the Ancient Near East', *Petits Propos Culinaires*, 42: 45–52.

Sturgeon, Launcelot (1823), *Essays, Moral, Philosophical, and Stomachical, on the Important Science of Good Living*, London: G. & W.B. Whittaker.

Symons, Michael (1982), *One Continuous Picnic: A history of eating in Australia*, Adelaide: Duck Press.

Symons, Michael (1991), Eating into Thinking: Explorations in the sociology of cuisine, PhD thesis, Flinders University of South Australia.

Symons, Michael (1995), 'Simmel and gastronomic depth', *Simmel Newsletter*, 5(1): 23–34.

Symons, Michael (1996), 'The postmodern plate: Why cuisines come in threes', in David Walker, ed., *Food, Diet, Pleasure*, complete issue of *Australian Cultural History*, 15: 69–88.

Symons, Michael (1998), 'From agape to eucharist: Jesus meals and the early church', *Food & Foodways*.

Tacitus (1971), *The Annals of Imperial Rome*, trans. Michael Grant, Harmondsworth: Penguin.

Tannahill, Reay (1988), *Food in History*, London: Penguin.

Tanzer, Helen H. (1939), *The Common People of Pompeii: A study of the graffiti*, Baltimore: Johns Hopkins Press.

Theophrastus (1973), *The Characters* [together with Menander, *Plays and Fragments*], trans. Philip Vellacott, Harmondsworth: Penguin.

Thomas, Northcote W. (1924), 'The week in West Africa', *Journal of the Royal Anthropological Institute of Great Britain and Ireland*, 54: 183–209.

Thompson, Deborah Ann (1991), 'Anoxeria as a lived trope: Christina Rossetti's "Goblin Market"', in Evelyn J. Hinz, ed., *Diet and Discourse: Eating, drinking and literature*, special issue of *Mosaic*, 24(3–4): 89–106.

Thudichum, J.L.W. (1895), *The Spirit of Cookery: A popular treatise on the history, science, practice, and ethical and medical import of culinary art*, London: Frederick Warne.

Toussaint-Samat, Maguelonne (1992), *A History of Food*, trans. Anthea Bell, Cambridge (Mass.): Blackwell.

Valdes, Maria Elena de (1995), 'Verbal and visual representation of women: *Como agua para chocolate/Like Water for Chocolate*', *World Literature Today*, 69(1), 78–82.

Veblen, Thorstein (1899), *The Theory of the Leisure Class: An economic study of institutions*, New York: Macmillan.

Veyne, Paul (1987), ed., *A History of Private Life*, vol. 1, *From Pagan Rome to Byzantium*, trans. Arthur Goldhammer, Cambridge (Mass.): Belknap Press [series eds P. Ariès & Georges Duby 1987–91].

Veyne, Paul (1990), *Bread and Circuses: Historical sociology and political pluralism*, trans. Brian Pearce, London: Allen Lane.

Vidal, John (1997), *McLibel*, London: Macmillan.

Visser, Margaret (1992), *The Rituals of Dinner: The origins, evolution, eccentricities, and meaning of table manners*, New York: Penguin.

Waines, David (1984), 'A prince of epicures: The Arabs' first cookbook', *Ur*, 3.

Waley, Arthur (1956), *Yuan Mei: Eighteenth century Chinese poet*, London: Allen & Unwin.

Walker, Harlan (1991), ed., *Proceedings of the Oxford Symposium on Food and Cookery 1991: Public Eating*, London: Prospect Books.

Walker, Harlan (1996), ed., *Proceedings of the Oxford Symposium on Food and Cookery 1995: Cooks & Other People*, London: Prospect Books.

Walker, Thomas (1928), *The Art of Dining*, London: Grant Richards & Philip Sainsbury at The Cayne Press [from *The Original*, 1835].

Waring, Marilyn (1988), *Counting for Nothing: What men value and what women are worth*, Wellington (New Zealand): Allen & Unwin.

Warner, Richard (1791), ed., *Antiquitates Culinariae: Or curious tracts relating to the culinary affairs of the Old English*, London: R. Blamire [reprinted Prospect Books, London, n.d.].

Warren, Peter M. (1994), 'Minoan palaces', in *Ancient Cities*, special issue of *Scientific American*: 46–56 [July 1985].

Wason, Betty (1962), *Cooks, Gluttons and Gourmets: A history of cookery*, Garden City (New York): Doubleday.

Watson, Andrew M. (1974), 'The Arab agricultural revolution and its diffusion, 700–1100', *Journal of Economic History*, 34(1): 8–35.

Watson, Lyall (1971), *Omnivore: Our evolution in the eating game*, London: Souvenir.

Weber, Max (1968), *Economy and Society: An outline of interpretive sociology*, 2 vols, Berkeley: University of California Press.

Weber, Max (1976), *The Protestant Ethic and the Spirit of Capitalism*, trans. Talcott Parsons, London: George Allen & Unwin [1904–5].

Wheaton, Barbara Ketcham (1983), *Savouring the Past: The French kitchen and table from 1300 to 1789*, London: Chatto & Windus.

Wheeler, Sir Mortimer (1968), *The Indus Civilisation*, Cambridge: Cambridge University Press.

Wilder, Laura Ingalls (1968), *The Long Winter*, Harmondsworth: Penguin [1940].

Wilkins, John (1991), 'Public (and private) eating in Greece 450–300 BC', in Harlan Walker 1991: 306–10.

Wilkins, John, David Harvey & Mike Dobson (1995), eds, *Food in Antiquity*, Exeter: University of Exeter Press.

Wolberg, Lewis Robert (1937), *The Psychology of Eating*, London: George G. Harrap.

Wollstonecraft, Mary (1985), *Vindication of the Rights of Woman*, Harmondsworth: Penguin [1792].

Woods, Vicki, Jonathan Meades, Patrick O'Connor & Ann Barr (1982), 'Cuisine Poseur', *Harpers & Queen*, Aug.: 66–70, 140.

Woolf, Virginia (1945), *A Room of One's Own*, London: Penguin [1928].

Woolley, Sir Leonard (1954), *Excavations at Ur: A record of twelve years' work*, London: Ernest Benn.

Xenophon (1971), *The Economist of Xenophon*, trans. A.D.O. Wedderburn & W.G. Collingwood, with a preface by John Ruskin, New York: Burt Franklin [reprint of 1876 translation].

Yü, Ying-shih (1977), 'Han', in Chang 1977: 53–83.

Zeldin, Theodore (1977), *France 1848–1945*, vol. 2, *Intellect, Taste & Anxiety*, Oxford: Oxford University Press.

INDEX

INDEX

Burke, Edmund 33, 34, 35
Burton, Robert 168
butchers, butchery 5, 9, 124, 135,
140–1, 144, 152, 153, 191, 214, 242,
243, 278, 299, 300, 301, 311, 314, 320;
see also sacrifice; slaughter

Cadmus 203, 208, 297
cafés, coffee-houses 2, 24, 311, 314, 341,
357, 358
cakes 75, 76, 102, 134, 168, 209, 241,
256, 257, 260, 264, 308, 317, 325, 329,
336, 345
calendars 159, 162, 163, 164, 254, 260,
276
cameline 317
Camous, Mama 302, 319, 320, 321
canning see bottling
capitalism 102, 164, 191, 235, 245, 285,
295, 308, 330, 344; see also market
economy
Capon, Robert Farrar 46, 85, 155–6, 337
Carême, Antonin 55, 93, 110, 119, 174,
287, 288, 289, 290, 353
carinderia (street restaurant) 308
carrying 40, 191, 212–13, 216, 219, 222,
229, 231, 279, 302, 304, 307, 311, 337;
see also bark trays; baskets
carving 6, 42, 43, 121, 133, 137, 138,
140, 146–51, 152, 155, 171, 191, 264,
288, 291, 350
casseroles 35, 42, 67, 70, 77, 193, 293,
320
Çatal Hüyük 227, 302
caterers 41, 118, 124, 174, 209, 272,
290, 305, 316, 317, 318
Cathy (Cathy Guisewite) 338
cats 218, 251
cauldrons 43, 58, 67, 69, 70, 80, 83, 85,
201, 227, 242, 276, 277, 329
caviar 101, 294
cellars 175, 195, 283, 314, 319
ceramics 69, 192, 227, 233, 237
Cervio, Vicenzo 147
Chang, K.C. 53, 280, 304
charcoal 49, 57, 65, 74, 77, 78, 79, 80,
85, 87, 282, 304, 311
charity 111, 172, 273
Charles, Nickie 102

Charpentier, Henri 319–21
Chaucer, Geoffrey 61, 99, 312, 313
cheese 6, 36, 44, 56, 57, 80, 95, 118,
155, 169, 171, 191, 204, 236, 237, 257,
283, 298, 313, 314, 317, 341, 348
chefs 2, 7, 10, 11, 55, 100, 110, 137,
139, 170, 258, 267, 269, 275, 279, 285,
289, 292, 293, 296–8, 315, 318, 320;
see also individual names
chemistry 52, 59, 86, 93, 108, 113, 120,
160, 209, 222, 325, 331, 336
Cheng, F.T. 26, 85, 134
Chequerboard ice-cream 6, 7
Chicago World Fair 84
Childe, Vere Gordon 188, 225, 229,
236–7, 238, 245
chimneys 66, 76, 78, 82, 85, 232, 278,
325
chimpanzees 211, 212, 217, 219, 222
Chinese, China 26, 46–8, 55, 61–2, 63,
69–70, 78–9, 94, 113–14, 118–19, 123,
134–5, 137, 151, 152, 159, 160, 164,
169–70, 175, 194, 225, 227, 235, 238,
245, 251, 267, 276–80, 301, 302, 304–6,
307; see also individual dynasties
chores 28, 53, 190, 191, 202, 324, 326,
327, 343; see also repetition
Chou Dynasty 69–70, 137, 237, 277–8
Christian, David 113, 283, 284
Christmas 20, 163, 164
chula (range) 79
Cinderella 25, 29
cities xi, 4, 9, 111, 129, 238, 239, 245,
246, 253–4, 273, 279, 289, 295,
299–318, 331, 335, 344
civilisation xi, xii, 120, 161, 173, 181,
187, 190, 196, 202, 203, 204, 207, 210,
221, 225, 227, 236–9, 245, 247, 250–1,
343, 356
pudding of 9, 187, 188, 190, 202,
321–2, 330, 339
see also individual civilisations
civilising process (Elias) 106, 151–2, 222
Cleisthenes 206–7
climate 67, 71, 225, 230, 337
clocks 130, 158, 159–60, 161, 167
clothing 22, 48, 54, 127, 259, 338
clowns 192, 352, 353–4, 355, 357
coals 56, 57, 60, 61, 65, 67, 76, 77, 83,

378